COLLECTION MANAGEMENT
FOR THE 21ST CENTURY

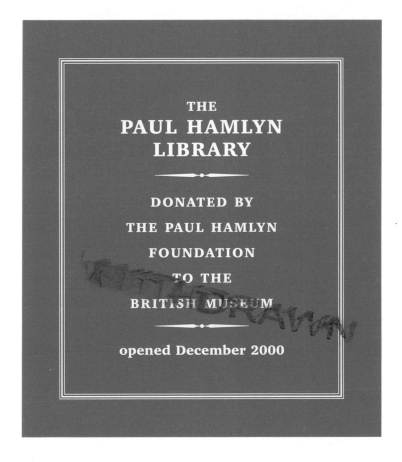

**Recent Titles in
the Greenwood Library Management Collection**

Collection Management for the 21st Century

A HANDBOOK FOR LIBRARIANS

Edited by
G. E. Gorman
and Ruth H. Miller

THE GREENWOOD LIBRARY MANAGEMENT COLLECTION

GREENWOOD PRESS
Westport, Connecticut • London

Library of Congress Cataloging-in-Publication Data

Collection management for the 21st century : a handbook for librarians
/ edited by G. E. Gorman and Ruth H. Miller.
    p.   cm.—(The Greenwood library management collection, ISSN
0894–2986)
  Includes bibliographical references and index.
  ISBN 0–313–29953–6 (alk. paper)
  1. Collection management (Libraries) I. Gorman, G. E.
II. Miller, Ruth H. III. Series.
Z687.C663 1997
025.2'1—dc20   96–2774

British Library Cataloguing in Publication Data is available.

Library of Congress Catalog Card Number: 96–2774
ISBN: 0–313–29953–6
ISSN: 0894–2986

First published in 1997

Greenwood Press, 88 Post Road West, Westport, CT 06881
An imprint of Greenwood Publishing Group, Inc.

Printed in the United States of America

The paper used in this book complies with the
Permanent Paper Standard issued by the National
Information Standards Organization (Z39.48–1984).

10 9 8 7 6 5 4 3

Contents

VIII. The Recent Literature

Introduction

G. E. Gorman

Mea culpa, mea maxima culpa—a confession is in order at the outset. This professional reference on collection management derives from a personal view of what is likely to be important in coming years, rather than by any consensus among practitioners that these are the pressing issues of our time. Over a period of years, wide professional reading in current monographic and serial literature on collection development and collection management has suggested that certain topics are likely to have enduring interest, and to open exciting new possibilities, as we turn the page on one century in modern librarianship to see what will unfold on the page of a new century. The result, in this volume devoted to development and change in the rapidly evolving field of collection management, is a set of contributions based around eight nodes: the future for collection management (one chapter); the technological contribution to collection management (two chapters); selection of materials in an electronic environment (two chapters); future practices in collection evaluation (two chapters); electronic document delivery and resource preservation (two chapters); organization and budgeting in collection management (two chapters); cooperative collection development and management (three chapters); and the recent literature (one chapter).[1]

There is yet a second confession—practitioners were not polled to determine their choices of "best authors," but again a set of personal criteria was employed in selecting possible contributors. In choosing possible authors, several questions were asked. First, does the candidate write on issues of current and enduring interest to the profession? Second, does this person exhibit a lucid and intelligent grasp of key issues and emerging trends? Third, does the author's writing generally offer a critical, reflective approach rather than mere description or blithe acceptance of the status quo? Finally, does an author write in a way that makes one feel, like Oliver Twist, keen to say, "Please, Sir, may I have some more?" In answering these questions the intention has been to draw together a group of writers who, individually and severally, write with erudition and a sense of practicality on topics of pressing interest to information professionals. The final selection thus includes eighteen authors (from Australia, Britain, Hong Kong, New Zealand, Singapore, and the United States) writing on fourteen discrete but interrelated subjects; all of the contributors are experienced librarians, primarily but not exclusively in academic libraries, or library science educators. The names will be familiar to most readers, but no other collection draws together this specific group of individuals writing on these particular topics—this volume thus presents a new perspective.

In the recent past, "collection development" was a blanket phrase that denoted the process of building collections of library materials to serve the needs of specific user populations. It included inter alia policy issues, selection and weeding strategies, collection evaluation, use and user studies, all aimed at creating the most appropriate, but discrete and institutionally based, collections for the educational, recreational, and informational requirements of identifiable client groups. While "collection development" continues to be used in the literature, there is a growing preference for "collection management," which choice reflects a somewhat subtle paradigmatic shift both from discrete institutional collections to a wider library world and from narrower issues specific to collection building to a rather daunting range of issues drawn from wider aspects of professional practice. In broad terms these issues encompass ". . . a process of information gathering, communication coordination, policy formulation, evaluation and planning."[2] More specifically, collection management generally is thought to involve the following activities: budgeting and resource allocation; selection, relegation, and withdrawal of stock; choice of media and format; storage services and facilities; preservation, conservation, and binding; monitoring of collections; organization and staffing; performance measurement; collection administration; systems development and new technology; resource sharing and networking.[3] That is, collection development is being subsumed in a wider, emerging field called collection management, which continues to exhibit that high degree of flux characterized by Osburn in 1990 as ". . . the rapid evolution of an unnamed, dispersed, slipshod operation for which the responsibility was ambiguous into an activity that is perceived as inherently pervasive."[4]

As collection development continues to evolve into collection management, the two areas together become increasingly difficult to define. Rapidly shifting emphases, driven in part by information technology and in part by economic factors, further mean that any definitions established today will be different tomorrow. Nevertheless, within this changing environment there are emerging issues that, because of their broad focus, are likely to remain significant as we cross from one century to the next. It is these issues that form the foci in the present volume, which opens in Part I (The Future for Collection Management) with a scene-setting analysis of the future relationship between collection development and scholarly communication in a networked environment. In Chapter 1, John Budd and Bart Harloe assess the impact that changes to the system of scholarly communication are having on the theory and practice of collection development in academic libraries. They posit an evolving future in which libraries will be less concerned with the management of artifacts than with the management of intellectual content. This chapter raises important issues for the future of libraries and seeks, more than any other in the collection, to posit a challengingly different climate for collection development. The views of Budd and Harloe should be borne in mind when reading subsequent chapters, as many of them quite subtly support their provocative predictions.

To emphasize this changing climate, Part II of the book looks at The Technological Contribution to Collection Management, with chapters on new (the Internet) and well-established (integrated library systems) technologies as management tools. In Chapter 2, Thomas Nisonger analyzes the relationship between the Internet and collection management in libraries at various levels and then focuses on identification, microevaluation, selection, macroevaluation, and acquisitions, while also addressing the Internet's implications for the core collection, cooperative collection development, document delivery, and collection management staffing. Thus, in this chapter there is already some confirmation of Budd and Harloe's view that we are moving from a concern with artifacts to intellectual content.

Chapter 3, by Mary Casserly and Anne Ciliberti, presents a very readable report on a small-scale, descriptive study of the degree to which academic library personnel perceive the data produced by their integrated library systems to be useful for collection development decision making. From a sample of academic library personnel using one of two major integrated systems, the authors found that the data generally were perceived as both available and useful, although less useful than available. In several categories of data, however, significant differences were found between the user ratings of the two systems, suggesting that there is yet room for improvement in the way that information technology serves the needs of decision makers in collection development. Putting the chapters by Nisonger and by Casserly and Ciliberti together, one sees that both established and new technologies may work together to improve the quality of decision-making and management practices in collection management.

Although no one doubts that the technological revolution has changed forever the way in which collections are managed, it is to be hoped that best practices from today will inform our utilization of this technology in the future. Nowhere should this be more apparent than in the subject of Part III, Selection of Materials in an Electronic Environment. In Chapter 4, Peggy Johnson reminds us of the degree to which selecting and managing electronic information resources is a challenge for many librarians. But while the format may be new, there may be assistance from current professional practice in the form of collection development policies. Johnson suggests that a collection development policy for electronic information can identify the questions to ask and guide answers that correlate with library priorities. To be effective such a policy must address issues of selection criteria, formats covered, responsibility for decisions and consultation, sources of funding, licensing considerations, and the changing nature of the medium.

Chapter 5, by William Monroe, is the second chapter dealing with selection in an electronic environment. In it the author focuses on the decision-making aspects of collection development, suggesting that, the Internet and other communication technologies notwithstanding, libraries will continue to have a role as selectors and organizers of information—a much needed recognition that an electronic future need not spell the end of libraries in a traditional sense. What emerges from these two chapters is that the electronic future of libraries can but benefit from the continued use of "best practice" in the form of carefully devised collection development policies and the use of collection development librarians as selectors of materials in any format.

If, in an electronic future, the selection of materials will remain important in the overall collection management strategy, so too will collection evaluation, the subject of Part IV. The two chapters here deal first with methodological issues and then with procedural matters. In Chapter 6, "Collection Development and Performance Measurement," our antipodean colleague Philip Calvert treats the enduring issue of collection measurement, which we believe will become increasingly important in a future of greater collection sharing and rationalization. Calvert looks at the whole issue of how collections are measured, suggesting that a mix of quantitative and qualitative measures is perhaps more appropriate. Based on his own New Zealand research, he employs a multiple constituencies model of organizational effectiveness for this mix of collection evaluation measures. Certainly, any process aimed at improving librarians' ability to gauge the "goodness" of collections is to be commended, and what Calvert proposes offers more hope for such improvement than other suggestions of recent years.

Having thus established a likely methodological basis for future evaluation, it is appropriate to look at how a methodology might be put into practice using staff at various levels. In Chapter 7, Sheila Intner's concern is expressed about the deprofessionalization of collection development work—a trend that appears to have been slow to arrive in the United States, as librarians in many other countries have lived through this and emerged unscathed, and have benefitted from the practical perspectives that paraprofessionals and library technicians bring to the collection development process. In the U.S. library environment, meaningful decisions (for example, allocating funds, designing evaluations, and setting methodologies) are moving "up the line" to senior management, while other tasks are moving "down the line" to lower-level staff. This leaves the professionally qualified librarian with the harder decisions, ones that genuinely shape collections. For Intner, though, the trend also poses important questions, for example, in terms of professional education and staffing, that are not being addressed as yet.

Such traditional collection development activities as selection and evaluation are not the only features that will be absorbed into and changed in the emerging collection management environment—so too will such aspects as document delivery and preservation, but with profound changes implicit in their continuation in a digital era. Part V, therefore, looks at the future in terms of Electronic Document Delivery and Resource Preservation. In Chapter 8, Graham Cornish maintains that in an electronic environment libraries will become increasingly significant as intermediaries between authors/publishers, copyright managers, and users. Many traditional library functions will be modified or replaced; acquisitions will be redefined in terms of facilitating access, and use will become a greater function of electronic accessibility. Who will request documents, who will supply them, and who will pay are all areas where fundamental changes will take place in a dramatically changing information industry.

If an electronic future will see significant changes in how we provide access to documents, it then follows that a process toward the end of the information chain, preservation, is also likely to be affected. Indeed, the interrogative title of Chapter 9, "The Preservation of Electronic Records: What Shall We Do Next?", suggests that the preservation of digital information is an emerging area in which new questions will require new answers. Through a series of questions about the role of preservation and who should be involved in it, Ross Harvey notes several possible models for cooperative action and describes the likely involvement of libraries in the management and organization of electronic resource preservation. Both Cornish and Harvey convincingly argue that two important aspects of collection management, access to materials and retention of materials, are already profoundly challenging collection managers.

No less challenging will be issues of staffing and finance, traditionally seen as the preserve of management as distinct from collection development. In an era of collection management, however, the same professionals will deal with these issues as with selection, preservation, and access. Thus, Part VI in the book turns to Organization and Budgeting for Collection Management, offering one chapter on each of these facets. Bonita Bryant (Chapter 10), using data from a variety of resources, searches for clues to the organization of collection development in the next century. Her research suggests that collection development may become a separate division in increasingly fewer libraries, as collection development officers' span of responsibilities are broadened. She also suggests that collection development librarians will perform more reference duties as subject specialists who select in a "format-blind" environment and teach library users to access information electronically (in addition to providing whatever sort of reference service and liaison with faculty). As a consequence, new patterns of organization will emerge as libraries accommodate new media as part of their information resources.

If organizational patterns are likely to change, so too will budgeting for collection management, according to William Fisher and Barbara Leonard in Chapter 11. In their view, budgeting will become more difficult, and budgetary issues will impact significantly on how information resources are delivered and managed. Buying, borrowing, and transferring information as well as document delivery, access, and ownership will all be affected. Neither Bryant nor Fisher and Leonard suggest that collection managers *qua* managers are in for an easy time; their views, then, may offer advance warning of the need for more proactive management.

Part VII deals with perhaps the most pervasive collection management issue to arise in recent years, Cooperative Collection Development and Management. In Chapter 12, Richard Wood focuses on the facilitators of and barriers to cooperative collection development. In so doing he examines a wide range of variables that can work for or against cooperation through networks or consortia. Within this general theme Wood offers a comprehensive summary of how networks have developed, reviews their strengths and weaknesses, and points the way to a positive future in which networking functions as an integral part of any library service. A similarly positive view is taken by Gay Dannelly in Chapter 13. She assesses the general nature of current library programs in cooperative collection development and services and considers the nature and effectiveness of two programs: OhioLINK and the Committee on Institutional Cooperation (CIC). This case study approach substantiates many of the views expressed by Wood, showing how several variables come into play in actual cooperative ventures.

If Wood and Dannelly represent the received wisdom with regard to cooperative collection management, Dan Hazen plays the devil's advocate in Chapter 14. Drawing on examples of cooperative collection development in the field of Latin American Studies, he assesses achievements, possibilities, and challenges and suggests that, rhetoric aside, the impact of cooperation has been limited. While recognizing that technological change may generate a new framework for action, his analysis suggests that the cooperative aspirations of collection managers may well exceed their reach. This is a challenging note on which to conclude the discussion of cooperation, which has achieved almost canonical status in the obeisance paid to it by consciously "modern" collection managers.

Finally, co-editor Ruth Miller seeks to bring order to the chaos of literature relevant to the several topics explored in this volume. In Chapter 15, she highlights the major trends in these topics through a survey of the major publications. This survey will not only assist those trying to map the terrain for the first time but will also aid those who are seeking new approaches and further ideas relevant to their own libraries.

Having reached the end of what one trusts is a stimulating professional reference that will serve as a benchmark for future thinking in collection management, there is a sense of excitement and challenge, but also of apprehension and misgiving, about the evolution of library collections and services in the new century. The excitement and challenge arise from a recognition that librarians are moving into largely uncharted waters, and that only careful navigation using accumulated professional knowledge from the present will ensure that libraries will continue to provide what their users have a right to expect—the right information at the right time. The apprehension and misgiving emerge from sensing that the library profession has become so enamored of the technological future, with its remarkable ability to manipulate data in the process of developing information, that it has lost sight of far more important issues. In T.S. Eliot's words,

> Where is the wisdom we have lost in knowledge?
> Where is the knowledge we have lost in information?

There was a time when collection development meant the creation and organization of collections of knowledge through a complex intellectual process—filtering out the dross, selecting for a known group of users, providing "the best" within a specific social and organizational context. Today collection development is more about access to information than about the quality of knowledge. Here we come full circle to the first chapter in this volume and can do no better than to concur with Budd and Harloe's reminder about the logical congruence of collection management, information, and knowledge: "[collection] management is an intellectual activity dependent on individuals' ability to comprehend what information producers are trying to communicate, to divine the needs and desires of information seekers, and to conjoin the two on the basis of what the mind endeavors to create [that is, knowledge]." As we turn the page to the 21st century, this idea should be implanted in the mind of every collection manager.

NOTES

1. A further area of particular personal interest, education for collection management, has not been included here; this will now be the subject of a separate monograph drawing on expertise in Britain, North America, and Australia.

2. Charles B. Osburn, "Collection Development and Management," in *Academic Libraries: Research Perspectives*, ed. Mary Jo Lynch and Arthur Young (Chicago: American Library Association, 1990), p. 1.

3. See the brief outline of collection management and it constituents in D. G. Law, "Collection Management—Chore or Necessity?" *National Acquisitions Group Newsletter* 12 (1991): 17–19.

4. Osburn, "Collection Development and Management."

PART I

The Future for Collection Management

Collection Development and Scholarly Communication in the 21st Century: From Collection Management to Content Management

John M. Budd and Bart M. Harloe

INTRODUCTION

This chapter represents an attempt to forecast the increasingly complex and dynamic interplay between the evolving system of scholarly communication and the collection management function of academic libraries. Thus, it explores in some depth and detail the current and future system of scholarly communication, assesses its impact on the traditional concepts and practices that have formed the basis of what the library profession currently refers to as collection development and management, and then sketches a future scenario where libraries move from collection management to "content management."

THE END OF AN ERA?

In the era of electronic access there is a need for a new vocabulary for describing what it is that we do, a vocabulary that focuses on content and transcends the very static dichotomy of "ownership and access."[1] To recapitulate that argument: The current crisis of scholarly communication is being driven by the rapidly escalating cost of traditional printed journals, especially in the sciences.[2] As a direct result of this crisis, many academic libraries have found that the classical model of collection development, one that assumed the existence of large, self-sufficient research collections as the foundation of the system of scholarship, simply no longer works. In light of this development, academic libraries will need to redefine their role, their mission, and the very language used to describe what it is they do. As Branin has argued, librarians must manage the "intersection" between two different systems—one print and one electronic.[3] In the near future, a network-based strategy for "content management" must be developed. In the era of electronic access, academic libraries will become "logical gateways" to local and external resources, based upon the following set of strategic assumptions:

• first, that academic libraries will be focused on developing core collections of highly used materials that reside physically on-site, as well a body of resources that we might call "core access," that is, "that body of information that is not locally held but which is, nevertheless, essential" to the user community;[4]

• second, that resource sharing and cooperative collection development become more realistic options in a networked environment;

• third, that various forms of expedited document delivery, commercial and noncommercial, will be integrated into the library as gateway;

• fourth, that it will be necessary to collaborate closely with local campus users and with local campus support groups (faculty and computer center staff) in order to ensure that the proper resources are provided in the most cost-efficient and effective way over the network.

However, as Battin has written, the era of electronic access is based upon a fundamental contradiction:

Approximately 90 percent of the information needs of the academic and research programs depend on this essentially nineteenth-century information system. It coexists with an emerging twenty-first century information system that currently serves only 10 percent of those needs. The coexistence contributes to a frenetic schizophrenia among students and faculty, who expect the efficiency and convenience of electronic facilities from traditional library services and the comprehensive literature coverage of traditional library collections from electronic systems.[5]

Perhaps the challenge of the next few decades is to attempt to reduce the schizophrenia by building a more rational support system for scholarly communication. In what follows, first the nature of the changes affecting that system is explored, and then certain strategies for dealing with "content management" in the 21st century are suggested. In so doing, of necessity a primary question that underlies much of the current debate about the future of libraries is considered: whither collections and whither collection development and management?

Scholarly Communication in the 21st Century

Any discussion of the future of collection management has to begin with an examination of the production of formal communication. This is a matter touched on briefly in the past, but a proposal for an evolution from *collection management* to a state that is centered on *content* management requires a deeper probe into the structure of scholarly communication.[6] The first realization must be that scholarly communication has quite a conservative past; as a system, it has been slow to react to short-term developments of media or means of dissemination. There has, though, been one constant that has all but defined the scholarly communication system—growth. Throughout this century, especially, there has been enormous growth in the output of scholars and researchers in the form of books, journal articles, technical reports, and so on. The effects of this growth on libraries have been long recognized and frequently documented.[7] There are also effects on the scholars and researchers themselves. No matter how narrow the field of specialization, the literature of that field is, in most instances, too much for any individual to be able to keep up with. David Mermin points out that browsing the literature of physics is no longer possible, and hasn't been for quite some time. He further urges his fellow scientists to fight the temptation to contribute to newly formed journals by not sending them papers and not serving on editorial boards.[8] It is not likely that Mermin's request will be heeded; there are other forces influencing the formal communication of research and scholarship.

HOW DISCIPLINES COMMUNICATE

It is imperative for workers within the scholarly communication system, and especially librarians, to understand that communication patterns are not constant across disciplines. In large part, the nature of the object of study influences how the object will be treated and how that treatment will be communicated. The same means of study does not suit examination of subatomic particles and *King Lear*. Likewise, the same means of communicating the results of examination does not suit such different objects. The physical scientist generally deals with discrete objects, is able to structure a particular method of study (such as an experiment), and communicates the research results according to a model that is widely accepted in the discipline. One reason for the level of standardization of both method and reporting is that the object of study is a physical entity. It can be described in precise terms; it can be examined in a somewhat, though certainly not absolutely, deterministic fashion. Further, the process of research has stages that are also fairly discrete. Since the world of the physical sciences is aimed steadfastly at progress, and since it is a competitive world (with prestige, academic rewards, and potential funding on the line), the process of communication encompasses the reporting of the stages of inquiry and the swift publication of results. Among the pressures under which scientists work are the practical need for timely reporting and the need to stake intellectual claims. The resulting literature is large and growing, and claims to be providing precisely what the scientific community demands. From the library's point of view, this means an increasing number of journals, increasing size (numbers of pages per year) of existing titles, and increasing prices.

Because the humanities are not mentioned in the same paragraph as the sciences does not mean that there has been no growth in humanities literature. The means of communicating, however, is very different in the humanities. For one thing, a particular focus of inquiry is not necessarily discrete, but may well be an installation in a larger, perhaps even a lifelong, effort at understanding a specific object of study. Another important difference is that the object of study is seldom a physical entity, but is more likely to be a text or set of texts (in the most general usage of the word text). Because of this integral difference, the means of study must be quite different. The humanities, by and large, do not depend upon measurement and observation, but on interpretation and exegesis. While it is true that in every discipline the core purpose is achieving a more complete understanding of the object of study, the way in which understanding is reached in the humanities incorporates the process of creating the object itself. At all levels and at each stage of inquiry the humanities scholar, of necessity, delves into the formation of the object, asking how it came about and how to gain some grasp of the malleability of the object. Thus, the humanities are far more indeterminate than the sciences; for this reason, the humanities must eschew deterministic methods of inquiry.

Between the sciences and the humanities lie the social sciences. These disciplines, to varying degrees, embody elements of both of the other two broad disciplines. The social sciences literatures, then, display features of the other two. There has been growth in the periodical literature in most of the social science disciplines. There has also been vigorous publication activity in other formats, principally books. The reasons underlying the two means of communication center on the bifurcated approach that social scientists have toward their objects of study. On one hand, there are many researchers who choose to adopt the stance that the object of study sufficiently emulates physical objects, so the methods of the physical sciences can be applied to the social sciences. Those who embrace such a stance say that the means of communication can also resemble that of the physical sciences; so there are journals that report what appear to be discrete studies of physical objects. It may be said that these individuals emphasize the *science* in the social sciences. On the other hand, others would maintain that the object of study is human and, so, not merely physical. The proponents of such a view use more interpretative methods, and the journals and books through which they communicate publish work that is less discrete and involves methods akin to those of the humanities. For these scholars, the *social* in the social sciences is emphasized.

A USER-CENTERED APPROACH TO SCHOLARLY COMMUNICATION

While discussion so far has dealt with the production of information, the other side of the coin has definite importance for our consideration of the future of collection management. Production is not the sole function of the system; what is produced is produced for a reason, and that reason incorporates some conception of use. An awareness of the need for attention to the user in the process of scholarly communication has been expressed in the past. Martell, for instance, observed more than a decade ago that

In theory, the academic library is sensitive and responsive to changing client needs for information. In practice, the library is relatively insensitive and unresponsive to these needs. . . . The creators of knowledge within the university should benefit from an enlightened library policy that actively encourages organizational efforts to understand the range of user needs and changes in needs.[9]

A necessary element in achieving a user-centered focus is understanding the purposes that drive creation of the artifacts comprising part of the scholarly communication system. There are two competing ideas that can be used to express the motivating purposes. One is the relativist stance; that is, the position that social structure drives the system and the players are motivated by such factors as tenure, salary, and prestige. The other is the realist stance; that is, that scholars see as their purpose the extension of knowledge through inquiry and formal communication of the results of that inquiry. These two stances are extremes, and reality exists on a continuum between the two, with the most appropriate position being toward the realist end of that continuum. Given such a position, it follows that a user-centered approach to scholarly communication means the library and librarians assume that scholars and researchers are engaged in the work they do out of at least a partial motivation to contribute to the growth of knowledge. Success, then, is a function of the degree to which the users can make contributions of this sort. Moreover, it is essential that librarians realize that their activities have not simply social or organizational functions, but an epistemic function as well. It would be impossible to assume the role of content management without such a realization.

We have briefly addressed the need for user-based approaches to collection management elsewhere. An integral part of such an approach is a definition of what the library has to offer to its community. We have maintained, and still maintain, that the library offers much more than simply artifacts. While it is true that artifacts (using the term as broadly as possible) allow for communication between a producer and a user of information, the package itself (book or CD-ROM) is not the essential element of the communication process. The user is not so much interested in the information package as in the information itself. Librarians must accept that the thinking of the past is insufficient to meet the key goals of the library. As has been observed, "Product [has been] defined as what the library has or what it has access to . . . , rather than as the content that might be needed at a particular place and time."[10] A realization based on this observation necessitates a revision of the library's purpose and a fresh look at the dynamics that influence use of the information base. One factor behind use of the scholarly communication system is the desire for knowledge growth. This factor means that when we use the word "information," it connotes much more than the available morass of data; it refers to both the collection and interpretation of those data into a meaningful and informing presentation. An active role is required to produce a presentation that informs; the passive acquisition of artifacts cannot achieve the user-based goal.

Once stated, however, this goal is not easy to accomplish. The bulk of data available militates against meaning. Weaver realized the paradox surrounding the amount of data and the quest for meaning nearly half a century ago. Weaver uses the word "information" very specifically: it expresses the degree of freedom of choice that exists in choosing any particular message. In a library collection, the user has an enormous amount of choice among various, and sometimes competing, bits of information. The greater the amount of choice, the more difficult it is for the user to make sense of what exists. According to Weaver, "One has the vague feeling that information and meaning may prove to be something like a pair of canonically conjugate variables in quantum theory ... [that is, that information and meaning may be] subject to some joint restriction that condemns a person to the sacrifice of the one as he insists on having much of the other."[11] With a great deal to choose from, the identification of relevant materials becomes ever more difficult. It is especially cumbersome for a user to find meaning if the librarian's role is passive. If, on the other hand, the librarian is active in the quest for meaning, for informing, then the possibility for success is heightened. Even with such an active posture, informing is not easy; the problem is not merely one of bulk of data, but of interpretation. Interpretation is not synonymous with awareness; the pressures on interpretation are exacerbated by an increasing inattention to the critical faculty that is necessary to reading.

THE FATE OF READING IN A NETWORKED WORLD

The pressures on an individual's critical faculty are made greater by the proliferation of information sources, including networked information. There can be little doubt that the structure of electronic media has altered the possibilities for writing and, so, for communication generally. As writing changes, either necessarily or not, the nature of reading must also change. Bolter addresses this dynamic from the point of view of writing. He asserts that electronic media recreate "writing space," which he defines as "the physical and visual field defined by a particular technology of writing."[12] Since writing is spatial, alterations to the space result in alterations in absorption of what is communicated in that space. Networked information is largely constructed of hypertext, which can include a multitude of links. Landow points out that hypertext changes conceptions of the beginning of a text, because a reader can "enter" the text at any point through any of the existing links. If hypertext alters the concept of beginning, then it also alters the concept of ending. "Readers cannot only choose different points of ending, they can also continue to add to the text, to extend it, to make it more than it was when they began to read.''[13] One result of the transformation enabled by hypertext is that the reader can be in a constant state of reinterpretation, since the text is mutable, since it is, in effect, versions of a metatext. The mutability of the text complicates the formation of meaning; as Said writes, ''we see that the beginning is the first point (in time, space, or action) of an accomplishment or process that has duration and meaning. The beginning, then, is the first step in the intentional production of meaning.''[14] With multiple beginnings there are multiple intentions; those intentions are no longer structured by the author (as is the case of a linear text). Moreover, there are multiple endings; by extension, the ending is the final step in the intentional production of meaning.

One implication of hypertext and networked information is that meaning is even more individualized than it is with traditional texts. Reader-response criticism tells us that the process of reading is as dependent on the intentional state of the reader as of the writer. Hypertext serves to all but remove the intentional state of the writer, so that the reader's state can be transformed from one reader to another and within one reader over time. To an extent, this occurs naturally in the process of reading linear texts. However, with hypertext, the text in question becomes less a literal text (a structured object that exists in stable form before the reader begins to apprehend it) and more a figurative text (an object with almost indeterminate structure that does not have a preexisting stability). Therefore, as Bolter notes, ''The role of the reader in electronic fiction therefore lies halfway between the customary roles of author and reader in the medium of print.''[15] One question this begs is whether all readers are equipped to engage in the function of writer as well. A more serious question regards what happens to understanding in an atmosphere of instability; is the result multiple opportunities for meaning formation, or a state of confusion with no way to take the first step toward meaning?

The magnitude of the number of choices that may be available to readers is seen by some as the most important factor inhibiting serious thought. Birkerts may be a typical exponent of such an opinion:

The explosion of data . . . has all but destroyed the premise of understandability. Inundated by perspectives, by lateral vistas of information that stretch endlessly in every direction, we no longer accept the possibility of assembling a complete picture. Instead of carrying on the ancient project of philosophy—attempting to discover the ''truth'' of things—we direct our energies to managing information.[16]

Of course, the outcome of reading is dependent on the purpose of reading. However, there are purposes that encompass understanding, comprehension, critical assessment. In order to accomplish these purposes, there is the need for contemplation of a narrative. This is not to say that the structure of narratives need be limited, but there has to be an effort at communicating an intended meaning. Bolter is speaking of employing technology to create multiple intentional states, with the intentionality of the reader assuming primacy. Birkerts implies that the intentionality of the author is an important element in written communication. Birkerts also asserts that there are disciplinary differences; that the means of communication used in one discipline will not necessarily fit another. His focus is on the humanities and the kind of reading that has been prevalent as a means to knowledge. His assessment of the place of reading in the formation of knowledge acknowledges the disciplinary differences. "In the humanities, knowledge is a means, yes, but it is a means less to instrumental application than to something more nebulous: understanding. . . . [I]t ultimately seeks to fashion a comprehensible narrative."[17]

It may be that some readers (or information users in some senses) do have an instrumental purpose for the reading they do. In fact, the likelihood that this is so magnifies the need for the librarian to comprehend content and the ways in which it may be used. Richard Lanham issues a challenge to this profession that cannot be ignored. "Librarians of electronic information find their job now a radically rhetorical one—they must consciously construct human attention-structures rather than assemble a collection of books according to commonly accepted rules."[18] Lanham speaks of a need for "architects of great skill" to meet the challenges of a changing world.

If educating our students for the world they will live in, for a competitive global economy and the unprecedented high level of daily symbolic processing that comes with it, is to be a dominant university purpose . . . , then we must find ways to bring these new contracts onto campus and to understand them. We must modify our departmental and disciplinary structures so that this vital conversation can occur, and be prepared to modify them much more after the conversation has occurred. I am not sure where the conversation should take place. The library, or library school, seems a logical place.[19]

Lanham's admonition strikes at the core of this paper—that there needs to be a transformation, characterized by a new vocabulary, from a concentration on the thing (the book, the article, the Web site) to the content communicated.

SPEAKING OF INFORMATION RETRIEVAL

For millennia libraries have been repositories of the graphic record. Over the course of these millennia this function has been possible because the graphic record has been embodied in physical artifacts that have been selected, acquired, and stored. The very notion of retrieval has been problematic since the first clay tablets were placed in the first libraries. We need to question seriously if our retrieval mechanisms are genuinely more sophisticated than those that were present at Alexandria. There is no doubt that the discussion surrounding access has embraced ideas that were previously foreign to the discipline and this discussion has been engaged in by an increasing number of people. In the light of the foregoing observations, there is more to be said on the searching, retrieval, and presentation of information.

GETTING TO THE SOURCE

It is becoming more readily recognized that the traditionally used means of access in libraries are less than adequate for the complexity of users' needs. It might be argued that the tools are a deterministic response to an indeterminate query. In partial defense of the past, there have been practical obstacles to providing anything other than this means of access. In the days of card catalogs (and certainly before), physical space was a major limiting factor: a library could afford to file only so many subject cards before the catalog would require more space than was available. In the early days of automation, when storage costs were high, a similar constraint held. We have entered an era wherein the limitations of the past do not necessarily tie our hands, and we, as a profession, are making strides in the consideration of possibilities that, while perhaps not completely nondeterministic, present arrays of options that were not previously presented. For instance, one option that is being mentioned is the inclusion of chapter titles in bibliographic records. While this suggestion may have some potential, DeHart and Matthews have found that misleading terminology may be introduced with the inclusion of chapter titles.[20] This problem may well be enlarged when one information source, such as a library's catalog, includes information from a number of disciplines which may employ the same, or similar terms, but with substantively different meanings. Reliance on the texts themselves, however, may not improve retrievability. There seems to be an assumption that the text offers completeness of terminology, as well as precision of expression and usage. Blair and Maron report that full-text searching leads to only limited success.[21] For instance, suppose a searcher enters the term "technology" to find items on libraries' incorporations of technological developments and does not retrieve relevant items, because that specific term does not appear in the text, although such terms as "computers" and "automation" do.

If text and such items as chapter headings provide little assistance with retrieval, then both users and libraries must rely on the efficacy of enhancements to access, such as the library's catalog. While there may be questions regarding how well libraries achieve access through their catalogs, there is little doubt about the purpose of cataloging. Mann outlines the three principal goals of cataloging and classification: "(a) promoting predictability of retrieval, as opposed to guesswork (with specificity being a crucial condition of predictability within subject cataloging and classification); (b) promoting serendipity in retrieval; (c) promoting depth of access to books."[22] There are some distinct obstacles to success, however. As Allen observes, some users know about the structure of the library's catalog, but that knowledge tends not to translate into success with retrieval.[23] Moreover, there is no guarantee that any two indexers will describe a given book in the same way. As is true of reading, indexing is an interpretive process; there is the potential for differing opinions as to the core subject of a book and the relative "aboutness" beyond the core subject. All of the vagaries that surround access and retrieval center on language—its indeterminacy, its problems of semantics and usage, its social aspects.

FROM COLLECTION MANAGEMENT TO CONTENT MANAGEMENT

It must be admitted that the transformation from concentration on managing collections (physical objects, their placement and storage, and their economics) to managing content is not an easy one, either conceptually or practically. For one thing, it is much easier to manage things than ideas. For the vast majority of its history the library has tacitly equated the *package* with the *content*, so the library's responsibility has been to preserve and make accessible the artifact, assuming that the content would then be preserved. The most absurd extension of this idea is embodied in Walter M. Miller's novel *A Canticle for Liebowitz*, in which a meaningless physical artifact is preserved, but can in no way "inform" its readers any longer. All this is not to imply that content has been utterly ignored by librarians. As was noted in the previous section, librarians have striven to create access mechanisms aimed at enhancing the retrievability of content. Even in the realm of collection management, the act of selection is based overwhelmingly on content and the match of content with community. It is not our intention to indict the profession wrongly. On the other hand, it is easy to become trapped in a discourse that creates ascendancy for the physical over the conceptual. As Strauch has said, "We have a mission to collect materials that appeal to our user base over time, and to make them locally, readily available."[24]

The use of a different vocabulary has been urged, not merely to express the vision of use and users of information, but to assist in altering our thought regarding use of scholarly communication. Strauch's rhetoric incorporates a particular piece of the past (and present)—attention, through language, to the package in which information is delivered. It is true that the medium does have an impact on the absorption of information. Without becoming too McLuhanesque here, one has to recognize that the medium does affect the message; that, for instance, a book is not received in the same way that electronic information is. A focus on content does not ignore the physical; it embraces an awareness that the physical affects the content and its reception. For much of the past the medium has been a choice of the producer. The writer has traditionally chosen the book; the artist may have chosen the painting or the sculpture. At present, a number of texts written for the printed page are available electronically. The change of medium cannot help but have an impact on the way the content is communicated. Also at present, some information users elect to use the printed word, the linear text; others opt for a hypertext presentation. There are questions raised by this observation regarding the media themselves and their longevity, but there are more pressing (for the purposes of consideration here) questions of the responsibility of libraries and librarians for meeting the needs of users. Again, there are both conceptual and practical aspects of this matter.

DUAL SYSTEMS: PRINT AND ELECTRONIC

This section heading suggests that there is the possibility for some debate regarding the state of scholarly communication and its place in academic libraries. To an extent, this is true. However, there are realities that must be accepted before we engage in revolutionary discourse. There is certainly the technological capability for large-scale transformation of the communication system, but technological concerns are not the only ones to consider. Libraries have extensive collections of print materials. It is likely that there will not be sufficient financial support to transfer the information that is currently available in print media to electronic media. The cost of such a transfer would be prohibitive. Because of the probability that these print materials will remain in collections, there is the need not only to maintain but to enhance access to them. Of course, this assumes that the content of the materials remains of use to the institutional communities. If that assumption is correct, then it is the *content* that becomes the most important factor in the equation. We must add a cautionary note here. If libraries were to diminish access to print materials (by transformations in their catalogs and/or by the elimination of secondary access tools) then, in the natural course of events, the content of these materials might very well be used less and less over time. A library that makes a particular item less accessible, intellectually and physically, can ensure that there is little demand for that item. It should also be noted that access as determined by the library is not the sole means of access. A principal piece of the scholarly mechanism is the citation, which, de facto, becomes a mode of access that is imbedded in the content itself.[25]

If there is indeed intellectual access to the products of the scholarly communication system, then the cost of providing the information itself must be considered. There are numerous estimates of the cost of providing content in print on paper (including the costs of selection, acquisition, cataloging, shelf maintenance, and circulation). It is clear that the provision of print materials to users is expensive. The question to be asked is: Is the electronic medium less expensive? The answer to this question is not clear. The entire infrastructure of networked information is less than stable at present. It is unclear who, in a matter of just a few years, will have control of the technical mechanism for information transfer and how much users of the mechanism will be charged. Also, many of the formal communication efforts, such as electronic journals, are still in experimental stages. As such, much of the cost of production, including editorial effort, is subsidized. Is the present level of subsidy going to continue? Probably not. Crawford and Gorman provide a guess at the costs of providing information solely in electronic media at the University of California,

Los Angeles: "A 'virtual' UCLA library would produce as much paper *every year* as is now contained in the library and involve spending $160 on printing on demand for every $100 now spent on *all library collections, programs, and services*."[26] We do not take their estimate as gospel, but it is likely that many users will want to capture the retrieved information in print, at least in the short term.

As Buckland notes, "It would seem very foolish to expect any scenario involving an 'either/or' dichotomy—*only* paper collections or *only* a paperless library. Some balance will be needed between selected materials on paper, presumably the more heavily used and the less volatile material, and selective recourse to electronic documents for as much of the rest as available."[27] Buckland's assessment is a cogent one that should be attended to by all librarians. There is a problem with it, however. It is an assessment that is still deeply entrenched in the management of physical artifacts; in fact, the statement features a fixation on the thing, as he refers to "less volatile *material*" and "electronic *documents*." Apart from availability (by that we mean whether specific information exists in only one medium), there are aspects intrinsic to the content that have an impact on the means of communication. Even someone as steeped in electronic media as Louis Rosetto, founder and editor of *Wired* magazine, recognizes that there is something about differences in content that affects the means of absorption: "Paper is completely random-access; it's high resolution; it's portable; it's almost interactive in the way it gives you the ability to determine the pace, to go backward or forward. Paper is still the best way of delivering high thought content."[28] Given the current state both of technology and of human inclination, there are advantages that have to go to print when it comes to some kinds of content. It is incumbent upon the librarian to acquire a deep understanding of the phenomenon of "reading" (for lack of a better term) and of the essential character of content.

So where are we in the history of dual systems? At an early stage, but at a stage where other factors outside the library (including the economics of all information production, the academic rewards system, and the nature of information use) are changing much more slowly than the technological landscape. At the time of this writing it must be acknowledged that there are few electronic journals (both in real terms and especially relative to the number of print journals). Since the capability certainly exists for the proliferation of electronic journals, there must be reasons for the small numbers. We would suggest that it is the political, social, and economic elements that are having the most profound impact on the medium at this time. Not only do authors overwhelmingly seek to publish in peer-reviewed outlets, but also they seek to read peer-reviewed sources. The preponderance of information necessitates employing whatever filtering mechanism might be available. This brings us to the point we wish to emphasize most strongly—that the academic library is no mere storehouse of physical artifacts; it is a gateway to the world of scholarly communication. The concept of library as gateway transcends the access/ownership debate. In essence the distinction is meaningless; what is important is that the librarians are able to communicate with users and know the communication system. This concept redefines the librarian's role.

HOW WILL THE LIBRARY MEDIATE?

This is not a rhetorical question; it is the single most important question for librarians to consider now and in the future. Our position is that the librarian is a manager. This, of course, is not a novel idea, but in the past the management aspect of librarianship has focused on (in temporal order) the physical packages of information, the buildings in which they are stored, the people who oversee them, the money to acquire them, and the technology to enhance access to them and, in some extreme visions, to replace them. Our view of management is different; management is an intellectual activity dependent on individuals' ability to comprehend what information producers are trying to communicate, to divine the needs and desires of information seekers, and to conjoin the two on the basis of what the mind endeavors to create. In this vision of management the items of prior management initiatives are not ignored, but they are all rethought in the context of content. Finances, space, physical plant, and people are all still essential to the library enterprise (in fact, people are even more essential in this scheme).

One of the first targets in a program to move the profession toward content management (which, we might add, not only replaces "collection management," but is larger than that concept) is to revisit our terminology in an effort to unify the purpose of mediation. And the first term to come under scrutiny is "information." The word is currently used to denote anything that librarians and libraries have to do with as well as the product of all scholarly work. For some years writers have suggested that "knowledge" replace "information," since there is a process not just of distillation, but of growth that is associated with research and scholarship. This, however, is also a problematic word, while the scholar has undoubtedly increased his or her knowledge through inquiry, there is no guarantee that the reader will be likewise enriched. The growth of knowledge is, first, a personal phenomenon, and once personal knowledge grows, it becomes a societal phenomenon. Librarians should certainly be concerned with epistemological matters, but we cannot, through coercion, exhortation, or any other means, impose knowledge on users of libraries. What we can do is enable users to enrich their knowledge bases. The enabling function of librarians centers on one thing—mediation focused on content.

The corollary to this imperative is that librarians must understand that users approach the content base of the library (the "information") from stances that are influenced by a variety of factors. Earlier we presented a brief discussion of the difficulties of retrieval. A reason for the difficulties is that users are attempting to apprehend content in personal contexts that are complex. The complexity strikes at the concept of relevance itself. We tend to think that relevance is determined solely by an objective judgment of a user or reader of particular content. While content is predominant in relevance decisions, other factors enter the fray. Barry points out such factors as the user's own experience and beliefs, the sources of the document (especially its perceived quality and reputation), the document as a physical entity (how easily it might be obtained and how much it might cost).[29] On the face of it, these findings may suggest that librarians should attempt to assess, or at least to direct, the intuitions of users regarding relevance. This is not an easy task, though, as Sperber and Wilson point out. In investigating cognitive aspects of relevance they acknowledge that there are problems with intuitions of relevance, the most serious of which is the fact that the intuitions are relative to contexts. The contexts are part and parcel of both the content under consideration and the personal stance (beliefs, assumptions, existing knowledge) of the individual. The content may or may not have a contextual effect on the individual; it may change the person's beliefs or alter assumptions, it may reinforce the existing context, or it may have no effect. Moreover, the contextual effect is, at the same time, cognitive and perceptual. That is, it may result in a change in thinking, or it may result in a change in perceived appearance. The distinction is a subtle one, which adds to the complexity.[30]

Given that relevance is problematic, there must be a strategy for librarians to address the role of mediation. Froehlich suggests that content assumes an ascendant position, that it becomes essential, since it becomes the key to interpretation, and interpretation is integral to the determination of relevance. The means, in fact, of mediation is interpretation. Froehlich states, "Hermeneutics can provide a productive framework for modeling systems and user criteria. . . . Interpretation is the act of placing a text . . . into a context so that the set of interpretations that frames the information collection will concide with the set of interpretations that frames the context of a user's information need."[31] This suggestion is not accidental; it meshes with the concepts put forth by Sperber and Wilson because of the connection between interpretation and context (broadly defined). It is difficult here to discuss in sufficient depth the nature of interpretation. But some mention must be made of the purpose of a hermeneutical approach to the mediation process. First, a definition of hermeneutics would be helpful, and one is provided by Palmer: It is "the process of deciphering which goes from manifest content and meaning to latent or hidden meaning. . . . [It] is the system by which the deeper significance is revealed beneath the manifest content."[32] For mediation to be realized, the interpretive process must extend beyond hermeneutics as just defined. It depends on principles that include intentionality. "[I]ntentionality is dependent upon the 'I,' the perceiver (the consciousness), and the object (that which may be perceived). . . . A failure of the user-library interchange may, at times, be due to a lack of commonality. That is, the library creators, the 'I' who structures intellectual and physical access, may not have an 'other' in mind."[33]

THE ART OF THE POSSIBLE

When we speak of what is possible, we have to be aware of what we mean by "possible" and also what is implied by that word. In the technological realm much is possible; unfortunately, much of what is possible is not affordable. In libraries we are generally careful to present what we do in terms (explicit or not) of public good. In one sense this means that we structure services, content, and access in such a way that the library benefits as large a portion of the community as it can. The goals that most libraries establish for themselves look outward; for instance, the academic library exists to support the teaching and research missions of its parent organizations. What is done in the library is intended for, or at least is justified by, the needs of the academic community. In another sense, the possible may refer to what can be done, irrespective of either need or cost. Eventually, cost will be a consideration in organizations like libraries that do not, by and large, generate their own income or control their own financial resources. The other aspect—the possible irrespective of the need—represents a temptation for libraries, and a temptation that we must be aware of. Reconciliation of what is possible with what is needed is not a simple task; sometimes technological possibilities enable us to alter our thinking, which may lead to alterations of behavior.

COMBINING THE BEST OF THE PRINT AND ELECTRONIC WORLDS

The previous discussion of mediation can help inform the issues pertinent to this section. If interpretation is at the heart of the library's mediation function, then medium is not what to turn to first in seeking the most efficacious means for reaching our goals. As has been stated elsewhere, "Decisions . . . should be based first on the needs of the community and then attention should focus on the content required to meet the need. Only after that should the package (or actual container) be considered. . . . Success, in library terms, should be redefined to reflect, not quantity, but provision for need."[34] Some communication is unique to a certain medium; that is, there are some things that are currently obtainable only in the form of a book, or journal article from a print source, or a World Wide Web site. It becomes incumbent upon librarians to be cognizant of the source of content and then to use that source to meet the needs of the community. The medium, then, is not exactly irrelevant (since librarians must have the capacity to incorporate that medium into the provision of content to the user), but it is certainly of secondary, if not tertiary, concern. Some combination of print and electronic formats, given the constraints of content attached to a single medium, becomes a necessity that requires little choice on the library's part.

Not all content is this simple, however. In an increasing number of instances there are choices of media. Particular content may be available in print, or via some electronic means. The issue of combination, or at least of selection, of media becomes an important one. What, in such a case, governs the decisions by librarians? The overriding concern is a fit of the nature of the content and the uses to which it will be put. It is conceivable that a library user simply wants a brief passage from a specific work, perhaps even a literary work. The most effective means of providing this content to the user may be to gain access to a networked source in which the specific passage is readily retrievable. In another case, an individual may want to spend a considerable amount of time with the content, thinking about it, rereading it, making notes about it, considering its relation to other content. For this user, a physical package may be more effective—one the individual can carry about, one that is amenable to sustained reading. It becomes clear that no common answer suits all uses and all users. The library's responsibility is to weave all of the aspects of use—need and purpose for the content, the content itself, the medium by which the content is delivered—into the provision of a service that meets the user's need. It also becomes clear, once again, that the terminology that has been in common usage falls short in describing the essence of the library's purpose. It is not sufficient to refer to "access" or "retrieval" in the absence of the user's need.

The notion of combining the *best* of print and electronic media implies that no medium, in itself, embodies the capacity for meeting every need, other than the most visceral one for form absent of substance. Libraries, however, exist to concentrate on substance first, and only then on form (or at least they should so concentrate now and in the future). Also implicit in the above notion is the importance of distinguishing the possible from the desirable. There are instances in which it is possible to store and retrieve information electronically, but the storage and retrieval may be accomplished at greater cost than by alternative means and with an inferior process and product. It is vital to recall the admonition of Louis Rosetto. It is also vital to connect his statement with that of Birkerts, who reminds us that not all uses of content are instrumental, not all involve discrete bits of information employed in practical application. A particular medium, in and of itself (whether it be print on paper or hypermedia), does not necessarily contain the most effective uses of content. Lanham reports that he upset attendees at a multimedia conference when he referred to new products purporting to be the teachers of the future as "mindless products." "The programs offered not a teacher or a curriculum or a book or a lesson plan, or even the table of contents for any of these. They supplied only the raw material, the parts list, for them. These programs employed every animated effect that multimedia can have except the animation of a human mind."[35]

It should be clear to us in libraries that the combination of the best of print and electronic media is dependent on what Crawford and Gorman refer to as the intelligent use of technology. Intelligent use involves "seeking answers to problems rather than seeking applications of interesting new technology; weighing the cost-effectiveness, cost-benefit, and, above all, impact on service of any proposed innovation; rethinking the program, service, or workflow that is being automated rather than automating what one has.''[36] It should be emphasized that this is in no way a Luddite approach; that it is a recognition that libraries must be open to technological possibilities. At the same time, it is a realization that the openness to those possibilities should not close one off to the nature of the content need that the user genuinely has. The combination of openness to medium and openness to need yields a fruitful expression of fitting content with the user who wants that content. "In the aftermath of the excitement [surrounding some technologies or media] . . . there remains the need for deliberate thought regarding what information [or content] is best stored and transmitted electronically and what is best fitted to other media.''[37]

THE GOOD OF THE READER IN THE SCHOLARLY COMMUNICATION SYSTEM

This section brings us full circle in examining the future of scholarly communication. The word ''reader'' is purposely employed here to enforce the idea that those who are intimately involved with scholarly communication are critical consumers of its output. They are not passive vessels into which the work of others is poured. They are skeptical, they are inquisitive, they are seeking knowledge (which is a very *active* process). What they seek is the content that facilitates their inquiry, and they must make judgments about that content based on what it communicates to them. They are interpreters of the world of content, but their interpretation depends, at least to some degree, on the interpretation that enables them to obtain the content. The interpretation of which we speak is that of the library and librarian. This interpretation is realized through access mechanisms, such as the library's catalog, and the librarian's own comprehension of the content base (which extends beyond the library's physical collection) and of the user's expressed need. In the realm of content management the elements of user need, librarian interpretation, content itself, and access to the most effective medium are all intertwined in a web that defines, ultimately, the success of the library.

A cautionary note is needed at this point. The good of the reader cannot be a tacit assumption in the information structure that includes producers, mediators (including the library), suppliers, and storers. Contrary to the assessment of some, such as Nicholas Negroponte, digital or electronic data do not simply and intrinsically exist forever.[38] As Stoll observes, sometimes things disappear.

You probably think that digital archives are permanent. Then consider Coffee Line. For the latest scoop on coffee beans, we'd call the Dialog system to sip information on growing, marketing, and packaging. Here's where we'd get the number of tons of Kona coffee shipped. All updated weekly. Well, it's gone. Log into Dialog and we see this greeting: ''Coffee Line is unavailable as of October 1.'' Why? It was uneconomical to carry.[39]

This illustrates that access to content can be tenuous, not necessarily because of a property of the content itself, but because of a connection between content and medium. This warning should be heeded in the context of the good of the reader, especially since much of scholarly communication is, by its nature, esoteric. Does the choice of medium for access determine the obtainability of the content? This is not a trivial question.

At this point, we wish to offer one more distinction between the thoughts of Negroponte and Stoll that is relevant to the overall assessment of the future of collection (content) development. Negroponte addresses the issue of where intelligence resides in the use of media. He says,

A newspaper is also produced with all the intelligence in the transmitter. But the medium of large-format paper provides some relief to the "sameness" of information, as it can be consumed differently, by different people, at different times. We browse and flip through pages, guided by headlines and pictures, each of us treating very differently the identical bits delivered to hundreds of thousands of people. The bits are the same, but the reading experience is different.[40]

Negroponte ignores, as does the discourse of collection development, the content and quest by the reader for meaningful content. To him, and to some ways of thinking in our profession, relevance is determined by medium, or factors other than content. Stoll offers a different assessment: "information is not knowledge. . . . Minds think with ideas, not information. No amount of data, bandwidth, or processing power can substitute for inspired thought."[41] Such a notion is central to a transformation to content management.

COLLECTION MANAGEMENT STRATEGIES FOR THE 21ST CENTURY

Atkinson has said, "If we understand selection as that activity that results in acquisition, then it is the user in the online environment who becomes the selector."[42] Atkinson further argues that the logic of the process that we are currently following means that ultimately "collection development as a separate library operation . . . probably will not survive the eventual disappearance of paper as the primary . . . medium of scholarly information exchange."[43] However, a more likely possibility for the first decades of the 21st century is the continued evolution of a mixed system—part print, increasingly electronic—that will affect the work of the different disciplines in different ways.

Thus, the exact role that content managers might play will be determined in part by the kind of disciplinary discourse that a library seeks to support. In the sciences, for example, librarians working as content managers may be integrated into a fully collaborative venture, as was recently suggested by the Association of American Universities Research Libraries Project on managing scientific and technological information: "The emergent model views each scientific community as a knowledge management system, and it calls upon scientists, information technologists, and librarians to act as partners in all components and activities of that system.''[44] In the sciences, the Human Genome Initiative might serve as an example of this kind of scholarly communication process.

Yet this sort of collaborative model may not make sense for the other disciplines in the humanities and the social sciences. Further, the fully collaborative model assumes that commercial publishers will stand aside as scholarly communities work to become self-publishing ventures on the Net. This is an unlikely scenario. In fact, progress toward networked electronic journals in all the disciplines may be slower than anticipated because of real and perceived problems with copyright. As Metz has stated,

Under current circumstances, too much success in electronic publication could be fatal to publishers. Currently publishers are very concerned about the ease with which electronic publications can be copied and shared. From their point of view, one of the critical advantages of the print medium is that it converts intellectual property into a physical commodity whose use can be limited and monitored and whose replication and redistribution is inconvenient and unsatisfactory. In the absence of a mechanism to prevent the duplication and redistribution of electronic text, publishers of profitable journals will regard the electronic text with the same fear and suspicion that the entertainment industry has had of dual head VCRs or digital audio tape, both of which have faced legal and economic roadblocks despite their technological advantages.[45]

For the near term, it looks as though librarians will be focusing on improving the delivery of journal articles *after* they have been published, rather than actively collaborating on the publishing of scholarly journals. In this context, content managers may pursue a dual strategy, one that emphasizes expedited document delivery utilizing commercial services where appropriate, and at the same time working toward the development of a network-based system of ''regional libraries that would provide a nationally organized structure for managing scientific and technological information. Among other things, such a system could collect and store serial publications that could then be distributed electronically to local users.''[46]

In the social sciences and humanities, because scholars will likely continue to communicate through the book for some time to come, content managers will be worrying much more about the fate of the book and, in the short run at least, devising strategies that will maintain part of the library's resources budget for the acquisition, storage, and eventual retrieval of these printed artifacts. In the longer run, content managers in the social sciences and humanities will be engaging more and more in retrospective content management, that is, developing criteria and strategies for selecting and then converting major segments of the traditional canon into electronic form that could then serve scholars.

CONCLUSION: CONTENT MANAGEMENT AS A FORM OF MEDIATION

In the next ten to twenty years, issues of retrieval, identification, selection, and ranking will dominate the work of those content managers attempting to develop and implement library programs and services. This is because, as Lynch has written,

There is simply too much information, and more and more of it is on the network. Not only is there too much information overall, but increasingly users will find that there is too much relevant information on the network. Thus, there will be a growing emphasis on precision in searching and on quality ranking and selection than simply identifying what is likely to be relevant information.[47]

And because users will be relying upon content managers to organize, select, and provide context for the information on the Net, there is likely to be a need for more library mediation, not less. Here are some of the critical activities that content managers might be expected to engage in as they seek to meet the needs of users in a networked 21st-century world:

- They will be responsible for evaluating, selecting, and ranking content—that is, the ideas, data, and graphic images—that embody and reflect the needs of the scholarly community within which they work.[48]
- They will attempt, wherever possible, to maintain the content that is discovered and make it accessible by means of "logical gateways."
- Because users will be faced with "multiple versions of the same object" in a networked environment, content managers will be expected to select the appropriate versions, whether it be print, electronic, multimedia, or a combination thereof.[49]
- Coping with the context of content will become increasingly important—mediation in this sense means that the "metadata" added by content managers will be essential to situating the information so that users can find, use, and then understand what it is that they have found.[50]
- Organizing resource sharing and content delivery systems that are sensitive to the variety of cooperative and for-profit arrangements that will be available in the networked world.
- Dealing with the issue of copyright in a way that protects the interests of the academic community while still meeting the legal obligations of an evolving copyright law.
- Finally, a very basic sense, content managers will continue to mediate between authors and readers, insofar as libraries serve as gateways to the information provided by publishers.

It is important to recognize that form does shape content to a certain extent and that consequently, "print yields a particular kind of discourse."[51] Electronic forms of information will also shape discourse, and it is the role of content specialists to mediate between these different discourses in order to make sure that users have access to the appropriate forms of discourse for the particular discipline. Because disciplines will continue to drive the scholarly communication process, it will be important for librarians to have both subject and bibliographic expertise. In this way, content managers may become the indispensable go-betweens as we move further into the 21st century.

NOTES

1. Bart Harloe and John M. Budd, "Collection Development and Scholarly Communication in the Era of Electronic Access," *Journal of Academic Librarianship* 20 (May 1994): 83–87.

2. The literature on the "serials crisis" is voluminous. For an excellent background report, see *Report of the ARL Serials Prices Project* (Washington, DC: Association of Research Libraries, 1989).

3. Joseph Branin, "Delivering on Promises: The Intersection Between Print and Electronic Systems in Libraries," *Information Technologies and Libraries* 10 (December 1991): 322.

4. Harloe and Budd, "Collection Development and Scholarly Communication," p. 86.

5. Patricia Battin, "Introduction," in *Campus Strategies for Libraries and Electronic Information*, ed. Caroline Arms ([Bedford, MA]; Digital Press, 1990), p. 3.

6. Harloe and Budd, "Collection Development and Scholarly Communication," p. 86.

7. To note just one recent treatment of the growth of literatures and the effects on libraries, see Anthony M. Cummings et al., *University Libraries and Scholarly Communication* (Washington, DC: Association of Research Libraries, 1992).

8. N. David Mermin, *Boojums All the Way Through: Communicating Science in a Prosaic Age* (Cambridge: Cambridge University Press, 1990), pp. 57–62.

9. Charles R. Martell, Jr., *The Client-Centered Academic Library: An Organizational Model* (Westport, CT: Greenwood Press, 1983), pp. 22–23.

10. Harloe and Budd, "Collection Development and Scholarly Communication," p. 86.

11. Warren Weaver, "Recent Contributions to the Mathematical Theory of Communication," in Claude E. Shannon and Warren Weaver, *The Mathematical Theory of Communication* (Urbana: University of Illinois Press, 1963, c1949), p. 28.

12. Jay David Bolter, *Writing Space: The Computer, Hypertext, and the History of Writing* (Hillsdale, NJ: Lawrence Erlbaum Associates, 1991), p. 11.

13. George P. Landow, *Hypertext: The Convergence of Contemporary Critical Theory and Technology* (Baltimore: Johns Hopkins University Press, 1992), p. 58.

14. Edward W. Said, *Beginnings: Intention and Method* (New York: Columbia University Press, 1985), p. 5.

15. Bolter, *Writing Space*, p. 158.

16. Sven Birkerts, *Gutenberg Elegies: The Fate of Reading in an Electronic Age* (Boston: Faber and Faber, 1994), p. 75.

17. Ibid., pp. 136–37.

18. Richard E. Lanham, *The Electronic Word: Democracy, Technology, and the Arts* (Chicago: University of Chicago Press, 1993), p. 134.

19. Ibid., p. 135.

20. Florence E. DeHart and Karen Matthews, "Subject Enhancement and OPACs: Planning Ahead," *Technical Services Quarterly* 7, no. 4 (1990): 35–52.

21. D. C. Blair and M. E. Maron, "An Evaluation of Retrieval Effectiveness for a Full-Text Document Retrieval System," *Communications of the ACM* 28 (March 1985): 289–99.

22. Thomas Mann, *Cataloging and Classification Quality at the Library of Congress*, Opinion Paper No. 5 (Washington, DC: Library of Congress, 1994), p. 4.

23. Bryce Allen, "Individual Differences, Values and Catalogs," *Technicalities* 11 (July 1991): 6.

24. Katina Strauch, "Don't Get Mired in It: Make Some Bricks," *Journal of Academic Librarianship* 18 (March 1992): 12–13.

25. Ross Atkinson, "The Citation as Intertext: Toward a Theory of the Selection Process," *Library Resources and Technical Services* 28 (April–June 1984): 109–19.

26. Walt Crawford and Michael Gorman, *Future Libraries: Dreams, Madness, & Reality* (Chicago: American Library Association, 1995), p. 143.

27. Michael Buckland, *Redesigning Library Services: A Manifesto* (Chicago: American Library Association, 1992), p. 59.

28. Louis Rosetto, quoted by Horace Bent in *Bookseller*, July 30, 1993.

29. Carol L. Barry, "User-Defined Relevance Criteria: An Exploratory Study," *Journal of the American Society for Information Science* 45 (April 1994): 149–59.

30. Dan Sperber and Deirdre Wilson, *Relevance: Communication and Cognition* (Cambridge, MA: Harvard University Press, 1986).

31. Thomas J. Froehlich, "Relevance Reconsidered—Towards an Agenda for the 21st Century," *Journal of the American Society for Information Science* 45 (April 1994): 130.

32. Richard Palmer, *Hermeneutics: Interpretation Theory in Schleiermacher, Dilthey, Heidegger, and Gadamer* (Evanston, IL: Northwestern University Press, 1969), pp. 43–44.

33. John M. Budd, "An Epistemological Foundation for Library and Information Science," *Library Quarterly* 65 (July 1995): 312–13.

34. Harloe and Budd, "Collection Development," p. 85.

35. Lanham, *The Electronic Word*, p. 218.

36. Crawford and Gorman, *Future Libraries*, p. 10.

37. Harloe and Budd, "Collection Development," p. 85.

38. Nicholas Negroponte, *Being Digital* (New York: Knopf, 1995). On page 13 Negroponte states, "Digital books never go out of print."

39. Clifford Stoll, *Silicon Snake Oil: Second Thoughts on the Information Highway* (New York: Doubleday, 1995), p. 186.

40. Negroponte, *Being Digital*, pp. 19–20.

41. Stoll, *Silicon Snake Oil*, pp. 192–93. Stoll owes an unacknowledged debt to Theodore Roszak, who has constructed a powerful narrative based on the concept expressed by Stoll. See Roszak, *The Cult of Information: The Folklore of Computers and the True Art of Thinking* (New York: Pantheon Books, 1986).

42. Ross Atkinson, "Access, Ownership, and the Future of Collection Development," in *Collection Management and Development: Issues in an Electronic Era: Proceedings*

of the Advanced Collection Management and Development Institute, ed. Peggy Johnson and Bonnie MacEwan (Chicago: American Library Association, 1994), p. 100.

43. Ibid., p. 102.

44. *Reports of the AAU Task Forces: On Acquisition and Distribution of Foreign Language and Area Studies Materials. A National Strategy for Managing Scientific and Technological Information: Intellectual Property Rights in an Electronic Environment* (Washington, DC: Association of Research Libraries, 1994), p. 61.

45. Paul Metz, "The View from a University Library," *Change* 27 (January/February 1995): 30.

46. *Reports of the AAU Task Forces*, p. 49.

47. Clifford Lynch et al., "Nature of the NIDR Challenge," unpublished draft of a white paper on network information discovery and retrieval prepared for the Coalition for Networked Information, by Clifford Lynch, Avra Michelson, Craig Summerhill, and Cecilia Preston (April 1995), p. 6.

48. For an example of how the group of content managers dealt with the process of selecting and ranking internet resources, see Samuel Demas, Peter McDonald, and Greg Lawrence, "The Internet and Collection Development: Mainstreaming Selection of Internet Resources," *Library Resources and Technical Services* 30 (July 1995): 275–90.

49. Lynch et al., "Nature of the NIDR Challenge," p. 5.

50. As Clifford Lynch has remarked, "with seamless navigation within a distributed, autonomously managed set of information resources, users tend to lose context for information that they retrieve, and this context is often important in helping the user access the reliability, timeliness, and bias of information resources." In "Networked Information Resource Discovery: An Overview of Current Issues," pre-publication draft (1995), p. 7.

51. Cummings, *University Libraries*, p. 109.

PART II

The Technological Contribution to Collection Management

2

The Internet and Collection Management in Academic Libraries: Opportunities and Challenges

Thomas E. Nisonger

INTRODUCTION

Five years ago many librarians had never heard of the Internet. Today the Internet (often simply termed "the Net") makes headlines in the national media. It has been observed that since the "race to the moon" in the 1960s, no technological issue has received as much publicity as the "information superhighway."[1]

This chapter examines the relationship between the Internet and collection management in libraries on three levels: (1) use of the Internet to perform traditional functions for traditional materials (for example, using the Internet to help select books and serials or evaluate the collection), (2) the application of traditional collection development functions to the Internet (evaluation and selection of Internet resources), and (3) the impact the Internet's existence will have on traditional functions and materials (selecting fewer print resources because they can be accessed electronically on the Internet). There are at least five major variables in analyzing the relationship between the Internet and collection management: (1) collection management functions (for example, selection, evaluation, etc.), (2) library type (academic, public, school, or special), (3) information resources on the Internet (electronic journals, listservs, databases, etc.), (4) access modes for Internet resources (such as file transfer protocol [FTP], World Wide Web [WWW or the Web], or telnet), and (5) time frame. However, this chapter focuses on collection management functions in academic libraries in the context of the present technological environment.

This chapter explores, in the context of the Internet, such collection management functions as identification, microevaluation, selection, macroevaluation, acquisitions, resource sharing, and document delivery. Although intellectual freedom and censorship are usually considered within the domain of collection management, these topics will not be discussed here. The chapter's objective is to outline major issues rather than provide definitive answers. Both descriptive (describing what libraries are actually doing) and prescriptive (suggesting what libraries can or should do) approaches are used. The focus is on the utilization of the Internet rather than on technological issues. Information for this chapter is based on reviewing the literature, surfing the Internet, monitoring several listservs pertinent to collection management, as well as the author's background as a collection development practitioner, teacher, and researcher.[2]

Because the word "traditional" is frequently used in this essay, a working definition is in order. Traditional resources include books, serials, government documents, maps, audiovisuals, and microformat materials. Traditional library functions are the identification, selection, evaluation, acquisition, borrowing, processing, and interpretation of information resources, usually in the form of distinct bibliographic units.

THE INTERNET

This section is relatively brief because it is assumed that most readers are generally familiar with the Internet. The Internet is a "network of networks." Its origin has been traced to the ARPANET, founded in 1969 by the U.S. Department of Defense for military purposes.[3] In January 1995, there were estimated to be over 25 million Internet users from more than 100 countries, with Internet traffic growing at 10 percent a month.[4] Librarians' initial use of the Internet focused on three applications: electronic mail (including listservs and discussion groups), remote log-in via telnet (most frequently to other libraries' online public access catalogs, or OPACs), and file transfer using FTP. Later, librarians' attention began to focus on gophers and then on the World Wide Web. The term "gopher" popularly refers to a menu-driven directory structure that provides access to Internet resources, or, more technically, the software that uses a client/server protocol to access the resources and create the menu. The first gopher was developed at the University of Minnesota in 1991. Gophers can be created for campus-wide information systems, libraries, academic departments, nonacademic organizations, and/or organized on a subject or geographical basis. There were at least 520 gophers by June 1993 and reportedly 1,000 in early 1994.[5] The Web uses hypertext transfer protocol (HTTP) to provide links among textual and multimedia documents. The Web was developed at the European Particle Physics Laboratory in Geneva, beginning in 1989. The number of sites on the Web has grown dramatically, increasing from 1,000 in April

1994 to 110,000 by October 1995.[6] The Web can be accessed through such graphics-oriented Web browsers as Mosaic or Netscape Navigator, as well as text-only browsers such as Lynx. An Internet gopher or Web site can contain both primary information created by the site's sponsor and secondary information in the form of links to external sites.

OPPORTUNITIES OFFERED BY THE INTERNET

"Access versus ownership" and " 'just-in-time' versus 'just-in-case' " have been catchy but somewhat simplistic collection development slogans for a considerable time. Likewise, the "virtual library," the "digital library," and "the library without walls" are frequently heard but ill-defined terms. It does not take much imagination to perceive that the Internet offers an opportunity to give real meaning to these terms by facilitating rapid access to information resources external to the library. At a minimum, the Internet offers a potential to save money, shelf space, and library staff time while simultaneously increasing the rapid provision of information to patrons; in effect, helping address the issue articulated by Melvil Dewey in 1877, "the problem before us . . . is to make libraries better—their expenses less."[7]

The phrase, "serendipitous use of automated technology," has been used to describe the utilization of technology for performing functions apart from the technology's original, intended purpose.[8] Numerous examples pertaining to collection management could be cited. *BIP Plus*, the CD-ROM version of *Books in Print*, was originally created as a technical services tool, but has been used for collection development and research. Bibliographic utilities, such as OCLC, RLIN and WLN, were created to support the cataloging function, but their archival tapes of cataloging records can be used for collection management, such as longitudinal analysis of a single library's collecting patterns or overlapping holdings among a group of libraries. In many ways the Internet's entire history illustrates the serendipitous use of technology. It was created for military reasons during the Cold War but soon became a scientific research tool. Only in recent years have librarians realized its potential applications to their profession. There are undoubtedly innumerable opportunities for collection management librarians to use the Internet in new and creative ways that are not now readily apparent.

At a maximum, the Internet could fundamentally alter library operations or even the definition of what constitutes a library, resulting in what Lynch terms "transformation."[9] Because the Internet can deliver information directly to the end user, a question arises whether libraries will even be needed in the future. These issues are speculated upon briefly later in this chapter.

PROBLEMS WITH AND LIMITATIONS OF THE INTERNET

At present, there are a number of generally recognized problems that hinder the effective utilization of the Internet: (1) the Net is not particularly user-friendly; (2) one often experiences technical glitches such as dropped lines or traffic jams; (3) the Internet is undergoing dynamic, rapid change; (4) surfing the Internet can become addictive and waste one's time; (5) numerous unresolved copyright issues abound; (6) some of the available resources require passwords; (7) numerous ostensible links on the World Wide Web are unavailable because they are still "under construction"; (8) intrusive advertising is beginning to appear on the Net; and (9) security is a problem.

There are additional difficulties more directly relevant to the collection management of Internet resources: (1) the totality of resources on the Net is unknown; (2) good bibliographical control of known resources is lacking; (3) resources on the Internet are inherently unstable, here today and gone, changed, or moved by tomorrow; (4) available information may be inaccurate, outdated, or generally useless since there is relatively little quality control on the Net (the opposite side of this issue is that the Internet is more democratic because anyone can post information without a gatekeeper); and (5) many of the Net's resources are not archived. However, it is reasonable to assume that some of these problems will ultimately be resolved.

These and other issues complicate planning for, as well as writing about, the Internet's effective utilization by librarians. Due to rapid technological change, the near future may witness presently unforeseen innovations. As the 1990s began, who would have predicted the Web's present importance? Moreover, how such issues as copyright, cost, and scholarly acceptance are eventually resolved will significantly influence the way collection management librarians use the Internet, and its impact on their work.

LITERATURE REVIEW

To illustrate the rapidly proliferating literature concerning the Internet, keyword searches in the *Library Literature* CD-ROM database under the term "Internet" retrieved 253 items published through December 1993; 406 entries published through June 1994; 770 through March 30, 1995; 917 through June 29, 1995; and 1,113 through September 28, 1995. Identical keyword searches retrieved 1,136 items from *Library and Information Science Abstracts*, 718 from *Information Science Abstracts*, and 374 from the *ERIC* CD-ROM databases, published in 1995. There is obviously considerable overlap among the databases. Moreover, searches under "web" (World Wide Web) and "gopher" retrieved additional entries not included in the figures cited above.

Many of these are short news items or book reviews rather than substantive works. Frequently occurring themes among the more substantial items are technological issues, Internet training, providing access to patrons, the impact on libraries, and resources available on the Internet. The Internet is also extensively covered in the popular press and the literature of many disciplines other than library and information science. Several journals are exclusively devoted to the Internet, including *Internet World*, *World Wide Web World*, *Internet Research*, and *Internet Reference Services Quarterly*.[10] A number of library science periodicals such as *Online, Technicalities, Database, Medical Reference Services Quarterly*, and *Computers in Libraries* have regular columns about the Internet. Several library and information science journals, such as *Library Trends, Education for Information*, and the *Reference Librarian*, have devoted special issues to the Internet.

From 1990 to the early autumn of 1995, nearly 600 books about the Internet, mostly practical guides and "how-to" manuals, were published in North America.[11] An annotated bibliography of approximately 35 Internet user guides and directories published through 1994 was complied by Lewis and Watstein.[12] A number of books have examined the Internet in the context of libraries, including McClure, Bertot, and Zweizig's report for the U.S. National Commission on Libraries and Information Science, *Public Libraries and the Internet*; McClure, Moen, and Ryan's *Libraries and the Internet/NREN*; *The Internet Library*, edited by Still; *The Internet Initiative*, edited by Valauskas and John; and *Emerging Communities: Integrating Networked Information into Library Services*, edited by Bishop.[13] These volumes contain little or no direct analysis of collection management issues. Indeed, despite the fairly large literature on the Internet itself, relatively few publications address the relationship between the Internet and collection management. In early 1995, Cassel asserted, "collection development issues relating to Internet resources have yet to be addressed in the literature."[14] Later that year Demas, McDonald, and Lawrence stated, "thus far little of a practical nature has been written about exactly how collection strategies, selection methods, and criteria are changing to assimilate networked resources."[15]

A few items provide general introductions or overviews. A brief section entitled "collection development" in Benson's *The Complete Internet Companion for Librarians* offers examples of how the Internet can support traditional collection development. Addresses are given for obtaining, on the Net, book reviews and a list of authors who sell their own books, while an exercise illustrates telneting to another library's OPAC to observe the holdings in a particular subject as an aid to selection.[16] Ensor discusses the collection development aspects of establishing a library gopher.[17] Johnson, comparing the Internet to a Nintendo game, introduces electronic mail, remote log-in, and file transfer to collection development librarians and suggests potential collection development applications for each. She inventories eight types of Internet resources that can be utilized through telnet: OPACs, electronic journal archives, full-text book archives such as Project Gutenberg, software archives, campus-wide information systems, vendor databases, subject databases, and bulletin boards.[18] Both Balas and Makulowich briefly explain how the Internet, through newsgroups, online chats, and bulletin boards, can provide reviews, commentary, tables of contents, and publisher information that assist book selection.[19] The Cornell University library's electronic library collection development model, including but not limited to Internet resources, is depicted by Demas.[20] This article introduces the concept of a "genre specialist," discussed later in this chapter. Britten's introduction to building Internet collections includes the assertion that "libraries must address the need to incorporate network-based information into the traditional work of collection management."[21] Demas, McDonald, and Lawrence later describe efforts "for mainstreaming selection from the Internet into ongoing collection development activity" at Cornell's library, arguing, in effect, that traditional collection development principles can be applied to the Internet. They append collection development policy excerpts and a taxonomy that breaks down Internet resources into fifteen categories, such as reference, discussion groups, "gophers, gateways, and networks," U.S. government publications, and "staff use resources."[22] Zhou explores the Internet's potential impact on research library collection development, asserting that ". . . radical changes will take place in research libraries' collection-development activities if scholarly communication becomes largely electronic."[23] Tedd examines how the Internet can promote resource sharing among academic libraries in Europe. [24]

Several articles about the construction of gophers or Web pages discuss microevaluation/selection criteria and/or collection development issues for Internet resources. Among these are the following: York, based on selecting government information sources for the University of Michigan Library's gopher; Riley and Shipman, also based on the Michigan gopher; Cassel, who briefly recounts the selection and deselection criteria for two Internet sites at Binghamton University; Swann and Rosenquist-Buhler, who developed a research gopher at the University of Nebraska, Lincoln; Dutcher and Arnesen for two subject-oriented gophers at the National Library of Medicine; McFarland and others for the Health Sciences Library gopher at St. Louis University; and Piontek and Garlock for a World Wide Web page.[25] In a similar vein, both Santa Vicca and Starr discuss microevaluation criteria for selecting Internet resources to support the reference function, while Morville and Wickhorst address selection criteria for Internet resource guides.[26] The criteria of these authors overlap, but they generally include both the traditional (such as "purpose, authority, scope, audience, cost, format, special features") and the new (such as ease of access and descriptive information about the source).[27]

Evaluation of networked or Internet resources has been dealt with in a number of articles. Gurn suggests four evaluation criteria for Internet service providers: "accessibility, authority, interactivity, and conviviality," which he defines as "user-friendliness."[28] McClure proposes four evaluative measures for networked information services: extensiveness (how much was provided), efficiency (cost), effectiveness (how well user needs were met), and impact (the difference made in user productivity and effectiveness). McClure then discusses ten data collection techniques including focus groups, user logs, network-based data collection, interviews, surveys, and observation.[29]

The Internet and collection management have also been addressed in a number of public presentations. Johnson's presentation on "Collection Development and the Internet" and Kelly's talk on collecting "free" electronic resources on the

Internet have been reported in *Library Acquisitions: Practice & Theory*.[30] Many
other presentations on this topic have not been summarized in the literature.

A few items address the Internet's role in acquisitions. Both Benson and
McCoy list some Internet resources (for example, bookstore addresses and publishers' catalogs) of potential interest to acquisitions librarians.[31] Blackwell
North America's New Titles Online (NTO) database of more than 200,000 current titles, available to Blackwell customers over the Internet, is described in
Technicalities, which explains that this information can be used for verification,
firm orders, approval plan administration, and collection development.[32] Marshall depicts use of this system by the Georgetown University library to transmit
orders to Blackwell over the Internet.[33] The Yankee Book Peddler's use of FTP
on the Internet to transmit bibliographical information on the weekly approval
books for the Michigan State University Library is described by Granskog.[34]
Hale analyzes the Internet's impact on the acquisitions workflow at the University of Nevada, Las Vegas (UNLV) Library. She reports that 33 percent of
UNLV's domestic firm orders are obtained by remote log-in over the Internet.
Use of the Yankee Book Peddler's Folio system for ordering books on the Net
reduced receipt time from 11–12 weeks to 6–7 weeks. Moreover, accessing the
Library of Congress OPAC was found to be more effective than OCLC or *BIP
Plus* for preorder verification.[35]

Document delivery over the Internet is also covered in the literature. Ariel, a
system developed by the Research Libraries Group (RLG) for document transmission over the Net, is described by Jackson.[36] Ariel's use by the Health Sciences Libraries Consortium (in Pennsylvania and Delaware) and by two
Pennsylvania State University libraries is reported.[37] In summary, this review
indicates that the constantly increasing literature concerning the Internet includes
numerous contributions relevant to library collection management. But as of late
1995, a systematic analysis had not yet been published.

THE INTERNET AS A COMMUNICATIONS DEVICE
TO ASSIST COLLECTION MANAGEMENT OF
TRADITIONAL MATERIALS

While computers were originally invented for number crunching purposes, it
is generally recognized that computers now facilitate communication. This section will discuss how, through the communication process, the Internet can assist
traditional collection management and acquisitions.

There are at least 700 to 1,000 library OPACs that can be accessed on the
Internet.[38] One can directly telnet to their addresses or access them through
gophers or Web sites. Information on holdings for other libraries can assist both
selection and deselection decisions. For example, one wishing to assist selection
by identifying titles in a specific subject could access the OPAC of a library
with strong holdings in the area. Whether a busy collection manager would
spend the time to assess OPACs to assist routine book selection is debatable.

Nevertheless, serials selection or cancellation decisions could be assisted by checking availability in nearby libraries. This technique's use in resource sharing and the checklist evaluation method are discussed in subsequent sections.

Discussion lists or listservs on the Internet assist the performance of traditional library functions by serving as a communication medium among librarians, and sometimes nonlibrarians such as vendors. The current *Directory of Electronic Journals, Newsletters and Academic Discussion Lists* annotates 161 "academic discussion lists" for library and information science.[39] Some important lists relevant to collection management are enumerated below:

Listname	Topic	Address
COLLDV-L	collection development	listserv@vm.usc.edu.
ACQNET	acquisitions	listserv@lester.appstate.edu.
SERIALST	serials in general, but covers serials collection management	listserv@uvmvm.uvm.edu.
COLLIBS	collection development in Australian academic and research libraries	listserv@is.su.edu.au.
WEB4LIB	creation of library Web sites	listserv@library.berkeley.edu.
GIFTEX-L	gift and exchange issues	listserv@ukcc.uky.edu.
BACKSERV	duplicate exchange among libraries	listserv@sun.readmore.com.
BackMed	duplicate exchange of medical back issues	listserv@sun.readmore.com.

An interesting but unanswered question concerns how collection management librarians actually utilize listservs. Based on their analysis of three listservs relevant to reference, Cromer and Johnson identified eight categories of messages: specific queries, responses to queries, summaries of responses, presentations of issues, discussions of issues, general announcements, conference announcements, and job postings.[40]

There are home pages on the WWW for most types of major players on the contemporary library and information science scene, including academic libraries, national libraries, publishers, journals, bibliographic utilities, book wholesalers, serial subscription agents, standards organizations, library and information science education programs, and professional organizations. Access to publisher home pages and catalogs can obviously assist the selection and acquisitions process. As a specific example, using the Internet to verify the cost and availability of a video can save the cost of a long distance phone call.[41] As of November 28, 1995, the WWW Virtual Library provided access to 508 publishers. Another use of the Web is the creation of Web pages by collection managers to communicate information to their constituents.

Specific types of information available on the WWW that would assist the collection management or acquisitions function are summarized below. Most of these can be accessed through AcqWeb:

Bookstore Names and Addresses

Book and Video Reviews

Lists of Award-Winning Books

Best-Seller Lists

Serial Back Issue Dealers' Catalogs

Stock Availability and Price

Currency Exchange Rates

Publisher Electronic Mail Addresses

Publishers' Catalogs and General Information

Vendor Policies and Services

Bibliographic Utility Policies and Services

Postal Information

Telephone Information

That electronic mail facilitates communication among librarians and with vendors is so self-evident that no further discussion is required. Finally, readers interested in relevant Usenet newsgroups are referred to Makulowich and Balas, who list about a dozen newsgroups devoted to books.[42]

SELECTION OF INTERNET RESOURCES

Selection of information resources has been the oldest and most fundamental collection development function. In abstract terms both traditional and Internet resources are selected through an essentially identical three-step process: identification, microevaluation, and selection. Microevaluation refers to the evaluation of a specific item, while macroevaluation is the evaluation of a collection or set of resources. The Internet's use in the selection (and acquisition) of traditional library materials was discussed in the preceding section. This section's major focus will be on the identification, microevaluation, and selection of Internet information resources.

Identification

Identification of a particular resource's existence is a logical prerequisite to selection. Traditional library materials are identified through reviewing sources, publishers' advertisements, approval plans, and so on. Identification (sometimes referred to in the literature as ''discovery'') of Internet resources presents more of a challenge because of rapid changes on the Net and its continuing lack of good bibliographical control. But the Internet's resources can be identified through both print publications and the Internet itself. Printed guides to Internet resources abound. As examples, one can mention *Internet World's On Internet 94: An International Guide to Electronic Journals, Newsletters, Texts, Discussion Lists, and Other Resources on the Internet*, or the *Gale Guide to Internet Databases*.[43] *Internet Resources: A Subject Guide* compiles a series of Internet guides in various subjects from *College & Research Libraries News*.[44] Moreover, published "webographies" are beginning to appear.

Many tools are simultaneously available in print and on the Net itself. One could cite, among numerous possible examples, the *Directory of Electronic Journals, Newsletters, and Academic Discussion Lists*, which is available on the Association of Research Libraries' gopher, or the *Internet Compendium*, which is available on the Internet through the Clearinghouse for Subject-Oriented Internet Resource Guides.[45]

A number of Internet tools have been developed for identification of information sources on the Net. Archie locates information on anonymous FTP sites, while VERONICA performs subject searches of gopherspace and provides access to identified gophers through customized menus. Use of these tools is explained in innumerable Internet guidebooks, so there is no need for further elaboration here. As of November 1995, an Indiana University School of Library and Information Science Web page provided access to seventeen Internet search tools.[46]

Tools for identifying sites on the World Wide Web include Yahoo, Lycos, the WWW Virtual Library, and the World Wide Web Worm.[47] Web tools usually are based on the following approaches: (1) menu-like subject directories or indexes, (2) keyword searching, or (3) both. Most Web searching tools are fairly primitive and do not include Boolean searching. The present effectiveness of these tools in identifying Internet resources for collection management librarians remains an unanswered question. For a useful evaluation of numerous Web searching tools see Courtois, Baer, and Stark.[48] Other approaches for identifying Internet resources include: (1) patron or staff suggestions, (2) monitoring other gophers and Web sites, (3) listservs (for example NewJour can help identify new electronic journals), (4) published reviews, (5) Usenet newsgroups, and (6) serendipity while surfing the Net.[49]

Microevaluation

In the second step, the identified item's intrinsic merit is evaluated. Microevaluation can be internal (done by the selecting librarian) or external (furnished by a third party such as a book or software reviewer). The two are often combined as the selector reaches an internal evaluation that incorporates external evidence.

Most traditional microevaluation criteria, including factual accuracy, currency, overall quality, and nonbiased perspective, also apply to Internet resources. The author's qualifications and publisher reputation are separate traditional criteria. On the Internet the distinction between author and publisher is often blurred, but the issuing agency's authority remains a critical factor. Several traditional microevaluation criteria (for example, factual accuracy, currency, and assessment of quality) may actually be more important for Internet than for print resources. This reflects the well-known fact that with the exception of some peer-reviewed electronic journals, the Internet lacks gatekeepers to perform a quality control function. There are additional microevaluation criteria unique to the Internet. Reliability of access and the source's stability are, due to the Internet's volatility, particularly critical criteria.[50] Other criteria are ease of access and whether there is documentation, so-called "About Files," or FAQs that can assist with its use.

Microevaluation of Internet resources can be challenging because, as pointed out by Johnson, many items on the Net do not have a formal title page that provides basic information about the source.[51] Nevertheless, a number of Internet tools provide evaluation of World Wide Web sites. McKinley, as of the fall of 1995, included a brief descriptive annotation for each of the 80,000 Web sites it accessed.[52] Moreover, 20,000 of these were evaluated through a one-to-four star rating system applied to the overall site and to each of four criteria: coverage, organization, currency, and ease of access. Pointcomm rated 3,500 World Wide Web sites (each considered by Pointcomm to rank among the top 5% of all Web sites) using a 0–to-50 scale for content, presentation, and "experience," subjective reaction to the site.[53]

Beginning in 1994, the "Best of the WWW Contest" provides annual "Best of the Web Awards," based on voting, for the best overall Web site as well as for the best campus information system, commercial service, educational service, entertainment site, professional service, navigational aid, and the most important service concept.[54] Four technical awards are also granted for the best in document design, use of interaction, use of multimedia, and technical merit. While the validity of these awards and their relevance to Internet selection by librarians is not yet established, one is tempted to speculate that someday there might be Internet awards with the same prestige as the Pulitzer Prize, National Book Award, or Newbery Medal.

Selection

In the final step, a decision to select or not select the item is made. What does "selection" of an Internet resource mean? Buckland cogently argues that it means "privileging" the resource by providing patrons with easier access to it than to other resources, such as including it in a gopher.[55] Other examples not explicitly mentioned by Buckland would be creating a link on a library's World Wide Web home page, or deciding to subscribe to an electronic journal available on the Internet.

As with microevaluation, most traditional selection criteria also apply to the

Internet. Foremost among these are: relevance to user need, projected use, whether the source's intended audience and purpose matches the library's clients, and the library's collecting priorities. Additional criteria unique to the Internet include whether an Internet site is the best source of information on a subject and whether the Internet is the best format for conveying the information.[56] Cost, a significant selection criteria for traditional materials, is usually not a factor in Internet selection, since most resources are free.

RELATIONSHIP BETWEEN COLLECTION MANAGEMENT OF TRADITIONAL AND INTERNET RESOURCES

Many observers have stressed that traditional collection management principles also apply to the selection of Internet resources—a point with which I agree. For example, Seiden and Nuckolls state, "any issues which are considered in the development of policies for traditional library materials should also be considered in developing electronic library collections."[57] Swann and Rosenquist-Buhler assert, "Providing collection development in an electronic environment is really quite similar to traditional collection building, since evaluators attempt to select information they feel will be most relevant to the academic community they serve."[58] Collection management of Internet and traditional resources is fundamentally the same in many respects. The three-step process outlined above applies to both. Internet and traditional selection are both done for the primary objective of meeting user information needs. Both require knowledge of those needs, subject expertise, stated objectives, policy making, and setting priorities. Librarians or information professionals using the Internet face the same responsibility outlined several decades ago by Ortega y Gasset in *The Mission of the Librarian*: the obligation to separate from the vast number of available resources (Ortega used the term "torrent of books") the small portion that best meets their clients' information needs.[59] In fact, as the Web increases in size, the filtering process will become even more critical.

How does collection management of Internet resources differ from traditional library collection management? A number of key distinctions (not listed in priority order) are stated below.

One selects rather than collects.[60] This is a self-evident yet crucial distinction. One usually selects Internet resources in order to provide access to them, whereas traditional resources are collected for the purpose of ownership and housing in the library. In exception to this generalization, software or electronic journals on the Net might actually be acquired.

Traditional space and cost restrictions generally do not apply to Internet resources. Resources accessed on the Internet do not consume library space. There are, of course, costs associated with establishing and maintaining an Internet connection. However, once connected to the Internet, most resources can presently be accessed free of charge. There are exceptions to the above statement. Some resources on the Internet, for example the *Encyclopedia Britannica*, are not free, while such traditional resources as books and periodicals are occasionally received free. The extent to which Internet resources continue to be free is a critical but uncertain issue.

The Internet offers resources that have not generally been collected by libraries in the past. An example is preprints. As of June 1995, an estimated 70 preprint servers were available on the Internet, of which the best-known were probably the Los Alamos National Laboratory, Physics Service, founded by Paul Ginsparg, and the International Philosophical Preprint Exchange, managed by the University of Chiba's Philosophy Department.[61]

Internet selection decisions are often macro, whereas traditional selection decisions tend to be micro. Macro refers to "en bloc" selection of an entire group of resources with a single decision; micro selection is on a title-by-title basis. Linkage to a Web site (or including a site in a gopher) is clearly macro because every resource on the site is simultaneously selected. Again, there are exceptions to the preceding generalization. Selection of an electronic journal on the Internet would be at the micro level, while a traditional blanket order for all the publications from a particular publisher would be macro selection.

Duplication is a less important issue on the Internet. Innumerable gophers and Web sites provide links to the same original sources. Consequently, when a library selects other gophers and Web sites to be included on its own gopher or Web page, many of the same original resources might be duplicated. Since Internet resources can be accessed free of charge, this is not, at present, an important concern.

One might select unneeded and unwanted sources.[62] Because much Internet selection is at the macro level on a "take it or leave it" basis, when one links to a Web page a connection is made to all resources on the site, and many unneeded resources may be included. As with the point made above, this is seemingly not a major concern as long as Internet resources continue to be generally accessible free of charge. Nevertheless, the inclusion of "fun" resources that would not normally be collected by libraries has been questioned.[63]

Internet resources tend to be dynamic, while traditional resources tend to be static. It is generally well-known that many Internet sites undergo rapid change. In fact, the adjective "volatile" is often used to characterize the Internet. Some traditional resources, such as serials, do change from issue to issue, but most remain in a fixed format after they are selected.

Traditional and Internet resources require different kinds of collection maintenance. Collection maintenance is defined as the handling of resources after their acquisition. For traditional materials it entails decisions concerning binding, weeding, relegation to remote storage, multiple copies, and replacement of missing items. Due to the Internet's rapidly changing nature, gophers and World Wide Web pages require constant maintenance to ensure that external links have not changed their addresses, ceased existence, or lost their currency. For example, links on the University of Michigan's ULibrary Gopher are checked at least once every two weeks.[64]

Most traditional selection/microevaluation criteria apply to Internet resources, but the relative importance of specific criteria may vary while additional criteria also become relevant. This point has been elaborated upon in the text of the preceding section.

Traditional resources are much more likely to be selected without direct examination than are Internet resources. With the exception of items received on approval, most books are selected without directly examining them. In fact, one reason for the founding of approval plans was to allow direct viewing before selection. In contrast, one presumes (there is no systematic research on the issue) that the creators of gophers and Web sites almost always examine Internet resources before creating links to them.

Most traditional resources are used by one patron at a time, while Internet resources can have multiple users.[65] Again, there are exceptions. Audiovisual items are sometimes used by more than one patron, while Internet resources requiring passwords can be limited to a set number of simultaneous users.

The library is more likely to create or "publish" Internet resources than traditional resources. A library's World Wide Web home page may be viewed as its own creation or publication. Only on rare occasions does a library publish traditional resources, as, for example, when it attempts to market its collection development policy.

Unlike traditional resources, many Internet resources are not packaged in bibliographical units. Traditional collection management tends to focus on information contained in such distinct bibliographical units as book or serial titles. While electronic books and serials are available on the Internet, the Net's information is often found in something other than a conventional bibliographical unit, such as a site, file, menu, or link.

Level of access is more critical in Internet than in traditional selection. Most traditional selection is a binary decision to select or not to select, although access level is occasionally a factor—for instance, the purchase of multiple copies to increase availability. At Cornell University's Mann Library, selectors must designate one of five "tiers of access" for a new electronic resource. Tiers 1 through 3 offer availability over the campus network through the Mann Library Gateway at declining access speeds ("instantaneous," "slower," and "not . . . continuously available"); tier 4 resources are available for use on a local area network in the library, while tier 5 resources are used at a stand-alone work station in the library.[66] In effect, higher-level tiers offer quicker, more convenient access to patrons. Likewise, most gophers and Web sites have several hierarchical levels. Consequently, collection management of Internet resources often requires not only their selection but an assessment of their overall importance and relevance to patron need in order to determine the appropriate access level.

Unlike traditional materials, there are many unresolved archiving/ preservation issues for Internet resources. Libraries ensure that their traditional materials are adequately preserved through binding and preservation programs. Yet there are presently no mechanisms that guarantee the archiving of Internet resources. Internet publishers can not be depended upon to permanently preserve their own resources, while it is generally not feasible for libraries to do so, although some Internet resources, such as electronic journals, can be downloaded and preserved. At present there are several unresolved issues concerning the archiving/preservation of Internet resources are. Who does the archiving: the resource creators, libraries, consortiums, national or regional agencies? Which resources are archived? For how long are they archived? What archiving methods are used? There is a real concern that unarchived Internet resources may eventually disappear from the scholarly record.

THE INTERNET AND MACROEVALUATION

Traditionally, macroevaluation focuses on the entire collection as opposed to the microevaluation of a specific item. In the evaluation of Internet resources the distinction between micro and macro blurs. A library's gopher or Web site could, depending on one's perspective, be viewed as a single source or a collection of sources. Nevertheless, evaluation of the Internet's overall effectiveness and efficiency in fulfilling patron information needs is clearly at the macro level.

Over the last several decades a host of techniques have been developed for macroevaluation of traditional library collections. Collection-centered techniques, which focus on the collection itself, include the checklist method, comparative statistical data, the Clapp–Jordan formula, and the RLG Conspectus. Client-centered methods, which concentrate on the client's use of the collection and how well client information needs are being met, include use studies, Orr's Document Delivery Test, and Kantor's availability study. The American Library Association's *Guide to the Evaluation of Library Collections* outlines the established evaluation approaches along with their benefits and drawbacks.[67] The literature on academic library collection evaluation through early 1992 is summarized by Nisonger.[68]

Established, authoritative methods for evaluating the Internet's effectiveness in libraries have not yet been developed. Present evaluation appears to be in an early, exploratory stage, and frequently draws on general evaluation methods. For example, the Woodstock Library (in New York state) reportedly used "structured interviews, evaluation forms, logs, background data, questionnaires, and site visits" for Internet evaluation.[69]

The Internet can be used in traditional collection evaluation. One of the oldest, most traditional approaches to collection evaluation is the checklist method, whereby a list of items is checked against the holdings of the library under evaluation. A basic issue in this approach's implementation concerns locating an appropriate list to check. The American Library Association's *Guide to the Evaluation of Library Collections* lists fifteen possible sources for checklists, including "printed catalogs of the holdings of important and specialized libraries"—an often-used source in evaluation projects.[70] A checklist for evaluating one's own library could easily be generated by remote log-in to the OPAC of a library known to have a strong collection in a particular subject. Subject or keyword searches in the OPAC would identify titles for the checklist. An obvious question concerns how one determines which library holds an appropriate subject collection. Ash and Miller's *Subject Collections* is a classic print work that would be of assistance.[71] The creation of an online directory to the strengths of collections accessible by OPACs, as advocated by Drabenstott and Cochrane, would also be helpful.[72]

Remote log-in to an OPAC can also be used to evaluate another library's collection. This tactic could be used by researchers to assess whether it would be worthwhile to visit a distant collection on a research trip, or by academics considering where to spend a sabbatical or whether to accept a job offer from an institution.[73] This technique's effectiveness would be limited if the library being accessed has not completed retrospective conversion of its entire collection.

A number of traditional collection evaluation methods have potential application to Internet evaluation. An availability study tests whether a patron can successfully locate an item on the shelf at the time he or she is searching for it. Lack of success may be because the item was not acquired by the library (acquisitions failure); the item was checked out (circulation failure); the item was lost or misplaced (library operations failure); or the patron was unable to find a correctly shelved item (user failure). Kaske claims that the concept of availability is no longer relevant in the electronic age because many patron needs are fulfilled by resources external to the library.[74]

I would argue that with some modification the availability model is applicable to Internet evaluation. Just as a patron may be frustrated because a desired book is checked out, someone accessing an electronic resource might receive a message "file server not responding." A test could be designed to measure patron success on the Net as well as analyze the causes of failure. If the patron was unsuccessful, was it due to technological error, the fact that a password was required, the patron's lack of skill, or some other factor? A complicating but not insurmountable problem would be that most traditional availability studies presuppose the patron is seeking a specific bibliographical item, a condition that often might not apply to Internet users. (Research is needed to determine how patrons actually use the Internet in a library setting.) The checklist approach, discussed above, could be used to evaluate the coverage of a Web site or gopher. Perhaps the biggest difficulty would be locating a valid, up-to-date list of Internet resources in a particular subject, although the evaluator could compile such a list.

In the past, data on volumes held, current serial subscriptions, and material expenditures have been major components for evaluation of a library's entire collection and specific disciplines as well as for comparison among libraries. A significant unresolved issue, at present, concerns how electronic journals and books are counted in library statistics, as they can be accessed by patrons but are not physically housed in the library. It seems exceedingly probable that in the future such collection-centered evaluation approaches as holdings statistics will decline in importance.

In the final analysis, the most critical evaluation criteria concern how well and how cost-effectively patron information needs are met. McClure, cited above, has recently emphasized the importance of user-based evaluation of networked information services.[75] There is also need for new, client-centered evaluation approaches to assess how well the library—as a system that integrates both print and electronic resources—is responding to patron need.

THE INTERNET AND THE CORE COLLECTION

The "core collection" has long been an important concept in collection development thought. The core refers to the most basic, fundamental, and important materials that form the center or heart of the collection. In the words of Intner, "core collections are the nucleus of needed materials no self-respecting library would be without—the 20 percent of existing information stock that satisfies 80 percent (or more) of users' requests."[76] Core lists have been compiled for subjects, formats, and library type as well as these variables in combination with each other. They can assist in selection, collection evaluation, plus deselection and weeding.

The Internet has been used to identify core materials for the print collection. Stein reports that during a serials cancellation project at the University of Delaware Library, core periodicals in the "fashion, textile, and apparel merchandising/manufacturing" field were identified by accessing the OPACs of eight other large university libraries with strong collections in that area. Titles held by five of the eight libraries were defined as core. Furthermore, the Internet was found to be a better method than the OCLC database or mailed surveys for obtaining serials holding information from other libraries.[77] This approach could also be used in serials selection and cooperative collection development decisions.

The core concept is obviously applicable to Internet resources, especially when constructing a gopher or World Wide Web site. It is evident that one would want to include links to the core items. How does one know what constitutes a "core" Internet resource? This question is not answered in the published literature. Yet, it seems clear that many of the methods used to identify core print and other traditional items, such as subjective judgment, identification of highly used items, overlap analysis, and published lists, could also be used for determining core Internet resources.

One can cite examples of research that might be used to ascertain core Internet resources, even though this was not necessarily the authors' intended purpose. Tillotson, Cherry, and Clinton found that of 1,325 sites available to University of Toronto Library users, the top ten accounted for 33 percent of the total connections, while 80 percent of the connections were to 13 percent of the sites—a finding reminiscent of Trueswell's famous 80/20 Rule that 80 percent of the circulation is accounted for by 20 percent of the books. The three authors note that similar Internet usage patterns have been observed at Texas A & M, University of California, Santa Cruz, and Memorial University of Newfoundland libraries.[78] Parenthetically, Haworth Press has announced that a forthcoming issue of *Collection Management* will be devoted to the 80/20 rule in cyberspace.[79] A 1993 study of nearly 100 gophers by Seiden and Nuckolls found that some sources such as the *CIA World Fact Book*, the *Chronicle of Higher Education*'s "Academe," and U.S. Supreme Court decisions were repeatedly included.[80] In the fall of 1995, Kuster was tabulating the external links on over 150 public library World Wide Web sites in order to determine, among other things, the most frequently linked to sites.[81]

Published lists of the "best" Internet sites may be viewed as the equivalent of core lists. As examples, one should note lists of the 100 "most interesting" Web sites and the 10 best government Internet sites.[82] As with traditional core lists, it would be prudent to consider the list's authority, scope, and purpose before using it.

One is tempted to speculate that due to the Internet and electronic resources, the core concept will assume a more significant role in collection management. As print collections become smaller—a trend already suggested by Perrault's research on the United States' declining national research collection—libraries may tend to concentrate on collecting the core, while providing non-core materials to patrons through external access mechanisms.[83] Under this scenario, identification of core print materials will be more critical because the core will make up a larger proportion of the print holdings.

In the past most core lists have been restricted to a specific format, but a trend toward multiformat core lists that integrate print with Internet resources can already be discerned. For example, Musser's recently published list of titles dealing with climate and global change included both print periodicals and Internet discussion groups.[84]

THE INTERNET AND ACQUISITIONS

Acquisitions is closely connected to collection management, yet it is an analytically distinct function. For the purpose of this discussion, acquisitions is defined as the technical process of ordering, receiving, and paying for an item, after the intellectual decision to select it has been reached. One can cite numerous ways in which the Internet facilitates the acquisition of traditional library resources: electronic transmission of orders, cancellations, and claims; access to vendor databases; transmission of approval plan information; general communication with vendors through electronic mail; and preorder verification by accessing other library OPACs.

By early November 1995, more than a dozen academic library acquisitions departments had established their own home pages on the Web. These pages typically provide clients with information about departmental staff and book ordering procedures, while containing links to other sites pertinent to library acquisitions.

The application of the acquisitions function to Internet resources is problematic because the Net's resources are generally not ordered, physically received, and paid for in the usual sense. Nevertheless, standard acquisitions procedures will still be relevant in some circumstances. For example, an electronic journal subscription over the Internet might require ordering, payment, monitoring that issues have been received, and claiming of missing issues. (While a majority of electronic journals on the Net are now free, this will probably change in the not too distant future.) In other instances payment for Internet resources may take the form of licensing, pay per use, or payment for a set number of simultaneous users.

THE INTERNET AND COOPERATIVE COLLECTION DEVELOPMENT

Cooperative collection development and resource sharing have been major collection management themes for at least two decades, although many observers have been disappointed with the results. The Internet can support traditional cooperative collection development by facilitating the dissemination of holdings information and the rapid transmission of documents between libraries. To illustrate the former, libraries could check each others' OPACs to ensure they are not ordering duplicate copies of a title already held by a cooperative collection development partner. As an example of the latter, in 1992 and 1993 the Pennsylvania State University's life sciences and medical libraries (separated by approximately 120 miles) canceled a combined total of almost $12,000 worth of current serials subscriptions. Then, using Ariel, the library that retained a subscription would transmit over the Internet copies of requested articles to the library that canceled the title. Copyright fees were paid.[85]

Innumerable opportunities abound for modified forms of cooperative collection development in regard to Internet resources. A gopher or Web link to another library's gopher or Web site clearly represents a form of resource sharing and, unlike conventional interlibrary cooperation, can usually be implemented without a formal agreement or the other library's permission. The WWW Virtual Library, administered by CERN in Geneva, Switzerland, compiles subject-oriented Web sites created at many different institutes. Britten advocates an American Library Association Virtual Library Collection modeled on the WWW Virtual Library to avoid "needlessly building dozens of similar collections" on the World Wide Web by academic libraries.[86] As with traditional cooperative collection development, there is always the danger that another library whose resources are being relied upon will discontinue its efforts.

Likewise, electronic journal collections may be viewed as a form of cooperative collection development on the Net. The "Ejournal SiteGuide," accessible through AcqWeb, contains links to approximately thirty electronic journal collections including the WWW Virtual Library and the Library of Congress.[87] Particularly noteworthy is the CICNet Project which, as of April 1995, archived 880 electronic journals.

THE INTERNET AND DOCUMENT DELIVERY

In an era emphasizing access, document delivery is inextricably connected with collection management. The Internet supports traditional Interlibrary Loan (ILL), commercial document delivery, and access to external information resources that transcends the traditional ILL/document delivery model.

The Internet, in a number of ways, can facilitate the traditional ILL function for print materials. Both initial patron requests and library requests to lenders can be sent through electronic mail. Ariel, a system developed by the Research Libraries Group for transmitting documents over the Internet and installed in over 350 libraries by the spring of 1993, allows more rapid, higher resolution, and less expensive transmission than that provided by facsimile machines.[88] Some libraries also use Ariel to transmit the original request to the lending library.[89] The British Library Document Supply Centre in conjunction with the University of East Anglia is experimenting with document delivery over the Internet.[90] The Association of Research Libraries' North American Interlibrary Loan/Document Delivery (NAILDD) Project for upgrading ILL and document delivery services among academic and research libraries includes support for electronic document delivery.[91] An increasing number of libraries now post information about ILL policy on their Web pages along with electronic forms for patrons to submit requests. Accessing other library OPACs for holdings and circulation information can also facilitate the ILL function. Lynch notes that the Z39.50 standard allows software programs to search remote OPACs for this purpose.[92]

During the last half decade an increasing number of libraries have turned to commercial document delivery services. A noteworthy feature of these services on the Net, such as CARL's UnCover, is that the end user can directly order a document without the intervention of a librarian. The issue of "disintermediation" presents an interesting set of questions that are beyond this chapter's scope.

Both ILL and commercial document delivery are tied to the old paradigm of providing print documents to patrons. Yet the Internet offers the opportunity to completely bypass the print format through electronic access to electronic documents. The number of electronic journals on the Internet is constantly increasing. *Alex: A Catalog of Electronic Texts on the Internet* provides direct access on the Net to 1800 book titles, as of March 1995.[93]

However, as cogently argued by Lynch, it is unlikely that conventional ILL will, to any appreciable extent, be applied to electronic resources on the Internet.[94] Free items can usually be accessed directly without the intervention of another library. Paid-for resources will be licensed rather than sold and the license agreements will probably prohibit sharing with other libraries.

THE INTERNET AND STAFFING FOR COLLECTION MANAGEMENT

The Internet can potentially impact numerous collection management and acquisitions staffing issues including workflow, education and training, staffing level, and departmental organization. However, it is difficult to isolate the Internet's impact on collection management staffing from that of other factors such as downsizing, budgetary considerations, and the increasing importance of electronic resources in general. This essay will focus on one unresolved but fundamental issue: who will select Internet resources? Possible theoretical models for organizing Internet selection responsibilities include: subject, format, genre, committee, or a combination of approaches.

Organization by format implies that Internet resources will be selected by individuals with technological expertise who probably do not take part in other collection management activities. On the other hand, organization by subject implies that the collection development staff who select traditional materials will also be responsible for Internet resources within their subject domain. Cornell University's Mann Library has organized electronic collection development according to "genre." So-called "genre specialists" perform collection management functions for a particular type or "genre" of electronic information, such as applications software, bibliographic files, full text, numeric files, or multimedia, regardless of the format, which might be CD-ROM, floppy disk, magnetic tape, or remote access through the Internet.[95] Committees can incorporate a variety of perspectives, including both subject and format expertise. In actual practice, many libraries use a mixture of approaches.

More research is required to ascertain how libraries are assigning Internet responsibilities. Organization by subject seems the best approach because Internet resources would be "mainstreamed" with regular selection. Some Internet collection maintenance functions, such as checking that gopher and Web links are still valid, can be handled by nonprofessional staff.

THE INTERNET'S CHALLENGES FOR COLLECTION MANAGEMENT LIBRARIANS

It is almost a cliché to state that the Internet offers one of the most exciting and fascinating challenges confronting the library profession in the mid-1990s. Specifically, what are these challenges for collection management specialists? They must demonstrate that their traditional skills and knowledge base, subject expertise, setting priorities, interpreting user information needs, evaluating resources, and so on, are both relevant and needed in an electronic environment.

Collection managers must master basic Internet skills themselves. Libraries will soon be expected to have their own home pages on the World Wide Web and selection skills will be needed. Countless issues require research. A major challenge is to analyze the Internet with dispassionate objectivity, identifying areas of effectiveness and ineffectiveness while viewing the Net as neither panacea nor threat.

New evaluation techniques must be developed. Written policy statements will be necessary concerning selection criteria, access issues, archiving, and preservation for Internet resources. In the near future, an increasing number of resources will be simultaneously available in both print and electronic format, especially as commercial and university press journal publishers begin issuing their established journals electronically while continuing the paper version. Consequently, collection managers will frequently have to decide whether a specific title will be housed locally in print format, accessed electronically, or, in some cases, both. Both policy guidelines and title-by-title microdecisions will be required. As Demas succinctly states, "The challenge to this generation of librarians is to seamlessly knit together a multiplicity of formats and access mechanisms into one intellectually cohesive, user-friendly set of information resources and services."[96]

FUTURE PROSPECTS

This chapter's focus has been on the Internet and collection management in the context of the present environment (late 1995). Since this volume's title is *Collection Management for the 21st Century*, some speculation concerning the Internet's future impact on collection management seems warranted.

Lynch's distinction between "modernization" and "transformation" can help clarify the discussion.[97] Modernization means doing better and more effectively what libraries have always done. Most of this chapter has focused on the Internet's role in modernization. In contrast, transformation represents a fundamental change in what libraries do. I would contend that while the Internet may lead to the transformation of libraries in the long run, in the near term it can contribute to modernization by assisting the performance of traditional functions.

In the short and perhaps the intermediate term, the Internet will undoubtedly help accelerate already existing trends toward smaller collections and an increasing emphasis on access rather than ownership. The Net will enhance, through providing access to externally held resources, the meeting of patron information needs. Yet collection management will become more complex because collection managers will face more choices; for example, should patron need for a journal title be met through a print subscription, access to the electronic version on the Internet, or document delivery?

Basic changes will almost certainly occur on a gradual, incremental basis. Zhou outlines a three-stage process for the migration from the print to electronic format over several decades: traditional acquisition of traditional resources, computerized acquisition of traditional resources, and computerized acquisition of electronic resources.[98] Bauwens offers a similar three-level framework: electronic access to real libraries, OPACs; electronic access to virtual collections with delivery of print documents, such as UnCover; and "electronic access to virtual collections consisting of electronic documents."[99] These schemes might seem to imply a uniform linear progression from stages 1 through 3.[100] In reality, the transition pace may vary among disciplines and among institutions.

The Internet's long-term impact on libraries cannot be foreseen. Potentially, the Internet might "transform" or alter the definition of what constitutes a library; for example, digital libraries could replace collections of print materials. This outcome is alluded to in statements by Lee Teng-hui, the president of Taiwan, and the computer guru Nicholas Negroponte, among others. President Lee recently commented to a distinguished American library consultant that the concept of a traditional library is as antiquated as the village well. Lee expects to receive both water and information in the modern way, delivered to him personally through a plumbing system or a computer network, rather than the outdated approach of having to journey to an external point, such as a well or library, and carry the commodity home.[101] Nicholas Negroponte recently expressed a similar concept in *Wired* magazine, proclaiming that in the future "every book" can be obtained "with a keystroke, not a hike."[102] Will the Internet, through its capacity to deliver information directly to homes and desks, eventually replace the library? If so, within what time frame? Will librarians be active agents or passive pawns in the Internet's ultimate impact on their profession? Will cybrarians replace librarians and webographers replace bibliographers? Answering these questions is probably impossible at this time and certainly beyond this chapter's scope.

SUMMARY AND CONCLUSIONS

This chapter's major themes may be summarized as follows: (1) the Internet can be used for more effective performance of traditional collection management functions, "modernization" in Lynch's terms; (2) the Internet presents numerous opportunities and challenges to collection management librarians; (3) traditional collection management skills are necessary for effective utilization of the Internet; (4) there are many similarities yet critical differences between collection management of traditional and Internet resources; and (5) the Internet's ultimate impact on libraries and collection management cannot, at present, be predicted, especially since there may be unforeseen technological developments in the future.[103]

NOTES

1. William A. Britten, "Building and Organizing Internet Collections," *Library Acquisitions: Practice & Theory* 19 (1995): 243.

2. Readers interested in Internet resources pertaining to collection management/ acquisitions are advised to consult the AcqWeb home page on the World Wide Web. AcqWeb's URL is: http://www.library.vanderbilt.edu/law/acqs/acqs.html. All Web addresses reported in this chapter were current as of December 1995.

3. Dennis G. Perry, Steven H. Blumenthal, and Robert M. Hinden, "The ARPA-NET and the DARPA Internet," *Library Hi Tech* 6, no. 2 (1988): 51.

4. Lucy A. Tedd, "An Introduction to Sharing Resources via the Internet in Academic Libraries and Information Centres in Europe," *Program* 29 (1995): 43.

5. Peggy Seiden and Karen A. Nuckolls, "Developing a Campus-Wide Information System Using the Gopher Protocol: A Study of Collection Development and Classification Issues," *The Reference Librarian*, nos. 41/42 (1994): 276, 278, 281–82; Dan Lester, "I May Be a Cyclops, But I'm Not an Internaut," *Technicalities* 14 (March 1994): 8.

6. "Energizing the 'Net," *USA Today*, 30 October 1995, p. B1.

7. Evan St. Lifer, "A New Era for ALA?" *Library Journal* 120 (October 1, 1995): 38, who cites *Library Journal*'s March 31, 1877 issue.

8. Thomas E. Nisonger, "The Use of CD-ROM to Investigate the In-Print/Out-of-Print Subject Patterns for Books," *Library Resources & Technical Services* 39 (1995): 123.

9. Clifford A. Lynch, "The Transformation of Scholarly Communication and the Role of the Library in the Age of Networked Information," *Serials Librarian* 23, nos. 3/4 (1993): 7–8.

10. According to a Haworth Press announcement, *Internet Reference Services Quarterly*'s first issue was scheduled to appear in the spring of 1996.

11. A keyword search in the September 1995 *Books in Print Plus* under the term "Internet" retrieved 584 items. Two books scheduled for publication in 1996 should be noted. Advertisements indicate that Elizabeth Thomsen, *Reference & Collection Development on the Internet: A How-to-Do-It Manual for Librarians* (New York: Neal Schuman, 1996) will cover the use of bulletin board systems, commercial providers such as Compuserve, electronic mail and listservs, Usenet newsgroups, FAQs (Frequently Asked Questions), and electronic texts in collection development, while Kristen L. Garlock and Sherry Piontek, *Building the Service-Based Library Web Site: A Step-by-Step Guide to Design and Options* (Chicago: American Library Association, 1996) will include planning the content of and maintaining a library's Web home page.

12. Janice S. Lewis and Sarah B. Watstein, "Getting on the Information Superhighway: Books about the Internet," *Booklist* 90 (May 15, 1994): 1708–9.

13. Charles R. McClure, John Carlo Bertot, and Douglas L. Zweizig, *Public Libraries and the Internet: Study Results, Policy Issues, and Recommendations* (Washington, DC: National Commission on Libraries and Information Science, 1994); Charles R. McClure, William E. Moen, and Joe Ryan, *Libraries and the Internet: Perspectives, Issues, and Challenges* (Westport, CT: Meckler, 1994); Julie Still, ed., *The Internet Library: Case Studies of Library Internet Management and Use* (Westport, CT: Mecklermedia, 1994); Edward J. Valauskas and Nancy R. John, eds., *The Internet Initiative: Libraries Providing Internet Services and How They Plan, Pay and Manage* (Chicago: American Library Association, 1995); Ann P. Bishop, ed., *Emerging Communities: Integrating Networked Information into Library Services: Papers Presented at the 1993 Clinic on Library Applications of Data Processing, April 4–6, 1993* (Urbana-Champaign:

Graduate School of Library and Information Science, University of Illinois at Urbana–Champaign, 1994).

14. Rachel Cassel, "Selection Criteria for Internet Resources," *College & Research Libraries News* 56 (February 1995): 92.

15. Samuel Demas, Peter McDonald, and Gregory Lawrence, "The Internet and Collection Development: Mainstreaming Selection of Internet Resources," *Library Resources & Technical Services* 39 (July 1995): 277.

16. Allen C. Benson, *The Complete Internet Companion for Librarians* (New York: Neal-Schuman, 1995), pp. 311–18.

17. Pat Ensor, "The Volatility of Electronic Collection Development, or, the Care and Feeding of a Gopher," *Technicalities* 14 (July 1994): 10–12; Pat Ensor, "The Volatility of Electronic Collection Development, or, the Care and Feeding of a Gopher, Part 2," *Technicalities* 14 (September 1994): 4–6.

18. Peggy Johnson, "Collection Development and the Internet," in *Collection Management and Development: Issues in an Electronic Era: Proceedings of the Advanced Collection Management and Development Institute, Chicago, Illinois, March 26–28, 1993*, ed. Peggy Johnson and Bonnie MacEwan (Chicago: American Library Association, 1994), pp. 63–79.

19. Janet Balas, "In Celebration of Books," *Computers in Libraries* 15 (May 1995): 28–30; John S. Makulowich, "Books, Books, Books—Browsing in Cyberspace," *Database* 18 (June/July 1995): 88–90.

20. Samuel Demas, "Collection Development for the Electronic Library: A Conceptual and Organizational Model," *Library Hi Tech* 12, no. 3 (1994): 71–80.

21. Britten, "Building and Organizing," pp. 243–49.

22. Demas, McDonald, and Lawrence, "The Internet and Collection Development," pp. 275–90.

23. Yuan Zhou, "From Smart Guesser to Smart Navigator: Changes in Collection Development for Research Libraries in a Network Environment," *Library Trends* 42 (1994): 648–60.

24. Tedd, "An Introduction to Sharing Resources," pp. 43–61.

25. Grace Ann York, "New Media/Traditional Values: Selecting Government Information on the Internet," *Collection Building* 14, no. 3 (1995): 7–9; Ruth A. Riley and Barbara Lowther Shipman, "Building and Maintaining a Library Gopher: Traditional Skills Applied to Emerging Resources," *Bulletin of the Medical Library Association* 83 (April 1995): 224; Cassel, "Selection Criteria," pp. 92–93; Julie Swann and Carla Rosenquist-Buhler, "Developing an Internet Research Gopher: Innovation and Staff Involvement," *Journal of Academic Librarianship* 21 (September 1995): 373–74; Gale A. Dutcher and Stacey J. Arnesen, "Developing a Subject-Specific Gopher at the National Library of Medicine," *Bulletin of the Medical Library Association* 83 (April 1995): 229–30; Mary Ann McFarland and others, "Developing a Health Sciences Library Gopher: More Involved than Meets the Eye," *Bulletin of the Medical Library Association* 83 (April 1995): 218–19; Sherry Piontek and Kristen Garlock, "Creating a World Wide Web Resource Collection," *Collection Building* 14, no. 3 (1995): 16–17.

26. Edmund F. Santa Vicca, "The Internet as a Reference and Research Tool: A Model for Educators," *The Reference Librarian*, nos. 41/42 (1994): 229–33; Susan S. Starr, "Evaluating Physical Science Reference Sources on the Internet," *Reference Librarian*, nos. 41/42 (1994): 269–73; Peter S. Morville and Susan J. Wickhorst, "Build-

ing Subject-Specific Guides to Internet Resources," *Collection Building* 14, no. 3 (1995): 26–31.

27. Santa Vicca, "The Internet as a Reference," pp. 229, 231–32.

28. Robert M. Gurn, "Measuring Information Providers on the Internet," *Computers in Libraries* 15 (1995): 42.

29. Charles R. McClure, "User-Based Data Collection Techniques and Strategies for Evaluating Networked Information Services," *Library Trends* 42 (1994): 591–607.

30. Margaret Maes Axtmann, "Advanced Collection Management & Development Institute, March 26–28, 1993: A Report," *Library Acquisitions: Practice & Theory* 18 (Summer 1994): 210–11; Margaret Maes Axtmann, "The New Collection Management: Internet & Other Networked Resources for the 'Wired' Collection Manager: An ALCTS Preconference," *Library Acquisitions: Practice & Theory* 19 (1995): 114–15; Rachel Miller, "Access, Resource Sharing, and Collection Development: Report of a Conference," *Library Acquisitions: Practice & Theory* 19 (1995): 482–83.

31. Benson, *The Complete Internet Companion*, pp. 308–11; Patricia Sayre McCoy, "Technical Services and the Internet," *Wilson Library Bulletin* 69 (March 1995): 37–38.

32. "Internet Access to Blackwell's New Titles Database." *Technicalities* 12 (June 1992): 10–11.

33. David L. Marshall, "The Internet Connection for Electronic Ordering," *Computers in Libraries* 13 (March 1993): 26–28.

34. Kay Granskog, "PromptCat Testing at Michigan State University," *Library Acquisitions: Practice & Theory* 18 (1994): 419–25.

35. Marylou Hale, "Automated Library Acquisitions and the Internet: A New Model for Business," in *New Automation Technology for Acquisitions and Collection Development*, ed. Rosann Bazirjian (New York: Haworth Press, 1995), pp. 65–82.

36. Mary E. Jackson, "Document Delivery Over the Internet," *Online* 17 (1993): 14–21.

37. Valerie M. Bennett and Eileen M. Palmer, "Ariel on the Internet: Enhanced Document Delivery," *Microcomputers for Information Management* 10 (1993): 181–93; Valerie M. Bennett and Eileen M. Palmer, "Electronic Document Delivery Using the Internet," *Bulletin of the Medical Library Association* 82 (1994): 163–67; Nancy I. Henry and Esther Y. Dell, "Ariel: Technology as a Tool for Cooperation," *Bulletin of the Medical Library Association* 82 (1994): 436–38; Esther Y. Dell and Nancy I. Henry, "A Resource Sharing Project Using Ariel Technology," *Medical Reference Services Quarterly* 12 (1993): 17–27.

38. Tedd, "An Introduction to Sharing Resources," p. 48.

39. Lisabeth A. King and Diane Kovacs, comps., *Directory of Electronic Journals, Newsletters and Academic Discussion Lists*, 5th ed., ed. Ann Okerson (Washington, DC: Association of Research Libraries, Office of Scientific and Academic Publishing, 1995), pp. 383–405; the URL is: gopher://arl.cni.org:70/11/scomm/edir/edir95.

40. Donna E. Cromer and Mary E. Johnson, "The Impact of the Internet on Communication among Reference Librarians," *Reference Librarian*, nos. 41/42 (1994): 150–54.

41. Telephone conversation with Kristine Brancolini, Indiana University Libraries, Media Services, on November 21, 1995.

42. Makulowich, "Books, Books, Books," p. 88; Balas, "In Celebration," p. 29.

43. Tony Abbott, ed., *Internet World's On Internet 94: An International Guide to*

Electronic Journals, Newsletters, Texts, Discussion Lists, and Other Resources on the Internet (Westport, CT: Mecklermedia, 1994); *Gale Guide to Internet Databases* (Detroit: Gale Research, 1995).

44. Hugh A. Thompson, comp., *Internet Resources: A Subject Guide* (Chicago: Association of College and Research Libraries, 1995).

45. King and Kovacs, *Directory*; Louis Rosenfeld, Joseph Janes, and Martha Vander Kolk, *The Internet Compendium* (New York: Neal-Schuman, 1995); the URL is http://www.lib.umich.edu/chhome.html.

46. The URL for the Internet search tools page is: http://www-slis.lib.indiana.edu/Internet/search_me.html.

47. The URLs are: for Yahoo, http://www.yahoo.com/weblaunch.html; for Lycos, http://www.lycos.com/; for the WWW Virtual Library, http://www.w3.org/hypertext/DataSources/bySubject/Overview.html; and for the World Wide Web Worm, http://wwwmcb.cs.colorado.edu/home/mcbryan/WWWW.html.

48. Martin P. Courtois, William M. Baer, and Marcella Stark, "Cool Tools for Searching the Web: A Performance Evaluation," *Online* 19 (1995): 14–32.

49. Susan Grajek and R. Kenny Marone, "How to Develop and Maintain a Gopher," *Online* 19 (1995): 38.

50. Dutcher and Arnesen, "Developing a Subject-Specific Gopher," p. 230.

51. Peggy Johnson, "Desperately Seeking Sources: Selecting On-Line Resources," *Technicalities* 15 (August 1995): 4.

52. McKinley's URL is: http://www.mckinley.com/.

53. Pointcom's URL is: http://www.pointcom.com/; "Web Site Rating Directories Increase," *Library Journal* 120 (October 1, 1995): 14; and the author's direct examination of McKinley and Pointcom.

54. The Contest's URL is: http://wings.buffalo.edu/contest/.

55. Michael Buckland, "What Will Collection Developers Do?" *Information Technology and Libraries* 14 (September 1995): 158.

56. York, "New Media," p. 8.

57. Seiden and Nuckolls, "Developing a Campus-Wide," p. 292.

58. Swann and Rosenquist-Buhler, "Developing an Internet," p. 373.

59. Jose Ortega y Gasset, *The Mission of the Librarian*, trans. James Lewis and Ray Carpenter (Boston: G.K. Hall, 1961), p. 22.

60. Cassel, "Selection Criteria," p. 92.

61. "Darwinism and the Internet: Why Scientific Journals Could Go the Way of the Pterodactyl," *Business Week*, no. 430 (June 26, 1995): 44; the URL is http://xxx.lanl.gov/; the International Philosophical Preprint Exchange's URL is: http://www.l.chiba-u.ac.jp/IPPE.html.

62. Ensor, "The Volatility of Electronic Collection Development . . . Part 2," pp. 4–5.

63. McFarland et al., "Developing a Health Sciences," p. 218.

64. Riley and Shipman, "Building and Maintaining," p. 223.

65. Neal K. Kaske, "On My Mind: Materials Availability Model and the Internet," *Journal of Academic Librarianship* 20 (1994): 317.

66. Demas, "Collection Development," pp. 76–80.

67. American Library Association, Resources and Technical Services Division, *Guide to the Evaluation of Library Collections*, ed. Barbara Lockett (Chicago: American Library Association, 1989).

68. Thomas E. Nisonger, *Collection Evaluation in Academic Libraries: A Literature Guide and Annotated Bibliography* (Englewood, CO: Libraries Unlimited, 1992).

69. Denise A. Garofalo, "Internet Use by Rural Public Libraries: An Examination of Two Programs in the Hudson Valley of New York State," in *The Internet Initiative: Libraries Providing Internet Services and How They Plan, Pay and Manage*, ed. Edward J. Valauskas and Nancy R. John (Chicago: American Library Association, 1995), p. 87.

70. *Guide to the Evaluation of Library Collections*, pp. 5–6.

71. Lee Ash and William G. Miller, comps., *Subject Collections: A Guide to Special Book Collections and Subject Emphases as Reported by University, College, Public, and Special Libraries and Museums in the United States and Canada*, 7th ed., rev. and enl. (New Providence, NJ: Bowker, 1993).

72. Karen M. Drabenstott and Pauline A. Cochrane, "Improvements Needed for Better Subject Access to Library Catalogs via the Internet," in *Emerging Communities: Integrating Networked Information into Library Services: Papers Presented at the 1993 Clinic on Library Applications of Data Processing, April 4–6, 1993*, ed. Ann P. Bishop (Urbana–Champaign: Graduate School of Library and Information Science, University of Illinois at Urbana–Champaign, 1994), p. 79.

73. Laine Farley, ed., *Library Resources on the Internet: Strategies for Selection and Use* (Chicago: American Library Association, Reference and Adult Services Division, 1992), p. 6.

74. Kaske, "On My Mind," p. 317.

75. McClure, "User-Based Data," pp. 592–95.

76. Sheila S. Intner, "The Meaning of Core Collections," *Technicalities* 13 (July 1993): 4.

77. Linda Lawrence Stein, "What to Keep and What to Cut? Using Internet as an Objective Tool to Identify 'Core' Periodical Titles in a Specialized Subject Collection," *Technical Services Quarterly* 10, no. 1 (1992): 3–14.

78. Joy Tillotson, Joan Cherry, and Marshall Clinton, "Internet Use Through the University of Toronto Library: Demographics, Destinations, and Users' Reactions," *Information Technology and Libraries* 14 (1995): 192–93.

79. From a Haworth Press advertisement dated July 1995.

80. Seiden and Nuckolls, "Developing a Campus-Wide," pp. 279, 284.

81. Richard Kuster is a Ph.D. student in Indiana University's School of Library and Information Science.

82. Don Willmott, "The World-Wide Web: A Guided Tour of 100 Hot Web Sites," *PC Magazine* 14 (April 11, 1995): 37–42; Bruce Maxwell, "The 10 Best Federal Government Internet Sites," *Database* 18 (August/September 1995): 42–47.

83. Anna H. Perrault, "The Shrinking National Collection: A Study of the Effects of the Diversion of Funds from Monographs to Serials on the Monograph Collections of Research Libraries," *Library Acquisitions: Practice & Theory* 18 (1994): 3–22.

84. Linda R. Musser, "Climate and Global Change Serials and Internet Discussion Lists," *Serials Review* 20 (1994): 59–80.

85. Henry and Dell, "Ariel: Technology," pp. 436–37.

86. Britten, "Building and Organizing," p. 247.

87. The URL is: http://unixg.ubc.ca:7001/0/providers/hss/zjj/ejhome.html.

88. Jackson, "Document Delivery," pp. 15, 17.

89. Based on a conversation with Jay Wilkerson, Indiana University Library, on November 15, 1995.

90. Tedd, "An Introduction to Sharing Resources," p. 50.

91. Mary E. Jackson, *North American Interlibrary Loan/Document Delivery Project ILL/DD Management System: Summary Description* (Washington, DC: Association of Research Libraries, 1995). Accessible on the ARL gopher at the following URL: gopher: //arl.cni.org:70/00/access/ill/naildd/mgt.

92. Clifford A. Lynch, "System Architecture and Networking Issues in Implementing the North American Interlibrary Loan and Document Delivery (NAILDD) Initiative," *Journal of Library Administration* 21, nos. 1/2 (1995): 146.

93. *Alex*'s URL is: http://www.lib.ncsu.edu/stacks/alex-index.html.

94. Clifford A. Lynch, "The Roles of Libraries in Access to Networked Information: Cautionary Tales from the Era of Broadcasting," in *Emerging Communities: Integrating Networked Information into Library Services: Papers Presented at the 1993 Clinic on Library Applications of Data Processing, April 4–6, 1993*, ed. Ann P. Bishop (Urbana-Champaign: Graduate School of Library and Information Science, University of Illinois at Urbana–Champaign, 1994), pp. 123, 124, 130.

95. Demas, "Collection Development," p. 74.

96. Ibid., p. 72.

97. Lynch, "The Transformation of Scholarly Communication," pp. 7–8.

98. Zhou, "From Smart Guesser," pp. 652–57.

99. Michel Bauwens, "What Is Cyberspace?" *Computers in Libraries* 14 (April 1994): 44.

100. These authors do not claim a uniform, linear progression from lower to higher levels.

101. This anecdote was related to the author by David Kaser, Distinguished Professor Emeritus, Indiana University, School of Library and Information Science.

102. Nicholas Negroponte, "Bits and Atoms," *Wired* 3 (January 1995): 176.

103. The author gratefully thanks Judith Serebnick, Associate Professor Emerita, and Howard Rosenbaum, Lecturer, at Indiana University's School of Library and Information Science, for providing valuable feedback on a draft of this chapter; and Cynthia D. Bergquist, my graduate assistant, for photocopying articles.

3

Collection Management and Integrated Library Systems

Mary F. Casserly and Anne C. Ciliberti

INTRODUCTION

In the past fifteen years integrated library systems (ILS) have become the *sine qua non* of library automation. Designed to integrate various technical applications such as acquisitions, cataloging, and serials control with a central bibliographic database, these systems capture, store, and produce vast amounts of important data. Their information by-products have the potential to tell us much about all aspects of the library and its use.

Collection development librarians have long recognized that data pertaining to collection use, size, growth, and cost are critical to the formulation of sound collection development decisions. Consequently, they are aware that the selection, management, and evaluation of their collections would be enhanced by information from each integrated library system module. However, despite the overwhelming volume and sophistication of ILS data, there is evidence to suggest that the information needs of collection managers have not been adequately addressed.

The research described in this chapter represents the first effort to examine empirical data about collection development librarians' perceptions about the availability and usefulness of data reported by their integrated systems relative to the size, use, growth, and cost of their collections.

BACKGROUND TO THE PROBLEM

As we pass into the last half decade of the 20th century, there appear to be three environmental factors that suggest it is a propitious time to examine the state of the art of library automation as it relates to collection management in libraries. These factors pertain to changes in the scope and nature of collection management, the rise and sophistication of library automation efforts, and the role and use of management information data in library organizations.

The first and most basic of these factors is the tremendous change in our view of collection management over the past twenty to thirty years. As a discipline, collection management has evolved beyond its historical roots in acquisitions to encompass such issues as selection, budgeting, preservation, and grantsmanship. As Barker suggests, successful collection management professionals are now "strong managers," with better communication and interpersonal skills, more background in automation and cataloging, and more skill with budget management.[1] Lynden extends Barker's definition to include issues of access and collection maintenance as well as collection analysis and evaluation.[2] Collection management is therefore no longer preoccupied solely with obtaining library materials as quickly and cheaply as possible, but rather extends to all aspects of collection building, maintenance, use, and planning.

At the foundation of this new understanding of collection management is the second environmental factor, the indisputable and ubiquitous rise in the use of automation. The manual routines of the past, first replaced by the batch data processing of single functions such as cataloging and circulation, have given way to fully integrated, online automated systems. The library systems of today not only perform the discrete functions of acquisitions, serials, cataloging, circulation, and the public catalog, but they do so in an integrated fashion. Working from a common bibliographic core with a common command structure, data elements are linked throughout the system, providing the opportunity to track both materials and transactions. Without redundant keying, materials can be tracked as they progress through the system from selection to shelf, and transactions can be monitored from catalog consultations to circulation.

However, as marvelous as these technological advances of integrated systems are for putting materials into the hands of users efficiently and effectively, an equally important feature is their ability, both realized and potential, to provide management information data about the system's transactions. In fact, as Cortez points out, an important criterion for "measuring the effectiveness of library automation systems is their ability to manipulate and generate information for management use."[3] As Hawks further notes, the management information value of automated library systems has been recognized by systems designers and vendors, for most systems are designed with a dual function: to support daily operations as well as to provide managers with useful information for decision making.[4]

The evolution in libraries of the role and importance of management information for decision making and resource allocation is the third environmental factor that has arisen in the last ten years. Traditionally, management information data have been viewed principally as a concern of only the top-level administrators. Decisions regarding the allocation of staff and dollars emanated from administrative offices. However, in recent years, this traditional view has given way to a new organizational understanding of management and management information needs. Today, more and more libraries are flattening their hierarchical organizations and are pushing managerial decisions down to the operational level. This trend, coupled with an increased reliance on empirical data in the form of management information, has resulted in a new emphasis on management information at the departmental or team level. Bruer recounts the story some years ago of almost all attendees at a library conference describing themselves as library managers. He underscores this trend by explaining that management is a term which can refer to many levels of policy and responsibility and that it is a mistake to "assume that management and the consequent need for management information applies only to the high levels of administration."[5]

Given the current reality of these three environmental factors (broader scope of collection management concerns, increased use of integrated library systems, and a recognized need for management information at operational levels), to what extent has useful management information been made available to collection management practitioners?

WHAT DOES THE LITERATURE SAY?

A sizable body of literature surrounding the issue of automation and collection management has developed since the late 1970s. However, the only relevant empirical study located is a doctoral dissertation written by Neuman in 1986.[6] This dissertation documents Neuman's efforts to examine the extent to which a group of Association of Research Libraries members follow the Management Information System model in planning for collection development. Based upon survey results from library directors and collection development officers, Neuman found that although many libraries were using automated tools to assist in collection development decision making, use of the institution's Management Information System/Decision Support System was not widespread. Further, she found that despite the fact that 88 percent of the responding libraries were automated or were implementing the automation of library operations, data from these systems was not being used for collection development planning and decision making. The automated tools cited as being used were generally spreadsheet or statistical programs and none was based upon an automated library system module. Neuman concludes that increased use of data from automated system modules for collection development purposes is likely to increase as automation efforts become more prevalent.

The remaining body of literature on the topic of automation and collection management consists of articles describing the use of automated tools or the need for integrated system data useful for collection development. Articles documenting some of the automated products and services useful for collection management purposes include Lynden's description of how the RLG Conspectus and various CD-ROM bibliographic products can contribute to the information arsenal of collection managers.[7] In their article about the use of automation for collection development in Colorado libraries, Sasse and Smith describe the local integrated system as a prime source of management information. They also note the value of national bibliographic utilities such as OCLC and RLIN and the usefulness of data prepared by commercial vendors such as Ebsco and Blackwell North America. Another source they describe is the Collection Analysis CD (CACD) developed by OCLC and AMIGOS.[8]

Although the products and sources of data described by these authors vary, they are similar in that they exist outside the context of the integrated library environment. Consequently, their ability to provide valuable information for collection management purposes is limited, not only because the data they provide are not comprehensive, but in many cases because of their cost and the staff expertise needed to cobble together and use them. Meador's and Cline's development of a Macintosh-based Bibliographer's Workstation capable of providing pathways to other databases and of storing data useful for the collection bibliographer is evidence of the type of support that could be required to generate the data needed for sound collection management decision making.[9] Gleeson's and Ottensmann's article describing how data from automated cataloging and circulation systems can be statistically manipulated and programmed to offer management information provides another example of the expense and effort often required to optimize data from externally automated systems.[10]

From the point of view of both expense and accessibility the ILS emerges as the most efficient source of collection management data. Reed-Scott describes many opportunities collection managers have to utilize management information obtained from integrated systems. She concludes that

It is clear, then, that automated systems have an immense potential to enhance collection management processes. Yet the practical problem of digesting the massive amount of data generated by these systems has not been dealt with effectively. There is a real danger of information overload because the systems' capability to generate data far outstrips the collection development managers' capability to analyze and interpret the data. Given the variety, complexity and quantity of potential data, there is a need for effective collection management information systems. These systems will become essential if collection managers are to exploit the machine-generated data for improved decision-making and effective use of collection resources.[11]

Several other authors support the view expressed by Reed-Scott regarding the potential value of integrated library systems for collection management data. Hawks, writing in 1986, 1988, and 1992, has been particularly interested in the issue and has followed its evolution through various phases of automation. As early as 1986, in an article about the GEAC Acquisitions System, Hawks reviews five categories of management information reports provided by the system. Although she recognizes that "acquisitions does not operate in a vacuum" and that it "is tightly coupled to collection development as well as to cataloging and circulation," the collection management reports she describes are based upon acquisitions data and do not include data captured from other system modules.[12]

Two years later, in another article about integrated library systems, Hawks discusses more fully how many of the individual system modules, such as acquisitions and cataloging, can provide important data for collection management purposes. She concludes that one important benefit of integrated systems stems from their interconnectedness, which enables them to discern relationships among data which in manual systems might not be recognized.[13]

However, despite her initial optimism about the potential value of integrated systems, in 1992 Hawks concludes that many of the second generation integrated systems still lack the ability to capture data normally considered by systems as "transitory," such as circulation transactions once the loaned item has been discharged.[14] In a second article that year, Hawks develops this idea further, noting that system users are "calling for the correlation of data on circulation, acquisitions, interlibrary lending and borrowing, and search behavior to assist in making informed collection assessment and management decisions."[15] She concludes that

Despite their abundant statistics and ability to quantify data, local automated systems do not always yield the information needed. Standard reports designed by the systems vendor may be rigid, inflexible and unsuitable for the purpose at hand. It may still be necessary to develop statistics, particularly comparative statistics, manually. As a result, collection management must look beyond traditional sources of information and develop non-traditional opportunities.[16]

Two articles published in 1993 further document dissatisfaction with the current state of integrated library systems with respect to collection management information. Johnson, noting that integrated systems should be able to provide such information, suggests that the problem is that few systems are designed with the requisite programs for generating useful reports.[17] While acknowledging that some management data are available, Sanders notes that they are generally not in the form needed or are not conveniently accessible; some are not available at all.[18]

Sanders, in this same article, describes the attributes of a truly functional, integrated, ideal collection management system. Describing work done with Hawks in preparing an RFP for an integrated system for Ohio libraries, she describes a system that would be flexible, user-friendly, capable of providing routine and unique reports, able to capture and store transitory data, and able to operate on a real-time basis. Functionally, such systems would be capable of providing quickly and flexibly a myriad of data such as statistics about the cost of collection building, about current collection attributes and patterns of collection growth, and about collection use and users.[19]

The potential inherent in automated library systems to form the basis for management information systems in libraries studied by Neuman, is also examined by Cullen and Chaudhry. Cullen acknowledges the vast potential of automated systems to provide important data, but also notes their failure to provide focused, useful data in manageable forms of output. She asserts that librarians should adopt a more "bottom-up" approach to the development of library management information systems and carefully examine and use the system data which can be successfully turned into information for decision making.[20] Chaudhry writes about this same problem and suggests that it is partly due to librarians' lack of knowledge about the types of data capable of being produced as well as an unclear understanding of their information needs. In an attempt to clarify the situation, Chaudhry developed a checklist of reports and statistics which can reasonably be expected to be generated by automated library systems and then evaluated six system software packages in terms of their capabilities and potential for delivering management information support. He found that while none of the systems he reviewed was impressive in this regard, the coverage of most systems was fair. He concluded, however, that the ultimate solution is not only continued development of system capabilities for more comprehensive and flexible output, but more clearly conceptualized and articulated statements of information needs from librarians.[21]

Two types of management information often desired by collection development practitioners, which have not been generally recognized by system designers, are data about interlibrary loan borrowing and online catalog search behavior. In most systems the circulation module reports provide data about interlibrary loans, counting those transactions as any other circulation transactions. However, an area of particular interest for collection development librarians is data about collection failures or items borrowed from other libraries because they were unavailable locally. Although the major bibliographic utilities such as OCLC have developed sophisticated interlibrary loan systems, these systems are not integrated into the host library's own system and they do not provide the kind of data reports most useful for the practitioner. While it is easy to understand that such systems cannot operate from the host library's central bibliographic database (because the materials were never acquired) as most other modules do, system vendors have developed sophisticated acquisitions modules which also rely upon bibliographic data not initially present in the local database. The fact that acquisitions systems have been successfully integrated suggests that systems could be designed to integrate interlibrary borrowing functions and report features useful to collection development librarians.

Online catalog search behavior is a second area of interest for collection development practitioners. However, unlike interlibrary borrowing, most systems do provide automated transaction log components capable of recording patron keystrokes and commands as entered into online catalog workstations. Although a few authors such as Hawks and Sandore recognize the enormous potential such logs can provide collection managers about how users search catalogs, what they are looking for, and how successful they are, two factors mitigate the use of such powerful management data for collection development purposes.[22]

The first limitation related to transaction logs is that most systems provide massive quantities of largely undifferentiated raw data which are extremely labor-intensive to analyze. As Flaherty concludes, "We need more systems with versatile, easy to use logging software that give library staff as well as system developers and programmers access to transaction log data."[23] Library staff in general, and collection development librarians in particular, must lobby for system designers to develop programs capable of massaging raw log data into meaningful reports. The second factor limiting the potential value of transaction logs for collection development purposes is that, with the few exceptions noted above, many librarians are unaware of the existence of the logging component in their systems. Flaherty suggests that the availability of log data "may be among the best kept secrets."[24] This lack of knowledge, combined with what Sandore calls the "difficult nature" of logs, has precluded many librarians from obtaining valuable information about their collections and their users' behaviors.[25]

In conclusion, the literature surrounding the issue of automation and collection management suggests that there are many automated opportunities and pathways for obtaining data useful to collection managers. Some of these opportunities are provided by commercial products and services, external to the library's own systems. Others, however, have evolved from stand-alone acquisitions systems to modules in fully integrated library systems. The latter, particularly those in their second generation of evolution, are often capable of producing vast amounts of data across a variety of subsystems. However, despite this potential, there appears to be considerable dissatisfaction with the systems' abilities to produce meaningful, easily accessible management data specifically tailored to the diverse needs of collection managers. The purpose of this research is to explore, from an empirical perspective, the degree to which two popular integrated library systems currently in use provide useful management data for collection development purposes.

RESEARCH METHOD

The investigators chose a descriptive approach to this study with the knowledge that the results of their effort might form the basis of future quantitative studies of collection development management information needs. This research design was largely determined by the absence of a solid foundation of empirical data on information needs in this area of librarianship. For the sake of manageability, the investigators decided to limit the study to two vendors, Data Research Associates (DRA) and Innovative Interfaces Incorporated (III), choosing to build on their familiarity with these systems to create a viable data collection instrument.

Innovative Interfaces, Inc. (III) has been providing products to automate libraries since its founding in 1978. Its first product, the OCLC-CLSI Interface, was followed, in 1981, by the INNOVACQ acquisitions and serials control system. III introduced its fully integrated INNOPAC public catalog and circulation system in the mid-1980s and currently markets a wide range of OPAC modules including cataloging, circulation, acquisitions, serials control, materials booking, and Internet gateway. Libraries using III systems range in size from small, specialized libraries to major research libraries and multitype library systems. Currently, more than 300 public, academic, law, medical, and special libraries located throughout the United States and abroad are users of III systems.

Founded in 1975, Data Research Associates (DRA) entered the library automation marketplace with products and services designed to maximize minicomputer-based library applications. From its inception, DRA software has pioneered the design concept known as "client/server" computing. Although the earliest software releases housed both client and server functions on the same computer, the system was designed to separate "client" functional tasks from the central database called the "server." Today DRA provides automation systems and networking services adaptable to libraries of all types and sizes. Its original Data Research System currently supports cataloging, circulation, acquisitions, serials control, and public access catalog modules. Recent purchases of the Inlex and MultiLIS library systems have expanded DRA's library automation presence to more than 500 library systems representing more than 1,700 individual libraries located on five continents.

The investigators began developing the survey instrument to be used in this study by formulating a list of the data that they judged to be pertinent to collection development/management librarians and which, according to both the DRA and III system documentation, were available or could be generated by these systems. This list formed the basis of a questionnaire which was developed during the spring of 1995 and pretested by the collection development/management librarians who attended the Association for Library Collections & Technical Services (ALCTS) New England Collection Management and Development conference held at Wellesley College in July 1995. The comments received from these conference participants resulted in modifications in wording and format. The final product was a three-page questionnaire consisting of four parts. In Part A, respondents were asked to identify themselves by title, provide information on the size of their libraries' budgets and staffs, and name the ILS vendor and modules in use at their institutions. In Part B, a list of categories of data related to collections, users, online catalogs, and costs were presented. Respondents were asked to indicate the degree to which these data were available from their ILS and the degree to which they found them useful. Parts C and D consisted of a series of open-ended questions concerning the existence and usefulness of additional types of collection management data received from respondents' ILS, vendors, or other sources.

Due to the descriptive nature of the study, the investigators were not required to achieve a representative sample of all DRA and III sites. Consequently, they chose to focus on academic, nonconsortial libraries in the United States and samples of fifty sites for each vendor were randomly selected from the vendors' user directories. Questionnaires were mailed to the collection development or collection management librarians at these sites, but if the person with this title could not be identified from the system directory or from the *American Library Directory*, the questionnaire was addressed to the library director. Respondents were asked to return the questionnaires within four weeks and follow-up letters and questionnaires were sent to those who did not respond to the initial deadline. A total of fifty-four questionnaires were returned for a final return rate of 54 percent, and all but five responses were judged useable.

The returned questionnaires were sorted by vendor and the responses tabulated. Using Excel, the means of the responses to each data category were calculated as were the means for the responses given by respondents from III sites, respondents from DRA sites, respondents with collection development/management titles, and those with director, other administrator or staff titles. T-tests were performed on the means in order to compare responses from III users and DRA users, and those with collection development/management titles and other respondents. Excel calculated the t-value and then the probability associated with it.

FINDINGS AND DISCUSSION OF THE DATA

The responses provided on each of the forty-nine useable questionnaires were analyzed and the findings are presented in Tables 3.1 through 3.10. As these tables indicate, responses were tabulated collectively, by ILS vendor, and by title of respondent. Data from Part A of the questionnaire indicating respondents' titles, the size of the libraries' materials budgets, and their levels of staffing of professional librarians are described in Tables 3.1 through 3.3 as simple counts and percentages. Numeric ratings obtained in Part B pertaining to the availability and usefulness of various categories of data are summarized as arithmetic means. Although the study was designed to examine responses to these questions in general, t-tests were performed to determine if significant differences occurred between the mean scores from III respondents and those from DRA respondents. These results are shown in Tables 3.6 through 3.10. Responses to the open-ended questions in Parts C and D of the questionnaire are also summarized in the text which follows.

Table 3.1
Title of Respondent by ILS Vendor

Title	III Number	%	DRA Number	%	Total Number	%
Directors	9	34.6	12	52.2	21	42.9
Collection Development/Mgt	9	34.6	4	17.4	13	26.5
Other Administrators	3	11.5	3	13.0	6	12.2
Staff	5	19.3	4	17.4	9	18.4
Total	26	100.0	23	100.0	49	100.0

The Respondents

The data presented in Table 3.1 indicate that of the forty-nine respondents, nearly half (42.9%) were directors and slightly more than one-quarter (26.5%) were from collection development/management librarians. Other administrators accounted for 12.2 percent of the responses and other staff for the remaining 18.4 percent. These responses indicate that nearly half of the ratings provided in Part B regarding the availability and usefulness of ILS data for collection development purposes were provided by library directors who presumably have varying degrees of familiarity and involvement with collection development issues. Conversely, only about one-quarter of the ratings were from respondents specifically identified as having collection development responsibilities.

The data in Table 3.1 also present the titles of respondents categorized by ILS vendor used. Of the 49 respondents, 26 (53%) were from III libraries and 23 (47%) were from DRA libraries. Although the numbers of DRA and III libraries are nearly equal, a higher proportion of DRA respondents were directors (52.2%) than III respondents (34.6%). With respect to the number of respondents designated as collection development/management librarians, the situation was reversed; 34.6 percent of the respondents from III libraries were so designated compared to only 17.4 percent of the DRA respondents.

The distribution of respondents by size of material budgets is presented in Table 3.2. Overall, more than three-quarters (77.6%) of the respondents reported materials budgets of $1 million or less. Of these, 20 (40.8%) reported materials budgets of between $100,000 and $500,000. Only one-fifth or 20 percent of the respondents indicated their materials budgets were in excess of $1 million.

When the data in Table 3.2 are examined by type of ILS vendor, it can be noted that 87 percent of the responding DRA libraries reported materials budgets of $1 million or less, whereas only 69.3 percent of the III libraries indicated

Table 3.2
Materials Budget by ILS Vendor

Title	III Number	%	DRA Number	%	Total Number	%
Less than $100,000	0	--	2	8.7	2	4.1
$100,001-$500,000	8	30.8	12	52.2	20	40.8
$500,001-$1,000,000	10	38.5	6	26.1	16	32.7
More than $1,000,000	7	26.9	3	13.0	10	20.4
N/A	1	3.8	0	--	1	2.0
Total	26	100.0	23	100.0	49	100.0

budgets within this range. The largest number of responding DRA libraries, 12 or 52.2%, fell within the materials budget range of $100,001 to $500,000 in contrast to the range of $500,000 to $1,000,000 into which the largest number of responding III libraries (10 or 38.5%) fell. Similarly, 7 or 26.9 percent of the III libraries reported materials budgets over $1 million, whereas only 3 or 13 percent of the responding DRA libraries reported comparable budget sizes.

The number of the professional librarians (expressed at full-time equivalents) employed at the responding libraries is presented in Table 3.3. In general, the data indicate that more than half (61.2%) of the respondents were from libraries employing fewer than 10 professional librarians. Conversely, none of the respondents were from libraries employing more than 60 professionals. Thus, 81.6 percent of all respondents reported their level of professional staffing at twenty or fewer.

When the data in Table 3.3 are reviewed by type of ILS vendor used, it can be seen that the pattern of staffing reported by III libraries follows the pattern established by the libraries as a total group. Just as approximately 80 percent of all responding libraries reported staffing levels of 20 or fewer, 84.6 percent of the III libraries fell into this category. With respect to the responding DRA libraries, slightly fewer (78.3%) reported this level of staffing. In terms of the lower end of the staffing levels, DRA libraries are similar to the III libraries in that more than half (69.6%) employed fewer than 10 professionals. However, unlike the III respondents in which 15.4 percent of the reporting libraries employed more than 21 professionals, 21.7 percent of the DRA respondents reported employing professionals of this number.

The data in Table 3.4 indicate that 61.5 percent of the respondents with collection development/management titles came from libraries with budgets between $500,001 and $1 million and only 22.2 percent of those with other titles

Table 3.3
Professional Staff Size by ILS Vendor

Number of Librarians	III		DRA		Total	
	Number	%	Number	%	Number	%
Less than 10	14	53.8	16	69.6	30	61.2
10-20	8	30.8	2	8.7	10	20.4
21-30	3	11.6	3	13.0	6	12.3
31-60	1	3.8	2	8.7	3	6.1
More than 60	0	--	0	--	0	--
Total	26	100.0	23	100.0	49	100.0

work in libraries with budgets in this range. With respect to size of professional staffs, Table 3.5 indicates that 61.5 percent of those with collection development/ management titles work in libraries employing staff of similar size. Almost 58.4 percent of the respondents with titles other than collection development/management reported working in libraries with materials budgets of less than $500,000 (Table 3.4) and nearly 78 percent reported staff sizes less than 10 FTE professionals (Table 3.5).

The data indicate that the librarians responding to this study work in small to medium-sized libraries with respect to both materials budget and staffing. Only 2 of the 49 respondents report materials budgets less than $100,000 and only 10 with materials budget greater than $1 million. In terms of staff size the vast majority of respondents report that their libraries employ fewer than 20 FTE professionals. Responding III libraries report larger materials budgets than do the DRA respondents, with 65.4 percent reporting budgets in excess of $500,001 in contrast to 39.1 percent of the respondents from DRA libraries. The respondents from III and DRA indicate overwhelmingly that their libraries employ 20 or fewer librarians, although slightly more DRA respondents report staffing levels greater than 20 professionals than do III respondents. In terms of titles of respondents, nearly half of all respondents were directors and only one-quarter were designated as collection development/management librarians, and respondents from DRA libraries were more likely to be directors than those from III libraries. The data also indicate that, in general, those with collection development/management titles represent libraries with large materials budgets and greater numbers of professional staff than do those with other titles.

Data Availability and Usefulness

In Part II of the questionnaire respondents were asked to rate, on a 5-point Likert scale, 18 data categories in terms of their availability and usefulness. In

Table 3.4
Materials Budget by Respondent Title

Materials Budget	Collection Development/Mgt		All Others		Total	
	Number	%	Number	%	Number	%
Less than $100,000	0	--	2	5.6	2	4.1
$100,001-$500,000	1	7.7	19	52.8	20	40.8
$500,001-$1,000,000	8	61.5	8	22.2	16	32.7
More than $1,000,000	4	30.8	6	16.6	10	20.4
N/A	0	--	1	2.8	1	2.0
Total	13	100.0	36	100.0	49	100.0

the case of availability a "1" was equal to "easily available" and a "5" indicated "not available." Likewise for usefulness, a "1" indicated "very useful" and a "5" indicated "not useful." Consequently, the higher the numerical rating given by the respondents the less useful or available they found the data.

The mean responses to the data categories in Part II of the questionnaire are presented in Table 3.6. The mean responses for the availability of data from the respondents' ILSs ranged from 1.31 to 2.49. On average the respondents found information on the number of items borrowed (1A), the number of reserve items used (1B), number of patrons who have used/borrowed library materials (2), number of items in the database (4A), and number of items ordered and received (6A) to be the most available types of collection development/management data. All of these categories had means of 1.5 or less. Data categories 3A-3E received higher ratings from respondents and mean responses to these five categories of information about OPAC searches ranged from 2.14 to 2.49. The number of items loaned to other libraries (1C) was the only other category to have a mean response of over 2.0.

Respondents indicated that, for all categories, data were less useful than available, that is, the mean usefulness responses are higher than the mean availability responses. The mean usefulness responses range from 2.03, information about vendor performance (6C), to 3.29, number of records retrieved/displayed during searches (3B). As was the case with respect to availability, respondents found information about OPAC searches to be the least useful category of data with mean responses to the five types of data in this category ranging from 3.00 to 3.29.

The mean responses from respondents using III and DRA are presented in Table 3.7. Also included in this table are the t-score probabilities for each pair of means that were calculated in order to determine where significant differences

Table 3.5
Professional Staff Size by Respondent Title

Number of Librarians	Collection Development/Mgt Number	%	All Others Number	%	Total Number	%
Less than 10	3	23.1	28	77.7	31	63.3
10-20	8	61.5	2	5.6	10	20.4
21-30	2	15.4	4	11.1	6	12.2
31-60	0	--	2	5.6	2	4.1
More than 60	0	--	0	--	0	--
Total	13	100.0	36	100.0	49	100.0

exist between III and DRA responses. The data in this table indicate that the mean responses of III users ranged from 1.32, number of items in the database (4A), to 2.36, number of items loaned to other libraries (1C). The range of responses from DRA users was greater than the range of III mean responses. DRA users indicated that with a mean of 1.27 they found the number of items borrowed within a specified time period (1A) to be the most easily available data, and that with a mean of 4.50 they found data about OPAC search activity (3E) to be the least available type of data. In 13 out of the 18 categories the means indicate that III users rate data more easily available than do DRA users. However, the t-tests indicate that this difference is significant at the .05 level in only 5 categories. These are: number of searches conducted (3A), number of records retrieved/displayed during searches (3B), number of searches conducted by type of search command (3C), number of successful searches (3D), and requests from users for materials to be purchased/replaced/acquired (5B).

The mean responses from III and DRA users to questions concerning data usefulness are compared in Table 3.8. The mean responses from III users ranged from 1.54 to 3.43 with these respondents finding data category 5B, requests for materials to be purchased/replaced/ acquired to be the most useful data category, and category 3B, number of records retrieved/displayed during searches to be the least useful. DRA users also found category 3B, along with 3C, number of searches conducted by type of search command, to be the least useful data category. The means for these categories were 3.07. DRA users indicated that the number of items lost, missing, or damaged (4B) was the most useful data category. A comparison of the mean responses from these two user groups indicates that for all parts of the data in categories on circulation of materials, information about users, OPAC searches, and the collection, DRA users indicated that these data were more useful than their III counterparts. The reverse

Table 3.6
Mean Responses to Availability and Usefulness of Collection Management Data

Data Categories	Mean Responses	
	Availability	Usefulness
1. Circulation of Materials		
A. No. of items borrowed	1.31	2.40
B. No. of items used in the Library	1.42	2.47
C. No. of items loaned to other libraries	2.16	2.68
2. Information about Users		
A. No. who have used/borrowed materials	1.43	2.22
3. Information about OPAC Searches		
A. No. of searches conducted	2.14	3.05
B. No. of records retrieved/displayed	2.34	3.29
C. No. of searches conducted by type		
of search command	2.45	3.15
D. No. of successful searches	2.45	3.00
E. Data about OPAC search activity	2.49	3.14
4. Information about the Collection		
A. No. of items in the database	1.50	2.07
B. No. of items lost/missing/damaged	1.79	2.20
C. No. of items on hold/in transit	1.77	2.58
D. No. of items added to the database	1.84	2.25
5. Feedback Directly from Users		
A. Online suggestions/messages received	1.68	2.09
B. Online requests for materials to be acquired	1.89	2.11
6. Acquisitions Information		
A. No. of items ordered and received	1.50	2.16
B. Cost of items ordered and received	1.59	2.08
C. Information about vendor performance	1.79	2.03

was true for the categories related to feedback from users and acquisitions information. The t-tests indicate that in only 4 data categories, 4B, 4C, 5A and 5B, were the differences significant at the .05 level.

The mean responses from respondents with collection development/management titles are compared with those of all other respondents in Tables 3.9 and 3.10. With respect to availability (Table 3.9) the mean responses from collection development/management librarians range from 1.38 for number of items borrowed (1A) to 2.27 for number of items "on hold" or "in transit" (4C). The mean responses from those with other types of titles indicate that they, too, found the number of items borrowed to be the most available type of information. This group's mean responses ranged from 1.29 to 2.59 and indicate that

Table 3.7
Comparison of Mean Responses to Availability of Collection Management Data by ILS Vendor

Data Categories	Mean Responses		
	III	DRA	Probability of T
1. Circulation of Materials			
A. No. of items borrowed	1.35	1.27	.650937
B. No. of items used in the Library	1.38	1.48	.670459
C. No. of items loaned to other libraries	2.36	1.90	.283086
2. Information about Users			
A. No. who have used/borrowed materials	1.52	1.33	.365255
3. Information about OPAC Searches			
A. No. of searches conducted	1.48	3.00	.000184
B. No. of records retrieved/displayed	1.64	3.31	.000197
C. No. of searches conducted by type			
of search command	1.50	3.72	1.95E-07
D. No. of successful searches	1.50	3.75	4.8E-06
E. Data about OPAC search activity	1.50	4.50	.174865
4. Information about the Collection			
A. No. of items in the database	1.32	1.70	.171548
B. No. of items lost/missing/damaged	2.00	1.55	.136973
C. No. of items on hold/in transit	1.83	1.68	.693645
D. No. of items added to the database	1.80	1.89	.809808
5. Feedback Directly from Users			
A. Online suggestions/messages received	1.38	2.05	.099258
B. Online requests for materials to be acquired	1.46	2.45	.024377
6. Acquisitions Information			
A. No. of items ordered and received	1.46	1.57	.678980
B. Cost of items ordered and received	1.46	1.80	.243292
C. Information about vendor performance	1.76	1.83	.868708

they believe data about OPAC search activity (3C) to be the least available type of data.

A comparison of the mean responses of these two groups indicate that for the majority of the categories the means of these two groups differ by less than .2. It should be noted that none of the t-tests indicate that the differences between the mean responses from the collection development/management librarians and those of the other respondents are significant at the .05 level.

The responses to data usefulness are compared in Table 3.10. Here the responses from both those with collection development/management titles and those with other titles covered a wider range and were higher than the mean

Table 3.8
Comparison of Mean Responses to Usefulness of Collection Management Data by ILS Vendor

Data Categories	Mean Responses		
	III	DRA	Probability of T
1. Circulation of Materials			
A. No. of items borrowed	2.64	2.14	.245222
B. No. of items used in the Library	2.71	2.19	.248070
C. No. of items loaned to other libraries	3.05	2.28	.129687
2. Information about Users			
A. No. who have used/borrowed materials	2.41	2.00	.326245
3. Information about OPAC Searches			
A. No. of searches conducted	3.16	2.88	.524979
B. No. of records retrieved/displayed	3.43	3.07	.469619
C. No. of searches conducted by type of search command	3.21	3.07	.763941
D. No. of successful searches	3.13	2.79	.473602
E. Data about OPAC search activity	3.27	2.93	.499700
4. Information about the Collection			
A. No. of items in the database	2.33	1.75	.156999
B. No. of items lost/missing/damaged	2.60	1.68	.024745
C. No. of items on hold/in transit	3.00	2.00	.042156
D. No. of items added to the database	2.40	2.05	.421287
5. Feedback Directly from Users			
A. Online suggestions/messages received	1.68	2.60	.010354
B. Online requests for materials to be acquired	1.54	2.89	.000902
6. Acquisitions Information			
A. No. of items ordered and received	2.04	2.33	.530011
B. Cost of items ordered and received	1.91	2.33	.345403
C. Information about vendor performance	1.95	2.15	.639535

responses for availability. The respondents with collection development/management titles rated requests for materials to be purchased/replaced/acquired (5B) as the most useful data category with a mean of 1.42, while their least useful data category, data about OPAC activity (3E) received a mean of 3.57. Respondents with other titles rated cost of items ordered and received (6B) as the most useful with a mean of 1.92, and indicated that with a mean of 3.18 the number of records retrieved/displayed during searches (3B) as the least useful data category. As was the case with the responses to availability the means for the majority of the categories are within .2 of each other. The t-tests indicate that the only category for which the difference in mean responses is significant

Table 3.9
Comparison of Mean Responses to Availability of Collection Management Data by Respondent Title

Data Categories	Mean Responses		Probability of T
	Collection Development/Mgt	All Others	
1. Circulation of Materials			
A. No. of items borrowed	1.38	1.29	.586567
B. No. of items used in the Library	1.38	1.44	.840015
C. No. of items loaned to other libraries	1.92	2.24	.837910
2. Information about Users			
A. No. who have used/borrowed materials	1.54	1.40	.546792
3. Information about OPAC Searches			
A. No. of searches conducted	2.00	2.19	.702078
B. No. of records retrieved/displayed	2.20	2.39	.727954
C. No. of searches conducted by type			
of search command	2.00	2.59	.305506
D. No. of successful searches	2.00	2.59	.369858
E. Data about OPAC search activity	2.11	2.60	.434537
4. Information about the Collection			
A. No. of items in the database	1.62	1.46	.611574
B. No. of items lost/missing/damaged	2.15	1.65	.137179
C. No. of items on hold/in transit	2.27	1.59	.109764
D. No. of items added to the database	1.85	1.83	.974229
5. Feedback Directly from Users			
A. Online suggestions/messages received	1.67	1.86	.133140
B. Online requests for materials to be acquired	1.25	2.12	.083661
6. Acquisitions Information			
A. No. of items ordered and received	1.54	1.48	.833502
B. Cost of items ordered and received	1.62	1.58	.899650
C. Information about vendor performance	1.92	1.71	.639005

at the .05 level is category 5B, requests for materials to be purchased/replaced/acquired.

Other Useful Collection Management Data

A series of open-ended questions in Parts C and D of the survey asked respondents about kinds of data other than those listed in Part B which they found useful for collection development/management purposes. Although few respondents answered each of the 4 questions, 43 or 80 percent provided thoughtful responses to at least one of the questions. The question presented in Part C

Table 3.10

Comparison of Mean Responses to Usefulness of Collection Management Data by Respondent Title

Data Categories	Mean Responses		Probability of T
	Collection Development/Mgt	All Others	
1. Circulation of Materials			
A. No. of items borrowed	2.38	2.41	.955555
B. No. of items used in the Library	2.54	2.44	.839105
C. No. of items loaned to other libraries	2.38	2.77	.535803
2. Information about Users			
A. No. who have used/borrowed materials	2.10	2.26	.745303
3. Information about OPAC Searches			
A. No. of searches conducted	3.10	3.03	.894444
B. No. of records retrieved/displayed	3.71	3.18	.374856
C. No. of searches conducted by type of search command	3.25	3.13	.831506
D. No. of successful searches	3.14	2.97	.768084
E. Data about OPAC search activity	3.57	3.03	.392344
4. Information about the Collection			
A. No. of items in the database	2.42	1.94	.301146
B. No. of items lost/missing/damaged	2.55	2.10	.341852
C. No. of items on hold/in transit	3.00	2.45	.356997
D. No. of items added to the database	2.33	2.22	.812142
5. Feedback Directly from Users			
A. Online suggestions/messages received	1.58	2.27	.094368
B. Online requests for materials to be acquired	1.42	2.36	.046245
6. Acquisitions Information			
A. No. of items ordered and received	2.23	2.12	.816251
B. Cost of items ordered and received	2.38	1.92	.310893
C. Information about vendor performance	2.00	2.05	.911998

asked respondents to identify categories of collection management data provided by their ILS other than those listed in Part B. Of the 43 respondents who chose to answer any of the open-ended questions, 16 or 37 percent responded to the question in Part C. The most frequently cited data category was circulation statistics by call number range used for budgeting or allocating purposes. Other categories of ILS data mentioned were inventory control, acquisition fund reports, material type and format reports, and author/title data from unsuccessful OPAC searches.

Part D of the questionnaire consisted of three questions about the use of collection management data from sources other than the respondent's ILS. The first question pertained to manually collected data and of the 43 respondents who chose to answer any of the open-ended questions, 25 or 58 percent responded to this question. The most frequently cited manually collected data was in-library use data, including periodical use surveys. Interlibrary loan borrowing data was the second most heavily cited category, with several respondents also citing user suggestions, reference questions, and building use counts as other types of data manually collected.

The second question in Part D asked about vendor-provided data useful for collection management decisions. Of the 43 respondents to questions in Parts C and D, 24 or 56 percent answered this question about vendor-provided information. Of these, 15 reported using book jobber data about approval plan activities, prices, and publishing statistics, and 12 reported using periodical vendor data about journal subscriptions, prices, subject distributions, and cost studies. Some respondents cited more than one category of data. The third category listed by several respondents pertained to data provided by an electronic indexing service regarding local use of its database.

The final question in Part D queried respondents about use of data from other automated systems not integrated into their ILS. Only 18 or 42 percent of those who chose to answer questions in Parts C and D responded to this question. Of the responses given, the most frequently cited source was data from CD-ROM network logs. Other responses included electronic indexing service search activity, interlibrary loan statistics, and data from stand-alone acquisitions systems.

SUMMARY AND CONCLUSIONS

The capability of integrated library systems to provide meaningful, easily accessible data about a library's collection and its use has been amply questioned in the professional literature. In fact, most writers on the topic have expressed dissatisfaction with their systems' report functions. They have observed that the data summaries are too massive, too complex, too rigid, not in a useable format, or not comprehensive enough. Further limitations are that the data cannot be easily manipulated and that correlation between data from different modules is lacking. This small descriptive study was undertaken to examine this problem and gain some perspective on this issue based upon empirical data from the field. The study was descriptive in nature and as such can only be considered a first step in the full exploration of the issues related to the need for and use of information for collection management decision making.

The forty-nine librarians who participated in this study were from small to medium-sized libraries in terms of their materials budgets and the number of professionals on their staffs. Twenty-three of the respondents used DRA and twenty-six used III. Only about a quarter had titles indicating that most of their responsibilities were related to collection development or management. The majority were, in fact, library directors. Although there was some initial concern that the questionnaires had not been completed by the targeted audience (those responsible for collection development) the size of the libraries represented suggests that the directors and respondents with other titles may indeed be the persons with primary responsibility for collection development matters. The lack of significant differences in all but one of the mean responses by those respondents with collection development/management titles and those with other titles suggests that these groups have similar perceptions of data availability and usefulness, and is further evidence that the questionnaires were answered by those responsible for collection development. Additional support for this contention can be found in a study by Casserly and Hegg in which the authors found a wide variety of titles used by persons responsible for collection development and conclude that the lack of consensus concerning title and organization for collection development exacerbates the problems of collecting data on collection development from the appropriate library personnel.[26]

This study provides a snapshot of the availability and usefulness of eighteen types of collection management data as perceived by those responsible for collection development in small and medium-sized libraries using either the III or the DRA integrated library system. The study found that in these settings the collection management data derived from the integrated library systems were perceived as being both available and useful. However, the respondents consistently indicated that the data were less useful than available.

In general, collection management information about circulation, users, the collection, and acquisitions, as well as feedback from users, was seen by respondents as easily available. In contrast, data about how the OPAC is being searched were perceived by respondents as less easily available and were also seen as the least useful of the data categories included in this study.

At first glance the finding that management information was perceived as available and useful by collection management librarians seems to contradict the literature review, which turned up a significant number of authors who contend that management information is unavailable and/or difficult to access. However, the study focused on what can be considered the most basic types of management information. In fact, many of the data listed in the eighteen categories have been considered so essential to library management that, prior to the advent of the ILSs, they were collected manually. The authors cited in the literature review, especially those writing within the last several years, have focused on more sophisticated types of management information, including cross tabulation of data from more than one module of the ILS. The findings of this study suggest that ILSs are doing some of what has been done manually reasonably well, but they cannot provide the same quality of data about the more complex aspect of system use, especially aspects related to how users conduct their research. Specifically, they suggest the need for improvements in the design of OPAC transactions logs and the need for more training to be conducted in their use. On a more general level, however, they point to a need for ILS developers to look beyond the types of management information traditionally gathered in libraries and move toward designing systems that provide the more sophisticated information that collection developers have requested.

It was not the intention of this study to focus on the comparison between the III and DRA integrated library systems. However, the responses do point to differences in the designs of the collection management information components of these two systems. III users indicated that they perceived information about OPAC searches and requests for materials to be purchased/replaced/acquired to be more easily available than did DRA users. DRA users found two aspects of information about the collection, number of items lost, missing, or damaged and number of items "on hold" or "in transit" to be more useful than III users. The reverse was true for the two categories of data pertaining to feedback directly from users. Overall, however, III and DRA users generally shared the perception that the eighteen types of data included in the questionnaire were less useful than available, suggesting that the data available to users from both systems cannot be easily employed in collection management decision making.

The responses to the open-ended questions in Parts C and D of the questionnaire suggest that those responsible for collection development consult a wide variety of data from book and periodical vendors, as well as from systems outside the ILS, such as their CD-ROM networks. In addition, they are still manually generating some of the data they need, especially related to the in-house use of materials. Again, these findings point to additional information needs and suggest areas for further development of integrated library systems.

FUTURE RESEARCH

The sample in this study consisted of a relatively small number of respondents using only two types of integrated library systems. While the results do identify some areas in which improvements could be made in ILS information management systems, a broader survey incorporating a wider variety of integrated systems is warranted. A further step would be to solicit input from collection managers regarding management information that is needed or desirable, but not available. Included in this category would be data derived by correlating information from more than one module, such as subject use by patron status or circulation by date of acquisition. Finally, an analysis of the information needs and a realistic look at how, and by whom, this information could be used would be helpful to both developers of integrated library systems and the library staff charged with selecting and implementing such systems.

NOTES

1. Joseph W. Barker, "Acquisitions and Collection Development: 2001," *Library Acquisitions: Practice & Theory* 12 (1988): 245.

2. Frederick C. Lynden, "Collection Management by Automation," *Library Acquisitions: Practice & Theory* 13 (1989): 177.

4

Collection Development Policies and Electronic Information Resources

Peggy Johnson

INTRODUCTION

Today's rapidly changing information formats and mechanisms for information access and delivery offer libraries wonderful opportunities and daunting challenges. The complex issues surrounding the selection and management of electronic information resources present many questions and few simple answers. This chapter seeks to frame these issues and identify the questions that should be addressed. Answers will vary from library to library. A case for developing collection policies for electronic resources is presented and approaches for developing a policy are suggested.

THE VALUE OF COLLECTION POLICIES

This chapter begins with the conviction that collection development policy statements are necessary library planning documents. Although the value of collection policies is not universally accepted, the prevailing view among library professionals is that a collection development policy statement is a necessary tool leading to consistent, informed decisions.[1] Throughout this chapter, the terms "library collections," "collection policies," and "collection management and development" refer to the entire collection of information to which the library provides access, as well as resources which it acquires. The ideal collection policy is a living document, reviewed and revised regularly to keep it current and meaningful. A dynamic policy organizes and guides the processes of acquiring and providing access to materials and information sources, integrating these into coherent collections, managing their growth and maintenance, and making decisions about preservation, withdrawal, and cancellation. Policies facilitate consistency and communication between collection management librarians and are information tools for working with the library's community.

To understand the value of electronic resources collection policies, one must first understand the benefits of collection policies to libraries. The purposes that collection policies serve fall into two categories. Policies both inform and protect. They are usually directed both to an internal audience and to a broader community outside the library. A collection policy describes past collection practices and existing collections for library staff, users, administrators, trustees, and consortia partners. It identifies both strengths and weaknesses of the existing collection. A policy defines collecting goals and presents a plan for future collection development, thus providing a means to measure progress toward meeting these goals.

Policies describe the user community, define the institutional mission, and identify user needs. They match collection development and management practices to the community, the institution's mission, and educational and research needs. This information provides a conceptual framework to guide external and internal budget preparation and allocation. A well-crafted policy informs a library's governing and funding body about the library's directions and provides a clear and carefully articulated rationale for its collection goals and practices. It demonstrates accountability by presenting a plan for careful management of fiscal resources and describing the results of funding decisions. A good policy statement can improve the library's ability to compete for resources within a complex and competitive institutional environment. It also aids in preparing grant proposals and planning fund-raising and development initiatives by providing supporting information. A collection policy guides internal fund allocation and matches goals with available resources.

Collection policies provide the information needed to establish priorities for the library. Priorities for collection management decisions (selection, deselection, preservation, storage) are guided by collection goals. In addition, collection policies provide the context for decisions about cataloging, retrospective conversion, space allocation, budgeting, and fund-raising priorities. They can guide those individuals responsible for managing personnel, fiscal matters, space, and other resources in support of collections. By establishing collection management priorities, policy statements guide in establishing staffing needs and allocating available personnel.

Policy statements serve as a vehicle for communication with the library's staff, administration, and constituencies. While describing the library collection and its strengths and weaknesses, they also formally document practice. Within the library, policy statements serve to coordinate selection when responsibilities for selection are dispersed among many selectors and over several physical locations. As such, policies provide a control and consistency. They foster shared values among selectors and can serve as training documents for new collection management librarians. Policy statements can be used externally in various ways. They provide information for accreditation surveys and in response to inquiries about the impact of new academic and research programs on library resources.

Collection policies can serve a particularly important function in supporting cooperative collection development. The policy statement explicitly identifies all active cooperative programs in which the library participates. These may include cooperative collection building, resource sharing, regional storage programs, shared access to electronic files through networks, and perhaps shared subject specialists. By documenting what the library does and what it plans to do with collecting levels by discipline, a policy provides the means to develop and maintain cooperative collection development and resource sharing programs. Using a common policy format and standard terms facilitates cooperation.

In addition to informing about past, present, and future practices and priorities, collection development policy statements protect the library against illegal, unethical, or unreasonable pressures. Polices can serve to protect intellectual freedom and prevent censorship. This may be handled by including the *Library Bill of Rights* and other intellectual freedom statements in the policy, or preparing a statement tailored to the local community. This portion of the policy serves both to protect the library against censorship and to affirm the library's commitment to intellectual freedom and fair, equitable access, not insignificant issues when dealing with electronic information resources.

A collection policy protects the library from pressures to acquire or provide access to inappropriate and irrelevant materials. A statement can provide a guarantee against undue special interest pressure from those who demand that the library purchase or provide access to certain materials. The statement should be written so that the guidelines for collection management (such as selection and deselection) protect as well as inform. Materials are rejected because of collection guidelines, not because of who may or may not wish their acceptance.

Policies can protect by providing guidelines for handling of gifts. Carefully written guidelines can help the library avoid the burden of unwanted, inappropriate, and undisposable items and specify the conditions under which the library accepts gifts. This portion of the policy addresses the specific economic, social, and political situation in which a library exists. By defining policy and procedures for accepting or declining, appraising, accessioning, acknowledging, and processing gifts, both the library and the potential donor are protected legally and practically. Gift policies apply to library staff members who wish to donate materials (for example, review copies) as well as potential donors outside the libraries.

As budget allocations decrease, materials costs increase and formats proliferate, libraries need protection as they plan to cancel serials, weed, and withdraw materials. These decisions often provoke vocal reactions from users. Libraries need a rationale documented in a policy statement with which to explain their actions. Substituting access to information in electronic formats for physical ownership of print resources and changing from one form of electronic information access to another can be equally inflammatory. Making clear the operating principles (assuming they are rational and acceptable) under which these decisions are made protects the library from charges of bias and irresponsible behavior. A policy should define the process through which materials are identified for withdrawal, cancellation, and replacement, and by whom.

Collection policies provide guidelines within which the library selects and manages its collection of information resources. These guidelines are a contract between the library and its community, supplying a framework within which complex decisions are made with consistency and reason. The most complex decisions librarians face these days are those surrounding acquisition of and access to electronic information resources. These decisions need special attention.

THE IMPORTANCE OF COLLECTION POLICIES FOR ELECTRONIC RESOURCES

This section explores the particular complexities of selecting and managing electronic information resources and the value of an electronic resources collection policy in guiding decisions. Not only are the issues associated with electronic information complex, they are also unique and unfamiliar. For this reason, if only in the short term, collection development and management decisions for electronic resources require special attention. Demas, who has written extensively on the need to integrate electronic information resources into library collections and services, recommends an electronic information collection policy as a vehicle for coordinating the development of print and electronic components of collections.[2] The need for a policy that fosters a consistent and coherent approach to all library resources is compelling.

So much about electronic resources is different from traditional library resources that a different kind of attention is needed from selectors. Electronic information is delivered in new and rapidly changing formats. The supporting hardware, software, and telecommunication options are unfamiliar. Even the terminology and skills necessary to understand and use electronic information resources are different from those associated with traditional resources, and they are changing rapidly. Having to consider the logical format of the data, which may vary greatly from system to system and file to file, is a new and different part of selecting resources.[3] Librarians have difficulty identifying what is available and finding substantive reviews. The routine reviewing infrastructure that has existed for print, audio, and video is only slowly developing for electronic information resources. A policy can provide a framework that suggests the decisions that need to be made, the questions selectors need to ask, and the context in which these activities occur.

The high prices of electronic resources justify special attention. Collection policies guide budgeting decisions, and the decision to acquire or access a single electronic resource can have significant dollar implications. Total cost (which may include hardware, access software, site preparation, technical support, connect costs, maintenance, and more) and, consequently, the potential financial risk of a poor choice, is often notably higher for electronic resources. Dannelly speaks of the high costs of investing in quickly outdated equipment, software, and network functions.[4] The speed with which new options (information resources, hardware, and software) appear makes for a volatile environment. A policy makes clear the need to consider cost implications of the infrastructure necessary to access electronic information. These costs go far beyond those of traditional materials. The equipment and facilities consequences of electronic resources are new and different. Libraries need policies to guide decisions about funding the infrastructure and about technical feasibility.

Negotiating licenses and pricing structures is a new phenomenon for most libraries. Collection policies protect libraries in legal and ethical matters through provision of guidelines for decision making. Purchase and lease agreements with contractual clauses addressing limitations on access, ownership of discs and tapes, restrictions on downloading and duplicating support documentation, copyright restrictions, and liability from patron use of information are not typical with print resources. A collection policy will clarify who has responsibility for selecting electronic resources and who has authority for negotiating and signing contracts. A library is well served if legal considerations are addressed in a collection policy.

The importance of vendor support and reliability in the selection process is new. While a publisher's reputation has been a consideration in selecting print resources, availability of continuing support by and accessibility of the producer have not been an important selection criterion. Decisions about preservation of information are constants in collection management, but preservation and archival responsibilities have different implications when the medium is electronic. Library service implications take on new importance. Selecting traditional resources has not often required the selector to consider the skills the users will need, how they will be taught, and who will teach them.

Among the challenging decisions libraries must make regarding electronic resources are procedures for acquiring, cataloging, processing, and managing electronic resources. Collection policies provide guidelines and help establish library priorities for cataloging and processing. A policy for electronic resources addresses institutional priority for intellectual access to these materials. A policy may state that all electronic resources selected for acquisition or access (regardless of physical location or format) will be cataloged. While a policy may not typically include the local procedures for acquiring, cataloging, processing, and managing electronic resources, it may refer to them and make them available in an appendix.

One aspect of selecting electronic resources for acquisition or access sets it apart from selecting other resources. This is the complexity of getting sufficient information to make an informed decision and the need to cross traditional library organizational boundaries to do so. Even libraries that do not have a formal electronic resources selection policy often have a document addressing who is involved in the decision-making process. Selection decisions can never be made in isolation. This becomes especially critical with electronic resources. Collection policies describe the organizational context of collection development and management. A policy for electronic resources will specify who should be consulted (automation staff, legal counsel, reference staff, senior administrators, computer center staff) and who has authority and responsibility for decisions. Policies provide a communication vehicle and provide institutional consistency. This is a primary function of a collection policy that addresses decisions about electronic resources.

MAKING DECISIONS ABOUT ELECTRONIC RESOURCES: CONTEMPORARY PRACTICE

The literature suggests that many librarians are concerned about the best way to manage electronic information resources. Cibbarelli, Gertel, and Kratzert explicitly state, "Librarians need to establish a framework within which they may address important questions regarding the options for delivering information in an electronic environment."[5] Writers emphasize the importance of selection that is blind to format and delivery mechanism, and speak of mainstreaming the responsibilities for electronic information collection decisions along with integrating these resources into the library's collections and services.[6]

Jan Kennedy Olsen sees this as consistent with libraries' continuing mission of connecting the scholar to the information. Users should not have to be concerned with type of access or format. Libraries will continue to share resources, though this will increasingly be through electronic means. Libraries will greatly expand their storage capacities though electronic formats.[7] Just as library users should not have to worry about formats, so, too, library selectors should not exclude electronic information resources from selection decisions simply because the format is electronic and the decisions are complicated.

Bosch, Promis, and Sugnet assert that the advent of electronic formats has complicated the selection process. They state, "Added to the traditional criteria associated with collection development policy and user needs are new concerns related to technology costs for the same information in different formats, additional staffing needs, and additional user demands."[8] They endorse the importance of written procedures for selecting resources. Their *Guide to Selecting and Acquiring CD-ROMs, Software, and Other Electronic Publications* is a useful tool that covers policy and procedural issues in detail. They suggest that within selection criteria for electronic resources fall policy concerns, service concerns, technical concerns, and cost considerations.[9]

Lancaster asserts that electronic resources present a set of problems that have not been encountered by librarians in the past.[10] He sees the challenge of integrating electronic resources with more traditional forms as an obvious problem. Costs involved in acquisition of and access to electronic information present difficulties. Equally troubling is access and what collection development really means in an electronic environment. The role of the selector will change dramatically. He concludes, "Nevertheless, collection development, whatever form it takes, still requires policies. . . ."[11]

Demas, McDonald, and Lawrence stress the need for bibliographers to develop a cohesive process for selecting materials in all formats.[12] The authors focus on key collection policy issues surrounding Internet resources and present an excerpt from a collection policy statement developed at the Mann Library at Cornell University. They describe a project at Mann Library to establish preliminary collection development policies and guidelines for networked resources. These policies were built around a taxonomy of Internet resources categories and included collecting intensity levels for each category. The authors suggest that electronic resources policies are broader than traditional policies because they include questions, problems, policy issues, guidelines, and a list of selection tools for identifying Internet resources.

Cassel also considers criteria for selecting Internet resources in a report of a Binghamton University Libraries project.[13] This library has chosen to develop a separate Internet resources selection policy that incorporates criteria used to collect traditional materials and recognizes unique criteria for electronic resources. Cassel's report suggests that extensive Internet resources and ease of access are compelling reasons to develop a policy with criteria used to select and deselect them.

Dickinson has written *Selection and Evaluation of Electronic Resources*, aimed at providing advice for the selection of electronic resources.[14] Her premise is that decisions about these resources need special attention. She suggests selection criteria and questions to ask when comparing and evaluating various products. She does not address selection policies or consider the need for overarching policies other than to suggest that decisions should be guided first by the needs of the patron community.

LaGuardia and Bentley believe that existing collection development policies are inadequate for the acquisition of electronic resources and stress the need for new policies to address the peculiarities of new formats. They see too many new questions needing answers and not being addressed in existing policies. They endorse the use of collection policies to guide collection management decisions. If these policies do not identify important issues such as those surrounding electronic resources, then policies must be written that do so.[15]

Intner explores the importance of written procedures for software selection and developing selection priorities that reflect collection goals and objectives. Selection should be made based on objective criteria, set up in advance, and written in measurable terms. Although, by definition, selection involves subjective judgments, a more objective process can lead to better performance. Intner suggests that policies assign priorities to selection criteria. She acknowledges the trade-offs between software features—for example, between size, speed, ease of use, and economy—yet stresses the value in clarifying the relative importance of these features, and any others that apply to resources under consideration.[16]

Duszak and Koczkodaj discuss the difficulty in selecting CD-ROMs and note the amount of time frequently devoted to nonproductive discussion about what the best resources are. They propose an approach to selecting these resources called a ''consistency driven knowledge acquisition model.'' They emphasize that this model should be used within the context of well-established guidelines for book and paper collections. The authors include a list of selection criteria, many of which are applicable to most electronic information resources.[17]

Ferguson says that much of the value of writing an electronic resources collection policy is realized in the process of writing it. This is because problems and questions must be confronted and a written policy provides a vehicle for recording these decisions. He describes the process of writing a collection development statement for electronic information at Columbia University and suggests four selection problems that should be addressed in the policy: how to find the best access medium to meet users; what criteria to use; how to pay for electronic resources; and how to modify conspectus definitions so they include electronic resources as well as print formats.[18]

Other authors consider the legal implications of lease and license agreement. Warro writes that electronic formats pose new legal challenges for libraries. He identifies potential problem clauses dealing with customer service, payment and delivery, exclusion of warranties and limitation of liability, termination, indemnification, assignment, and governing law. He recommends adding a standard rider and gives an example.[19] Dannelly observes that leases and licenses for electronic information ''are anything but standard, except in the inclusion of legal terminology.''[20] Issues of copyright application, ownership of electronic information, and rules of access are particularly troubling, and consultation with university counsel is often recommended.

Hazen, while criticizing static collection development policies, does not discount the importance of documents that can guide collection management. He recommends recasting documentation about *all* research resources associated with a library's users and the fields they represent. Libraries need to use flexible descriptions that encompass all formats of information and resources, both local and remote, and create documents that can adjust as methods and materials evolve. Hazen stresses the importance of focusing continuously on users' priorities and needs.[21]

Despite ongoing discussion in the literature, only selected libraries have prepared collection development policies that address electronic resources. An Association of Research Libraries SPEC Kit, published in August 1994, reported that only five of thirty-five libraries receiving electronic journals had collection development policies addressing making electronic journals available.[22] The American Library Association's Reference and Adult Services Division, Collection Development and Evaluation Section, Collection Policy Committee, recognizing wide interest in developing electronic information policies, collected and analyzed several policies during the winter of 1993/1994.[23] In the process of identifying common elements, the committee found that these statements contain more detailed administrative elements than are usual in print collection policies.

Practitioners and theorists agree on the need to apply consistent criteria and standards to the acquisition of any resource, no matter what the format. Especially as selection responsibility for electronic resources is distributed to individual selectors ("mainstreamed"), the library must be confident that all decisions are being made within the same framework. Libraries are beginning to consider how they make decisions regarding electronic resources and how they should be making them. This leads to documenting the library's criteria, areas of concern, priorities, practices, and responsibilities through the preparation of written electronic resources collection policies. The next section suggests possible approaches to creating a collection development policy for electronic resources.

CRAFTING AN ELECTRONIC INFORMATION RESOURCES COLLECTION POLICY

A collection development policy for electronic resources should be consistent with other collection policies in the library. The *Guide for Written Collection Policy Statements* is an excellent starting point, covering format, content, and style.[24] The approach presented here draws heavily on the standard approach to preparing collection policies recommended in the *Guide*.

Classed Analysis Policy

Collection development policies are usually prepared according to one of three formats or models: classed analysis, narrative, or a combination of elements from these two. The classed analysis model describes the collection, current collecting levels, and planned future collecting levels in abbreviated language and numerical codes, most typically according to the Library of Congress classification scheme. This format grew out of libraries' need to develop an effective, consistent way of defining subjects and levels of collecting. The conspectus, developed by the Research Libraries Group (RLG) and also used by WLN, is the most well-known classed analysis format. The conspectus approach to assessing collections and defining collecting practice, though challenged by some as too dependent on individual perceptions, has become accepted as a tool that is adaptable, widely applicable, and useful for sharing and comparing collection practices.

In the traditional classed analysis approach, subject categories are defined by classification range and subject descriptors. Each category is assigned a series of numbers for (a) existing collection strength, (b) current collecting intensity, and, when the library wishes, (c) desired collecting intensity. The numbers, often called collection depth indicators, range from 0 (out of scope—nothing is collected) to 5 (comprehensive—collecting is exhaustive, inclusive, and intensive). Language codes also are given for each category. In addition, scope notes can be used to describe special features of parts of the collection.

A library may choose to adapt the classed analysis model to electronic information resources. Instead of using a subject-based classification system (Library of Congress classification or Dewey Decimal classification), the library may develop classes of electronic resources. Three possible classifications are suggested below; a combination of these may be appropriate. The purpose is to describe electronic resources in a way meaningful to the library and its selectors and to develop a classification scheme that supports consistent decision making.

One approach looks at information content and develops categories of what Demas calls "information genre."[25] Collection depth indicators are then assigned to these categories or classes of information. Such a list will consider electronic information as the following:

- Bibliographic information (citation-based with searchable fields; includes online public access catalogs, indexes, abstracts, and bibliographies)
- Numeric and statistical data (often raw data; includes genetic sequences and geographic information, spatially referenced data, demographic and sociometric data, economic and financial data, scientific and technical data)
- Applications software (general and subject-specific)
- Textual files (often called full-text; includes structured and formatted text and free text files)
- Courseware and instruction files
- Sound files
- Image files
- Multimedia (combination of sound, graphics, animation, and video)

Another approach to classifying electronic information is to organize it by type of resource, that is, to define format genre appropriate to electronic information resources. Collection depth indicators can be assigned by these categories. Each can be further subdivided and collection depth indicators assigned to each separate subcategory. Possibilities are as follows:

- Reference resources (includes directories, dictionaries, bibliographies, online public access library catalogs, other catalogs, abstracts and indexes, current awareness/table of contents services, encyclopedias)
- Monographs (includes new monographs, reprints, scholarly works, popular works, museum catalogs)

- Journals/serials (includes newsletters, news services, referred journals, nonreferred journals)
- Discussion groups (includes listserv lists, computer bulletin boards, Usenet newsgroups)
- Numeric files
- Gopher servers, gateways, and network servers
- Archives (includes archives of software, graphic images, sound)
- Video conferences
- Games
- Government publications
- Library staff resources

The third possible approach to categorizing electronic resources suggested here is based on mechanism of delivery/access. A library may find it more meaningful to apply collection depth indicators to these categories or classifications of electronic information. Such a list might identify the following approaches to acquiring and accessing electronic information:

- Single user, circulating
- In-library use only, via stand-alone workstation (may be floppy, loaded on hard drive, CD-ROM)
- Mounted on local mainframe on demand
- Permanently mounted on local area network
- Permanently mounted on wide area network
- Permanently mounted on local mainframe
- Remote resource via gateway (on local menu)
- Remote resource on Internet, with local pointers (via gopher servers or World Wide Web)

Each of these approaches should be used in concert with subject-based analysis or subject-based narrative collection policies. Collection depth indicators based on type of electronic resource, information content, or means of access provide guidance. They can occasionally be used as independent mandates, such as one finds in policies that deal with traditional resources. For example, just as a library may have a policy that it does not collect popular fiction, it may have a policy that it does not collect computer games. The most important part of using collection depth indicators is to understand how the library's selectors are collecting and to reconcile practice with library mission, goals, and objectives. Use of classifications or categories of electronic information provides a useful way of discussing these resources within the context of subject-based policies and priorities. The traditional classed analysis (based on familiar classification schemes) has the advantage of offering a widely used format for sharing information with other libraries. The models proposed here are not in common use and could not provide a useful vehicle for communication outside a single library.

The second common type of collection policy, the narrative model, is text-based. A general policy consists of narrative descriptions, one for each subject, discipline, or subcollection, with policy statements that cover special considerations for specific collections, types of materials, and exceptions. The purpose is to give a focused view of subjects and collection management as practiced in the library preparing the policy. An advantage of the narrative model is use of terms to describe local programs and collections that are also local and immediately familiar.

Many libraries use both classed analysis and narrative policies. Although both are subjective, the classed analysis, by using standardized divisions and terminology, provides a vehicle for clear division and coordination between selecting responsibilities and measurement of progress toward stated goals. Narrative policies, by their nature, are more descriptive and can define the context in which selection and collection management occurs.

Narrative Policy

A narrative collection development policy statement has several standard elements. If the library has a general collection policy, the information in this document is not repeated in the section or separate policy dealing with electronic resources. All policies begin with an introduction that sets the stage for the policy statements and guidelines that follow. A special policy addressing electronic resources will refer to the library's general or overarching policies. The guidelines that follow must be coherent with the library's mission, goals, objectives, and priorities. The policy will begin by stating the purpose of this particular policy, why it is needed, and the audience to whom it is directed.

The introduction usually describes the community and types of users served and these users' needs. Reference should be made to the electronic information needs and expectations of different types of users. Types of users may include undergraduates, graduate and special students, faculty, distance education, general public, ethnic communities, government employees and officials, extension agents. The policy describes academic programs, degrees granted, research centers, specializations, and other subject needs. If the library is an academic library, the statement should address the library's responsibilities to the off-campus community and to any other constituencies that it may serve beyond its primary users on campus. Description of the user community is followed by a statement of library priorities related to primary and secondary users. Definition of users and the priorities assigned to meeting their needs is particularly critical when developing policies for selection of and access to electronic resources.

Limitations affecting collection development and management are an important part of the introduction. This is the point to note any factors that may limit the library in achieving its goals. The proliferation of new technologies for information delivery, escalating monograph and serial prices, and reduced or steady state budgets may affect the library's ability to achieve all its priorities for electronic information delivery and access. The library may address misconceptions about the imminence of a paperless society and responsibilities for preservation of both printed and electronic resources. Limitations may be financial, technical, legal, or institutional.

A brief overview of the library and its electronic information resources (owned, leased, accessed) should follow. This includes a history of acquisition and access and description of subject areas and formats that have been and are being emphasized or deemphasized. The quality and character of electronic resources collections are evaluated in broad terms, as is current collecting practice. The policy lists any cooperative collection development and resource sharing agreements that deal with electronic resources. These will include formal agreements to share purchase or lease of resources, including access to remote resources. The policy may identify memberships in networks, consortia, and other cooperative groups and systems that may be relevant to future electronic information cooperative agreements. Here is an appropriate place to include library goals about maximizing financial resources and the evolving nature of shared electronic resources.

Polices and guidelines follow the introduction. If the library has chosen not to use one of the classed analysis models suggested previously, the narrative policy will enumerate types of electronic information resources that are selected and not selected, referencing those that apply only to certain subjects. Some policy issues that have been addressed in the library's general policies may be given special attention in a policy for electronic resources. These may include policies covering gift electronic files, preservation and deselection of electronic resources, disposing of superseded and unneeded materials, equity of access, and censorship.

The policy describes the library's collection development organization—that is, how decisions for electronic resources are handled. It locates responsibility for collection building and management within the library structure and staffing. The specific tasks of evaluation, selection, collection, maintenance, budget management, faculty liaison, withdrawal, cancellation, and so on, are identified and assigned. Correlating decision-making responsibility with type of electronic resource is particularly important. One of the classed analysis approaches to electronic resources could be used to distinguish the types of decisions that reside with individual selectors and those that require wider review. The policy should make clear the types of electronic resources that have system-wide impact and those that do not. This will vary from library to library.

Assigning responsibility for decisions is a central part of a collection development policy. Who is ultimately responsible, who is responsible for day-to-day selection and collection management, and who is consulted in the process of making a decision should be clarified. As noted earlier, the boundary-spanning nature of selecting and managing electronic resources in most libraries means that many individuals and units (other selectors, reference librarians, acquisitions librarians, legal advisors, technical advisors) should be involved. The library usually develops a formal mechanism for consultation, even if all decisions about electronic resources do not require system-wide approval. Libraries may appoint a standing committee (similar to a standing serials review committee) or develop a checklist of individuals who are consulted. The common feature in both approaches is broad representation from library units and librarians with varying responsibilities and expertise. The goal is to bring together the necessary expertise to make informed decisions.

Libraries find it equally useful to include a policy statement that addresses shared and distributed responsibilities of the library, computing center, and campus network in acquiring and providing access to digitized information. The aim of this policy is to avoid confusion and conflict in providing access to electronic information resources across the institution. Demas frames the question to be answered as "How does our investment in electronic publications relate to the institution's existing computing and information environment?"[26] This portion of an electronic resources policy should be developed through discussions with representatives of the computing center, campus network, and university administration so that the library's policy is consistent with the institution's information policy and plans for an institutional infrastructure.

An important portion of an electronic resources collection policy focuses on budgeting issues. This section will consider both sources of funds and responsibility for expenditures. Libraries typically have a salaries budget, a supplies and equipment budget, and a materials budget. Each library faces decisions about sources of funding to cover costs associated with acquiring, servicing, managing, and accessing electronic information. Possible costs include initial purchase for separate items and back files, continuing leases, contracts, and subscriptions, hardware, furniture, software and search engines, loaders, connect time to remote files, storage and file refreshing, initial wiring and telecommunication installation, upgrades, continuing technical support, staff and user training, documentation, and more. Even free electronic resources have financial consequences found in the preceding list. An electronic resources policy will make clear which of these costs are to be covered by the materials budget and which are covered by other budgets. Some library electronic resources budget policies are a consequence of institutional policies that specify how allocations and expenditures are tracked at the institutional level.

A second aspect of budgeting policy concerns allocation of funds for electronic resources and responsibility for expending these funds. Several models are possible. A library may have a central fund line used for all electronic resources. At the opposite end is the model in which all funds are allocated to subject lines, and individual selectors manage these fund lines in the same way they have managed fund lines for more traditional library materials. They may make cooperative purchases with other selectors, but no resources are funded "off the top." A middle ground retains some money in a central fund for re-sources of system-wide interest (perhaps major catalogs, a general periodical index and matching full-text file, a current awareness service, an encyclopedia) and other decisions are funded at the individual subject line level. Policies that speak to allocation of funds for electronic resources must be consistent with the policies that address responsibility for selection decisions.

The library's criteria guiding selection decisions are an integral part of a collections policy. These are the attributes of information sources that selectors consider when making a selection or access decision. They will include standard criteria that are applicable to all types of resources and special criteria that are critical when selecting electronic information resources. Standard criteria are fairly consistent from library to library, though the relative importance may vary. Materials in all formats are evaluated for relevance to program needs, scope of treatment (completeness, geographic and chronological coverage, depth, breadth), ability to fill gaps, uniqueness of content or treatment, quality of schol-arship, quality of physical product, currency of information, frequency of up-dating, accessibility of information, language, cost (immediate and continuing), reputation of publisher, and special features. Each library will have its own variation of this set of criteria, to be used in explaining how materials are se-lected and rejected.

The features that are unique to electronic information resources necessitate what LaGuardia and Bentley call a "supplemental set of technology-based cri-teria."[27] These criteria address the features that are unique to electronic infor-mation resources. They are particularly important because many electronic information resources are available in delivery formats that can be compared and contrasted with each other and with paper versions. A policy guiding se-lection will identify the following considerations when evaluating and choosing among electronic resources and between electronic and paper resources:

- Network, hardware, and software compatibility, plus compliance with industry stan-dards

- Availability of network, hardware, and software resources and cost implications

- Availability of electrical and telecommunication lines and cost implications

- Continuing costs, which may include electricity, telecommunications lines, systems support, maintenance, upgrades in hardware and software, and their predictability

- Quality of interface, which includes ease of use for library users and staff

- Effectiveness and efficiency of retrieval or search engine

- Training implications for staff and patrons

- Service implications and levels of staff support needed

- Potential use, which includes size of user community, frequency of use, need for remote and on-site access

- Reliability of vendor and availability of vendor support, which may include technical support, training, documentation

- Licensing considerations, which may include forfeiture of back issues, constraints more severe than copyright law, and limitations on use

- Pricing considerations, which may include discounts for retaining hard copy, number of simultaneous users, definition of a user, and total potential user population

- Treatment of graphics, formula, and other nonstandard characters

- Support for information transfer, which includes support for file transfer protocols, downloading, and printing capabilities

Criteria guiding decisions about Internet resources can be considered a subset of criteria for electronic resources. Consideration should be given to the advantages and disadvantages of using pointers to remote resources at either the server level or the title level, providing reliable archival access, and downloading and maintaining Internet-accessible resources.

An electronic resources collection policy includes library policies that guide priorities for cataloging and preservation. The library may decide that standard policies apply to all formats or that priorities and practices are different for electronic resources. In either case, this should be confirmed by explicit policy statements. Some considerations may be unique. For example, a library may have a standard policy that all materials selected for the library are cataloged and selectors expect their selection decisions to be reflected in the library's catalog. The cataloging unit, however, may not be ready to add bibliographic records for electronic resources loaded and managed on a local mainframe or accessed via a gateway, even if these resources replace a more familiar print version of the same information. Preservation of electronic resources may involve moving files from one format to another. Documenting library priorities in policy statements confirms the importance of developing supporting practices and procedures.

The special nature of electronic resources collection policies often leads libraries to include appendices to the policy statement. This supplemental material may consist of some mechanism to guide decision making, such as a decision matrix, forms, checklists, or questionnaires to use when evaluating criteria and soliciting input from others in the library. The appendices may also include actual procedural documents. Libraries find it more practical to have such resources in an appendix, since they are tools for the decision process rather than policy guidelines.

Style

The most important advice for style, when preparing an electronic information resources collection development policy, is to make a document that is easy to use. The intent of a policy is to provide guidelines for decisions and a cumbersome, wordy document defeats this purpose. An effective policy identifies the questions that need to be asked when selecting electronic information resources and provides guidance in formulating the answers. It is neither vague nor theoretical. A collection development policy is a formal, official, documented policy of the library, but should be crafted so that it is easy to understand and practical to use. A policy that is well written will be used. It will not be put in a file and left there. A well-crafted policy describes what the library has done, is doing, and plans to do to satisfy its users. It will provide information about the library's prospects and benchmarks against which to measure progress. It is the written rationale for selection and collection management decisions for electronic resources and will be used regularly.

When preparing an electronic resources collection policy, libraries should remember what a policy is not. It is not a static document. To remain meaningful, a policy must be reviewed and revised regularly. This is particularly critical for a policy that is to address the rapidly changing universe of electronic resources. Most important, a collection policy is not a substitute for selection. It defines a framework and provides parameters, but cannot select specific titles. A policy is not prescriptive to the point of eliminating human decision. No matter how detailed the collection development policy statement may be, individual judgment is still necessary. Collection development policies can substitute for neither intelligent discernment nor an awareness of and sensitivity to the changing needs of the library's community. The most effective decisions are rational, based on explicit criteria, and linked to library objectives.

Writing the Policy Document

The first step toward developing an electronic resources collection development policy is a library-wide agreement that it has value and should be written. Only then should the people who will participate in writing and reviewing it be identified. These participants should be truly interested in and committed to the project. The most successful policy statements are the products of a working group. A collection development policy written by an individual is less likely to be a document that speaks for and to the entire library and its community. Project team members can be volunteers or assigned by administrators. The project team may be an existing committee or task force, perhaps already in place to deal with electronic resources. Dedication to the project, understanding of the time required, and expertise with various issues surrounding electronic information resources are critical. As with any working group or task force, the optimum size is between five and nine members. Others, who have specific knowledge of various aspects of electronic resources, may be invited to contribute to the work either as consultants or through assignment to specific tasks.

The process of preparing an electronic resources policy is strengthened if at least one member of the working group is a representative of an academic department. This faculty member should be someone who has displayed an active interest in the library, its collections, and its services and is familiar with electronic resources. Including teaching faculty on the project team serves two purposes. Faculty participation is important in preparing a policy that speaks directly to the needs of institutional research and teaching. The presence of collection users helps to ground the policy statement in the real world. In addition, extending an invitation to faculty members to participate in writing and reviewing a collection development policy strengthens faculty–librarian communication in all areas. Involving faculty members in library planning for electronic resources has the potential to improve understanding between academic departments and the library. Librarians who include library users in library planning increase the likelihood that they, in turn, will be included in academic planning.

Immediately after or at the same time the project group is appointed and charged with preparing an electronic resources collection policy, a project leader is identified. The leader should be someone who can take a long-range view of both the project and the policy statement. The leader should have a strong grounding in the library's existing collection policy statements. Equally important, the team leader must have both administrative support and acceptance by the project team. A model leader is one who has the interpersonal and organizational skills necessary to keep the team on task and schedule.

Once the project team and team leader are in place, project responsibilities are assigned. This is easier to do if an outline or preliminary table of contents for the finished product is prepared. This list of elements is used to assign responsibilities. The working group can then identify others within and outside the library who will be contributors, consultants, and reviewers and secure their agreement to participate. A schedule lays out the process of preparing a policy statement, noting those tasks that can occur simultaneously and those that are sequential. Writing an electronic resources collection policy and securing approval within the library (and outside, if appropriate) will take varying amounts of time, depending on the library. A target completion date should be made clear when the project starts.

The project team begins by reviewing existing documentation and gathering information. Both tasks, which can be done simultaneously, are necessary before writing can begin. The person or group charged with these tasks locates existing mission and vision statements, collection development policies, cooperative collection development and resource sharing agreements, planning documents, and other formal documents that speak to the library's role in its community. Gathering information involves surveying the library and the community in order to have all information necessary to begin writing. Focus groups and open hearings may be used. Data about primary and secondary users and their needs, academic programs, degree programs, and other subject needs are collected. The project team learns about the electronic resources the library presently collects and accesses. It will consider electronic information resources collected and accessed by institutional units outside the library. Also important to record are the informal, but generally accepted, criteria that guide selection decisions. Much of the writing of an electronic collection development statement may involve documenting practices and informal polices selectors already follow.

When the electronic resources collection policy is drafted, it is ready for review and revision. It should be shared widely within the library and reviewed by the library's community, as well. The library may consider having legal counsel review areas that deal with copyright, institutional cooperation, and responsibility for licensing and purchase agreements. Those individuals and units who will be following procedures found in appendices should review them carefully. The project team revises the policy document to fix problems and address any missed issues. The final version is approved by the appropriate library bodies (library council, management team, library director) and institutional bodies (senate committees, university administration, trustees, regents) and endorsed for implementation.

Implementing the final version is a misleading description, however, since no collection development policy is ever finished. Collection development policies, especially electronic resources policies, are works in progress. The document should include scheduled periods to evaluate, revise, and amend the policy. This is important to ensure it continues to be meaningful and effective. Regular reviews of a collection development policy can become a mechanism for reviewing a library's community, services, and collecting needs and the rapidly changing universe of electronic information resources. Regular reviews also measure the effectiveness of the policy and the degree to which it fulfills its intended purposes.

CRITICAL CONSIDERATIONS

The universe of electronic information expands and increases in complexity with astounding speed. A collection policy for electronic resources can provide a framework within which a library makes the decisions that will guide its future. Even if a library does not develop a formal policy that follows the models presented above, it is well served by recognizing a few critical considerations that confront all libraries when selecting and managing electronic information resources.

An important element of success is well-informed and well-prepared selectors. The people who make decisions about electronic information and contribute to these decisions need to understand the universe with which they are dealing. This includes learning about methods of access and delivery as well as about the information resources themselves. Selectors should have the hardware and software tools nearby so they can test, explore, and evaluate options. They need to know how to use the software and hardware effectively and they need ongoing opportunities to improve their skills. Besides personal expertise, selectors should have additional resource people within the library and institution to whom they can go with unanswered questions.

Resolving decision-making responsibility for electronic resources is essential. A policy is a logical place to make this clear. In the absence of a policy document, a library still needs to address this point. Without assigned responsibility, a library may ignore electronic information resources or develop an uneven collection. Some libraries assign decisions involving expenditures below a specified amount to individual selectors and above that amount to an administrator or an oversight committee. Division of responsibility may be on the basis of system-wide impact (cost and service implications). All decisions may be in the hands of one individual, though this encourages the belief that electronic resources can be ignored by other selectors. Assigning selection responsibility for electronic information resources to the staff members who select and manage other types of resources reinforces that all formats are necessary to build a comprehensive collection.

Another critical consideration is the library position on how electronic resources fit into its mission, services, and collections. The position endorsed throughout this paper is that electronic information resources should be integrated into the library's collections, services, and processes. While mechanism of access and delivery may not yet be transparent to users, they should not have to worry that important resources are missing simply because of format. Mainstreaming electronic resources into all library operations is an institutional value that underpins successful management of these materials.

The library's approach to budgeting for electronic information resources is a crucial aspect of their effective selection and management. A separate fund for electronic resources can serve to stress their priority. On the other hand, a separate fund line reinforces the uniqueness of these resources. Some libraries set target expenditures (either dollar amounts or percentage of total expenditures) as guides for selection activity. If a library sees value in including electronic resources among its suite of services and collections, it should develop a budget that supports this as a priority.

A final critical consideration is recognition that selection and management of electronic resources is never completed. Collection development and management are always dynamic activities. No decision is forever—materials are added and withdrawn as options and needs change. This is particularly true of electronic resources as the products and technologies evolve. Policies addressing electronic resources should be continually reviewed and revised. Selectors must work to stay current in order to make informed decisions. Someday, electronic resources will not present the special challenges they do now. Until that time, libraries and their selectors will need to devote extra energy to keeping on top of a rapidly changing resource.

CONCLUSIONS

The challenges that surround electronic information resources need not be daunting. Careful consideration of critical issues can go a long way toward positioning the library to address decisions effectively. An electronic information resources collection development policy can go a long way toward providing a framework for decision making. This is the recommended mechanism for dealing with the unique and often still unfamiliar aspects of electronic resources. If the library views its collection policy for electronic resources as a living document, its continual review and revision will keep it current with the changing universe of electronic resources. The importance and value of a collection development policy lies in the context it provides for every decision made in a library. It will help define the issues, identify the questions that need to be asked, and guide answers that respond to institutional priorities and library mission.

NOTES

1. While Dan C. Hazen, for example, has written a provocative paper questioning the value of collection development policies and suggesting they have outlived their purpose (see his "Collection Development Policies in the Information Age," *College & Research Libraries* 56 [1995]: 29–31), collection development policies on the whole are endorsed by numerous authors. See, for example, Bonita Bryant, ed., *Guide for Written Collection Policy Statements*, 2nd ed. Collection Management and Development Guides, no. 3 (Chicago: American Library Association, 1989); under revision with publication expected in 1996; David Farrell, "Policy and Planning," in *Collection Management: A New Treatise*, ed. Charles B. Osburn and Ross Atkinson (Greenwich, CT: JAI Press, 1991), pp. 51–63; and Elizabeth Futas, ed., *Collection Development Policies and Procedures*, 3rd ed. (Phoenix, AZ: Oryx Press, 1995).

2. Samuel Demas, "Mainstreaming Electronic Formats," *Library Acquisitions: Practice & Theory* 13 (1989): 229.

3. Pamela R. Cibbarelli, Elliot H. Gertel, and Mona Kratzert, "Choosing among the Options for Patron Access Databases: Print, Online, CD-ROM, or Locally Mounted," *The Reference Librarian* 39 (1993): 86.

4. Gay N. Dannelly, "Strategic Issues in Planning for Electronic Resources," *Technicalities* 14 (May 1994): 12.

5. Cibbarelli et al., "Choosing among," p. 86.

6. Sheila S. Intner, "Selecting Software," *Library Acquisitions: Practice & Theory* 13 (1989): 233–40; Diane Geraci and Linda Longschied, "Mainstreaming Data: Challenges to Libraries," *Information Technology and Libraries* 11 (1992): 10–18; Samuel Demas, Peter McDonald, and Gregory Lawrence, "The Internet and Collection Development: Mainstreaming Selection of Internet Resources," *Library Acquisitions: Practice & Theory* 39 (1989): 275–90; Rebecca A. Guappone, Beth J. Shapiro, and Scott R. Bullard, "Integrating Electronic Publishing into the Concepts and Practices of Collection Development: Selected Highlights of the Institute on Collection Development for the Electronic Library, Cornell University April 29–May 2, 1990," *Library Acquisitions: Practice & Theory* 14 (1990): 327–39; Demas, "Mainstreaming."

7. Guappone et al.,"Integrating," p. 329.

8. Stephen Bosch, Patricia Promis, and Chris Sugnet, *Guide to Selecting and Acquiring CD-ROMs, Software, and Other Electronic Publications*. Acquisitions Guidelines, no. 9 (Chicago: American Library Association, 1994), p. 9.

9. Ibid., pp. 9–11.

10. F. W. Lancaster, "Collection Development in the Year 2025," in *Recruiting, Educating, and Training Librarians for Collection Development*, ed. Peggy Johnson and Sheila S. Intner (Westport, CT: Greenwood Press, 1994), pp. 215–29.

11. Ibid., p. 220.

12. Demas et al., "The Internet and Collection Development."

13. Rachel Cassel, "Selection Criteria for Internet Resources," *College & Research Libraries News* 56 (1995): 92–93.

14. Gail K. Dickinson, *Selection and Evaluation of Electronic Resources* (Englewood, CO: Libraries Unlimited, 1994).

15. Cheryl LaGuardia and Stella Bentley, "Electronic Databases: Will Old Collection Development Policies Still Work?" *Online* 16 (1992): 60.

16. Intner, "Selecting Software," p. 237.

17. Zbigniew Duszak and Waldemar W. Koczkodaj, "A Consistency-Driven Approach to CD-ROM Selection," *Library Software Review* 13 (1994): 260–68.

18. Anthony Ferguson, "Interesting Problems Encountered on My Way to Writing an Electronic Information Collection Development Statement," *Against the Grain* 7 (1995): 16–19, 90.

19. Edward A. Warro, "What Have We Been Signing? A Look at Database Licensing Agreements," *Library Administration & Management* 8 (1994): 173–77.

20. Dannelly, "Strategic Issues," p. 13.

21. Hazen, "Collection Development," p. 31.

22. Elizabeth Parang and Laverna Saunders, comps., *Electronic Journals in ARL Libraries: Policies and Procedures*. SPEC Kit 201 (Washington, DC: Association of Research Libraries, Office of Management Services, 1994), p. i.

23. "Draft: Electronic Information Access Format Collection Policy Element, Revised February 1994," photocopy (Chicago: American Library Association, Reference and Adult Services Division, Collection Development and Evaluation Section, Collection Policy Committee, 1994).

24. *Guide for Written Collection Policy Statements.*

25. Samuel Demas, "Collection Development for the Electronic Library: A Conceptual and Organizational Model," *Library Hi-Tech* 12 (1994): 71–80.

26. Demas, "Mainstreaming," p. 229.

27. LaGuardia and Bentley, "Electronic Databases," p. 62.

5

The Role of Selection in Collection Development: Past, Present, and Future

William S. Monroe

INTRODUCTION

Library collections are built through the selection of items from a wider universe of material. Even in an age where "collections" are giving way to other means of access, this decision making remains at the heart of collection management, and needs to be so recognized. With today's static budgets, and library buildings filled to capacity, librarians must select the most important resources for their users, whether for purchase or for access. While electronic resources available over the Internet are predicted to spell the end of libraries, cooler heads are recognizing that libraries must play to their historic strengths. Libraries have always offered what the Internet resources so tellingly lack: selectivity and organization.

THE IMPORTANCE OF SELECTION

The promising technology of recent years, coupled with unpromising finances for libraries, has brought on a debate within librarianship over the very nature of the library and what it should be. Against a traditional image of the library as a collection of books (*bibliotheca* or "bookcase"), some would now propose the library as a service point or a node on a complex information network. In many ways this is a pseudo-debate, since the library, of course, has always been both of these things and what is really in question is proportion or emphasis.

The role of the library in the coming century will not change, nor will the major means of fulfilling that role: connecting people to the information resources they need. This goal has been, and will be, achieved through selection.[1]

Almost any library collection is built through the selection of certain items from a wider universe of material available. This is true of the average family's home library and of the largest national libraries. Even now, when "collections" are giving way to other means of access, and we could speak rather of "resource development," or perhaps "connection development," this decision making is essential—possibly even more important than it is for the purchase of books or journals, because there is less quality control over the resources available. Selection, whether of material containing information or of paths to information, lies at the heart of library service.

This centrality of selection follows from Atkinson's recent definition of the library's mission. "The primary function of the library," he says, "is not so much to provide access to information, as it is rather to reduce the amount of time needed by local clientele to gain such access."[2] Until recently, the surest way to reduce access time has been to own the desired item, and that is what libraries have sought to do.[3] In general, that goal was more easily met in the past than it is today, because we have a greater diversity of desires as well as an enormous quantity and variety of resources from which to select.

Ancient and medieval libraries did not need to be much concerned about selectivity. When books had to be copied by hand, one had to be glad for anything one could acquire. Even the largest libraries in the 12th century might have only 600 volumes.[4] It was only with the onset of printing, with its great increase in the availability of books, that libraries had to become more selective in what they acquired.[5] More recent has been the development of the omnivorous library, which would see nothing as out of scope for its collections.[6] More common is the practice of research libraries to build "just-in-case" collections; that is, trying to get into the collections anything we thought someone might conceivably need now or in the future. This has led to the tendency to measure the quality of a library by the quantity of its holdings.

But with the "information explosion" of our own time, there is a trend away from the omnivorous library. Some have even questioned the entire notion of a balanced collection and suggest aiming at meeting the immediate demands of current users.[7] The ability to meetiate needs through document delivery, and even traditional interlibrary loan, has led to an emphasis on access over ownership, which is, at once, both welcome and disturbing. Some of the excesses of the proponents of access over ownership may be reviewed elsewhere.[8] Most reasonable people would agree that most types of libraries will continue to collect resources as well as to provide access to items they do not own. Yet they can no longer collect at the same level to which they have been accustomed. Not only is the need no longer there, but neither is the money. It seems worthwhile to address here the role to be played by selection in what has otherwise been portrayed as a struggle between resources and services.

The role of selection has been little mentioned in relation to the larger themes of collection development and library services.[9] This could be because selection, like acquisitions, has been seen as somehow distinct from collection development, which is regarded as a "planning or policy-making function."[10] Atkinson, however, believes that this distinction "is not nearly as clear as is frequently assumed."[11] Selection is, in fact, part of the practice of collection management, whether one is deciding what to collect, what not to collect, what to weed, what to preserve, or what not to preserve. The role of selection in collection management needs to be reemphasized, and we must remember that selection implies selectivity.

Selection is not only important in the building of collections, but also in their long-term maintenance. In the past two decades, we have begun to replace "collection development" with "collection management," which takes a more holistic view of library collections than did the earlier focus on "building" collections.[12] It is time to give more thought to what shape collections should take, whether items already in the collections should be reformatted, and whether to retain some of these items at all.

There are probably still some libraries that operate on the principle that what was once added to the collections should always remain there; but few can realize this principle in practice. As collections deteriorate, and as space runs out, there is a need for selection once more. This can be seen either as putting the same material once more through the selection process (to determine whether it should be kept), or putting the entire collection through a *deselection* process (to determine what can be withdrawn).[13] Deselection can be a much more difficult decision than selection for purchase because it may be irreversible. However, collections will benefit if these decisions are not avoided.[14]

SELECTION IN THE LITERATURE OF COLLECTION DEVELOPMENT

The earlier literature of collection development placed great emphasis on selection, but this was at a time when most collection development librarians were selectors, rather than administrators.[15] Some of this early work is still of great value, and should be read more by today's collection development librarians. Helen Haines's *Living with Books*, despite its age, could serve as a useful vade mecum for any new selector.[16] A major characteristic of this early literature is the emphasis on quality. Haines repeats Drury's line, in saying that "Library service is not only the provision of books; it is the bringing of the right book to the right reader."[17] She goes even further in saying that the function of the library is to provide education, which "in its ideal fulfillment is not simply fact finding nor the assiduous pursuit of information. It implies the use of books for spiritual and intellectual as well as for material and vocational profit. . . ."[18]

In the postwar era, however, as colleges and universities were expanding, and their libraries growing tremendously, more emphasis was placed on growth.

Money was plentiful, as were the publications on which to spend it. Institutions began to compare themselves more than ever before by the size (and, to some extent, the content) of their libraries. This was the period when Clapp and Jordan published their famous formula for adequacy of library collection size.[19] It is also when the Association of Research Libraries began to publish its annual statistical report, which included the ranking of libraries by number of volumes held, a practice that is beginning to receive criticism.[20]

The Clapp-Jordan formula is only a quantitative measure, and does not pretend to assess the quality of the collection; but an attempt was made in this direction with the publication of *Books for College Libraries* in 1967.[21] It attempts to define just which 50,000 titles should form the core collection of a college library. In many ways it is both the product of a period of growth and a coping tool for less affluent times. While, by its very nature, it endorses the notions of quality and selection, it also is part of the mentality of growth, since it is meant only to be a "core" or "minimum" collection. It is always assumed the true collection will be much larger.

Edelman has drawn this distinction in a well-known article on selection methodology, where he points out the difference between selecting for "short-term demands" and for "long-term needs." In the first case, one must

identify and choose from the universe those titles that are likely to be requested. . . . The second objective deals with long-term needs and involves selection for collection building. The main criteria will have been defined by policy, but balance, reliability, and comprehensiveness, in that order, are the principal goals.[22]

But even in the climate of growth, there was always some form of selection taking place, and this selection was recognized as an important process. So important was it that, as budgets began to level off, theorists began to study the selection process. The goal, however, was not so much to determine how the collection development librarian could be more selective, but rather how the decisions could be made more efficiently. Models of the selection process which would appear to be moving toward the *automation* of selection began to be seen. Such is DePew's 1975 article, "An Acquisitions Decision Model for Academic Libraries."[23]

The modelling of the selection process need not explicitly be aimed at automating that process, but it carries implications beyond that of gaining a better understanding of this complex activity merely for its own sake. Models such as DePew's, or more recently that of Rutledge and Swindler, are too complex to be useful for routine selection.[24] Rutledge and Swindler point out that their model would be most useful for training selectors, and for setting priorities both for funding and for cooperative collecting agreements.[25] That also provides a step toward applying what Edelman called "microdecision making" to the making of "macrodecisions."[26] That is, if one can better understand how individual selection decisions are made, those same criteria can be applied in the profile of an approval plan or some other means of selecting a larger quantity of material with fewer decisions. Even the training aspect raises the question of where libraries are placing their priorities, for as library budgets have flattened, the response has generally been to cut staff and protect the materials funds.[27] As a result, selection has been dispersed among more staff, who often have little experience or training in collection development.

Despite the attempts to develop a theory of selection, it remains, as Katz has written,"an art form that, as such, rejects universal laws and formulas."[28] Still, it is helpful to analyze the process, in order to better understand what is really done, and how to do it better. Selectors should be aware of the criteria used to select, and all the introductions to the subject, as well as theoretical approaches, propose a list of such criteria.[29] These usually vary only slightly, and criteria can always be found which overlap or which are superfluous. A good list of this sort can be found in Gardner's *Library Collections*.[30]

- Authoritativeness (reputation of author or publisher)
- Accuracy
- Impartiality
- Recency of data
- Adequate scope
- Depth of coverage
- Appropriateness (level appropriate to users; the format is also considered here)
- Relevancy
- Interest
- Organization
- Style
- Aesthetic qualities
- Technical aspects (includes faithfulness of illustrations or sound)
- Physical characteristics (quality of package)
- Special features (bibliographies, notes, appendices)
- Library potential (potential use, or how an item fits a particular library)
- Cost (Is it permanent or ephemeral? Should it be purchased or rented or obtained through document delivery?)

It must be recognized that the criteria do not apply equally in all cases, but there is really a complex interplay among them. This interplay is so important that one could suggest that any single criterion means nothing, but is only valid in its relation with the others. On the simplest level, then, one could posit the relation between the library and the item itself. The library has a need or demand for the item (or has some degree of demand), and the item is selected according to the degree to which it fills that need (in comparison with similar items). This demand is what is recorded in the collection policy statement, as determined by user recommendations and/or through other interaction with the library's users.

The degree to which the item satisfies the demand is dependent on five characteristics, some of which have subcriteria:

Type:	Reference/nonreference Serial/nonserial Survey/textbook/specialized monograph Primary text/critical edition
Quality:	Authority Accuracy Currency Organization Physical characteristics
Level:	Should match the demand (popular, professional, research)
Format:	Paper, microform, CD-ROM, tape, video, online
Price:	Must be in relation to value (relative to quality and demand)

All of these criteria and subcriteria are interdependent, and we are not always seeking the highest level of each. Ancient and medieval scientific texts may be purchased even though they are not accurate or current in terms of the information they contain. One edition may be preferred over another, not because it is the latest, but because it carries more authority. The criteria used to select a critical edition of Pliny's *Natural History*, however, may not be as useful for a modern scientific encyclopedia.

The criteria for the item itself do not include subject, because that is a function of demand. It is assumed that there is demand for some subjects and not for others, and this demand is reflected in the policy statement. A specialized library may have *no demand* for most subjects, while a large research library would have *at least some demand* for almost any subject.

Some writers have suggested that price is not at issue, but cost is as much a factor as other elements, and *is* considered in relation to them. Rutledge and Swindler, for example, point out that "a costly microform collection or multi-volume set does not compete against a current book or a new journal subscription but against other possible expensive purchases."[31] In fact, these items are segregated just because of their price and format, and are often purchased at the end of the fiscal year, if enough money remains, at least if the demand for them is low. When demand is high, they may be purchased immediately, and then do directly compete against books or other formats.

In addition to selection criteria, it is important to consider the selection time frame, or chronology of selection. This gets less consideration both in introductory and in theoretical works, yet is critical in the way selections are made and collections are built. The major factor here is the way in which a potential selection comes to the notice of the selector. These may be divided into four categories:

Current material:
> Approval plans
> Notification services
> Publishers' notices
> Quick reviews (*Choice, LJ, NYTBR, Kirkus, Booklist*)
> National bibliographies
> User recommendation

Immediate retrospective:
> Reviews in scholarly journals (and other slow reviewing sources)
> National bibliographies
> User recommendation

Retrospective:
> Bibliographies
> Citations in the literature
> User recommendation

Occasional:
> Gifts
> Sales and auctions (including out-of-print dealers' catalogs)
> Personal and institutional collections (through gift or purchase)
> Created collections (microform and electronic resources)

As with the selection criteria, these categories are not mutually exclusive, and one might readily arrange them in different ways. They are important because, in practice if not in theory, different selection criteria are applied to them (or at least applied differently). Many books, for example, are purchased in the first category that would not be selected in the third, because of a need to add books which are new, despite the fact that their worthiness is unproven. In this sense, the most effective selection might be done retrospectively, when items show up in the secondary literature and in important bibliographies. But most libraries cannot wait that long, because users demand some of these books long before that. Unfortunately, it is not known which books they will demand, and most books will sit on the shelves unused.

The expertise of the selector enters here. More expertise is needed to select wisely from a batch of new, unreviewed books than from a list of recommended titles such as the American Historical Association's *Guide to Historical Literature*. It is also more important to know one's own collection in the first case, because there may not be time to verify whether the new book really fills a gap or is superfluous. But, here again, as the duty of selection has spread to more librarians, most of whom have other duties, this kind of knowledge of the collections is ending.[32]

THE FUTURE

It has long been recognized that no library can collect everything its users need or want. In recent years even the largest research libraries have been faced with this problem. Declining budgets (at least in terms of real dollars), rising prices, and increasing volume of publication seem to be affecting large research libraries even more than the smaller academic and public libraries. To some extent this may simply be due to higher expectations on the part of their clientele, and their librarians. Libraries today face great challenges and opportunities, if they are willing to make the right decisions. These decisions do not always mean change, for the fundamental mission remains the same, and there is a long history of achievement. But flexibility is important in welcoming change where it is needed.

Research libraries will continue to build "just-in-case" collections for some years to come, though the shape of these collections must change. At the same time, they must expect to have a smaller proportion of all the publications available, as their users must expect not to find everything they might want in a particular library. This implies a greater challenge than ever for collection development, and for those who select materials for the library. Selection is key, as Atkinson concludes, "The fundamental question of collection development, therefore, is not how useful the document is, but rather how useful it should be made."[33]

It is just at this point that technology offers help along with its challenges. Libraries no longer have to own all the resources which their users need. With full-text databases online, and interlibrary loan by fax and even e-mail, access can now be provided to a world of resources at a fraction of the cost of owning these resources. Of course, this works best for items of low demand; most people realize that the library still needs to collect those core items that are needed by hundreds of people each week. Or is it tens of people each month? The problem becomes one of where to draw the line.

Crawford and Gorman have recently pointed out some of the excesses of those who would consign books to the dustbin of history.[34] Electronic versions are suitable for some types of text and not for others.[35] But there is an intermediate step on the horizon, which could fundamentally change the way library collections are built. This is a technology which is appearing first in the music industry, and is aimed at delivering recorded music electronically to music stores, where it can be registered on a CD-ROM. IBM and Blockbuster Entertainment have joined forces to test this method:

The companies predict that stores would initially use the computer technology to obtain out-of-stock titles. But over time, as the nation develops vast new networks for electonic communications, music stores might close the stock room altogether and rely entirely on computerized delivery.[36]

This same technology could be used for movies, video games, and computer software, according to the companies involved.[37] But this technology has major implications for the distribution of books as well. New printing technology, such as the Xerox DocuTech printers, can transform digital texts into printed and bound copies.[38] A library with such a printer would no longer need to purchase books "just-in-case," but could simply download and print them as they are requested. They would still have physical collections, and they would probably continue to buy books which they know would be in greater demand. But they could save money and space by not filling up their shelves with "just-in-case" titles whose cases never arrive.

On the other hand, savings will not be made in this regard if all that is requested is ordered, even if ordered "just-in-time" rather than "just-in-case." As users are faced with a more and more bewildering array of resources, the role of the librarian becomes even more crucial, whether at the reference desk, in interlibrary loan, or in this new type of selection. Atkinson, again, has clearly identified the librarian's role in this new environment: "An essential responsibility of information services must be to assist users in determining *what* information they need to do their work."[39]

Librarians should be hired who are comfortable in this role, which is as fitting for a selector as for a reference librarian. When librarians are hired for these dual roles, as much emphasis should be placed on the need for subject expertise and the knowledge of scholarly communication and research methods as on experience with the Internet and the World Wide Web. Unfortunately, it is likely that budgetary realities will continue to move libraries away from the subject specialist selectors, and toward more "mechanical" means of selection.

An alternative to this model is an extension to collection development of the current interest in outsourcing various library services. Approval and blanket order plans are already a step in this direction, but further development will be seen in two directions. The first would be an arrangement wherein selectors work, not for individual libraries, but for consortia. Such an organization would permit not only a more effective use of a wider range of subject expertise, but also more efficient cooperation in building collections within the consortia. The second direction would be the growth of commercial services which would select materials for many different libraries.[40] This would have a great appeal in certain subjects where language and subject expertise are not readily available to most libraries, especially in area studies.[41] Either of these stategies might serve as a step toward reversing the declining trend in foreign acquisitions which the Association of Research Libraries has been studying, and toward assuring that American libraries acquire the foreign resources they may need in the future.[42]

CONCLUSION

It is in the nature of any research collection, and probably any library collection at all to collect beyond current needs. Yet, the diversification of our collecting interests has forced us to collect *less* (proportionally) of a *wider variety* of resources. A balance must be found by cutting out the less important materials rather than those of high quality, but for which there may be no immediate demand. Herein lies the role of selection. Unfortunately, it is a labor-intensive process, since it often involves item-by-item decision making. The more the selector knows about the field, the less labor-intensive selection becomes, but selectors today are less likely to be specialists in the fields in which they select.[43] If this model continues to be used, emphasis should be placed on staff development, encouraging selectors to gain more expertise in their subjects as well as in general collection management issues. And they must be given the time to develop familiarity with the collections they are overseeing.

More attention should be given to the appointment of selectors.[44] The importance of having knowledgeable selectors in collection management cannot be overemphasized. As Shreeves has written,

A major function of the collection development librarian is to serve as a gatekeeper, identifying that portion of the published universe which a given library chooses to acquire. . . . An effective bibliographer or selector should be familiar with the subject matter, including trends in research and publishing, knowledgeable about the strengths and interests of faculty and students, well informed about the book trade, and able to manage a budget. This bibliographer is judged, over the long term at least, by the collection he or she built. . . . [45]

If dual-role selectors are not given the time to develop the necessary knowledge and skills, then perhaps outsourcing selection, whether through consortia or to private constractors, may prove to be an answer to this problem.

Many libraries, even the largest research libraries (perhaps especially the largest), have never paid much attention to selection. When budgets were adequate, or even more than adequate in the 1960s and 1970s, the greatest problem these libraries faced was to spend the money quickly enough. Thus arose the approval plans, blanket orders, and standing orders for almost any identifiable series. These methods are, indeed, an excellent way to acquire many items without a great deal of labor, and a good way to be sure things are not inadvertently missed. They also eliminate much duplication of labor by getting core books in early, so that they are not ordered and reordered numerous times. But they also spend much of the budget on items that will never be used (and *should* never be used). As budgets become tighter, we need to put more emphasis on getting the resources we know our users are likely to need (whether now or fifty years from now), and depend on other methods to cover the more peripheral resources. But this means cutting the materials budget, not staff.

Mosher, in describing withdrawal of faculty from library collection development, once wrote:

There were two solutions available to libraries: (1) get a lot of money, spend it, and build comprehensively, under the premise that if you can get enough, you are more likely to get what your users need; or (2) hire specialists to identify and locate needed resources, and make sure that the library was effective in getting the materials it needed.[46]

Libraries really responded in both ways, especially the larger research libraries; but Mosher was right in pointing out that the second solution is the more effective one. This should be stressed in the current climate of flat budgets. Good collections will not be developed by cutting staff and automating the selection process. This is more likely to result in what Brownson has called "the vanilla library."[47] What is needed, instead, is to hire more expert collection development librarians, and let them *select*.

NOTES

1. I do not intend this chapter to be a guide to how to select material for libraries, nor as merely a review of recent literature on the topic. There are already many such works, and I owe a great deal to them. A few that I find especially useful are: Richard K. Gardner, *Library Collections: Their Origin, Selection, and Development* (New York: McGraw-Hill, 1981), pp. 179–99; Dan C. Hazen, "Selection: Function, Models, Theory," in *Collection Management: A New Treatise*, ed. Charles B. Osburn and Ross Atkinson (Greenwich, CT: JAI Press, 1991), pp. 273–300; Bill Katz, "Book Selection and Collection Building: Evolution of the Art," in *Recruiting, Educating, and Training Librarians for Collection Development*, ed. Peggy Johnson and Sheila S. Intner (Westport, CT: Greenwood Press, 1994), pp. 3–16; and John Rutledge and Luke Swindler, "The Selection Decision: Defining Criteria and Establishing Priorities," *College & Research Libraries* 48 (1987): 123–31.

2. Ross Atkinson, "The Conditions of Collection Development," in *Collection Management: A New Treatise*, ed. Charles B. Osburn and Ross Atkinson (Greenwich, CT: JAI Press, 1991), p. 38.

3. Compare, for example, the first line of Francis Drury's *Book Selection* (Chicago: American Library Association, 1930), p. 1: "The high *purpose* of book selection is to provide the right book for the right reader at the right time."

4. Robert N. Broadus, "The History of Collection Development," in *Collection Management: A New Treatise*, pp. 3–28. Broadus cites James Westfall Thompson, *The Medieval Library* (Chicago: University of Chicago Press, 1939), p. 130.

5. Ibid., p. 5.

6. Ibid., pp. 5–7.

7. See, for example, Carolyn Bucknall, "Balancing Collections, Balancing Budgets in Academic Libraries," *Journal of Library Administration* 14 (1991): 121–34.

8. William S. Monroe, "Redefining the Library: The Year's Work in Collection Development," *Library Resources & Technical Services* 36 (1992): 227–89; especially pp. 277–78 and 282–83.

9. This is not to say that selection has received no attention in general. See Monroe, "Redefining," pp. 280–81. A number of articles and even books have been aimed at selectors recently, including the series of ALA volumes: *Selection of Library Materials in the Humanities, Social Sciences, and Sciences*, ed. Patricia McClung (Chicago: American Library Association, 1985); *Selection of Library Materials in Applied and Interdisciplinary Fields*, ed. Beth J. Shapiro and John Whaley (Chicago: ALA, 1987). These

have been followed by books centered on selection in area studies, some of which are still in production. See also the theoretical work by John Rutledge and Luke Swindler, "The Selection Decision: Defining Criteria and Establishing Priorities," *College & Research Libraries* 48 (1987): 123–31, and the works cited therein, as well as that of Charles A. Schwartz, "Book Selection, Collection Development, and Bounded Rationality," *College & Research Libraries* 50 (1989): 328–43.

10. Atkinson, "The Conditions," p. 31. This is the distinction made by Hendrik Edelman, who defined collection development as "a planning function," while selection "is a direct function of collection development." See Hendrik Edelman, "Selection Methodology in Academic Libraries," *Library Resources & Technical Services* 23 (1979): 34.

11. Atkinson, "The Conditions," pp. 30–31. This distinction is exemplified in the series of Collection Management and Development Guides published by ALA. Of the five guides, the ones that touch on selection are the *Guide for Writing a Bibliographer's Manual*, ed. Carolyn Bucknall (Chicago: American Library Association, 1987), and the *Guide for Written Collection Policy Statements* (Chicago: American Library Association, 1989), both clearly intended for collection managers rather than for selectors.

12. See Paul H. Mosher, "Collection Development to Collection Management: Toward Stewardship of Library Resources," *Collection Management* 4 (1982): 41–49.

13. For a thorough treatment of the history of weeding library collections, see Loriene Roy, "Weeding," in *Encyclopedia of Library and Information Science*, 54 (1994), pp. 352–98.

14. There is a concern among librarians (and library users) about the possiblity of discarding the last surviving copy of a work, which I think is one of the great superstitions of librarianship. As a medievalist, I have a great appreciation for primary sources and the importance of preserving them. But I also am aware that we can conduct quite intensive and successful research in subjects for which very little (by our standards) sources survive. The historians of our own era will be faced with an impenetrable mountain of potential sources, and will be able to do little more than scrape the surface of it. While they may be sorely disappointed to not be able to locate some work for which they have found a reference, I am reasonably certain they will get along fine without it.

15. One can see this even in the titles of some of these early books: Lionel R. McColvin, *The Theory of Book Selection for Public Libraries* (London: Grafton, 1925), and Francis Drury, *Book Selection* (Chicago: American Library Association, 1930). For a good overview of the literature of selection, see G. Edward Evans, *Developing Library and Information Center Collections*, 3rd ed. (Englewood, CO: Libraries Unlimited, 1995), pp. 97–124.

16. Helen Haines, *Living with Books*, 2nd ed. (New York: Columbia University Press, 1950). The first edition was in 1935, and that was intended to update Francis Drury, *Book Selection.*

17. Ibid., p. 16. See note 3, above.

18. Ibid., p. 15.

19. Verner W. Clapp and Robert T. Jordan, "Quantitative Criteria for Adequacy of Academic Library Collections," *College & Research Libraries* 26 (1965): 371–88.

20. See Richard M. Dougherty, "Research Libraries Must Abandon the Idea That Bigger Is Better," *Chronicle of Higher Education*, June 19, 1991, p. A32. In all fairness, the ARL statistics consider many factors besides size of collections, but many of these still lend themselves to the implication that "bigger is better."

21. *Books for College Libraries: A Selected List of Approximately 53,400 Titles Based on the Initial Selection Made for the University of California's New Campuses Program* (Chicago: American Library Association, 1967). This was followed by a second edition, and now a third: *Books for College Libraries: A Core Collection of 50,000 Titles*, 3rd ed., 6 vols. (Chicago: American Library Association, 1988).

22. Edelman, "Selection Methodology," p. 36.

23. John N. DePew, "An Acquisitions Decision Model for Academic Libraries," *Journal of the American Society for Information Science* 26 (1975): 237–46. See also Charles W. Brownson, "Mechanical Selection," *Library Resources & Technical Services* 32 (1988): 17–29.

24. Rutledge and Swindler, "The Selection Decision."

25. Ibid., pp. 130–31.

26. Edelman, "Selection Methodology," p. 37. Ross Atkinson makes this explicit in "The Citation as Intertext: Toward a Theory of the Selection Process," *Library Resources & Technical Services* 28 (1984): 109.

27. Similar is the establishment of approval plans, which are often justified by the saving of staff time. See Robert F. Nardini, "Approval Plans: Politics and Performance," *College & Research Libraries* 54 (1993): 417–25, especially p. 419.

28. Katz, "Book Selection," p. 4.

29. There are numerous works which attempt to give criteria for materials selection. These vary greatly in usefulness. See, for example: Richard K. Gardner, *Library Collections* (New York: McGraw-Hill, 1981), pp. 184–188; Jean Boyer Hamlin, "The Selection Process," in *Collection Development in Libraries: A Treatise*, ed. Robert E. Stueart and George B. Miller, Jr. (Greenwich, CT: JAI Press, 1980), pp. 185–201; and, more recently, Rutledge and Swindler, "The Selection Decision," pp. 126–28.

30. Gardner, "Library Collections," pp. 184–88. Gardner, of course, explains these criteria more fully.

31. Rutledge and Swindler, "The Selection Decision," pp. 127–28.

32. Which is not to say there are not benefits to be gained from this type of organization. In many ways, it is good to have more librarians involved in collection management. The difficulty arises when the other aspects of the selector's job are perceived as more immediate, and while the more *routine selection* of new books gets done, the wider *collection management* activities tend to be pushed aside. See David G. Null, "Robbing Peter to Pay Paul: Balancing Collection Development and Reference Responsibilities," *College & Research Libraries* 49 (1988): 448–52.

33. Atkinson, "The Conditions," p. 38.

34. Walt Crawford and Michael Gorman, *Future Libraries: Dreams, Madness, & Reality* (Chicago: American Library Association, 1995).

35. Ibid., pp. 53–69.

36. *Washington Post*, May 12, 1993, pp. A1 and A16.

37. Ibid., p. A16.

38. Some publishers are already using this technology to avoid warehousing large stocks of books. See *Publishers Weekly* 242, no. 26 (June 26, 1995): 67.

39. Ross Atkinson, "Networks, Hypertext, and Academic Information Services: Some Longer-Range Implications," *College & Research Libraries* 54 (1993): 201. Of course, this has *always* been the role of information services, but many librarians have been mislead by the term *service*, so that they believe their role is simply to get their users whatever they *want*, without any concern over what they really *need*.

40. As with the outsourcing of cataloging, such services might first appear as extensions of existing services, such as approval vendors.

41. Many such arrangements have already been made by libraries, if only temporarily. I know of one case where two major research libraries were hiring the same person to select in modern Greek studies. The selector worked from her home, and was not an employee of either library. I think there is a potential market for such contract selectors on a much larger scale.

42. On this problem, see Barbara Walden et al., "Western European Political Science: An Acquisition Study," *College & Research Libraries* 55 (1994): 286–96.

43. Lynn B. Williams, "Subject Knowledge for Subject Specialists: What the Novice Bibliographer Needs to Know," *Collection Management* 14 (1991): 31–47.

44. Jasper G. Schad, "Managing Collection Development in University Libraries That Utilize Librarians with Dual-Responsibility Assignments," *Library Acquisitions: Practice & Theory* 14 (1990): 165–71, especially p. 168.

45. Edward Shreeves, "Between the Visionaries and the Luddites: Collection Development and Electronic Resources in the Humanities," *Library Trends* 40 (1992): 579–95.

46. Mosher, "Collection Development," p. 42.

47. Chuck Brownson, "The Vanilla Library," COLLDV-L@uscvm.bitnet, no. 134, August 10, 1993. Brownson concludes with the rhetorical question: "Ought the vanilla library, then, in times of tight budgets, reduce its approval plans and increase its expert selection?"

PART IV

Future Practices in Collection Evaluation

6

Collection Development and Performance Measurement

Philip J. Calvert

INTRODUCTION

Whenever collection development has been associated with measurement, it has almost always been in purely quantitative terms. It seems that throughout the 20th century the only way librarians have felt they could satisfactorily gauge the success or otherwise of their collection development is by enumerating how big the collection is compared with other similar institutions, and/or how much it has grown in a fixed period of time.

Measuring a collection in terms of its size and growth has obvious merits. One of the problems inherent in the development of sophisticated performance measures is that the mensuration itself can become excessively difficult or time-consuming, which inevitably will mean it is expensive because it uses staff time. Measuring collection size, however, is by comparison a simple matter which can be done in libraries of almost any type without the use of much staff effort. Similarly, collection growth rates are easy to calculate, and acquisitions departments have done so almost since the earliest libraries were founded. Perhaps because they have been used for so many years, or perhaps because they are, in fact, sound ways to evaluate collection development, librarians are comfortable with these measures and use them almost by instinct. Who can put their hands on their hearts and say they have never compared one library with another by simply looking at the number of volumes each contains? Collection size is also used as a surrogate for the worth of the librarians who manage them, and the career ladder is marked by rungs representing larger and larger collections. There is a further reason for using collection size as a measure of a library's success, which is that performance measurement is inherently political, and in the political field very simple measures are easily used and comprehended. If a funding body is happy to use collection size as a measure of the library's performance, then only a foolish librarian will not endeavor to make the collection grow without fail year after year. That is why our annual reports always include simple figures showing collection size and growth.

Librarians have enough on their plates already without making their lives unduly difficult, so if simple measures of collection size and growth are quick and cheap to gather, and if they satisfy both librarians and funders, why is there any need to look at other ways of measuring the performance of collection development? The simple answer is that growth is a thing of the past for some libraries because their funding agencies are less generous (or if one is really cynical, much meaner) than they used to be, and when the materials budget dwindles, collection growth is curtailed. Fewer volumes are purchased than in previous years. Total collection size itself may not grow if regular weeding is still being done, as it surely ought to be. This does not make good reading in annual reports, so, not surprisingly, librarians have recently become interested in other ways of measuring their library's performance. Total collection size does not seem to matter as much as it did even just a few short years ago, especially when one's own collection is not growing.

There are other reasons why librarians are taking a greater interest in performance measurement. As Ford says, "libraries are suffering reductions in budgets and are being required to demonstrate that they offer value for money"; the pressure for accountability to funding agencies is growing, and Ford's term "value for money" can be seen as a demand for libraries to show their effectiveness.[1]

The search for library effectiveness has been likened to the search for the grail—demanding, obscure, but enormously rewarding if successful. From Orr's first attempts to define effectiveness in 1973 to the present day, no totally satisfactory description of library effectiveness has been achieved.[2] Definitions are enormously important in research, and arriving at commonly accepted definitions in the search for library effectiveness has been almost as elusive as the grail itself, because every author seems determined to reinvent the wheel by producing new definitions of terms. Yet Lynch produced a simple and rational series of definitions in 1983 which can serve as a base for further cooperative research. Lynch defined measurement as "the process of ascertaining the extent or dimensions or quantity of something"; performance as "the doing of something, an activity"; evaluation as "the process of determining whether something is what you want it to be"; whereas effectiveness refers to "something which does well that which it is supposed to do." These are combined in a single, explanatory sentence: "The results of measurement can be used to evaluate the performance of a library and thereby determine whether or not it is effective."[3]

THE TRADITIONAL APPROACH

Librarians interested in methods for evaluating their collections have had a range of proposals put forward for the purpose, which, as McDonald and Micikas have pointed out, have always been subunit- or program-level approaches to library effectiveness [4]. Lancaster, and then Baker and Lancaster, summarized the many approaches found in the literature of library effectiveness, and argued that it is only by examining each aspect of library service and then adding the results together can a total picture of the overall effectiveness of the library be produced.[5] Lancaster found several such approaches to collection evaluation which were either quantitative or qualitative. Quantitative methods, as will be described shortly, are nearly always simple measures of collection size and growth, whereas qualitative approaches consist of a variety of methods, including simple list checking which involves comparing titles listed in an authoritative source such as *Books for College Libraries* against titles in the library's catalog. Other qualitative approaches vary from simple subjective expert judgment to actual analyses of use.

Of all the methods described by Lancaster, by far the best known is the Clapp-Jordan formula. This method, first published in 1965, has had numerous imitators, but basically the same approach can be found in them all.[6] A formula is used which includes numerous aspects of academic life such as numbers of faculty, numbers of students, both postgraduate and undergraduate, and so on, and for each of those aspects adds a number to a total which should eventually be translated into a total number of library volumes. If the library's actual collection is above the figure produced by the formula, it has performed well in collection development; if it is below the figure produced by the formula, it has performed poorly. There is a clear simplicity with this approach which can account for its popularity for so many years; it's a bit like the image of St. Peter at the pearly gates—you are either in or out based on a simple sum of your merit points. Unfortunately, there is no empirical substantiation for the Clapp-Jordan formula, for although the use of quantitative methods has given it a pseudo-scientific veneer used by librarians to justify the method to themselves and to their funding bodies, the actual figures are a phantom. Who has chosen the figures used in the formula (whether it be Clapp-Jordan or any of the numerous imitators), and where did the figures come from? This pure subjectiveness is a problem for those who wish to use empirical data to set targets. It is also a concern for those wishing to use performance measures as a way of being accountable to funding agencies, for if the targets have no objective basis, why should the funders pay them any attention? Yet this approach to measuring performance has a long tradition in libraries, matched by an apparent enthusiasm among librarians which shows little sign of flagging. For example, recently,

Clouston produced a new formula for collection size which is calculated using much the same sort of process as the Clapp-Jordan formula.[7]

Other very simple quantitative methods are still used throughout the world. As an example, the New Zealand university library statistics compiled each year for the New Zealand Vice-Chancellors' Committee are mostly concerned with easily quantifiable data such as collection size, number of transactions, staff numbers, and so on. In the United Kingdom, the much awaited Citizens' Charter, promoted by the Audit Commission, lists only five indicators for public library performance, only one of which is connected directly to the collection—"The amount spent per head of population on books and other materials," which is so familiar it could as easily have come from the end of the 19th century as the end of the 20th.[8]

Another approach to assessing performance is the use of standards set by a national or otherwise authoritative body, describing in simple, qualitative terms what the minimum levels of library provision must be. The weakness of this approach is that it emphasizes the minimum levels to be attained and can easily lead to complacency, if not by library staff, then certainly by the funders who see the standards as all they need to attain. England and Sumsion defend the use of quantifiable standards against attack by those who favor goal-setting by using the example of the Library Association's "Model Statement of Standards" which proposes "best practice" standards or benchmarks based not upon average or minimum levels but upon national upper quartile performance levels; in this case only the top 25 percent are above the standard.[9] Even so, although this addresses the problem of low benchmarks and a tendency to complacency, it does not satisfy the critics who wonder where the original figures came from.

THE INTERMEDIATE STAGE

In the 1980s, a new mood in library management began looking for something beyond traditional measures, usually based on inputs and easily measured outputs such as loan statistics. The apparent answer was in goal-setting. Demands for accountability continued to grow throughout the 1970s and 1980s across the whole of the public sector to the point management had to respond. Recognizing the need for analytical tools with which they could describe their library's performance, librarians looked at the prevailing theory of organizational effectiveness, which was goal-setting. One of the best examples of the use of goal-setting is the American Library Association's manual, *Measuring Academic Library Performance*, published in 1990. It stated that its purpose was to present librarians with instruments or measures which could (1) measure the impact, efficiency, and effectiveness of library activities; (2) quantify or explain library output in meaningful ways to university administrators; (3) be used by heads of units to demonstrate performance levels and resource needs to library administrators; and (4) provide data useful for library planning. [10]

Goal-setting, as used in the ALA manual, may have little direct bearing on collection development. Indeed, the ALA manual says little about the collection in terms of its size and growth. It is as if it were a deliberate attempt to break away from the input-dominated measures of the past. Attention shifts away from collection building to outputs such as reference satisfaction, which require more qualitative methods of measurement. The manual says

The measures are service-oriented. They do not cover the library's internal operations, such as technical services. Instead, they address the quantity and quality of services delivered to users. Technical services provide necessary support to public services, but the measures in this manual are concerned with the service as delivered to the user, not with the many intermediate processes within the library required to deliver those services.[11]

Are technical services library staff to be immune from performance measurement? Is there a danger their contribution will be overlooked? There is also the same problem already seen with using inputs as measures. Who says what is enough? If the goals are set by librarians for librarians, then they may have no significant impact on the people they are intended to satisfy. Goal-setting has its place, but librarians have continued to look for other means of measuring their libraries which cover the totality of operations and services, and include the views of customers and funders.

THE NEXT GENERATION?

Some recently published research has focused on the subject of organizational effectiveness itself, as this may shed some light on the library effectiveness debate. The work of Kim Cameron and others into organizational effectiveness has been used by three groups of researchers to date, and it is anticipated that more will follow. Most of Cameron's work is based on analysis of subjective perceptions of organizational performance of internal participants in organizations in the not-for-profit sectors of the economy, such as the police and higher education. He describes four different models of organizational effectiveness, and though there are other ways of describing organizations, the four models cover the subject in a satisfactory way, as other models will overlap with Cameron's four models (Open Systems; Goal Attainment; Internal Processes; and Multiple Constituencies).[12]

The Open Systems model looks at how well an organization exploits its environment to gather needed resources. In a library this frequently becomes a matter of measuring inputs such as the materials budget and/or the number of volumes added to the collection each year. As was noted earlier, this model has been popular with librarians for many years because it has two advantages: first, the figures are easy to collect, and second, the resulting data is relatively simple to analyze (for instance, if the materials budget has risen, it suggests the library has been successful, whereas a falling budget means a failure to perform).

The Goal Attainment model uses goal statements as targets and criteria for measuring success. In the last few decades of the 20th century this model has come to dominate thinking in the public sector of nearly all the anglophone library world, so it will be familiar to most readers. The library will use a strategic planning process, or something similar, to set goal targets for the future, usually within short-term or medium-term periods such as one year. Effectiveness is then judged by whether the library reaches or surpasses the target. Although some measures used in goal attainment can be quantitative, there is also considerable scope for qualitative measurement as well, such as in surveys of customer satisfaction with the collection. In this case the goal might be to raise the level of customer satisfaction with the collection to a 75 percent satisfaction level by the end of the planning year.

The Internal Processes model equates effectiveness with internal health, such as smoothly flowing processes and procedures. The cost of measuring effectiveness as determined by this model is extremely high, for it is not easily quantified, and depends instead on assessments of the organizational culture.

The last, and in terms of its popularity with librarians, the least, is the Multiple Constituencies model, sometimes called the Constituency Satisfaction model, the Strategic Constituencies model, or the Participant Satisfaction model. This equates effectiveness with the ability of the organization to identify and then meet the needs of its strategic constituencies. This model, more than any other, recognizes that libraries are social constructs, created by society for a particular purpose at a particular time. Even tyro librarians can see that not all libraries have the same purpose, but it may be easy for Western librarians to perceive only a narrow range of roles for libraries, especially those in the public sector. Only dramatic events such as the rise of the Third Reich can demonstrate that libraries can be used for roles other than those which we in the West so readily accept. By extension, therefore, if the role of libraries can be twisted in such a massive fashion, is it not necessary to recognize the social origins of our own libraries so we might better understand why societies are willing to fund our libraries as "public good" institutions?

It behooves librarians to ask themselves some critical questions about the social construct of libraries, and having arrived at some conclusions not to rest, but attempt to use the results in the context of organizational effectiveness. If it can be seen that local government officials play a large part in the all-important funding decisions which keep the library (and its collection) alive, then the local government officials, as a group or community, are a constituency of the library, or to use a different term, they are stakeholders in the library. For almost any library there will be a group which allocates funds to the library, and obviously that group is almost bound to be a stakeholder group. Perhaps even more obviously, libraries must have users, or patrons, or customers, and as a group they will be stakeholders as consumers of the products produced by the library. Library staff are almost certain to be stakeholders as decision makers within the library, though this may not be true in every situation.

The Multiple Constituencies model assesses how successfully the library meets the legitimate demands of its stakeholders. Such demands can be quantified. However, interpreting the results need not be trivial, for stakeholder groups may have quite opposite and incompatible demands, so if the library succeeds in meeting a demand from its customers who want more books on gardening to be purchased, this may be the opposite of the wishes of funders who might prefer austerity. Using this model thus requires a sense of balance between the conflicting needs of different stakeholder groups, and it is as well to remember at all times that libraries are social constructs and as such are in the political field. If this point is accepted, then Lynch's definition of effectiveness as "something which does well that which it is supposed to do," in which it is the stakeholder groups which have decided what the library should do. Now it can be seen that library effectiveness has a social environment in which all stakeholder groups are represented. This model of organizational effectiveness has a high degree of appropriateness for the 1990s and beyond, for stakeholder groups are becoming more insistent that their legitimate demands upon the library are heard. Funders want more efficiency and greater accountability. Customers want better quality service without higher expense. Library staff, caught in the crossfire, have their own agendas.

Research by two teams in the United States (McDonald and Micikas, and Van House and Childers) and one team in New Zealand (Calvert and Cullen) have used Cameron's work on organizational effectiveness as a means of assessing library effectiveness. The methods employed have been similar, first used by McDonald and Micikas in academic libraries, and by Van House and Childers in public libraries, and replicated by Calvert and Cullen in academic and public libraries.[13] The justification for a new approach to effectiveness is simply that all prior attempts have been purely subjective, using the point of view of the library staff and ignoring (passively rather than actively ignoring) the opinions expressed by other stakeholder groups.

Performance measures have nearly always been produced by library staff who first decide (without any empirical evidence) what are the dimensions of library effectiveness, in which a dimension is a cluster of indicators or measures, all of which deal with the same broad range of library inputs, outputs, or outcomes. Having chosen the dimensions, librarians then choose a few indicators which they believe will be used adequately, if operationalized into measures, to determine if the library is performing effectively. The weaknesses of this approach are that it is subjective, has no empirical base, and does not involve the stakeholders. Another difficulty is that measures tend to proliferate, pushing up the cost of actually taking the measures in the first place, let alone interpreting the mountains of data they produce. In the Multiple Constituencies model, as it has been used by the above-mentioned research teams, the process of arriving at measures is different. First, it assumes that the problem is not in writing the measures, for there is already a plethora of indicators in the literature, but in determining the dimensions of effectiveness. If only a small set of dimensions is chosen, it is then only necessary to use one or two measures for each dimension because the chosen measures serve as surrogates for all the other indicators in the dimension. Thus, when a set of measures is finally produced, it will be a parsimonious set of measures tailored to the needs of the library as determined by all of its stakeholder groups. To do this it is necessary to concentrate on determining the dimensions of effectiveness; then the measures will follow. As Abbott has said, "work on the subject has been for the most part repetitive, with little attempt to build on previous work in the development of new approaches," and it is hoped that this is the sort of new approach she has in mind.[14]

A brief description of the method employed in this research will now be given. The research can be conceptualized in two parts, even though not all the studies have actually been conducted that way. The first stage is a survey of the perceptions of library effectiveness among the stakeholder groups. To do this, a survey instrument is drawn up which lists a number of indicators of library effectiveness. There is no need to write new indicators as there is a multitude of indicators already available in the library science literature; indeed, the problem is to cull them and condense them to a manageable number. Even after combining similar indicators, there is still a high number for a questionnaire; the New Zealand public libraries study, for example, included 95 indicators in the questionnaire, but this does not, strangely enough, seem to have a major impact on response rates. It is not a typical social science artifact for ascertaining user satisfaction; it is a very specialized type of survey instrument whose antecedents are well understood and reported in the nonprofit and tertiary institution management literature, notably that of Cameron. The indicators are listed beneath a single question, which is phrased something like "please say how important these things are to you when trying to judge the performance of a public library," with a Likert scale (usually 1–5) from "Very Important" to "Less Important" for each indicator. The resulting data can be analyzed in a variety of ways. A simple ranking of indicators by the mean of the responses shows which indicators are perceived as very useful descriptors of library effectiveness, and which are not. Comparisons (done by using correlation tests) between pairs of ranked lists of indicators for each constituency will show if there is similarity or divergence between the opinions of stakeholder groups. Finally, it is possible to conduct a factor analysis of all the data to produce factors which are interpretable as the dimensions of library effectiveness.

At this point a degree of subjectivity enters the method, because factor analysis can produce as many or as few factors as requested, so researchers must choose the number of factors which seems both the best explanation of the data and the most robust. The second stage of the project is similar to the first and uses the same questionnaire, except that the single question is changed to read something like "please say how your library is performing on each of the following indicators." Usually, this questionnaire has only been given to library staff, as it is felt that other stakeholder groups will be incapable of responding adequately to a question about actual performance. It would be interesting if a study asked nonlibrary staff this question and then compared the results to see if there is a reason for not including the other stakeholders in this stage of the research. Data analysis proceeds as in the first stage. The factor analysis, which is optional in the first stage, is critical to the second stage, for it is at this point that the dimensions of library effectiveness are determined. Factors are interpreted as equalling dimensions exactly, and empirical evidence has suggested that there is good cause for this assumption. The highest loading indicator in each dimension is a good representation of the dimension itself, so that indicator can, if it is considered valid and measurable, be operationalized as a performance measure.

Absolute comparison between research findings has not been possible, because the number of factors drawn from the data sets is dependent upon the data, so this is an unpredictable number. McDonald and Micikas choose thirteen major dimensions and seven minor dimensions from their study of American libraries. One of the major dimensions is "Library Collection Adequacy," which they describe as "Criteria indicating sufficiency of support for user demands by the existing collection and additions to it, and the adequacy of the annual budget."[15] This dimension is composed of seven indicators, which are, in order of descending factor loading: existing collection contains materials of sufficient breadth and depth to support the curricula; size of collection is large enough to meet user needs; the library acquires materials to support faculty research; library users are able to secure needed materials from the collection; the library acquires materials to meet anticipated curricular needs; the annual budget is adequate.[16] It is interesting to see that an indicator which emphasizes the collection as support for the curriculum loaded higher than a measure of size. The last indicator in this list is also worthy of comment, because it could be expected that an indicator about the library budget would fall into a dimension mostly concerned with inputs, so the librarians in this survey associated the materials budget with indicators of collection adequacy in terms of meeting user needs. This is the Multiple Constituencies model at work rather than the Open Systems model of input measures.

In the New Zealand public libraries study, rather different results were produced, as might be expected. A dimension labelled collection management appeared as a result of the second stage factor analysis, in which the indicators were, in descending order of factor loading: newness of books, magazines, and other materials; state of repair of books, magazines, and other materials; quality of books, magazines, and other materials; total materials processed (purchased, cataloged) per year; speed and accuracy of reshelving materials; match of stock to community needs and demands; and amount of use of materials inside the library building. It is very interesting to see what one might call a qualitative statement as the highest loading indicator, as "newness" is surely relative. There is also a reminder to all librarians, even those away from the academic scene, that owning an item is no use to the customer unless it is accurately shelved.

The apparent emphasis on qualitative terms is in marked contrast to the dimension labelled financial inputs in which money spent on materials per resident per year is the highest loading indicator, total money spent on books and other materials is the third highest, number of items purchased per year is the fifth highest, followed by per-item expenditure on new items being added to stock. Then in the eighth and lowest loading of the indicators in the dimension is total stock of books, magazines, and other materials. This is interesting for two reasons: First, the factor analysis showed that there is difference in perceptions between inputs as measure of performance and qualitative indicators of the collection; and second, because the familiar measure of total stock is so poorly valued.

Even if the Multiple Constituencies model does not find favor with the library community, there is enough evidence here to suggest that a fresh look must be taken at performance measurement in relation to collection development. If not the Multiple Constituencies model and the methodology suggested here, then perhaps a different instrument which measures the attitudes of librarians regarding the contrast between "quality-driven" and "demand-driven" collection development, such as has been suggested by Hamilton and Weech, can be developed.[17]

THE FUTURE?

The philosophy and rationale underlying collection development has undergone dramatic change in recent years, as has been described elsewhere in this volume. The transition from a "just-in-case" library, in which the collection is built to satisfy customers within the four walls of the institution, has changed to a "just-in-time" approach, which uses developments in information technology allowing fast and accurate transmission of data across distance, to create a situation in which the library only seeks access to material wherever it may be stored in its original form, and then copies it for use by its own customers. Collection development must address what has been called the "anti-collection," that is, those items not held in the local collection. "Selection is . . . to a large extent, a continuous series of decisions about which items in the anti-collection should be moved to the collection. Once the decision is made to move an information unit from the anti-collection to the collection, that unit ceases to be of concern to collection development."[18] Of course, this does not deal with concepts such as network navigation in which the librarian/information manager operates as a guide and filterer of information on the Net, but it does force us to consider the need for performance measures to ascertain how effectively the library is meeting demand from customers for material outside its own four walls—the anti-collection.

What does the librarian understand by access to the anti-collection? If we only half understand the issues, then how can we write valid performance measures for this new service we are expected to provide for our customers? Part of the problem with any new development, particularly something as radical as a change to "just-in-time" access is that it is difficult to place it within our existing mental map of library effectiveness. Is remote access part of collection development, or is it part of customer service? The methodology utilizing factor analysis, described earlier, can suggest a solution to this problem. The McDonald and Micikas research shows that there is, as yet, no consensus on this matter. After analyzing the factor analysis for their research in U.S. academic libraries they conclude,

Very clearly, a tension exists here. The library's major constituencies associate its effectiveness with its ability to provide an adequate collection. Librarians on the other hand, understand that they will probably never be able to provide a fully adequate collection, as defined by the users. . . . Accordingly, librarians see the necessity of providing access to information beyond the local setting and place an emphasis on providing services that will allow that access.[19]

Librarians place more emphasis on access to materials as part of the information service, whereas college administrators and faculty place more emphasis on access to materials on-site, in other words, as a part of traditional collection development. The benefits of the approach suggested here are that indicators may float between dimensions as perceptions change. Should an aspect of remote collection development move in the common perception from collection building to information service, it will do so without a subjective decision having to be made by a small group of librarians. The stakeholders will decide.

CONCLUSION

Throughout the 1960s and 1970s, librarianship was under the sway of the methods then prevailing in the social sciences, due in part to a desire to justify library science as an academic discipline, which led to borrowing from other disciplines, and partly to the influence of Brookes and others whose work in information science was becoming more influential among librarians. At that time quantitative methods were much more acceptable in academia than qualitative methods. Quite simply, they were held to be more scientific. It is thus not surprising that suggested performance measures were almost entirely quantitative, because most scholars and librarians agreed that quantitative was best. This has gradually changed in the 1980s and 1990s. Scientific quantitative methods have been shown to be just as fallible as qualitative methods, if done poorly. At the same time, qualitative methods have been improved to the point that many researchers believe there is no intrinsic superiority of one over the other.

Practitioners, understandably, have been more reluctant to accept the validity of qualitative methods: They have had less exposure to them and, without solid experience of the relative merits of both methods, will hold to ideas instilled in them when they were at library school—which for many current library managers was during the heyday of quantitative methods. For practitioners there is also the basic need to justify what they do to funding agencies, and as many who sit on funding boards or committees will have had little exposure to changes in academic thought (or fashion?), quantitative methods are still the simplest and best. A recent study, which tries to compare quantitative and qualitative methods for collection evaluation, has found little to distinguish them. As Ephraim points out, "Quantitative data is not necessarily 'more objective' than qualitative data. A statistic is susceptible to misleading presentation and interpretation, just as a judgement may be based on insufficient information. An accurate, soundly based judgement may be as objective as a set of statistics."[20] The study upholds the hypothesis that the size of a collection closely correlates with the number of postgraduate degrees awarded, which is of some comfort to those librarians who still argue that the larger the collection, the better it is. The significance of the study, however, is that the method used to evaluate the collection is a mix of quantitative and qualitative measurement.

The research by Van House and Childers, and Calvert and Cullen has drawn the conclusion that no single model of organizational effectiveness satisfies all the requirements of defining library effectiveness. Although this paper may appear to malign the simple inputs approach, it still has some credibility and popularity with librarians and funders. In the early developmental stages of a new library it is easy to see that a pure inputs approach is suitable while the library has a growth spurt in its early years. The harsh reality of adult life, however, will probably mean that measuring inputs alone does satisfy the needs of the library managers in terms of accountability. Goal-setting is still in favor in the public sector, so in order to satisfy political pressures librarians must be willing to plan and measure performance with goal-setting techniques. What this paper argues is that the Multiple Constituencies model should also be used in the mature years of a library, that is, once its growth has eased and its customer base has been established.

NOTES

1. Geoffrey Ford, "A Perspective on Performance Measurement," *International Journal of Information & Library Research* 1 (1989): 12–23.

2. R. H. Orr, "Measuring the Goodness of Library Services: A General Framework for Considering Quantitative Measures," *Journal of Documentation* 29 (1973): 315–32.

3. Mary Jo Lynch, "Measurement of Public Library Activity: The Search for Practical Methods," *Wilson Library Bulletin* 57 (1983): 388.

4. Joseph A. McDonald and Lynda Basney Micikas, *Academic Libraries: The Dimensions of Their Effectiveness* (Westport, CT: Greenwood Press, 1994), p. 11.

5. F. W. Lancaster, *If You Want to Evaluate Your Library* . . . (Champaign: University of Illinois, Graduate School of Library and Information Sciences, 1988); Sharon Baker and F. W. Lancaster, *The Measurement and Evaluation of Library Services*, 2nd ed. (Arlington, VA: Information Resources Press, 1991).

6. V. W. Clapp and R. T. Jordan, "Quantitative Criteria for Adequacy of Academic

Library Collections," *College and Research Libraries* 26 (1965): 371–80; reprinted in *College and Research Libraries* 50 (1989): 154–63.

7. John S. Clouston, "How Much Is Enough? Establishing a Corridor of Adequacy in Library Acquisitions," in *Practical Issues in Collection Development and Collection Access: The 1993 Charleston Conference*, ed. Katrina Strauch et al. (New York: Haworth, 1995).

8. Len England and John Sumsion, *Perspectives of Public Library Use: A Compendium of Survey Information* (Loughborough: Loughborough University of Technology, Library and Information Statistics Unit, 1995), p. 107.

9. Ibid., p. 106.

10. Nancy A. Van House, Beth T. Weil, and Charles R. McClure, *Measuring Academic Library Performance: A Practical Approach* (Chicago: American Library Association, 1990), p. vii.

11. Ibid., p. ix.

12. Kim S. Cameron, "Measuring Organizational Effectiveness in Institutions of Higher Education." *Administrative Science Quarterly* 2 (1957): 604–29.

13. McDonald and Micikas, *Academic Libraries*; Nancy Van House and Thomas Childers, *The Public Library Effectiveness Study: The Complete Report* (Chicago: American Library Association, 1993); Philip J. Calvert and Rowena J. Cullen, "Further Dimensions of Public Library Effectiveness: Report on a Parallel New Zealand Study," *Library and Information Science Research* 15 (1993): 143–64; Philip J. Calvert and Rowena J. Cullen, "Further Dimensions of Public Library Effectiveness II: The Second Stage of the New Zealand Study," *Library and Information Science Research* 16 (1994): 87–104.

14. Christine Abbott, *Performance Measurement in Library and Information Services* (London: Aslib, 1994), p. 1.

15. McDonald and Micikas, *Academic Libraries*, p. 63.

16. Ibid., p. 159.

17. Patricia Hamilton and Terry L. Weech, "The Development and Testing of an Instrument to Measure Attitudes Toward the Quality vs. Demand Debate in Collection Management," *Collection Management* 10 (1988): 27–37.

18. Ross Atkinson, "Access, Ownership, and the Future of Collection Development," in *Collection Management and Development: Issues in an Electronic Era*, ed. Peggy Johnson and Bonnie MacEwan (Chicago: American Library Association, 1994), p 97.

19. McDonald and Micikas, *Academic Libraries*, p. 69.

20. P. E. Ephraim, "A Review of Qualitative and Quantitative Measures in Collection Analysis," *Electronic Library* 12 (1994): 237–41.

7

Integrating the Activities of Librarians and Paraprofessional Workers in Evaluating Academic Library Collections

Sheila S. Intner

INTRODUCTION

In 1986, Hafter's seminal study of cataloging librarians in academic libraries appeared, concluding that cataloging as a professional specialization within library and information science had been downgraded to the point where a master's degree was no longer thought to be necessary.[1] She attributed the phenomenon to the implementation of computer-based shared cataloging networks, such as OCLC, which provided so large a proportion of cataloging records to its academic library members that they could dispense with nearly all of their original cataloging.[2] Instead of professionally trained catalogers, libraries wanted lower-level, lower-paid people to operate the computers, search for existing records in the database, match up newly acquired books with the computerized records, and import the records into the library's catalog. It was a wasteful luxury to employ librarians with master's degrees in library and information science (and all sorts of other specialties, such as foreign language proficiencies and subject master's degrees) to do this kind of cataloging. Any person who could work a computer and match records on the screen to books in hand could catalog. A new category of nonprofessionally trained staff member arose, aptly called a copy cataloger, since he or she copied records from the network database into the local catalog system.

Hafter pointed out that the impact went beyond deprofessionalizing cataloging—moving cataloging from the realm of professional duties to a new category of paraprofessional jobs. She found other effects as well, including loss of control over the actual implementation of cataloging work, which was shifting to administrators, and threats to the status, authority, and autonomy of catalogers.[3]

The changes wrought by bibliographic networks are, indeed, far-reaching, but despite Hafter's negative-sounding conclusions, evidence fails to show that catalogs are less effective search tools at this writing, a decade later, than they were in the past. On the contrary, a great deal of evidence shows the opposite—catalogs now provide more information to searchers and they do so in many different ways. The function of current computer-based catalogs differs fundamentally from that of the traditional book or card catalog of the past. In practice, we now accept copy cataloging as an integral part of present-day cataloging operations and an essential factor in the development of contemporary ideas of the local library catalog as a double-barreled instrument: first, as always, the record of local holdings, and second, a gateway to the holdings of other institutions. The current vogue toward contracting with outside sources for cataloging, known as outsourcing, seems to be a development in the same vein as, but one step beyond, copy cataloging. Outsourcing is not new. Libraries have long sought to obtain cataloging from external sources such as the Library of Congress and the H. W. Wilson Company. But the way outsourcing is accomplished today, and its implications for local library staffing, differs from cooperative and commercial cataloging operations of the past.

Thinking about these phenomena raises questions about other professional activities, especially selection. Has a similar deprofessionalization occurred in this area also? Are there ''copy'' selectors or their equivalents? And if so, how are the activities of these paraprofessionals integrating with those of degreed librarians in the broader spectrum of functions we now call collection development—not just selecting titles, but being responsible for evaluating user needs and existing collections, setting goals and objectives for new purchases, and obtaining and allocating the funds to acquire the materials? It seems sensible to begin with a look at the professional literature. What does it indicate is happening? Does it provide sufficient evidence that a similar phenomenon is occurring to warrant further investigation? This chapter attempts to lay some initial groundwork in answering these questions and suggesting models for integrating paraprofessionals into collections work in the area of evaluation.

DEFINITIONS: CONTEXT FOR THE DISCUSSION

In order to clarify meaning and avoid misunderstanding in the balance of this chapter, the reader is asked to accept the following working definitions as the basis for discussion. ''Collection development'' is a contemporary term representing all the activities associated with building and shaping library collections, including planning, goal-setting, decision making, budgeting, and selecting, acquiring, and evaluating them. ''Collection development'' supersedes the earlier terms ''acquisitions'' and ''selection,'' and, for the purposes of this chapter, is considered synonymous with the terms "collection building," "collection management," "resource building," and similar terms, although it is not necessarily identical in literal meaning to them.

"Collection evaluation" is a part of collection development in which existing collections are measured, analyzed, and judged according to preset criteria for size, relevance, quality, and use. Evaluation methodologies may be categorized by their focus (user-centered versus collection-centered) or by the nature of their findings (objective/quantitative/statistical versus subjective/qualitative/interpretive). Specific methodologies include (but are not limited to) list checking, in which local collections are matched against bibliographies and/or catalogs of notable collections; soliciting opinions on adequacy and quality of local collections from users and/or experts; request analysis, in which requests for materials that could not be found in local collections are analyzed to determine weaknesses, while fulfillment of requests from other libraries is analyzed to determine strengths; and use studies, in which the circulation of locally held materials is analyzed to forecast distributions of future needs. All of these methods typically include gathering data, analyzing data, and interpreting the results. No matter how objective the method and its data, analyses, and reporting, eventually someone must decide the meaning for the individual library involved, which, by any definition, is a subjective act.

"Professional librarians" are defined as holders of a master's degree in library/information science and, for the purposes of this chapter, library subject specialists holding the doctorate in their area of specialization (such as Ph.D., J.D., M.D.), but having no master's-level degree in library and information science. It is a purely individual decision made by this author to equate the possession of a doctorate (plus experience in library operations) with the possession of a master's degree in library and information science, and it is based on the assumption that in many, if not all, libraries where librarians hold faculty status, the doctorate would merit the same status. "Paraprofessional workers" in libraries are defined as persons who have experience in performing or assisting in the performance of library operations and functions, but who do not possess a master's degree in library/information science or the doctoral degree in a subject area.

PARAPROFESSIONALISM IN THE LITERATURE

The publications discussed in this section do not plumb the depths of literature about paraprofessional workers in libraries, but have been chosen to reflect most of the principal elements found in the literature and, especially, to describe recent serious research done on the subject. Other papers in this area suggest similar hypotheses, articulate similar concerns, and offer similar solutions, although it would be far from accurate to imply that a consensus exists. On the contrary, the outlines of at least two positions in a continuing debate can be seen in the literature.

In the first position, paraprofessionals are not librarians, do not do the same work as librarians, and should not have librarian status without possessing the same knowledge (as evidenced by earning the requisite master's-level credential). In the second position, paraprofessionals really run libraries, quite often doing the same work as degree-holding librarians, and should be treated with more respect and given similar, if not equal, status as degree-holding librarians. (This seems to be the current "politically correct" view, if the opinions expressed in *Library Journal* editorials and some of the literature reported here may be taken to indicate the politically correct stance.)[4]

One can also discern a middle-ground position that accords paraprofessional workers a greater measure of status than heretofore, assessing their job descriptions objectively as falling between those of degree-holding librarians and ordinary clerical workers, and recognizing and acknowledging the increasingly important role they play in libraries of all kinds. Most serious studies of library operations tend to support this position and follow a tradition of such findings going back half a century or more.

It might seem unusual to find discussions of paraprofessionalism in the literature before automation and the contemporary economic crunch, but they were appearing regularly as far back as the 1940s, peaking in the 1960s and 1970s.[5] In a paper published in 1989, Nettlefold says the following:

Most authors assume that library paraprofessionalism developed in the latter half of the 20th century. Although true for English-speaking countries, this is not universal. It is also important to distinguish between the development of paraprofessionalism and the development of education and training for paraprofessionalism. The latter is a recent phenomenon, but the former is a counterpart of the evolution of library professionalism since the late 19th century, with many librarians working as paraprofessionals in all but name.[6]

Much of the literature about paraprofessional work in libraries discusses general issues such as recruiting, wages and benefits, status, and relations with librarians. Articles which address specific job tasks have tended to focus mainly on activities at the cataloging terminal, as Hafter did, or covering the reference desk, where, in libraries with very few degreed librarians, paraprofessionals may take their turns answering patron queries and guiding people toward relevant materials. Authors who discuss selection and other collection development work assigned to paraprofessionals may define them simply as not holding a master's degree in library and information science, and not specify whether they might have doctoral degrees in other subjects.

A landmark survey of the role of paraprofessional workers in academic libraries, funded by the Association of College and Research Libraries division of the American Library Association, was conducted in 1990 by Oberg, Mentges, McDermott, and Harusadangkul.[7] Response to their survey instrument was excellent—80 percent of a random sample of 488 public and private institutions from the 2,747 listed in the Carnegie Foundation's *A Classification of Institutions of Higher Education* (Carnegie sample) and 71 percent of 108 members of the Association of Research Libraries (ARL sample).[8] The two populations represent a broad spectrum of academic libraries, with special attention to the research university cohort that plays a leadership role within the academic community. Summarizing their findings, Oberg et al. state: "The collective portrait of paraprofessionals that emerges from this survey is that of a vital, growing force within academic libraries. Few traditional or newly created tasks are off-limits, and paraprofessionals are routinely assigned complex duties that a generation ago characterized the work of librarians."[9]

Book selection and collection development both were listed among tasks regularly assigned to paraprofessional workers; with 23 percent of the Carnegie sample and 21 percent of the ARL sample assigning the former, and 16 percent of the Carnegie sample and 19 percent of the ARL sample assigning the latter.[10] These statistics contrast with much larger proportions of libraries that assign leading tours of the library (40% of the Carnegie sample and 71% of the ARL sample) and copy cataloging (61% and 49% in the Carnegie sample and 92% and 91% in ARL sample, depending on whether Library of Congress or member library data are used)—the two tasks most frequently assigned to paraprofessional workers.[11] The discussion provides no further elaboration on specific collection development related duties that paraprofessionals perform or any limits on their performance, such as whether their selections must come from particular sources or require approval by a professional before being implemented; whether they can authorize budget adjustments, assess user needs, evaluate collections, and so on. Nonetheless, the authors comment that they find the numbers of libraries using paraprofessionals in collection development related activities surprisingly high.[12]

In a 1990 article surveying the relationship between job responsibilities and job satisfaction at nine campuses of the University of California, Kreitz and Ogden found that small proportions of paraprofessionals did collection evaluation and weeding (tasks combined by the researchers) "fairly often" or "very frequently," and that the percentage jumped between the two lower grades and two higher grades of library assistant.[13] While only one-fourth as many paraprofessionals as librarians evaluated collections and weeded materials from them, it is a clear result.[14]

The 1991 Feather River Institute examined the impact of automation on acquisitions and collection development. In a provocative paper given at that conference and published in *Library Acquisitions: Practice & Theory,* Sasse and Smith of Colorado State University Libraries suggested that future paraprofessionals could monitor selections made by means of automated matches between vendor databases and library set parameters constituting a rather precise "mechanical filter," a term coined by Charles Brownson several years earlier.[15] Nonetheless, they still envisioned that a collection development officer—presumably a librarian holding an M.L.S.—would evaluate the results, saying, the process would continue to need broad review by a collection development officer who would concentrate on methodology and results. With the aid of the bibliographer's workstation, collection specialists would concentrate on policies for acquisitions, access, and consortial agreements; they would also design and analyze user and use studies; design and refine research and curriculum profiles as well as design and implement collection assessment studies. Once library administrators realize what a wealth of evaluative data is available, they will expect collection developers to produce assessments of collections based on many factors—including how well user demands are met. They will also encourage improvements in other accountability measures.[16]

Among the results Sasse and Smith foresee developing from these more sophisticated evaluative processes is the initiation of new publications to fill identified gaps.[17]

Far fewer scholarly papers deal with public libraries than with academic libraries, but in 1991, Smith addressed the use of paraprofessionals at the reference desk in public libraries.[18] In his concluding section he stated,

The results of this survey support in many instances the findings of previous academic library studies . . . [that] nonprofessionals (particularly those at the associate level—the highest category for such personnel designated by the American Library Association) comprise an integral and important part of reference service. As in previous academic library studies, the nonprofessionals in this survey provide roughly one-third of direct patron contact at the reference desk. Further affirmation of the extent of nonprofessional reference responsibilities was evident in the significant amount of reference service provided by these employees without any supervision from professional librarians.[19]

Smith's focus is on assignments to reference desk service, not collections work, but one can reasonably expect that other reference-related duties might follow— at some point in the future if not immediately—in libraries where paraprofessionals staff the reference desk.

In "Reference Encounters of a Different Kind: A Symposium," Massey-Burzio describes a 1990 decision made at Brandeis University Library to end its practice of staffing the reference desk primarily with librarians, assisted by graduate students much of the time, and for a few hours a week, by graduate students alone.[20] In place of that arrangement, Brandeis substituted a two-pronged service: an information desk staffed only by graduate students and a research consultation service staffed only by librarians. The reasons for the decision included the need to deal with the familiar twin problems of insufficient staff and budget to provide enough librarians to cope with reference traffic at all hours; but, also, the recognition that recently acquired CD-ROM databases had created a traffic jam of reference queries that could not be handled in the traditional manner. The two-level deployment of differing levels of staff not only solved Brandeis's problem, but helped to improve service quality by sorting queries and matching the appropriate staff level with each type of query. The students could handle directional and ready reference questions, and refer difficult and more complex questions to librarians. This became known in the field as "the Brandeis model."[21]

Ray's report on a discussion about paraprofessional workers in collection development includes the remarks of two speakers: Jim Spohrer, from the University of California, Berkeley, and Jasper Schad, from Wichita State University. They describe how paraprofessionals contributed to collection development in their libraries, illustrating potential models for a large research university library and a medium-sized college library, respectively.[22] Spohrer says that deep cuts in numbers of professional positions have motivated the creation of a paraprofessional position called "curatorial assistant." Curatorial assistants, drawn solely from the two highest levels of Berkeley's library assistant ranks, are selected on the basis of previous experience, language abilities, and individual interests. Working with a designated librarian, they are assigned evaluation tasks comparing holdings to bibliographies, as well as nonevaluation tasks such as (but not limited to) selecting titles from brochures and notification slips, drafting letters and other documents, and translating foreign language materials for the librarian. According to Ray, Spohrer was pleased by the results of Berkeley's experiment with curatorial assistants and said he hoped to double the number of such assistants in the ensuing year.[23]

Schad consulted a number of colleagues in medium-sized academic libraries and discovered about one-third of them use non–M.L.S. selectors, mainly out of necessity, and generally in the subjects of area and language studies. But, Schad notes in Ray's report, when paraprofessionals are assigned to collection development, they performed the full range of activities, not just the ones thought to be within the capabilities of nonprofessionals, such as list checking or document preparation. Moreover, he says, "there might be a corollary to [the Brandeis] model for staffing collection development, but the difficulty comes in attempting to divide collection development work into its professional and non-professional components."[24]

Ray summarizes the problem, according to Schad, as follows:

Collection development is perceived as more complex than reference because it consists of ongoing plans and policies, unlike the typically single transactions at an information or reference desk. Effective collection development work is continuous, cumulative, and interactive. . . . [C]ollection development might be divided into the macro and micro decisions. The most critical function in collection development is planning, the macro; selection follows on this planning as a set of microdecisions.[25]

In the discussion following the speakers, Rick Lugg of Yankee Book Peddler said that in his experience of managing bibliographers with and without the M.L.S., he had observed no differences in their abilities to select and evaluate a book.[26] While this is not the same as evaluating the library's collections or assessing user needs for materials, it is part of numerous evaluative processes exerting influences of one kind or another on collecting. Unfortunately, neither

Ray nor the speakers specify whether the paraprofessionals held terminal degrees in their fields (the Ph.D. or equivalent).

Schad's idea of macro- and microdecisions describes well the process employed in an evaluation of a children's literature collection at Gustavus Adolphus College Library reported by Nevin in *Collection Management*.[27] Nevin says, "Although the focus here was children's books, the methodology may be applied to any specialized collection in the smaller academic library, provided that it is manageable in size . . . and that it is self-contained and has its own shelflist location."[28] Designed by a librarian working with a faculty member from the Department of Education, the project was carried out by a student specially chosen to perform the study.[29] Several methods were used in the evaluation, including complex list checking, a user survey, and analysis of call numbers for the materials being evaluated. The student's involvement ended after the study's findings were reported; and, subsequently, librarians applied the findings in making decisions to alter cataloging and classification practices, bibliographic instruction programs, and selection procedures.

In a 1994 posting on the COLLDV-L listserv, Anthony Ferguson of Columbia University noted,

for area studies bibliographers subject, language, and previous university library experience are the most important factors when hiring a new librarian. If you can get these three qualities plus the MLS so much the better. After hiring a good many area bibliographers I have only been once disappointed when I hired a non-MLS and that person lacked library experience.[30]

It may be that to Ferguson, working at Columbia University, "subject knowledge" means possession of an advanced degree, often a doctorate, not just a bachelor's degree with a major in the subject. At the same time, Ferguson acknowledges the importance of university library experience, equating it with subject knowledge and expressing the view that such experience goes far as a substitute for the master's degree in library and information science. Because the definition of paraprofessional in this chapter excludes holders of terminal degrees in a subject area, it is possible Ferguson's remarks do not apply to this discussion; however, they could if the bibliographers in question hold only master's degrees in their subject areas. Subject experts can be paraprofessional workers in libraries and, when this is the case, they might well be entrusted with evaluating collections and other professional collection development tasks.

The listserv discussion preceded a program jointly sponsored by two collection development groups within the American Library Association at its June 1995 annual conference.[31] The question the program's panel of four speakers addressed was whether collection development could be taught in library school or had to be learned on the job. This debate is important to the discussion in this paper since, presumably, if the consensus among librarians is that collection development work cannot be taught in library school, paraprofessionals must be considered as well prepared as librarians for it. Three of the four panelists (including this author) came down firmly on the side that held that library school coursework imparted much knowledge of value for a collection development librarian, even as they agreed it could not teach them everything of importance. The fourth, a practicing bibliographer at Harvard University, held that his library school coursework gave him neither useful theory nor practical knowledge for his job. The dissenter held both a Ph.D. in a discipline and an M.L.S., earned in that order, and claimed the subject degree was of far greater value than anything he was taught at library school. He claimed that subject knowledge, preferably at the doctoral level, should be followed by an apprenticeship under a master bibliographer to complete the preparation necessary for performing collection development work. Although not specifically stated during the program, one might conclude that the dissenter is but a step away from assigning all collection development responsibilities to nonlibrarians, provided they possess subject expertise and guided experience—two of Ferguson's three essential attributes.

A popularly written article surveying paraprofessional duties in special libraries, "The Paraprofessional in Today's Libraries," by Kainin, Eyler, and Ryan, reports many tasks generally reserved for librarians alone are being done by nondegreed staff. The tasks named are managing student staffing, including writing the budget for the student staff; hiring, training, and firing them; monitoring approval plans; selecting titles to be ordered from book lists; performing online searches and in-depth reference; overseeing circulation; supervising computer systems; and participating in library-wide planning and management on an equal footing with degreed librarians.[32] But looking carefully at the situations Kainin et al. describe, two explanations emerge: First, the settings are atypical—a special library or a highly specialized collection within a larger general library; second, the paraprofessional may be a subject expert even if the person does not hold the M.L.S. In the special library or specialized collection setting, staffing is not expected to follow the pattern typical of general academic and large public libraries, which tend to hire professionally educated librarians for management tasks. For the specialized library or collection, subject expertise is as critical as library and information science knowledge. One could debate eternally whether it is easier or more effective to teach a subject expert about librarianship or a librarian about the subject without ever coming to any firm conclusions. Anyone lacking one of the two kinds of knowledge has to learn a lot on the job, and having an advanced degree in one field does not substitute for failing to have it in the other.

The activities of paraprofessionals, as defined in this chapter, in relation to collection work are not always specified clearly. In Kainin's study the paraprofessional who selected titles for purchase, searched databases, and performed in-depth reference service was a subject expert holding an advanced degree. This is neither unusual nor atypical of large research libraries (or, for that matter, special libraries), where a doctorate may be thought a more important credential for a bibliographer than an M.L.S. However, the definition of paraprofessional used for this discussion excludes such experts, so the foregoing list of duties must be viewed accordingly. Other authors equate selection with collection development, which, while not entirely incorrect, is not all-encompassing. In an effort to describe how paraprofessionals function successfully in a particular institution, authors sometimes neglect to discuss whether the selections of paraprofessionals are reviewed and approved before purchase, and whether selection also included other activities as well.

The final word summarizing the literature in this section belongs to Oberg. In ''The Emergence of the Paraprofessional in Academic Libraries: Perceptions and Realities,'' Oberg did a preliminary exploration of the data from the Association for College and Research Libraries study he conducted with Mentges et al.[33] He concluded:

For decades, librarians have attempted to sort the professional wheat from the paraprofessional chaff by compiling lists of the tasks that putatively define each category. In most respects, this has been a singularly unrewarding exercise. Its one great virtue, however, has been to demonstrate that librarianship is more than the sum of its parts. Still, a new theoretical model of the profession, a lens through which librarians can view, organize, and evaluate practice, has yet to emerge.[34]

After relating this finding to Veaner's 1984 vision of librarianship as being discontinuous, involving two fundamentally different types of work performed by two different groups of workers, Oberg went on to say,

The inability of librarians to define their own role less ambiguously inhibits us from describing paraprofessionals more precisely, from explaining ourselves to clients who fail increasingly to distinguish between the two groups, and from exercising leadership in this important arena. The emergence of the paraprofessional as an active, vital force in our libraries compounds librarians' age-old identity crisis and challenges us to resolve at last the problem of our status.[35]

ROLE OF THE PROFESSIONAL LIBRARIAN

The activities nearly always reserved for professionals alone, both historically and at present in the mainstream perspective, are of two types: those requiring subjective judgments and those involving decisions about expenditure of resources. Two activities involving judgments that come to mind immediately are the evaluation of existing collections and the selection of new materials to add to them and currently held materials to remove from them. Because those activities are so obviously dependent on the possession of expert knowledge such as is taught in M.L.S. programs, they are easy to identify. Despite their importance, however, they should not outshine other activities that will affect—perhaps even more crucially—the definition and shaping of library collections: setting long- and short-term collecting goals and objectives; assigning priorities to those goals and objectives; and allocating funds among the library's subjects, audiences, and media. The evaluation of current collections and selection for purchase or removal depend to a large extent on both the allocation of funds and collecting goals and objectives. Budgets create monetary limits on the amount of material that can be acquired and, sometimes, the kinds of materials as well. Collecting goals and objectives define the territory of collecting; that is, they create boundaries on the scope, depth, and nature of selections as well as, indirectly, the deselections. The judgments made in setting goals and priorities and allocating funds fall quite clearly into the professional purview. They tend to be made by members of the library's top administration, who may or may not also have specific responsibility for other activities concerning collections. Often, even the library's top collections officer does not have the power to alter goals, priorities, and budgets set by the library's director and approved by the library's (and parent institution's) governing body.

One can see all collection evaluation as being defined and structured by previously made administrative decisions on collecting aims and materials allocations. The intention to continue building particular strengths or, alternatively, limiting support for traditional strengths in order to redress weaknesses, are what set the agenda and create norms for measuring the results when a collecting cycle ends. Perceived in this way, the activities involved in carrying out the agenda by making appropriate selections and deselections and gathering the data to ascertain whether norms were met, not met, or exceeded, possess far less judgmental authority. If one accepts this view of selection and evaluation activities as simply following predefined orders, these activities would not require the same types of expert knowledge gained through professional education and training, and could easily be assigned to competent and experienced paraprofessional workers, especially if their work was monitored carefully by a professional supervisor.

To a degree, the adoption of approval plans is based on the assumption that setting up the collecting parameters—the profile—is the task of a professionally educated librarian, while carrying out the individual selection decisions is not and can be done by the clerical staff employed by the approval plan vendor. These days, book wholesalers hire M.L.S.-educated librarians to advise library clients about what to buy and how to design their approval plan profiles as well as to advise their employers about how to design and market their products and services. Vendors, using the expertise of professionally educated librarians, are able to implement a variety of collection development services in addition to whatever discounts they may offer.

Large university research libraries generally employ either M.L.S.-educated librarians, often with master's degrees in the relevant subject areas, and/or Ph.D.-holding subject specialists (who may be called bibliographers) to develop the collections in each subject area important to the institution. In this context, "develop" means more than just selecting the books and journals to be purchased for the subject area or removed from existing collections, although those tasks may be included in the subject specialist's job description. It also means surveying, identifying, and monitoring the entire range of that subject's literature worldwide; interacting regularly with faculty teaching in the subject area, whether in a formally defined liaison capacity or on an informal basis; interacting with book, periodical, and nonprint vendors furnishing materials in that subject; assuming responsibility for profiling any approval plan or other gathering plans for that subject; directing and coordinating day-to-day selection and deselection activities if they are distributed among several staff members; making the day-to-day decisions that arise; and, possibly, making the strategic decisions as well—forecasting needs; setting goals, objectives, and priorities for it; allocating the budget; planning for preservation, security, and maintenance; and representing the subject area to other bibliographers, to the rest of the library, to same-subject peers at other libraries, and to those outside the library. One important and highly sensitive task such specialists may undertake is interacting with current or potential donors to the library who evidence interest in the subject area, as well as with the institution's alumni and development offices concerning the gifts. Large city public libraries, particularly those maintaining research-level collections, follow similar patterns, although there are no faculties with whom the bibliographers interact; but all the other activities have parallels if not exact duplicates. When collecting activities on a large scale are part of the library's operations, they may merit the attention of a highly educated specialist full-time, in addition to which the specialist may be assisted by other staff holding fewer credentials, lacking the subject specialty, or both.

Another important function exercised at the end of a collecting cycle that would warrant the attention of a professionally educated librarian or subject specialist is evaluating its outcomes. Assuming the decisions that set priorities among competing needs when those needs cannot all be satisfied are what define collecting activities, they cannot ensure that actual collecting will have the desired results. In this as in all other library functions and services, gaps are not uncommon between goals and results. When gaps occur, it is important to determine whether it was because of coincidental, unforeseen, and/or uncontrollable (and potentially redressable) circumstances; or, by purposeful, systematic efforts to ignore or undermine the library's stated agenda. Nearly everyone with some years of experience in practice has encountered moments when library staff members—intentionally, through ignorance, or merely from a lack of understanding—continue to act as they have in the past, perpetuating the status quo, even though their actions are inconsistent with changed goals and priorities, and are likely to cause problems both for the library and for themselves. Occasionally, such actions are purposeful and intended to confound the library's new agenda. More frequently, the implications of the new agenda are not made sufficiently clear to librarians in nonadministrative positions, who continue to do the same job they did in the past without realizing it is not the job the library wants done any longer. Someone in authority must address the problem and solve it, or face continued failure to reach library goals for as long as it is allowed to persist.

ROLES OF THE PARAPROFESSIONAL WORKER IN THE LIBRARY

Can paraprofessionals select materials to be added or removed from collections? The answer must be "yes," because they have been doing so in many communities all over the nation for many years, either because there are no professionally educated librarians available or, even when there are, because the salaries of these jobs are too low to attract persons holding master's-level credentials. But in parts of the country where professionals generally are employed as selectors, paraprofessionals can—and do—perform the same activities, according to the reports in the literature. Furthermore, some paraprofessionals consider themselves well prepared to do so, based on their knowledge of the information needs of local communities and whatever on-the-job training they may have received.

The emphasis of the literature on selection as the central activity in developing collections overshadows and obscures the activities of paraprofessionals in collection evaluation. Can paraprofessional library workers evaluate collections? Certainly, they can and do contribute to evaluation processes. But few surveys ask specifically about evaluation activities, which might be attributable to the fact that many libraries fail to perform formal evaluations on a regular basis, despite several decades of exhortation to do so from collections specialists. In the author's recent consulting experiences in academic library collection evaluation, it became clear that two factors influence decisions to use paraprofessional workers: the attitudes of library decision makers about doing so and the methods chosen to gather and analyze evaluative data.[36] To save money, maximize available work hours, and develop staff knowledge about evaluation, the author made efforts in every instance to employ paraprofessional workers. At one institution, the suggestion to include paraprofessionals was met with approval, and they participated as follows:

- attended focus interviews held to identify perceived needs and existing attitudes as well as to inform staff about the evaluation project;
- after taking a training session led by the author, selected books for inspection, inspected them, evaluated them, and compiled data about age and the condition of bindings and paper;
- gathered collection statistics running the OCLC/AMIGOS Collection Analysis Compact Disc;
- measured the shelflist to gather collection statistics for materials classified by the Dewey Decimal Classification and Library of Congress classified materials not covered by the Collection Analysis Compact Disc.

At a second institution, the suggestion to employ paraprofessionals was met with mild resistance. Subsequently, circumstances made it impossible for any paraprofessional workers to participate during the consulting phase of the project, which included focus interviews, shelflist measurements, and inspection of books on the shelf similar to, but not the same as, those done in the first library. The consultants initiated, but did not complete, the evaluation of the second institution's collection. Instead, they developed a model using two departments, tested the model with members of the professional staff as a test/training phase, and made adjustments to the procedures which the staff will eventually apply to the balance of the departments and collections. It is quite possible that paraprofessional workers eventually will contribute to the data gathering, for example, running programs with a Collection Analysis Compact Disc, which the institution planned to obtain, and extracting demographic data from college documents; it is less likely they will assist in conducting faculty surveys, another method selected by this institution for their evaluation.

A valid question is the expectation that paraprofessional workers will be employed similarly in different types and sizes of libraries. Consulting experiences described above occurred in two college libraries, both with graduate programs (including a few at the doctoral level), but with a distinct emphasis on the undergraduate mission. Other consulting and research performed by the author and associates at public libraries (varying from small towns in Massachusetts and Rhode Island to medium-sized cities in California and Utah) revealed similar variations from institution to institution over what work was considered appropriate for paraprofessionals. Just because a library serves the general public in contrast to an academic community, or just because it is very small does not mean that paraprofessional workers automatically will be assigned tasks that academic libraries or larger institutions will reserve solely for professional librarians. In this author's experience in teaching at two large research universities and conducting research at two others, it was not unusual to find paraprofessionals in middle management positions, supervising clerical technical service activities, such as monitoring serials, microforms, copy cataloging, and so on. Because the volume of these activities was extremely high—for instance, at one institution 33,000 serial subscriptions were active—monitoring serials occupied a sizeable staff and supervising them was a full-time job, but not necessarily one requiring a great deal of library and information science knowledge. Instead, communicating skillfully, building morale, accomplishing well-defined tasks accurately and promptly—activities we might deem general supervisory skills when they do not also include deciding what is to be communicated, what tasks must be done, by what methods and procedures, and when—comprise the bulk of these middle management positions. (It is not surprising that quite a few of the people holding these positions were enrolled in the master's degree program of the library school at the institution, having decided they could not improve their positions or their salaries without this credential.)

Considering the collection evaluation tasks to which paraprofessionals are being assigned in even the small number of libraries observed directly by the author, an important question is what kinds of skills they require. Do they require the kinds of general supervisory skills identified above, subject or language knowledge at baccalaureate or master's degree levels, simple observation and recording skills, or other non–M.L.S. program knowledge? If that is the case, it would seem logical that the staff performing the tasks do not require a professional library and information science degree. If, on the other hand, they require the kinds of knowledge taught only in M.L.S. programs, a mismatch exists between job descriptions and job preparations, making it difficult for the individuals to perform successfully. At the very least, paraprofessional workers entrusted with tasks requiring selected skills taught in library and information science programs might be subsidized to take one or a few courses directly relevant to their work, even if they do not wish to matriculate in a degree program. Schools of library and information science have a role to play in providing them with the tools for their job, or they will be culpable for abdicating an obligation to their field. Here is a topic where a large-scale study of current activity, both on the part of employing libraries and professional schools, could be fruitful.

IMPACT OF EMERGING ELECTRONIC METHODOLOGIES ON THESE ROLES

Many methods of evaluating library collections are currently in use, including developing descriptive statistics on collection size, age, and condition; checking holdings against printed library catalogs, bibliographies, and guides to the literature; surveying users and acknowledged experts about collection adequacy; examining requests for materials, and so on. Most methods require laborious effort to gather needed data—so much so that a whole literature has developed to help large libraries count hundreds of thousands (or more) of volumes by sampling their collections properly in order to collect credible data with less time and effort.[37] Obviously, the longer the data collection process and the more staff hours it consumes, the more expensive the evaluation project. For a good many libraries, the cost seems to outweigh the perceived benefits of a proposed evaluation, and evaluations are thought to be beyond affordability.

When computer systems began to be implemented in 1970s and 1980s, the opportunity to program them to count the materials ordered, cataloged, and circulated—automatically—and produce useful management reports was recognized, but not accorded sufficiently high priority to result in effective evaluations. With some systems, for instance, patrons might be assigned as many as 1,000 different categories, while materials could be assigned only 100 categories.[38] Management reports based on even that small number of categories could be helpful to collection developers, but lack of foresight on the part of librarians in utilizing available categories effectively left many libraries without even that small measure of help. With early computer systems, however, categories had to be identified and assigned before the computer system was utilized in the library. Librarians focused on making the system perform its central function or functions—ordering, cataloging, or circulating materials, which themselves required hundreds of difficult policy decisions to be made and incorporated into basic system programming. Little time and energy was diverted, as a result, to thinking about the design of management reports. By the time their potential importance became clear, it was too late to reprogram the system properly and assign categories to the thousands of records already entered into its database.

A proper desire to ensure the confidentiality of circulation records prompted computer system designers to arrange for check-ins to erase data about usage. The number of check-outs might be gathered and recorded in individual item records, but in order to make it useful for collection development purposes, the item record for each title in a group of books would have to be viewed separately and its data cumulated with the others either manually or by entering the data into another file. Nonetheless, in sample populations and/or targeted areas, such laborious methods could be warranted to save libraries from purchasing materials of questionable value.

The Research Libraries Group (RLG), in order to facilitate resource sharing, developed a uniform methodology for evaluating collections in specified subject areas, termed the RLG Conspectus.[39] The Conspectus prescribes a division of the collections using Library of Congress Classification number spans, and provides a schema of collecting levels ranging from collecting little or nothing to collecting exhaustively in all languages and media. Best of all, RLIN (Research Libraries Information Network), RLG's shared bibliographic network, maintains the network's Conspectus database online, so once entered, data are retrievable for a variety of purposes. By following the Conspectus, institutions can compare their holdings, knowing that all have defined subjects the same way and that quality judgments are based on the same set of assumptions about collection contents.

The Conspectus methodology appeared at just the right moment, when it was needed to satisfy libraries' quest for better methods of comparing collections, to be used both for evaluative and resource-sharing purposes. Before long, a translation for the Dewey Decimal Classification was devised, so Dewcy libraries would not be excluded from the growing bandwagon for Conspectus-based comparisons.[40] Conspectus-related work was not simple, easy, or quick, because, no matter how innovative the method, it was an inescapably large-scale data-gathering project intended for the nation's largest collections. To expedite their progress (and minimize their costs), librarians working with the Conspectus analyzed it carefully into component tasks and identified those that could be done by paraprofessional and clerical staff.

Another popular and powerful new computer-based tool for evaluating local collections to come on the scene consists of subsets of cataloging records from the databases of the bibliographic networks. These database subsets are being made available to OCLC member libraries by the AMIGOS Bibliographic Network and to Western Library Network (WLN) member libraries by the network.[41] Cataloging records for a specified period of time entered by the evaluating library are downloaded to an optical disk along with similar data for specified groups of libraries with which the evaluating library's collection can be compared. The disk is enhanced with software to manipulate the data, retrieve various kinds of evaluative information, and display or print it. Computer-based collection analysis disks furnish descriptive statistics, comparisons with an average of each of the library groups (called peer groups), and bibliographies of selected titles, but running the programs takes time and requires a computer operator to monitor the procedures, especially when long print runs are generated.

While Conspectus and collection analysis data from OCLC and WLN provide valuable information about book collections, they give no statistics about journal holdings. In the last decade, many studies have been instituted to determine which titles are the most heavily used, in order that those titles deemed expendable could be dropped. As materials budgets have been squeezed more intensely by a combination of inflation and diminishing dollar exchange rates, higher costs of subscriptions and their acquisition, and increased demand from users, libraries have responded by implementing journal deselection projects.[42] Many strategies have been employed, including user surveys, analyses of interlibrary loan records, feedback from online resources and document delivery services, among others. While attention rarely is focused on the status of the personnel who perform the studies by gathering and analyzing data from local automated systems and management report of commercial vendors, it seems a likely possibility that both librarians and paraprofessional workers have been involved.

INTEGRATING THE ROLES OF PROFESSIONAL AND PARAPROFESSIONAL WORKERS

Studies examining the activities of professional and paraprofessional workers in collection development seem to point clearly toward an increasing deprofessionalization of collection development activities—especially selection, but also evaluation—similar to that which occurred a little more than a decade ago for cataloging. It seems to be occurring for the same combination of reasons: technology and economics. Networked computer systems provide all sorts of collection-related data, including evaluative data, automatically. Armed with that data, selectors working for libraries and selectors working for vendors both can identify what materials are in greatest or least demand, or relate most closely to specified subject needs, and so on. Using carefully drawn institutional profiles and mechanical filters, anyone who can read a computer screen and compare bibliographic records can select titles. They also can see where needs match most closely with holdings or, conversely, where they diverge. By quantifying "strength" and "weakness" of collections, anyone can see what is happening. Comparing these data with predefined goals and objectives, anyone can say whether a particular subset of the collections is "good" or "bad," and there is no justification to have an M.L.S. librarian do it.

Two phenomena have occurred in connection with collection evaluation. First, evaluation has been divided into its component parts, and it has become obvious that some do not require professional education and training to execute properly, such as collecting data and analyzing it by means of standardized statistical tests; second, librarians have realized that all of the components do not have to be done by the same person. This author hypothesizes that the more meaningful decisions—setting the collection goals and objectives that will eventually be used as norms against which collecting will be evaluated, planning for income sources and allocating funds, designing evaluative projects and selecting appropriate methodologies for data collection and analysis—are moving "up the line" and being made by higher-level staff (members of a library's top management team) who usually hold the M.L.S., while the more obvious tasks of evaluation, like the more obvious tasks of selection and cataloging, are moving "down the line" and being done by lower level staff (either lower-level librarians or paraprofessionals) who report the results of their work to the decision makers in order to inform their decisions.

To see where professional and near-professional tasks divide, we must look to find where decisions involving subjective judgment are being made. Collection evaluation decisions are being split, on the one hand, into those that select appropriate methodologies for gathering data and set norms for interpreting them; and, on the other, those that merely apply the decisions by conducting specified data-gathering routines or comparing the results against the norms. This represents a new division between professional and paraprofessional tasks in collection development in general and collection evaluation in particular.

The split described here mimics the pattern that occurred ten years ago with cataloging, when it became apparent in large, carefully performed studies such as Hafter's that cataloging decisions had been divided into those that set the norms for cataloging and catalog systems, which moved up the line to administrators (as Hafter perceived with alarm), and those requiring searching and matching skills that could be done by trained paraprofessionals. Far from eliciting alarm, I believe the current trend should be seen as a positive, even a perfectly natural development made possible by maturing computer networks and our understanding of how to utilize them. Although it leaves the M.L.S. librarian with the tougher, riskier decisions to be made, these decisions happen to be the ones that, now, really shape the library's collection and all programs and services based on it. The trend should bring about responses in several areas, including library education and training for collection evaluation, and staffing patterns in libraries of all types and sizes.[43]

Two areas that beg for immediate and close investigation are the curricula covering collection development in library school programs and the deployment of collection development staff members in all types of libraries. Curricula should be examined to ensure that current M.L.S. students are being properly prepared for the work they will be assigned when they get into practice, not just the tasks of their first entry-level jobs.[44] For instance, they should be taught to think of collecting as more than just selecting titles, one by one, to be purchased for the library's shelves. Instead, they will have to know how to create long- and short-range goals for the collection, translate them into measurable objectives, devise funding plans to ensure they can be met, and evaluative projects to measure the results. Collection development librarians must be prepared to negotiate with vendors, lobby with funding bodies, guide selectors (some of whom probably will be knowledgeable paraprofessionals), and coordinate the differing agendas of individual departments and constituencies. Among the areas of knowledge required to perform these tasks successfully are research methods and statistics, risk management, problem solving, and finance. Learning how to write and speak fluently, easily, and persuasively, teach and train well, and interact comfortably with people at all levels is important. It would be marvelous if creativity could be taught in a classroom, but perhaps that goes beyond the realm of the possible. The curriculum should address time and stress management as well as decision making. While it must teach entry-level tasks (where else might the student-librarian be introduced to them?), it should go beyond them to the principles and theoretical constructs underlying both collecting itself and evaluation. That work is harder to teach and to learn, but far more important in today's networked environment than individual acts of selection and, ultimately, much more satisfying.

Similarly, librarians should want to ensure they are using staff well, not wastefully, by assigning appropriate levels of tasks to each level of staff employed by the library. Unfortunately, my personal storehouse of anecdotal evidence indicates that practitioners fail to have unblemished track records in doing this. Too many former students returning for visits to Simmons College reveal that they have been hired to do copy cataloging full-time, or most of the time, with reference desk duty ("teach-'em-how-to-use-Index X"-type bibliographic instruction lectures), or selection tasks filling out the balance. Too many people still seem to be saying that selecting books or answering reference questions is *always* M.L.S.-level work, without acknowledging the lessons we should have learned from the Brandeis model. While neophyte librarians might fruitfully be put to such tasks while they are "learning the ropes" of a new library, this teacher, for one, fervently hopes it is for a limited time only during which they receive the on-the-job training and gain the practical, hands-on experience needed to enable them to move on quickly to other, more responsible and meaningful tasks.

At the same time, there are colleagues who will disagree and dispute these interpretations. M.L.S.-educated librarians who have spent their entire careers selecting materials or cataloging books may believe themselves and their life's work demeaned by the idea that what they have done is not considered professional any longer. However, far from demeaning their efforts up to the time of this writing (although the handwriting has been on the wall for more than a decade), this author applauds their perseverance in accomplishing by hand the tasks that created quality collections in the nonautomated and minimally networked environment. I recognize and proclaim openly that the key factor making these new and different interpretations possible is technology—more specifically, technological advances in networking that make it possible to share computerized data in ways most library and information specialists could not have predicted twenty years ago. These colleagues above all others should be inspired and invigorated to realize how much more is being accomplished by both M.L.S. librarians and paraprofessionals—working together—to meet the expanding information needs of library patrons.

NOTES

This chapter is dedicated to the memory of my good friend, Elizabeth Futas, a leading librarian and educator, who was to co-author it with me. She died suddenly, without warning, on February 8, 1995, at a meeting of the American Library Association in Philadelphia. Her vision for building library collections included a profound respect for partnership among various levels of staff.

1. Ruth Hafter, *Academic Librarians and Cataloging Networks: Visibility, Quality Control, and Professional Status* (Westport, CT: Greenwood Press, 1986), pp. 63–78.

2. Ibid., p. 125. Specifically, she says: "... the actual practice of cataloging is being restructured so that routine and standardized records available in the database can be manipulated by library assistants and clerks, rather than catalogers."

3. Ibid.

4. For example, in a 1992 editorial, Berry says, "Despite the good wishes and intentions of the 'professionals' who have laid claim to the title 'librarian,' members of the new movement will have to take whatever power they can on their own. . . . They want both recognition and compensation when so-called 'professional' duties are reassigned to them, as they are so often in tough times." By putting 'professionals' in quotations, the author questions the truth of its characterization, both of the M.L.S.-holding persons who call themselves professionals and the tasks with which they have been identified, which he goes further to call "so-called." John N. Berry III, "The 'Other Librarians' Organize." *Library Journal* 118 (November 1, 1992): 8.

5. See Figure 1, Brian A. Nettlefold, "Paraprofessionalism in Librarianship," *International Library Review* 21 (1989): 530.

6. Ibid., p. 526.

7. Larry R. Oberg, Mark E. Mentges, P. N. McDermott, and Vitoon Harusadangkul, "The Role, Status, and Working Conditions of Paraprofessionals: A National Survey of Academic Libraries," *College & Research Libraries* 53 (May 1992): 215–38.

8. Ibid., p. 219.

9. Ibid., p. 231.

10. Ibid., Table 8, p. 225.

11. Ibid.

12. Ibid., p. 233.

13. Patricia A. Kreitz and Annegret Ogden, "Job Responsibilities and Job Satisfaction at the University of California Libraries," *College & Research Libraries* 51 (July 1990): 297–312.

14. Ibid., Tables 3 and 4, p. 303.

15. Charles W. Brownson, "Mechanical Selection," *Library Resources & Technical Services* 32 (1988): 17–30; Margo Sasse and Patricia A. Smith, "Automated Acquisitions: The Future of Collection Development," *Library Acquisitions: Practice & Theory* 16 (1992): 135–43.

16. Ibid., p. 142.

17. Ibid.

18. Daniel R. Smith, *The Characteristics, Use, and Training of Reference Nonprofessionals in Selected Southeastern Urban Public Libraries* (University of Illinois Graduate School of Library and Information Science Occasional Paper) (Urbana: University of Illinois, Graduate School of Library and Information Science, 1991), pp. 3–39.

19. Ibid., p. 26.

20. Virginia Massey-Burzio, "Reference Encounters of a Different Kind: A Symposium," *Journal of Academic Librarianship* 18 (1992): 276–86.

21. In reporting on a discussion held at the 1994 American Library Association midwinter conference, Ron L. Ray says, "This discussion of paraprofessionals' roles offered an opportunity . . . to examine whether a corollary of the 'Brandeis Model' for staffing a reference department was applicable or workable within collection development." Ron L. Ray, "Paraprofessionals in Collection Development: Report of the ALCTS CMDS Collection Development Librarians of Academic Libraries Discussion Group," *Library Acquisitions: Practice & Theory* 18 (Fall 1994): 317–20.

22. Ibid., p. 317.

23. Ibid., pp. 317–18.

24. Ibid., pp. 318–19.

25. Ibid., p. 319.

26. Ibid., pp. 319–20.

27. Susanne Nevin, "Evaluating the Children's Literature Collection: A College Library's Experience," *Collection Management* 19 (1994): 127–33.

28. Ibid., p. 127.

29. Ibid., pp. 127–28.

30. Anthony W. Ferguson, "Response to Tony Angiletta's Response on No. 475 Para-Professionals in Collection Development," COLLDV-L, May 24, 1994.

31. "Education Collection Developers: In the Classroom or On-the-Job?" Program sponsored by the Committee on Education for Collection Development, Collection Management and Development Section, Association for Library Collections and Technical Services, and the Collection Development and Evaluation Section of the Reference and Adult Services Division of the American Library Association, held in Chicago, Illinois, Saturday, June 24, 1995, at the American Library Association annual conference.

32. Mary T. Kainin, Wendee Eyler, and Susan Ryan, "The Paraprofessional in Today's Libraries," *Library Mosaics* 5 (May/June 1994): 16–18.

33. Larry R. Oberg, "The Emergence of the Paraprofessional in Academic Libraries: Perceptions and Realities," *College & Research Libraries* 53 (March 1992): 99–112.

34. Ibid., p. 108.

35. Ibid., p. 109. See Allen B. Veaner, "Librarians: The Next Generation," *Library Journal* 109 (April 1, 1984): 624.

36. In order to protect the anonymity of the institutions, citations to the unpublished reports of their consultancies are not given. However, the author directly observed all the activities herself and hopes the reader will forego the lack of cited documentation.

37. A recent example of such articles is: Beth M. Paskoff and Anna H. Perrault, "A Tool for Comparative Collection Analysis: Conducting a Shelflist Sample to Construct a Collection Profile," *Library Resources & Technical Services* 34 (April 1990): 199–215. In his bibliography of collection evaluation between 1980 and 1990–1991, Nisonger devotes a chapter to methodology containing five substantial articles of this type, including Paskoff and Perrault's. Thomas E. Nisonger, *Collection Evaluation in Academic Libraries: A Literature Guide and Annotated Bibliography* (Englewood, CO: Libraries Unlimited, 1992), pp. 23–25. Earlier literature included many more such titles.

38. This was the case with the automated circulation system purchased by the public library in which the author worked in 1978, and implemented the following year.

39. In his bibliography, Nisonger devotes a whole chapter to the RLG Conspectus and its counterpart for smaller libraries, the Pacific Northwest Conspectus. The chapter begins with a good description of the tools themselves and lists 60 articles about them, plus more articles about cooperative projects based on them, such as the North American Collections Inventory Project.

40. The Dewey translation was introduced as part of a cooperative project known as the "Library and Information Resources for the Northwest Program" (LIRN). Responsibility for it and a Library of Congress classification version of Conspectus for smaller libraries now is managed by the Western Library Network.

41. Nisonger also devotes a chapter to automated evaluation methodologies, in which these tools are mentioned and some of the early literature is cited. For several years, OCLC has distributed bibliographies of articles about the AMIGOS Collection Analysis Compact Disc that have grown from a single page to three pages.

42. A section of Nisonger's chapter "Evaluation of Serials" is titled "Serials Cancellation Case Studies," which includes twenty-seven articles.

43. For a discussion of some of the educational issues as they affected cataloging, see: Sheila S. Intner, "The Education of Copy Catalogers," in *Interfaces: Relationships between Library Technical and Public Services* (Englewood, CO: Libraries Unlimited, 1993), pp. 160–65.

44. An excellent description of what should be covered in a proper preparation for new librarians may be found in: Peggy Johnson, "Collection Development Officer, a Reality Check: A Personal View," *Library Resources & Technical Services* 33 (April 1989): 153–60. Johnson elaborated on the topic in her chapter, "Collection Development Is More Than Selecting a Title: Educating for a Variety of Responsibilities," in *Recruiting, Educating, and Training Librarians for Collection Development*, ed. Peggy Johnson and Sheila S. Intner (Westport, CT: Greenwood Press, 1994), pp. 113–26.

PART V

Electronic Document Delivery and Resource Preservation

8

Electronic Document Delivery Services and Their Impact on Collection Management

Graham P. Cornish

INTRODUCTION

The widespread use of electronic technology to produce, store, manipulate, and distribute information of all kinds is one of the great achievements of the information age. The arrival of digital technologies for handling text, sound, and visual images has made the possibilities almost limitless. Not only can material be manipulated within its own form, but multimedia packages can be created through information from different sources which can be downloaded, copied, edited, and repackaged to suit the individual user or to generate completely new products which can be made available on the open information market. These capabilities will inevitably be reflected (and should, in my view, be led) by radical changes in document supply services, and therefore will impact on the whole concept of collection management.

At one time, interlibrary loan was a minor activity carried out by junior staff on a quiet afternoon when there were few readers about requiring attention, but this is no longer the case. It is not sufficient to view interlibrary cooperation of this kind as merely a supplementary activity to support the needs of the few which cannot be met by the collection designed to meet the needs of the many; rather, interlibrary loan should be seen as an essential adjunct to collection management. It is, after all, a mechanism whereby a library satisfies the needs of a reader which cannot be met through the existing collection which was built through a combination of expertise and intuition. It often has been argued that, with continually improving capabilities of electronic document transfer, the time of comprehensive library collections is coming to an end. Libraries can, and should, concentrate on the core collection and rely on remote supply for everything else. The argument over access versus holdings is a long and complex one.[1] Although that argument as such does not intrinsically rest on document delivery being electronic, the capabilities of such systems to meet one of the basic requirements of document delivery systems (namely, speed) better than paper systems cannot be denied, although the other criteria—cost, quality of material, and reliability—may be no better, and can often be worse, than the paper environment. The argument has as much to do with storage space, staffing levels, equipment costs, user requirements, and records management. The specific benefit of electronic document delivery is seen to rest on all these arguments, and on others as well.

WHAT DOES IT MEAN?

Electronic document delivery can be seen in terms of both interlibrary and intralibrary supply. The two scenarios have some similarities but many differences, largely brought about by the differing attitudes of publishers to these technologically similar, but administratively different, situations.[2] For the purposes of this discussion, electronic document delivery means supplying a text in electronic form which is required by a reader, but which is not in the library being used by the reader at that time. The format in which it is supplied to the reader may be electronic or paper as a result of an electronic signal, but the transmission of the document will be done electronically. This rather cumbersome definition is important as the boundaries between fax and electronic delivery become less clear.

THE CHANGING ROLE OF THE LIBRARY

The role of the library is not limited to making available a range of publications and information to a specified group of users. The library is a crucial element in the publishing industry as such. While nobody questions that publishers publish for profit, the basis for the activities of the industry is to make the creativity of authors more widely known to the public. Indeed, aside from the recreational and education writing markets, most authors write not for profit but to make ideas more widely known, despite Boswell's cynical remark that "Nobody except a fool ever wrote except for profit." But no author or publisher can reach all potential readers of any work and therefore both need intermediaries. Although booksellers fulfill part of this role, they provide only those materials which are likely to sell, and therefore their role as intermediaries is limited to commercially attractive material. On the other hand, libraries are used by millions of people who never have any intention of buying their information nor have the economic power to do so. The library provides the interface between the publisher and the untapped, and untappable market, and therefore enables one aim of publishing—to reach the public—to be more effectively achieved. This achievement is largely at the expense of taxpayers throughout the world.

THE CHANGING NATURE OF DOCUMENT SUPPLY

Libraries have never been able to meet all the needs of their users from their own collections, and what we now call document supply (and once called interlibrary loan) can be traced back to the Middle Ages. Interlibrary loan is traditionally about transferring a document (rather than a copy of a document) from one library to another, thereby temporarily enriching the collection of one library while depleting that of another. On the other hand, we still think of document delivery as a system for supplying copies, but the meaning of ''a copy'' in the electronic environment is something which needs to be reconsidered. Where the document is held in paper form and an electronic copy required, then clearly a copy is made; but when the original document is held electronically, then what is transmitted may or may not be considered a copy, depending on all kinds of technical questions. At what point is a copy supplied? Does the mere transmission of an electronic version mean a copy has been provided, or does this not happen until that signal has reached its destination? When the signal reaches its destination, is it a copy immediately or only when downloaded or converted into paper? Does the fact that the signal has been received and can be viewed on the screen mean that delivery has been achieved? It is important to decide on these definitions, because their interpretation will become important when dealing with suppliers of text and the conditions under which material is supplied.

Today lending has given way to copying, and the number of photocopies provided by libraries through various networks and cooperative schemes is now several million a year worldwide, and growing, as recent U.K. statistics demonstrate.[3] While this copying took place in the same way as the traditional copying by libraries, publishers wcrc irritated but not unduly concerned about it. However, the growth of the document supply industry, focused as it is on a few major centers, concentrates the mind on the volume of copies being made and makes the process seem very unfair even if, in terms of the individual receiving the copy, it is no different from traditional library copying. Such systems will work only if they supply what is needed to the person who needs it at an affordable price. In addition, it has to be remembered that, even if a system can technically achieve everything the user wants, it may fall foul of legal or political constraints.

The document delivery industry is now moving to a stage where the real issues are concerned with electronic copying, storing, and transmission and the flexibility which this gives for repackaging to meet users' specific information needs. The role of the library will change from supplying information and documents to supplying packages of information. The desire for information is a constant feature of current cultural patterns, particularly in the industrialized world. The information may be supplied in various ways: newspapers, journals and books, radio, television, teletext, or online system. Document supply is one aspect of the way that demand is being satisfied. In the more sophisticated reaches of the information supply industry, librarians are not simply renamed "information scientists" but transmogrified into "knowledge scientists." A knowledge scientist is not expected simply to provide information but to interpret it for the customer. This particular trend leads those in this situation to receive requests for appropriate data, suitably packaged, on a given topic or aspect of a topic. The resulting package may be a mixture of statistics, manipulated data, law, company information, economic projections and predictions—and even some documents. The knowledge scientist will be required to obtain such documents either locally or from remote sources. The customer in this situation has little interest in where or how the document was procured so long as it supplies the information needs of the time. Although this is one extreme of the information supply spectrum, it is nevertheless symptomatic of an increasing trend in the information industry at all levels. Documents are vehicles for information in the widest sense. This naturally has a profound effect on the nature of libraries and of document supply. How long libraries can remain the information archive of society is an open issue at present, and technology does not necessarily hold all the answers.

WHAT CAN BE SUPPLIED?

Can a document supply service provide access to absolutely everything? Technologically, virtually anything can be supplied, and in a variety of formats, to meet different needs; but studies show that demand is likely to be for current material, often with scientific and technical content.[4] This is not to say that all demand is for this type of material. Also a distinction needs to be made between material which is currently in paper form and that which is produced in electronic format. There will certainly be a demand to convert paper copies to electronic form, and this will often form part of a wider collection management program for preservation purposes as well as considerations of storage, but this will only be possible with the agreement of the publishers in the long term, except where material is particularly old.

Although many countries may now permit the conversion of paper documents to digital form for preservation purposes, their subsequent transmission to those outside the library is at best problematic. This raises questions not only of document supply but also of the economics of digitization. If the use to which such electronic documents can be put is much more limited, perhaps the potential savings are not as beneficial as was at first considered, especially if a library fulfills a significant document supply role locally, regionally, or nationally. Even where electronic documents will be used only within a specific campus or community, publishers will be reluctant to grant such permission for digitization without adequate safeguards and may complain if legislation permits such copying; the process of digitization, even if intended for preservation purposes, inevitably will extend the ways in which such documents can be used within a campus and thus add value to the documents. This will be seen by publishers as unfair, and they may seek recompense in the form of additional royalties or fees. Several experiments are taking place at present, but these are often accepted by the publishing community only because they are experiments. Permanent arrangements will be viewed very differently. However, there is a growing demand also for older material which has been digitized for preservation purposes, and technology makes it possible to transmit high quality images as well as text. Where materials are produced in electronic formats, it is probable, as already happens, that the publishers will allow access to this material only under conditions which will probably limit the use of such electronic data for remote transmission and supply. In these circumstances it can be seen why photocopying is rapidly becoming an old technology whose threats are more perceived than real.

Although document supply was once a rather minor element in library provision, it has now become a major contributor to the flow of information, and in a rapidly changing technological age its role is becoming more crucial and its accomplishment easier.[5] Therefore, document supply systems need to be able to deliver documents in whatever form they are produced and needed. Digitization is one area of growing importance, but this must not be seen solely in terms of textual information. The rapidly growing industry for the conversion of old and rare materials into a format which enables them to be transmitted to anywhere in the world (with the appropriate receiving equipment) is itself having a major impact on document delivery and collection management.[6]

At the other end of the spectrum will be the increasing need to be able to supply documents which include sound and moving images as well as computer software and interactive media. Here the collection manager will face severe problems. The acquisition of these types of materials is not as straightforward as for printed materials and usually includes conditions of sale or licenses which prohibit the use of such materials outside the institution for which they have been purchased. Therefore, the ability of any one library to meet the requirements of another through interlibrary arrangements or document supply will become more limited. Requests for such documents as directories and encyclopedias between libraries is quite common, but as these reference materials are increasingly made available only in electronic form, at present on CD-ROM, they will not be available for loan.

An increasingly popular way of making documents available is reciprocity. This arrangement allows registered users of one library to have access to the facilities of another library, usually in the same geographical area. However, many electronic documents have attached to them not only site licenses but

user-group licenses as well, so that even an accredited user from another institution would not be allowed to use them.

It is therefore clear that document supply systems will not be able to continue
meeting all the needs of users that cannot be satisfied by their own libraries.
The clear implication for collection management is that libraries will be forced
either to expand their electronic collections, probably at the expense of traditional paper collections, or contract them because, increasingly, the paper documents will no longer be available. One crucial issue which collection managers
must face is the technical requirements of modern document supply systems.
There is little use in one library making documents available electronically if
the receiving library or user does not have access to the necessary equipment.
Material may be available but not in the form needed, and there may be no
legal way to overcome this barrier.[7] The traditional book or periodical can be
used by most people without formality. The new methods of transmitting and
storing information require the library to possess and maintain an increasingly
wide range of sophisticated equipment which may be charged against the collection budget in order to use what has been acquired. Most people are familiar
with the note on interlibrary loan forms: "not in microfilm—we don't have a
reader." This will become much more common when a range of hardware and
software is needed to operate CD-ROMs, interactive videodisks, and multimedia
packages. Those in less-developed countries will, of course, find themselves
even more deprived, but the gulf between the "haves" and "have nots," even
in developed countries, will become increasingly obvious. How many public
libraries will be able to afford such equipment from shrinking acquisitions budgets? Those in the academic sphere may be able to turn to colleagues in technical
departments for help, but many others eventually will be starved of information.
At one time, budgetary constraints could be balanced by increased use of interlibrary cooperation; but if this is not possible because of contractual or technical
reasons, then where will the desperate user turn?

WHO SHALL REQUEST?

Making requests for electronic documents is rapidly becoming one of the
major issues in electronic document delivery. Users will not perceive the need
for an intermediary and will simply search, request, and receive, sitting at their
desks. This obviously bypasses not only the librarian but the library collection,
which may well have the document ready to hand at little or no cost, whereas
the electronic delivery will certainly be expensive and may have serious restrictions placed upon it.

Does all this mean the end of the relationship between the users and their
libraries as far as document supply is concerned? The answer is almost certainly
"no."[8] The electronic information triangle, by which bibliographic citations are
identified, requests in electronic form generated, and the document supplied
through the electronic network in a matter of minutes, has been likened to the

Bermuda Triangle. In the Bermuda Triangle it is aircraft that disappear, whereas in the information triangle it is the reader who vanishes from the library. This almost certainly will not be the case. While the workstation may be the answer to the introvert reader's prayer, most human beings are interactive in nature and require the interface between themselves and other groups of people and systems. In addition, the good researcher will not rely only on electronic materials but will see the value of paper and older material stored in a central source, commonly called a library. The ability to browse documents and interact with other people working in both similar and very different disciplines is essential to intellectual growth and academic research and will not be displaced by an electronic screen.

Nevertheless, libraries will have to work much harder to entice readers to come in. The supermarket approach of telling people what they need rather than suggesting what they might want will have to be an integral part of library management in the future. Essentially, such marketing will have to include material not immediately available on-site in the library. If readers do not mind where documents come from, then the maximum exposure to available materials must be achieved, and their access should be made as easy and as quick as possible. Users will ask less and less frequently if a document is available; they will ask only the other two questions in document supply: how soon and how much?

If document supply is perceived to be part of the acquisitions procedure, which it certainly should be, then the question will arise as to who should control this freelance requesting of documents from elsewhere. If the library already holds the document required, then surely the user should be prevented from making an external request which will cost more and mean that the library is being underutilized. Where unit costs are being studied, any such decline eventually will have a significant effect on library budgets. At the same time, it may be that the library cannot or will not meet the particular needs of a user as regards speed, quality, or success. Where an institution is multicampus or even multinational, some users cannot go physically to the library to consult works. Others may find the investment of time and effort not worthwhile when the document can be delivered directly to them by a network far more quickly, and possibly using technology which ensures a better quality copy than the library is using on the local area network within the institution. Add to this the fact that many document suppliers now guarantee delivery if the work is held by them; then this compares badly with the library where a work may be unavailable for various reasons. The library may hold works in electronic form rather than in paper, and these can be delivered under the same quality and economic constraints as outside suppliers can achieve. Usually, such delivery will be cheaper than from an external source and can be guaranteed, because nobody "borrows" electronic documents, nor do they disappear to the bindery for several weeks. There will be pressure on collection managers to focus on documents in electronic form to make sure that maximum use is made of them and unit costs kept down or even reduced. Naturally, such products carry a higher price than conventional paper, precisely because they do offer multipoint access, often simultaneously, and the costing exercises then become more complex. They also totally inhibit the concept of interlibrary cooperation for the purposes of document supply.

WHO SHALL SUPPLY?

Patterns of interlibrary loan and document supply have changed radically over the years.[9] Beginning as an exercise in mutual support, they rapidly became activities in which a few supplied the needs of the many, although everyone in the system was both a supplier and a user. The growth of the document supply center changed this model for some countries so that it became much more focused on one, or at most a few, institution(s). Where such dependence was focused on one major resource, any decline in the services of that resource, or significant increase in the cost of its services, caused, and causes, serious information decline in parts of the world other than that primarily serviced by that resource. With the growth of online networks the emphasis has changed once again, and increasingly document supply is a cooperative activity in which a large number of libraries play a part. At the same time, growth of the commercial document supplier has led to a diversity of sources not previously contemplated. Thus, the simple answer to the question ''who will supply?'' is not, as some think it should be, either other libraries or other libraries within the organization, but anyone who can offer the right kinds of services to meet the needs of the user.

The situation is further complicated by the entry into the field of publishers themselves. As the producers of most of the documents which our libraries buy and collect, it would appear logical that publishers should join in the provision of such services; but they face severe restrictions when doing so. Publishers will want to supply direct to users in order to cut out the intermediaries (libraries, booksellers, database hosts) and provide direct access. Libraries will then become direct competitors with publishers and with each other. Document supply services will want to offer such access to a wide range of materials in both electronic and paper form, the latter converted into electronic form for the purpose of transmission. To continue to play this vital role, such services need to reach soundly based understandings with the other players in the information industry. Users need to be educated to understand the true value of the material they wish to use and the economic importance of it to the industry at large; information intermediaries need to remember they earn their living by exploiting the intellectual property of others; and copyright owners need to consider the importance that libraries play in disseminating their works.

With changing mechanisms, document supply is increasingly an activity undertaken by commercial organizations, subscription agents, and library cooperatives. This makes document supply into an industry rather than a library service.

At the same, time these new suppliers all offer a fairly limited repertoire rather than a wide variety of documents. Increasingly, document suppliers also concentrate on specific subjects such as engineering, law, or science. The development of document supply functions by online database vendors is having a major impact on traditional models of document supply. For example, some databases allow subject searches producing bibliographic records to be transmitted automatically to the appropriate document supply source (either a library or a commercial document supplier) without any further formality. This may not be the more usual source of supply and so will change document supply routes for that library, possibly permanently. Although databases offer ease of access and request, they may not necessarily provide sources which are the most efficient in performance terms.

Another model is that the online database does not itself offer document supply but rather a range of facilities for transmitting the request to document supply services with which it has reached agreement but which it does not itself control. Thus, a search on a database might offer BLDSC, INIST, and several academic libraries as possible alternative sources for a document, leaving the librarian free to choose within those offered. The difficulty here is that the choices offered may not include those which would have been selected if the librarian had not been faced with a predetermined list. Thus, several local sources may not be included on the database, although these are known to be readily available and easily accessible, possibly at little or no cost. Some utilities, such as OCLC, offer a rotation facility so that requests are directed to different libraries at different times to share the burden of supply. However, this can also undermine the individual librarian's free choice of the best source of supply for a particular user.

The changing technology means that delivery of documents to end users, for so long seen by publishers as beyond their capabilities, becomes a reality. This naturally alters publishers' attitudes to libraries, which are seen as being in competition. However, libraries and document suppliers can also be seen as agents for publishers, as their activities are interpreted as surrogate publishing. They can also bring benefits to publishers, as they reach markets beyond the publishers' capabilities and could therefore collect royalties as well as disseminate published works more widely.

In a fiercely economic world there may be a temptation for some collection managers to see their resources as ones from which they might generate some revenue by exploiting their role in the document supply industry. This is an industry which is very competitive, and careful attention needs to be paid to the detailed costs of any attempt to break into it. While demand is small, most libraries can manage to cope with interlibrary requests. When the volume grows, the demand must reach a critical mass before it becomes feasible to dedicate staff and resources specifically to this activity. Until that critical mass is reached, document supply can be a very demanding activity in both money and staff time. Once the critical mass has been passed, then constant monitoring of costs is essential to ensure that the mass continues to be accurately identified. Neither can document supply be seen as a pot of gold from a user viewpoint. The conflict between lending and reference has been discussed, classically by the "father" of document supply, Donald Urquhart.[10] This conflict can be reduced by the use of document supply rather than interlending, but there still remains a real conflict when the needs of browsing users are disrupted by the removal of material, even for photocopying activities.

In the case of documents acquired in electronic format, then, the concept of document supply becomes far more complex, as already remarked. Initially, libraries may see themselves as having little to do with electronic document supply when the material is already acquired in this form. After all, if they can access it, so can their users, often directly. When electronic publishing is still a small segment of the industry, this is likely to be have some truth, but the information overload which most users will suffer when they have unlimited access to electronic documents will soon require an intermediary to act as a filter, evaluator, and general guide. In this milieu the library should once again be able to fulfill the role of document supplier as, unlike paper, access to electronic documents can be multiple in nature. However, the whole question of licensing and royalties will once again creep in to thwart the library in its good intentions.

WHO SHALL PAY?

The problems in the area of payment and charging are complex. Electronic document delivery is not cheap. The technology needed to achieve high-quality services and copies is very expensive when the actions of digitizing, storing, transmitting, reproducing, and displaying are all examined individually. It may cost only a few cents to transmit a document, but someone has to bear the cost of investment in high-quality terminals, transmission modes (cable, satellite, etc.), technical support staff, and training of both staff and users. There are also considerable costs involved in the technology to set up scanners and store material digitally. Statistics show that many documents are used only once in document delivery systems, so the unit cost of digitizing a single document can be very high unless use is stimulated. There is also the issue of who will pay for access to electronic databases which are available only on subscription. This is a live issue already with librarians but will become even more controversial as such databases are used for remote access. Just who pays for the supply of the final copy (whatever that means) is an issue with which the paper world has grappled for many years already, and the electronic environment in no way changes the arguments in this area; it only heightens them because of the costs involved. One approach is to say that, when supply is direct to the user, it should be the user who pays. But why? If the library is responsible for document supply, surely it should bear the cost of that operation, however it is achieved. An alternative is to say that users pay for what they request unless it is through the library. This would almost certainly shift much use from the individual terminal to the library as such, with obvious consequences for budgetary administration.

This issue comes down to control. If document supply is part of acquisitions then it should be funded from that source; but if it is used instead of exploiting existing resources, then it should be viewed as a luxurious extra, and the library budget should not be involved. There is a general view within the library profession that interlending is a cooperative activity which is mutually beneficial to all libraries taking part in the exercise. Therefore, in this general climate of goodwill there is a prevailing feeling that interlending should be free. This feeling is based more on an innate reaction to the idea of cooperation than on any real financial or managerial theory or practice. "Free" has many meanings and applications, and it is important from the outset to understand these, identify them, and make sure that those involved in interlending really understand what "free" actually means.

A first principle in any operation is that any activity has a cost, either in cash terms or in other resources such as manpower, equipment, or consumables. Any participation in an interlending system will almost certainly require some expenditure in all of these areas, whether it is as a borrower or a lender. Staff at all levels in interlending need to be aware of these demands on resources so that decisions on priorities can be made in an informed way. The ratio of resources to request for interlending is higher than that for documents supplied directly from the library's own collection, and it may be necessary to justify such expenditure on these types of request. Areas where resources are most in demand in interlending must be identified. A difficulty in training staff to make decisions in this area is the vastly different circumstances in which they operate.[11] In a large academic or government library the quantity of interlending requests may well be sufficient to justify several members of staff being devoted solely to this activity. There may well be a proper managerial structure to operate the system. The activity will be fully recognized as an integral part of the library's services. At the other end of the scale, interlending may be an occasional activity in a small general public library, or a small part of the activity of a library or information unit operated by a single member of staff. In these circumstances a very different approach to the financing and management of interlending will be required.

At the same time, it seems unfair that a user might have to pay to obtain access to something which the library does not have, yet the same user does not pay for access to something which the library does have and for which it paid out of its own budget. On the one hand, it could be argued that users should not be penalized because the library could not anticipate their needs; on the other hand, should the library pay because users' needs take them outside the normal parameters of the library collection profile? Perhaps such needs should be paid for by those funds which are provided to enable such intellectual adventures to take place.

Where electronic documents are concerned, it is most unlikely that the library will acquire anything which is not firmly within its normal profile; and the more esoteric publications will probably be accessed through interested departments in academic and commercial libraries and by individuals as necessary in the public library sector.

THE LAW

All these wonderful things can be achieved technically, and our users can have access to almost anything in electronic form, if that is their desire or need. But will it be permitted? It seems most unlikely. In order to use material in this form it is necessary to assure the owner of the intellectual property that it will not be unreasonably exploited. Most owners fear the digital world, as it poses threats of unlicensed copying, distribution, and reuse. There is also the fear of works being changed and their meaning altered and authorship being wrongly attributed so that real creators do not gain from their work. Only where a rights owner can properly control a work and gain remuneration from it will there be any willingness to open up the electronic market. A combination of control, information, and remuneration will be necessary; otherwise the limitations which owners put on the use of their works will become so restrictive that users will not be able to use them for any meaningful research. This will add significantly to the cost of access to information and may distort the market for electronic document delivery.

Legal attitudes will also be changed considerably by the changing way that information is packaged. The emphasis on journal articles, rather than journal titles, is a trend to be noted, as it underlies a major change in attitude by publishers to their rights, apart from its impact on the patterns of document supply. Journals are convenient methods of packaging a group of materials with some mutual relevance. In electronic publishing this is less true. Individual articles can be stored in a database independently of one another but brought together through the medium of individual search strategies. Therefore, in this context the individual article becomes a published unit in its own right rather than being a unit within a package. The continued emphasis on the journal in the electronic environment is just one example of old concepts and jargon being forced to fit into a new situation where they may well be no longer appropriate or relevant. Until we divest ourselves of many of these paper-based concepts, many of the issues with which we are struggling will never be resolved.

However, there are signs of progress to resolve some of these issues, and projects such as CITED (Copyright in Transmitted Electronic Documents), and its practical application in distance learning in Project COPICAT, may yet show the way to enable electronic document delivery to become a reality rather than something which is technologically possible but legally prohibited—the worst scenario of all.[12]

THE FUTURE

What hope, then, is there for the traditional interlibrary activity as distinct from document supply direct to individuals? Probably quite a lot. In the first place, individuals, seated at their computer workstations, will rapidly realize that they are subject to information overload and will need assistance in identifying the best information sources for their needs. Second, it can be demonstrated quite easily that when individuals have access to unlimited resources, they start out with a type of "infomania" mentality. Everything that is remotely relevant to the subjects under consideration is retrieved and looked at, and then often rapidly discarded. This is a very costly exercise which leads to a further reason for users to return to the library environment. Even where libraries begin to charge commercial rates for document supply and information searching, these charges are still significantly lower than those which individual online hosts and other services will levy on the individual user. Some individuals may view the Internet as the salvation of their information needs, but this has a limited range of materials available, often excluding the most valuable items for research. In any case, there is a serious question mark over whether free Internet access and services will continue to remain free.

Putting together the human, technological, and economic aspects of information retrieval, it will only be a short time before the individual finds it not only preferable but necessary to return to the information warehouse—the library. Here, of course, a wide range of materials will be identified to meet researchers' needs, and the skilled librarian or information worker will then identify the best ways by which this material can be retrieved, and we shall return to the traditional interlibrary activity once again, albeit using quite different technological carriers.

NOTES

1. Eleanor A. Gossen and Suzanne Irving, "Ownership versus Access and Low-Use Periodical Titles," *Library Resources and Technical Services* 39 (1995): 43–52; Michael Wooliscroft, "Access and Ownership: Academic Libraries' Collecting and Service Responsibilities and the Emerging Benefits of Electronic Publishing and Document Supply," *New Zealand Libraries* 47 (1994): 170–80.

2. Karen Hunter and Jaco Zijlstra, "TULIP: The University Licensing Project," *Journal of Interlibrary Loan, Document Delivery & Information Supply* 4 (1994): 19–22; Jaco Zijlstra, "The University Licensing Program (TULIP): A Large Scale Experiment in Bringing Electronic Journals to the Desktop," *Serials* 7 (1994): 169–72.

3. Roy Huse and John Sumsion, *Inter-Library Lending Statistics* (Loughborough: Loughborough University of Technology, Library and Information Statistics Unit, 1995).

4. Graham P. Cornish, *Interlending and Document Supply in Europe* (Paris: Unesco, 1990).

5. Jeremy Rees, "Information Access versus Document Supply: The International

Visual Arts Information Network Project," *Interlending & Document Supply* 22 (1994): 20–24.

6. Mary Brandt Jensen, "Copying for the Future: Electronic Preservation," *Document Delivery World* 9 (1993): 29–31.

7. Graham P. Cornish, "The Philosophy behind International Interlending and Its Implications for the Visually Handicapped," *Interlending & Document Supply* 19 (1991): 7–10.

8. Graham P. Cornish, "The Superhighway and the Information Intermediary," in *Nordic Conference on Copyright Issues, Copenhagen, 22–23 September, 1994* (Esbo: NORDINFO, 1995), pp. 111–18.

9. Graham P. Cornish, *Model Handbook for Interlending and Copying* (Boston Spa: IFLA Office for International Lending, 1988).

10. D. J. Urquhart, "National Lending/Reference Libraries or Libraries of First Resort?" *BLL Review* 4 (1976): 7–10.

11. Graham P. Cornish, *Training Modules for Interlibrary Loan and Document Supply* (Paris: Unesco, 1991).

12. Graham P. Cornish, "Copyright Management of Document Supply in an Electronic Age: The CITED Solution," *Interlending & Document Supply* 21 (1993): 13–20.

9

The Preservation of Electronic Records: What Shall We Do Next?

Ross Harvey

INTRODUCTION

Who shall be responsible for ensuring continued access to electronic records in the 21st century? Who shall preserve electronic records? Will the library have a role? If it does, what is this role likely to be? This chapter poses these questions and provides some conjectural answers after beginning with a rehearsal of accepted—or at least relatively uncontentious—facts.

The preservation versus access quandary has been well documented and is well understood, even if the strategies for dealing with its contradictions are not always implemented as part of standard library practice. We can say, for instance, that key strategies for preservation are now commonly accepted as part of the professional practice of librarianship. These can be applied to enhance the accessibility of the library's collections to its users and to ensure at the same time that the artifacts which constitute the collection are maintained at an acceptable level of preservation. Such strategies include clearly determining priorities for preservation, relating preservation actions to institutional objectives, preferring methods which treat material economically in bulk (such as mass deacidification) over those which apply only to single items, implementing the practices of preventative preservation rather than reliance on ''after the event'' intervention by conservators, recognizing the important role which education and training plays, and accepting that librarians cannot leave the running to conservators but must take their preservation future into their own hands. Also important here, and significant for the discussion which follows, are strategies based on collaboration by all who have a stake in the preservation of library resources—librarians, archivists, administrators, conservators, authors, and publishers, among others.[1]

Preservation strategies have been formulated and their outcomes implemented in the context of the traditional library, that is, a library with a physical collection. These strategies and practices work best when applied to the artifacts (the *physical* objects) contained in library collections, because they have typically been developed in the context of conserving the artifact. More specifically, they have been developed for and applied to "traditional" artifacts used for information storage, which are usually printed materials. The library preservation world has not yet coped fully with the preservation aspects of other kinds of artifacts in its collections. It still persists in labelling these, using the pejorative term "nonbook materials" or the imprecise "audiovisual materials" or, even worse, "media." Preservation practice is still primarily focused on books. As we move to the virtual (or digital) library we must expect major changes in preservation practice as well as in all other aspects of professional practice. In the words of Margaret Hedstrom, written in the context of archives and records management, but entirely applicable to libraries,

We have to shift our mentality from paper-defined issues to a new electronic record-keeping culture. . . . We have to learn to like electronic records and not to fear them. In doing this we can liberate ourselves from the tyranny of paper practices, to really recognise and understand the benefits of electronic recordkeeping. Not to look at electronic records as a problem, but to look at them as an opportunity to do what we have been trying to do in the paper world much more effectively.[2]

While it is clear that preservation strategies and practices will be altered in the virtual library, the parameters of the changes are still in the process of being defined. The key questions include:

• What is the collection of the virtual library?
• What roles will preservation play in the virtual library?
• What preservation strategies and practices will be applied in the virtual library?
• Who will take responsibility for preservation in the virtual library?

WHAT IS THE COLLECTION OF THE VIRTUAL LIBRARY?

As the amount of information available in electronic form grows, so does libraries' reliance on it for providing information to their users. The rate at which electronic information sources have grown in recent years is well appreciated by librarians. Some representative figures indicating growth rates are as follows:

- between 2 and 7 percent per year for paper-based sources (books and print journals)
- more than 28 percent per year from 1985 to 1994 for online databases
- nearly 40 percent per year for online databases which contain full text
- more than 100 percent per year for CD-ROM databases.[3]

Faced with facts such as these, commentators on the virtual library have argued along the following lines. Information will increasingly be sourced from remote data files electronically accessed from the library. All information will eventually be accessed in this manner. The source of information will be of little relevance to users who, in particular, will not be concerned about whether their sought information comes from a printed source or an electronic one. The collection of information-bearing artifacts in the library will be of ever-decreasing significance as a source of information. In addition, these information-bearing artifacts will more and more become objects which store digital information (such as optical disks and magnetic tape), and the quantity of paper-based material to be housed and preserved will decrease. The preservation of these artifacts will become decreasingly significant as part of the library's collection management activities. The corollary is, of course, that there will be an increasing reliance on information maintained outside the library's collection.

Michael Buckland amplifies aspects of this argument. He poses this question: "What would collection developers do if and when the emerging environment of networked electronic resources were to lead to the absence or reduced significance of local collections?"[4] Preservation, he indicates, is one of four roles to be considered in this context: "If a document is to be available now and in the future, then at least one copy needs to be collected somewhere."[5] He notes that the role of local collections in the networked environment will alter considerably, and with it the role of the collection developer (and we can include here the role of preservation). Locally maintained collections will still be developed and maintained, but these "localized caches of electronic documents will be transient and transparent."[6] He sees that the role of the collection developer, traditionally that of "privileging" of documents by selecting and acquiring the documents in their artifactual form, and of making these artifacts accessible in local collections, will alter:

Hitherto the privileging of documents has been dominated by a binary division: items acquired for the local collection and those not acquired or not retained. In the environment of networked resources such an abrupt division seems improbable. A much finer gradation of degrees of accessibility and privileging seems likely.[7]

Further, Buckland notes that

Access and ownership, always separate in principle but hitherto rarely separate in library practice, are expected to diverge in the electronic network environment. One consequence is that "collection development" is much less limited to one's own materials, or that one can "privilege" the materials of others.[8]

WHAT ROLES WILL PRESERVATION PLAY IN THE VIRTUAL LIBRARY?

But we are still left with the question: Who takes responsibility for preservation of the "privileged" documents? For locally maintained collections there is probably no significant alteration from current responsibilities, although the techniques will be different from current practices; but who takes responsibility for the long-term maintenance of the remote electronic sources?

Part of the answer can be found by recollecting some of the traditional roles of libraries, those of the library as collector of heritage material, as repository of last resort for significant material. Although we might not all share Nicholson Baker's belief that "the function of a great library is to store obscure books," we probably can agree that this collecting and preserving function is a significant one.[9] While not all libraries need to perform this function, a surprising number do. The obvious examples spring readily to mind, such as research libraries with their objectives of supporting research, or national libraries with their legislative imperative to maintain a nation's published heritage for future generations. However, the small public library may not be exempt, with its collection of locally produced ephemera, for instance; and the business library may be required to maintain important documents relating to the company's founder or to the company's early years.

It seems clear there will still be local collections to be preserved, but these will be considerably reduced in size and of a different nature, consisting of much more electronic data. Because the library still needs to maintain and preserve these local collections in the virtual library environment, the issue then shifts to one of selection. The current reality is that "a decreasing share of the world's literature is on any one library's shelves"; "no library, however well-funded, can warehouse all the books a reader may need": this will become increasingly the case in the virtual library environment.[10] So *who* warehouses? And *what* do they select to warehouse? Who is concerned with preservation of the remotely stored information, upon which the library will come to rely more and more, and to which the library points? Although they will not be the only players, libraries will have a major stake in ensuring that the electronic data are preserved so that they can be used in the future.

One issue relating to selection is that of the volatility of much electronic information. In one of the few sources to address this issue, Ackerman and Fielding point out that in the virtual library environment the gap between local and remote sources will increase, and that "only some of the practices of the traditional library will carry over into the digital world, perhaps only for a narrow conception of the digital library."[11] They note that in a traditional library control over the collection is possible because publications are stable but that the same does not necessarily apply with many electronic information sources.

At one opposite is the World Wide Web. The Web nodes often change, in content, location, and even existence. On the other hand, the content in a location does not shift rapidly; it tends to remain relatively stable. There is no control by any given individual over the entire Web. An individual has control only over his nodes and the selection of pointers to others' nodes (URLs) that provide the capability for extended collections. At another opposite is Usenet or similar computer-mediated communication (CMC) systems. The locations (i.e., channel or topic) do not change, but the contents of any location (e.g., comp.sys.laptops) change constantly. The control over the collection for this type is also very low for any given individual.[12]

Ackerman and Fielding conclude that ''collections that are closer to those in traditional libraries can use more traditional control and maintenance mechanisms. Digital libraries that incorporate more individualistic, dynamic, and informal information may need to find new maintenance mechanisms.''[13]

WHAT PRESERVATION STRATEGIES AND PRACTICES WILL BE APPLIED IN THE VIRTUAL LIBRARY?

There is also the question of how electronic information can be preserved. One single fact has shaped the discussion about preserving electronic records: None of the present media for storing electronic records has a life expectancy anywhere near as long as paper and microfilm that have been manufactured to accepted archival standards and appropriately stored and handled. The two media most commonly used, magnetic tape and optical disks in various formats, both have restricted life spans which impose serious limitations on their use for preservation.[14] In 1988 this thinking was put into print by David Bearman:

We must begin by accepting the information life of specific recording formats as a fact of physics. While we can influence the production of new media and formats and encourage current information recorders to use formats with longer lives, the ''format life'' of any given format is the outside boundary beyond which we cannot rationally plan to retain the information without transforming the medium.[15]

Preserving the artifact (a principle on which much of traditional preservation practice is based) can be only a short-term expedient for electronic records. The key issues here are the fragility of each medium and the rapid rate of obsolescence of the operating apparatus, both software and hardware.

For the two media currently used for most electronic data storage, the factors which affect their longevity are their care and handling (including quality of storage conditions, care in handling, and number of times the medium is accessed), the quality of the manufacturing process and of the material from which the medium is manufactured, and the future availability of the technology to play back the tape. We can only exercise any real control over the first of these. For magnetic tapes, current informed estimates of life expectancy (assuming optimal storage conditions and handling procedures) are at least ten years for tapes where immediate access and playback is required, and considerably longer for tapes in archival storage.[16] It is worth reiterating that the exact life expectancy is heavily dependent on storage conditions and on the quality of handling. For optical disks the life expectancies are longer, although there is considerable variation, depending on the type of disk: Estimates vary from a minimum of 10 years to a maximum of 100 years.[17] Many other media exist for the storage of digital data and new media are being developed and promoted on a regular basis. (These include the promising write-once medium called Digital Paper whose "effectiveness continues to be hampered by its perplexing nonexistence."[18]) Those which establish themselves commercially will clearly need to be tested to determine their life expectancies.

Although these estimates of life expectancy are subject to change as more accurate tests are devised and applied, their implication is clear: The lifetime of optical disks of all kinds, and of magnetic tapes, is longer than that of their recording and playback technology. The precise life expectancies of the digital artifacts do not matter. What matters is that they have a life span shorter than the effective life span (obsolescence period) of the equipment. The key issues are as follows:

- Devices, processes, and software used to record, store, and retrieve digital information are being replaced with new products and methods on a 2- to 5-year cycle.
- Backward compatibility between versions of software and generations of hardware is not assured.
- Interoperability among competing hardware and software product lines is not assured.[19]

Attention is now being turned to migration as the key strategy for preserving electronic records. Migration refers to the transfer of digital data to new software or hardware configurations: it is

a set of organized tasks designed to achieve the periodic transfer of digital materials from one hardware/software configuration to another, or from one generation of computer technology to a subsequent generation. The purpose of migration is to retain the ability to display, retrieve, manipulate and use digital information in the face of constantly changing technology.[20]

The fragility of digital data imposes a real danger on such a strategy: "that owners or custodians who can no longer bear the expense and difficulty will deliberately or inadvertently, through a simple failure to act, destroy the objects without regard for future use."[21] Whereas with paper-based materials there was a strong possibility that artifacts would survive even if no longer actively maintained—indeed, the concept of "benign neglect" indicates that lack of active maintenance could be a positive advantage—with digital data the cessation of active maintenance very rapidly makes that data unusable.

Migration strategies are in the process of being developed. While migration strategies for large quantities of digital data such as census data are well established (as is noted below), the same cannot be said for more complex data such as multimedia documents. Procedures which are straightforward to implement need to be developed, and preferably they should be as automatic as possible so that they become part of the normal collection management procedures in libraries. One glimpse of how this could be done is offered by the Archival Preservation System (APS) designed and developed by the U.S. National Archives and Records Administration (NARA). The APS "transfers electronic records from the media used by the records creators (or from a network) to a medium chosen specifically for archival preservation"; "writes the archival copies of physical files in conformance with standard specifications for physical recording and labelling of physical files"; "automatically tracks all of the media volumes it writes, the physical files it copies, and the processes performed on them"; and "facilitates the eventual migration of physical files to new preservation media." Data can be input from a wide range of devices including open reel tape, 3480 cartridge, 4mm and 8mm tape cassettes, floppy disks, and CD-ROM; the output device was in late 1994 a 3480 magnetic tape cartridge drive.[22] An excellent summary of the range of migration strategies, their problems, and some guidelines is to be found in the September 1995 draft report of the Task Force on Digital Archiving, *Preserving Digital Information*.[23]

WHO WILL TAKE RESPONSIBILITY FOR PRESERVATION IN THE VIRTUAL LIBRARY?

Although we are starting to be clearer about the *how*, we are not much clearer about the *who* and the *what* of preserving electronic records. These two are very closely related. To address these questions we need to know more about who creates and maintains these electronic data at present and who has an interest in them being maintained into the future; in other words, who the stakeholders are. We may find a partial answer by developing a typology of electronic information sources of interest to libraries based on characteristics such as the type of file, who "publishes" it, who maintains it, who benefits from it commercially, and who benefits from it in other ways. If those who benefit, the stakeholders, can be more clearly identified, then the roles which they might play in the future in preserving the electronic data which make up the information sources can also be better delineated.[24]

The following example indicates some of the possible alliances of stakeholders which such a typology suggests. This approach is capable of considerable further expansion and should produce clear indications of where libraries could look for support.

Type of file: electronic journals

Who "publishes" it: publishers (commercial, professional societies, etc.)

Who benefits from it commercially: publishers, subscription agents

Who benefits from it in other ways: authors, information seekers

Who maintains it short term: publishers maintain for as long as it is marketable

Who maintains it long term: traditionally libraries; perhaps a new role for subscription agents and vendors; publishers.

Comment: One vendor, Ebsco, is "archiving these [electronic] items because we see it as a natural extension of document delivery, which is now one of our products or activities. We must archive or have access to archives of journals, whether electronic or paper, in order to meet the document delivery needs of our customers." Ebsco notes that "the archiving of E-journals will create a business or activity for whoever is best at providing that service."[25] Suggestions from other sources indicate that such a typology (for library purposes, as distinct from archives) would need to include, at the least, the following categories of electronic information sources:[26]

- electronic journals
- scientific data sets
- cartographic databases (including geographic information systems)
- legal databases (including patents, trademarks databases)
- expert systems (these are significant because they represent the current state of expert knowledge)
- textual data (including works which represent the creative process such as authors' works in progress)
- image collections
- newsgroups, listservs, and mail archives
- indexes and directories
- electronic search and display tools (including OPACs, citation databases)
- combinations of the above (including training packages and educational software).

Another possible typology, centered on mode of delivery rather than on the nature of the content, could include (but not be limited to):

- discussion lists and forums
- FTP sites
- general online services (for example, Compuserve, Prodigy)
- Campus Wide Information Systems
- distributed file servers (Gopher, WAIS, WWW).

When fully developed, such typologies will demonstrate that libraries cannot rely on the publishers or the creators to maintain electronic data files, for once the data have no commercial value, their maintenance will probably not be assured. The typologies will also clearly indicate that preservation responsibilities still lie with libraries, as they are one of the chief institutional users of electronic information sources and they may need continued access to these data even when their publishers, their creators or the body responsible for their maintenance is no longer interested in it. The reasons for this in the virtual library are no different from the collection-based library: The library still has a heritage role, and it is still the keeper of the collective consciousness. It may also adopt a new role, as maintainer or preserver of electronic data which are still useful and required but no longer generate enough income to be of commercial interest.

The idea of stakeholders has been developed further in the report of the Task Force on Digital Archiving.[27] This report suggests that the initial stakeholder in a digital object is its creator; after this stage it may become increasingly more public and in doing so additional interests in the digital object, that is additional stakeholders, will accrue. These could include editor and publisher, for example, and also the library as collector. Members of the public can also be stakeholders, as Margaret Hedstrom has pointed out in relation to government records, where their interest in access to these records lies in ''enhancing accountability; making maximum use of records acquired at public expense; conducting business with government; or carrying out research for personal or practical purposes.''[28] Libraries may need to consider how best to harness and use the public interest in pursuing their own imperatives in preserving electronic records. So there is a long list of possible stakeholders, all of whom need to be clearly identified in relation to each category of electronic information source, as also does their specific interest in each category.

An even more difficult question is *what* to preserve. Some selection is necessary, despite the common library professional's view that all information sources should be preserved. This has always been unrealistic, and will be no less so in the virtual library. Many of the traditional library's techniques for selection will apply in the virtual library, such as criteria used to assess quality of information—for example, whether an authoritative review process has been applied (moderated or refereed newsgroups as distinct from unmoderated newsgroups, for instance).[29] The library community may need to become more aware of the principles of archival appraisal and to apply them to the electronic information sources which it wants to preserve. This approach would result in the development of rigorous guidelines for sampling of specified categories of electronic materials, and would certainly lead to the exclusion of other groups. But we lack some basic information needed to develop a strategy for selection for long-term preservation, such as the answer to yet more questions: Who uses electronic information, and how is it used? Or do we simply leave the selection process to chance?[30]

COOPERATIVE ACTION IN DATA ARCHIVING

In the virtual library environment it seems to be an inevitable conclusion that libraries will need to act in consort with other stakeholders to ensure the preservation of electronic information sources. Cooperation is seen to be the key to further progress, as no single group will be able to develop adequate responses in isolation.[31] Donald Waters has summarized the likely key trends:

- stakeholders will invoke a variety of consortial models as the emerging digital environment gives rise to new ways of interacting and dividing labor and responsibility;
- collaborative models will likely include partnerships, federations, contractor/subcontractor relationships;
- organizations will form around intellectual discipline, types of material, functional role such as storage or cataloging, and across to regional, national, or international boundaries.[32]

Establishing data archives is one possible option. Successful data archives will require an amalgam of skills: Consortia will need to be formed consisting of librarians, archivists, publishers, and probably others too. A possible role for the library community to play in these consortia is in the capacity of instigator, organizer, and manager of such digital archive consortia. Models for the electronic data archives of the future which are worth examining can be found within already-existing organizations that archive electronic data. Some experiments with publishers in the late 1980s are also worth reexamining.

POSSIBLE MODEL 1: THE ESRC AND OTHER DATA ARCHIVES

Much of significance of preservation in the virtual library can be learned from the operation of social science data archives. One example is the Economic and Social Research Centre Data Archive (ESRC). Housed at the University of Essex, it was established in 1967 and currently has a staff of 26 and holds approximately 4,500 datasets.[33] The Archive provides a range of services from data acquisition, processing, and dissemination to information services and data use workshops and seminars.

Data for the Archive are acquired from academic, commercial, and public sector sources within the United Kingdom, with special attention being paid to acquiring data where holdings are out-of-date or where interest in the data is known to exist. Datasets are also acquired by regular deposit from data-producing agencies. The Archive does not own data but holds and distributes data under licenses signed by data owners. The Archive may administer some control over access to some datasets on behalf of the data owner. The area covered by data in the Archives is wide, ranging from agriculture and rural life, through education and industrial relations, to social welfare. Conditions of deposit of data include the payment of a handling charge and provision of full documentation by the depositing agency. At the time of acquisition the data are converted to the Archive's own software standard in order to guard against obsolescence; checks of the data's integrity are made, identification numbers are allocated, and then the data are stored on optical disks with backup copies stored on optical and exabyte media. The Archive's data take up twenty-five gigabytes of storage space on the University of Essex's main computer. Data can be disseminated to users in a variety of formats: magnetic tape, network file transfer, 8mm videotape, digital audiotape, transfer by portable cartridge tape drives, and floppy diskettes have all been used.

The Archive pays attention to providing intellectual access to the data in its collection. Datasets are indexed by subject using a thesaurus developed by the Archive. The catalogs and indexes and thesaurus form part of the BIRON (Information Retrieval On-line) system, which can be accessed by remote users over the Internet.

The ESRC Data Archive is by no means the only such data archive operating. Its Web site points to nineteen Web addresses for other data archives and social science information servers.[34] And almost forty are noted at the Web site of the Social Sciences Data Archives at the Australian National University, Canberra.[35] Collectively, these data archives have a wealth of technical and administrative experience about how to manage and provide access to large bodies of digital data. It is very likely that much of this experience can be transferred to the library context.

POSSIBLE MODEL 2: THE KNOWLEDGE WAREHOUSE PROJECT

Also of relevance is the Knowledge Warehouse Project formed by British publishers in the mid-1980s in conjunction with the British Library. It was based on the proposition that, as most paper publications also existed in electronic form (for example, for electronic typesetting), it would be possible to archive the electronic versions and further exploit them commercially in electronic form. Although this project did not proceed beyond the pilot stage, it is worth reexamining for any lessons it can provide about balancing the different requirements of publishers and libraries.

The aim of the Knowledge Warehouse Project was "to examine the establishment, maintenance and commercial exploitation of a central store in common electronic format, of all knowledge works published by [its publisher] members."[36] It was to be controlled by an independent trust. Principles were established about commercial exploitation of the data, right to compensation, and technical standards to be developed and adhered to.[37] The Project did not proceed beyond the pilot stage, apparently because initial funding of £1.25 million was not raised and because most publishers were not inclined to deposit electronic copies of their output.[38] With changed attitudes now current in libraries about the validity of commercial exploitation of information, and with a very different technical environment, an alliance between publisher and library stakeholders to operate enterprises like the Knowledge Warehouse Project could now be possible.

POSSIBLE MODEL 3: THE NATIONAL DIGITAL LIBRARY FEDERATION

Another initiative, the U.S.-based National Digital Library Federation, was formally established in May 1995 and reached agreement on overall objectives and principles in October. Its goals include:

* the implementation of a distributed, open digital library;
* the establishment of a collaborative management structure to coordinate and guide the implementation and ongoing maintenance of the digital library;
* the adoption of common standards and best practices to ensure full informational capture; to guarantee universal accessibility and interchangeability; to simplify retrieval and navigation; and to facilitate archivability and enduring access.[39]

Its members include libraries and archives and also the Commission on Preservation and Access. The Commission on Preservation and Access has been involved in similar earlier initiatives. One was the Digital Preservation Consortium, established in 1990 to preserve and improve access to significant digital information. Among its aims were the promotion of the development of the required infrastructure, including establishing the convertibility of preservation media (for example, microfilm to digital images at high production levels); defining and promoting shared methods and standards (such as production quality standards, data structure standards, bibliographic control standards); and increasing the quantity of materials in digital format.[40] The activities of these consortia, like those of the ESRC and other data archives, and of the Knowledge Warehouse Project, represent a considerable and significant body of knowledge on which to keep building.

THE SMALLER LIBRARY: WHAT CAN IT DO?

But is the only possible avenue for preserving electronic information through establishing and participating in large-scale cooperative activities? What can the smaller library do to prepare for the near future? (Remember that all virtual libraries will need to maintain local collections of electronic data.) While we are waiting for the major initiatives to be prototyped, the issues to be addressed, and the range of practical solutions to become better defined, we can start addressing most of the issues outlined in this chapter at both the personal level (the electronic data we generate on our own PCs or Macs—I suspect that very few of us have well-established procedures in place) and in smaller libraries which are not the Cornells or Yales (or in small units within larger libraries). For example, the following steps suggest themselves: (1) identify electronic records which are considered significant to preserve (perhaps final versions of journal articles, books, or other publications on a personal level; institutionally generated documents in a library context); (2) devise routines for migration of this data (here a significant factor is the plummeting cost of storage devices, both tape and optical disk–based); (3) document these procedures for migration; (4) carry out (as libraries have always done) an educational role aimed at raising the consciousness of library users about the issues of preserving electronic records; and (5) implement these procedures.

Even on a small scale such an exercise will be profitable, for example by suggesting some of the areas where problems will occur when the procedures are scaled up to larger operations.

CONCLUSION

Many questions about the preservation of electronic information sources in the virtual library need to be addressed. If we cannot answer these questions soon, what will become of such electronic information sources as the "A Day in the Life of Cyberspace . . . the first global portrait of human life in the digital age" collected in late 1995?[41] This paper suggests some possible avenues to explore. Libraries will need to play an active role in the preservation of electronic information sources. If they do not, much non-current digital data will rapidly disappear. Libraries will in the short term need to play a consciousness-raising role, which will later need to be expanded to an active managerial and organizational role. The consequences of not attending to these (and no doubt also other) questions are of enormous magnitude. If we fail to address these questions, we may condemn future generations to a life of ignorance; at the least we will deprive them of knowledge which is essential to make informed decisions about critical aspects of their lives. This, at least, is the view of the science fiction writer Isaac Asimov. In the following excerpt, the future of the universe in the far-distant future depends on whether knowledge about the past still exists and can be located and accessed.

"What do you mean we don't know the situation in 1,000 G.E. very well? There were computers then, weren't there?"

"Of course."

"And memory storage units? We should have all the records of 1,000 G.E. as we have of the present year of 12,020 G.E."

"In theory, yes, but in actual practice—It's possible to have full records of 1,000 G.E., but it's not practical to expect to have it. Records don't last forever. Memory banks can be destroyed or defaced as a result of conflict or can simply deteriorate with time. Any memory bit, any record that is not referred to for a long time, eventually drowns in accumulated noise. They say that fully one third of the records in the Imperial Library are simply gibberish. Naturally, records frequently referred to and frequently duplicated on various worlds and in various libraries—governmental and private—remain clear enough for thousands of years. . . ."

"Undesired knowledge is useless knowledge. Can you imagine all the time, effort, and energy expended in a continual refurbishing of unused data? And that wastage would grow steadily more extreme with change."[42]

NOTES

1. Based on Ross Harvey, *Preservation in Libraries: Principles, Strategies and Practices for Librarians* (London: Bowker-Saur, 1993), pp. 13–15; see also John Feather, *Preservation and the Management of Library Collections* (London: Library Association, 1991), especially Chapter 6.

2. Margaret Hedstrom, "Closing Address," in *Playing for Keeps: The Proceedings of an Electronic Records Management Conference hosted by the Australian Archives, Canberra, 8–10 November 1994*, ed. Stephen Yorke (Canberra: Australian Archives, 1995), p. 336.

3. S. Michael Malinconico and Jane C. Warth, "The Use of Electronic Documents in Libraries," in *61st IFLA General Conference Conference Proceedings, August 20–25, 1995* (URL http://www.nlc-bnc.ca/ifla/conf/ifla61/61–mals.htm).

4. Michael Buckland, "What Will Collection Developers Do?" *Information Technology and Libraries* 14 (1995): 155.

5. Ibid.

6. Ibid., p. 157.

7. Ibid., p. 158.

8. Ibid.

9. Nicholson Baker, "Discards," *New Yorker* 70, no. 7 (April 4, 1994): 78–79, quoted in Robert A. Gross and Christine L. Borgman, "The Incredible Vanishing Library," *American Libraries* 26 (October 1995): 902.

10. Ibid., p. 902.

11. Mark S. Ackerman and Roy T. Fielding, "Collection Maintenance in the Digital Library," in *Digital Libraries '95: The Second Annual Conference on the Theory and Practice of Digital Libraries, June 11–13, 1995, Austin, Texas USA* (URL http://www.csdl.tamu.edu/DL95/papers/ackerman/ackerman.html).

12. Ibid.

13. Ibid.

14. For a fuller version of this section see Ross Harvey, "From Digital Artefact to Digital Object," in *Multimedia Preservation: Capturing the Rainbow, 2nd National Preservation Office Conference, Brisbane, 28–30 November 1995* (to be published in 1996).

15. David Bearman, "Archival Methods," in *Archives and Museums Informatics Technical Report, 9* (Pittsburgh: Archives and Records Informatics, 1988, reprinted 1991), p. 24; italics added for emphasis.

16. John Van Bogart, *Magnetic Tape Storage and Handling: A Guide for Libraries and Archives* (Washington, DC: Commission on Preservation and Access and National Media Laboratory, 1995); this report is also available at URL http://www.nml.org/resources/misc/ commission_report/contents.html.

17. William Saffady, *Electronic Document Imaging Systems: Design, Evaluation, and Implementation* (Westport, CT: Meckler, 1993), p. 118, Table 5-1.

18. Paula Lieberman, "Taking Measure of Magnetic, Optical, and Magneto Optical Media and Drives," *CD-ROM Professional* 8, no. 7 (July 1995): 72.

19. Donald Waters, *The Social Organization of Archiving Digital Information. Draft 26 April 1995* (URL http://www.nlc-bnc.ca/documents/libraries/net/waters2.htm).

20. *Preserving Digital Information. Draft Report of the Task Force on Digital Archiving, September 1995* (URL http://www-rlg.stanford.edu/ArchTF/).

21. Ibid.

22. Kenneth Thibodeau, "Electronic Records Activities at the National Archives and Records Administration (NARA)," in *Playing for Keeps*, p. 44.

23. *Preserving Digital Information.*

24. Others have considered the typological approach worth pursuing. Don Waters, for instance, suggests a distinction between "meta-information (bibliographic catalogs, indices, data dictionaries, directory systems, etc.)" and "the documents and other objects to which they refer, such as monographic and serial texts, graphic and photographic images, sound recordings, data collections, software-dependent data objects (GIS and CAD), and hyper-media or compound documents, which combine some or all of the other types." He also suggests a basic categorization by ownership: individually owned materials (such as mail, notes, manuscripts, preprints, databases, etc.); corporately owned materials (employment and financial records, planning documents, reports, etc.); material "owned" by publishers (books, serials, films, recordings, etc.); and material "owned" by libraries, museums, and other educational institutions. Don Waters, "Some Considerations on the Archiving of Digital Information," January 1995 (URL http://www.nlc-bnc.ca/documents/libraries/net/waters1.htm).

25. Based on Wim Luijendijk, "Archiving Electronic Journals from the Serial Information Providers Perspective," in *61st IFLA General Conference Conference Proceedings, August 20–25, 1995* (URL http://www.nlc-bnc.ca/ifla/conf/ifla61/61–luiw.htm).

26. These include Steve Stuckey, "The Australian Archives' Policy on Electronic Records—The Technical Issues," in *Playing for Keeps*, p. 122; Maggie Jones, "Preserving Australia's Electronic Documentary Heritage," in ibid., pp. 163–72; Dennis Nicholson et al., *Cataloguing the Internet: Catriona Feasibility Study* (London: British Library, 1995), p. 65; Gary Marchionini and Hermann Maurer, "The Roles of Digital Libraries in Teaching and Learning," *Communications of the ACM* 38, no. 4 (1995): 67–75.

27. *Preserving Digital Information.*

28. Margaret Hedstrom, "Finders Keepers Losers Weepers: Alternative Program Models for Identifying and Keeping Electronic Records," in *Playing for Keeps*, p. 31.

29. This example is only one of several in a paper by Michael Lesk, "Preserving Digital Objects: Recurrent Needs and Challenges," in *Multimedia Preservation: Capturing the Rainbow* (URL http://community/bellcore.com/lesk/auspres/aus.htm).

30. This course of (in)action, which has the considerable attraction of requiring little effort, is noted in more detail by Maggie Exon, "Long-Term Management Issues in the Preservation of Electronic Information," in *Multimedia Preservation.*

31. But note a contrary argument for localized ultimate responsibility expressed by Maggie Exon, in *Multimedia Preservation.*

32. Waters, "The Social Organization."

33. Most of this description is based on information available from the ESRC Data Archive's Web site (URL http://biron.essex.ac.uk/).

34. URL http://dawww.essex.ac.uk/othserv.html. See also Edward Higgs, "Information Super-highways or Quiet Country Lanes? Accessing Electronic Archives in the United Kingdom," in *Playing for Keeps*, pp. 52–67.

35. URL http://ssda.anu.edu.au/foreign.html.

36. Michael William Day, *Preservation Problems of Electronic Text and Data* (Loughborough: Loughborough University of Technology, 1990), p. 141.

37. The detailed proposal is found in Robin Williamson, *Electronic Text Archiving* (Oxford: Elsevier Advanced Technology Publications, 1988).

38. Monica Blake, "Archiving of Electronic Publications," *Electronic Library* 7 (1989): 382; see also Day, *Preservation*, for an assessment of the Project's significance.

39. *Mission and Goals for a National Digital Library Federation* (URL http://www.nlc-bnc.ca/documents/libraries/net/digfed2.htm); see also *Commission on Preservation and Access Newsletter* 84 (November-December 1995): 1; *Commission on Preservation and Access Annual Report July 1, 1994–June 30, 1995* (Washington, DC: Commission on Preservation and Access, 1995), p. 6.

40. Donald J. Waters and Anne Kenney, *The Digital Preservation Consortium: Mission and Goals* (Washington, DC: The Commission on Preservation and Access, 1994).

41. See URL http://www.media.mit.edu/.

42. Isaac Asimov, *Prelude to Foundation* (New York: Bantam Books, 1989), pp. 150–51; some words have been omitted.

PART VI

Organization and Budgeting for Collection Management

10

Staffing and Organization for Collection Development in a New Century

Bonita Bryant

INTRODUCTION

For many years library literature has reminded practitioners that the library of the future will be electronic or paperless. Predictions for the all-electronic library with dates specified have failed to meet their deadlines, yet all librarians are conscious that, however near or far away that date is, it is coming and it will have dramatically changed how all library functions are performed by the time it is recognized as being here. One way of addressing a future whose manifestations resemble a mirage, changing in some way each time a new type of computer or software emerges, is to think about who will work in the library of the future and how these people will organize to accomplish their missions. Collection development librarians, who know that information may eventually cease to be published on paper and who know that existing collections will not all be scanned into electronic format, are beginning to have a better idea of what they will be doing in the next century than they did five or six years ago.

CHANGING FOCUS OF COLLECTION DEVELOPMENT

In 1991, Tyckoson predicted two areas in which the collection development librarian would need to change: (1) ''to allocate significantly more resources for materials that may not become part of the library collection,'' and (2) ''to select among several different levels of access to information.''[1] He described the levels as ownership of information in response to high demand, purchase of access to information in moderate demand, ordering material when it is needed, and deciding to neither own nor access materials not in demand.

In 1993, Atkinson established three principles for approaching the future of collection development: (1) ''traditional divisions of library operations not only are changing but also are blending into each other, primarily as a result of innovations in information technology''; (2) ''we must try to devote as much attention as possible to the process of the transition itself''; and (3) ''it is unavoidably abstract.''[2] He sees four roles for current collection development personnel in the transition from paper-based to electronic libraries: (1) ''protecting and maintaining mediation services for disciplines that continue to rely on paper''; (2) providing ''full-text retrospective conversion, which will be an enormous undertaking and will form the last major effort of traditional collection development''; (3) ''working with acquisitions to design the budgetary procedures for access to online information''; and (4) ensuring that ''selectors begin to learn more about, and to form closer administrative links to, what are now the cataloging and reference operations in order to prepare the way for what will be the inevitable fusion of selection with those two operations.''[3]

With these long-range visions and short-term caveats, it is clear that collection development librarians will have plenty of work to do in at least the early decades of the 21st century and not at all clear that their expertise will ever cease to be needed in the 21st-century information environment. To project what the collection development enterprise of the 21st century may look like, it seems sensible to determine whether forecasts for the library of the future have already engendered modifications in organizational structure and the roles of individuals engaged in collection development in academic and research libraries in 1995, and, if so, what changes may carry through to the year 2000 and beyond. Two methods have been used in this chapter: interaction with collection development librarians in some specific libraries, and a review of library literature. The results of these activities are interspersed in the text that follows.

THE ACADEMIC LIBRARY SITUATION

During the 1989/1990 academic year, the author visited forty-four academic libraries in the United States. The libraries spanned large academic and research libraries and those serving medium-sized and small institutions, although the majority (37) were members of the Association of Research Libraries, and twenty-two of them were represented on the ALA Chief Collection Development Officers of Large Research Libraries Discussion Group. Among other topics discussed on those visits was that of the organizational structure for collection development and the tasks performed by collection development officers (CDOs) and their colleagues bearing such titles as bibliographer, selector, subject specialist, and collection manager. The CDOs of all but eight of the libraries visited in 1989/1990 found time to respond to the author's 1995 inquiry about changes in organizational structure and staffing. Some information about the other libraries has been obtained from colleagues.

In 1989/1990, the electronic library was but a vision, with little tangible evidence beyond the automation of library functions themselves, commercial computer search services, and a growing number of CD-ROM installations. Few libraries had mounted databases other than local catalogs on their automated systems, and external networks offered little more than the capability to communicate with colleagues via e-mail and listservs. In many of the libraries visited, selectors yearned for PCs on their desks with plans to use them for word processing, desktop access to the library's automated system, and an introduction to electronic mail communication. Training for this much participation in automated library activities was combined with exploration of sophisticated searching techniques for online catalogs, commercial online search services, and CD-ROM products, especially for those selectors who also worked at the library's reference desk. Collection development officers had some facility in the use of spreadsheets and database management systems in managing budgets, if they were responsible for more than allocation of firm order budgets and the occasional cancellation project necessitated by increased costs for journal subscriptions and standing orders. Not many library automated systems were using acquisitions modules of integrated systems for managing budget or serials holdings.

By 1995, a whole new world of electronic publications and access to information had emerged. Libraries across the United States, both large and small, were developing World Wide Web home pages, distributing access to databases via OPACs and other networks, cataloging electronic journals for patron access, subscribing to remote bibliographic resources (some with customized interfaces for the library's clientele and some with full-text journal articles), and providing an array of electronic document delivery options. Collection development librarians were immersed in making decisions about what to purchase, what to access for a price, or what to simply point to on the Internet. Even those who advocated excluding electronic information costs from the traditional acquisitions budget in the early 1990s had finally acknowledged that supplying information in any format must be the purview of collection development librarians and funding for information resources. Most collection development librarians had embraced Buckland's perception that, regardless of information format, they are the appropriate decision makers for access to and ownership of information resources.[4]

A majority of libraries in 1989/1990 were interested in cooperation with other libraries to provide either a national or regional collection that could help subvert the ravages of cost increases threatening the concept of self-sufficiency. CDOs usually represented their institutions for these purposes. By 1991, the Research Libraries Group had disbanded its Collection Management and Development Committee, recognizing that little of use had resulted from expensive semiannual meetings. In only a few libraries were selectors involved in other cooperative efforts, even though CDOs agreed that only subject specialists could arrive at practical methods of collaboration in specific subject areas. Several RLG subject-oriented cooperative efforts (most notably Long Term Serials Projects) were conducted by telephone and e-mail among selectors; travel expenses prohibited meeting in person except at ALA or other professional meetings. Various segments of the American Library Association, the Special Libraries Association, and a few subject-specific organizations brought selectors together in discussions that yielded some viable cooperative projects. By 1995, regional collaboration had replaced nationwide efforts to counter fiscal trends that are reducing the number of monographs and journals a given library can afford; and, in most cases, it focused on access to electronic resources and interlibrary document delivery agreements.

THE LITERATURE ON COLLECTION DEVELOPMENT ORGANIZATION

Within this framework, a brief review of the literature about collection development organization is in order. Bryant reviewed the few published discussions of the organizational structure of collection development practitioners that appeared before 1987 when she first addressed this issue.[5] As the following exploration of collection development organization in specific libraries shows, the array of existing organizational patterns for collection development has not changed substantially since Sohn simultaneously published her report of a survey of Association of Research Libraries (ARL) libraries' collection development configurations,[6] and ARL published a SPEC Kit containing organizational charts, position descriptions, and other operating documents prepared that year by Bobick.[7] Also in 1987, Cubberley examined similar aspects of collection development activities in medium-sized academic libraries, basing descriptions on three broad types of organization and concluding that the optimal organization locates librarians with primary assignments in collection development in departments established for that purpose.[8] Cogswell described six models for collection management and development in his study at Johns Hopkins University's library, comparing the models' potential for success in performing eight principal functions of collection management.[9] He concluded that two models best meet that challenge: Model A—an assistant/associate director of a separate division of the library staffed by bibliographers with narrow subject responsibilities who operate exclusively within the Collection Management Division; and Model B—wherein the assistant/associate director supervises several bibliographers with broad subject assignments and chairs a collections advisory group that includes collection management librarians enlisted from other departments of the library.[10]

In the next few years, need was acknowledged for a fresh look at collection development organizations. In 1988, Bucknall urged experimentation with staffing collection development in order to "respond effectively to new directions opened as the knowledge base undergoes profound changes."[11] At the 1988 joint meeting of Association of Research Libraries and the Standing Conference of National and University Libraries at the University of York, Creth advocated adoption of a combined functional and team design to address the role of collection development in libraries.[12] In 1991, Creth further elaborated on this "new organization paradigm" in which a collection management administrator is responsible for coordinating teams of librarians from throughout the library who have appropriate subject knowledge.[13] Cline perceived the human resources in collection development as "one of the most important elements in bringing change to research libraries" when she addressed the 1993 Advanced Collection Management and Development Institute, enumerating the leadership qualities and staff competencies required to do so.[14]

ORGANIZATIONAL STRUCTURE AND THE COLLECTION DEVELOPMENT OFFICER

Organizational patterns are closely related to the hierarchy of leadership in libraries, and until recently, every library had its hierarchy. During the last decade or so, this was true for collection development in a variety of organizational patterns that nearly always included a position in the director's cabinet. Thus, a discussion of organizational structure and of the CDO position coincide in what follows next.

In 1989/1990 most of the libraries visited by the author had a collection development officer at the assistant director level as Cogswell recommended; sometimes this role was combined with responsibility for either public services or technical services. The original visits found twenty-six CDOs whose time was exclusively dedicated to collection development with, at most, additional responsibility for preservation and/or special collections. Ten libraries' CDOs were also assistant/associate directors for technical services. One CDO administered acquisitions along with collection development, but not other technical services units. Four held comparable positions for public services. Two libraries managed collection development with committees, one of which included selectors, reference, and technical services librarians, while the other included the coordinators of collection development from each of that university's five major libraries. In each case the chairperson position rotated among members. Only one small library had no official CDO.

Changes in the CDO position since then have been dramatic. By 1995, only twenty-two libraries of the 1989/1990 cohort still employed the same person as CDO. Of the remaining twenty-two, in six cases a new CDO was appointed to replace CDOs who had retired or moved to other libraries. One additional recruitment is in progress; three other libraries have not decided whether recruitment is their most desirable option. The small library with no CDO in 1989/

1990 has evaluated its collection development operations and assigned this function to the acquisitions librarian.

Other changes in organizational structure have occurred: two libraries have placed responsibility for collection development in a team framework without a CDO. Three have broadened the existing CDO's job description to include public services, and six have absorbed a vacancy in this manner to compensate for overall staff reductions. One library has included technical services in the CDO's purview, while another has seen fit to relieve the CDO from dual responsibility for some public services to an exclusively collection development role. In yet another library the position simply seems to have evaporated. The two committee-driven collection development organizations report that one has had the same chair for five years, while the other no longer operates officially but keeps communication lines open among its members.

During this six-year time span, twenty-three of the forty-four libraries have undergone a change in directorship. It is appropriate to ask whether new directors are the driving force in reorganization of collection development. For six of these libraries, the director's position is currently open or was filled only in recent months. Twelve of the new directors have influenced some of the changes in CDO positions cited above: One eliminated the CDO position; two created teams for collection development and have not replaced the CDO; two have responded to fiscal stringencies by absorbing the CDO role in the public services function of their libraries; four hired new CDOs; one has advertised this position; and two have not yet made decisions about their CDO vacancies. One can only speculate on the changes the six newest directors may make and whether the five who have been directors for a few years without instigating reorganization may find it necessary or attractive to make changes as CDO positions become vacant.

Among the twenty-one libraries retaining their 1989/1990 directors, eight vacancies in the CDO position prompted four "new hires" (with one recruitment still in progress), and four directors chose to absorb the vacancies in their existing organizations. None of the other directors has felt compelled to reorganize either the total library or only collection development. Thus, the 1995 "score" is as follows: Fourteen libraries have collection development as a discrete division; thirteen libraries combine it with public services; twelve combine collection development with technical services (or at least acquisitions); and two committees, two teams, and a CDO-less library complete the original forty-four.

Based on the trends demonstrated by the changes cited above, it appears likely that more CDO positions may be absorbed or eliminated. The fiscal problems of institutions of higher education may be expected to engender added modifications in organizational structure in their libraries. However, it is not necessarily money that has prompted all decisions to absorb CDO vacancies. Directors, CDOs, and other librarians (including collection developers) may well have been responding to the challenges of Tyckoson, Atkinson, and Buckland for reinventing the collection development organization in their libraries.

In a 1993 article, Robinson studied academic library collection development and management positions advertised in *College & Research Libraries News* from 1980 through 1991, finding little change over time in the library expectations for successful candidates.[15] A cursory review of recent issues of recruiting sources such as the COLLDV-L listserv, *College & Research Libraries News*, and *American Libraries* in 1995 reveals that libraries do continue to seek leadership for their collection development activities. All but one advertisement at the assistant director or department head level, however, indicate that the CDO role is combined with responsibility for either technical or public services, and that lone advertisement does include management of multiple special campus libraries in the CDO's responsibilities. Advertisements for CDO positions in several large libraries have appeared in the past five years only to go unfilled. As in the libraries studied by the author, it appears that these administrative positions are viewed as too expensive given parallel needs for librarians with electronic skills and given massive budget, and therefore staffing, restrictions, especially among state-supported universities.

Although the tasks performed by CDOs and collection development librarians in general have been the topic of frequent publication, those usually reserved for CDOs have rarely been systematically described. Johnson discussed what she considers the essential qualifications for CDOs: political skills, financial expertise, creative and analytic thinking, and communication skills.[16] An overview of collections, institutional programs, and financial resources for meeting user needs seems all the more necessary in an era when the library must choose between purchasing library materials and providing access to a myriad of electronic sources. Leadership skills are an essential addition to Johnson's litany of qualifications for CDOs, especially when efforts to persuade faculty of the need to contain costs while forsaking subscriptions to their favorite esoteric journals and to demonstrate the value of electronic titles to selectors clinging to paper must be made. Both Schad and Cline commented extensively on the importance of the leadership of the collection development enterprise.[17]

In 1992, Hamaker challenged CDOs to justify their positions both at a meeting of the Chief Collection Development Officers of Large Research Libraries Discussion Group and in print, but engendered no published response from them.[18] Small wonder, then, that libraries have placed great value on these traits for CDOs and other administrators, but have offered little recognition of the time required to prepare and implement acquisitions plans, to study use of collections and other information sources, and to usher faculty and students into the age of access and ownership. They have, instead, reduced the portion of administrative time devoted to collection development in their libraries. The unwillingness of library directors to invest in full-time CDOs may reflect financial pressures, a conviction that the electronic library must combine collections and public services, or a premature belief that the electronic library supersedes paper collections, so no collection development is needed.

Demas has updated our definition of CDO: "it is the role of the collection development officer to coordinate the systematic building of the library's base of information resources, regardless of format . . . leading a selection process which ensures that all the right questions are asked and all the right people are involved in the decision to acquire electronic publications.''[19] In this context it would seem as important as ever that CDOs have time to fulfill this challenge in the form of few other administrative responsibilities. Many libraries appear to see this role as a public services one. The trend in the 1989/1990 cohort has, however, not moved collection development out of technical services to confirm that vision. One may suppose that library directors place functions such as this in the hands of the people they see as most capable, wherever they may fit on the organization chart. Atkinson's three principles are certainly upheld by the changes in the CDO's locus in the library organization.

In libraries that have telescoped the CDO role into a position covering other administrative units, quite a few incumbents have reported that they can only address the most pressing issues of the moment in a broad span of library functions all competing for attention. Nevertheless, it appears that some libraries choose to view information resources and public services as a whole or to see collections and their acquisition and processing as a functional unit; a case can be made for each approach. No one has suggested that one combination is superior to the other, the same attitude that has dominated librarians' thinking about the various models of organizational structure for collection development for the last half century. The concept most touted for organizational structure has been (and continues to be) whatever works for the specific situation.

When CDOs were given broader responsibilities, such as merging collection development with public or technical services, several of them chose to create a position at departmental head level to manage the daily operations of collection development, usually reserving budgetary allocation and control for themselves. In 1989/1990 several libraries had appointed selected collection development librarians as cluster heads, each responsible for selectors in a broad subject area (usually humanities, social sciences, sciences). Some of these arrangements continue and have been adopted since then by other libraries, but some also have been disbanded. It remains to be seen whether these subject oriented librarians will find the management aspects of their new roles attractive, especially when they are busy fulfilling expectations for new types of instruction required by electronic resources, selecting resources from a widening pool of publications from traditional publishers and the as yet untamed Internet, and making themselves more available to library users as in-depth reference consultants and as liaisons with academic departments.

ROLES OF COLLECTION DEVELOPMENT LIBRARIANS

To address these concerns it is time to turn to an examination of the roles of collection development librarians who operate on the level of individual title decision making, the bibliographers, selectors, subject specialists, and collection managers whose work is bound together to produce the individual collections and services which CDOs have been expected to see as a whole. It is not as easy to digest the results of a 1989/1990 visit and a 1995 recap of current circumstances into the statistical panorama provided for CDOs above. Certainly, there were as many patterns of organization in the forty-four libraries studied as have been described in library literature over the years. No two were exactly alike then or now.

The same is true for the job descriptions of selectors. Cogswell listed collection management functions as: planning and policy making, collection analysis, materials selection, collection maintenance, fund management, user liaison, resource sharing, and program evaluation.[20] Cubberley extended this list to include include gift and exchange, approval profiles, searching titles, preparation of order forms, user surveys, circulation studies, desiderata files, and retrospective selection.[21] Whatever enumeration of activities an author may make, some are performed by CDOs and some by selectors; the mix varies from library to library. In 1995, CDOs described few basic changes in the roles of selectors other than a diversification of challenges as selection has become format blind.

Twenty of the libraries visited in 1989/1990 had some full-time bibliographers, ranging from one to fourteen in number. Two of these libraries report discarding this model completely, but in the others, although the number of full-time bibliographers may have increased by one or decreased by as much as six, the commitment to the traditional bibliographer position has not changed. One library with full-time bibliographers who do a number of public services tasks as well as building collections plans to add several more bibliographers over the next few years. Another library with some full-time bibliographers is currently considering redefining collection development and may opt to move to broadened roles for those who only do collection development tasks at present. Definitions of "full-time" varied from library to library at the time of the initial visit. Some libraries required bibliographer participation in public services; others did not. At a few libraries, these definitions had changed by 1995, always in the direction of more bibliographer involvement in public services. All of the libraries with full-time bibliographers also had an additional group of part-time collection development librarians with various titles, such as liaison officer, collection manager, fund manager, subject specialist, collection specialist, and selector. A wide array of administrative reporting lines existed (and still does) for these librarians, depending on what the library administration perceives as their primary responsibility.

The number of part-time collection development librarians has decreased in some libraries considerably, and rarely has it increased by more than a few. One library has found that the dispersal of responsibility for collection development among the entire librarian pool works well, but position vacancies require that advertisements for replacements include a subject background component as well as the original position's technical expertise; long-term employees contract for their subject assignments every three years.

ORGANIZATION OF COLLECTION DEVELOPMENT

Five dramatic changes in the organization of collection development have occurred at these libraries during the past six years. One library has abolished the full-time bibliographer concept and has merged collection development with "resource services" units responsible for electronic information services, liaison with faculty, instruction, and reference. That CDO has become associate director for all library programs, including technical and public services. Another library has disengaged its CDO from a variety of user services and has instituted increased CDO supervision of bibliographers as they perform collection development and liaison tasks with "office hours" and develop proficiency in electronic access. Two libraries have eliminated the CDO position and developed team management of the collection development function. Stoffle described this evolution at the University of Arizona Libraries at the 1995 ALA annual conference.[22] Another library has reorganized, combined CDO duties with responsibility for the operations of the main library on campus, appointed a chief bibliographer to manage along with a Collections Monitoring Group, and a collection management librarian, responsible for projects. A major change at another library combined its reference organization with the user services personnel in the institution's computing center; the selectors (all the reference librarians) report to the coordinator of collection development and electronic information. Flowers, Keck, and Lindquist address how Rice University Libraries manage collection development in this context.[23]

Coulter and Martin spoke about collection development paired with the acquisitions department at the 1990 Conference on Acquisitions, Budgets, and Collections.[24] A 1992 issue of *Library Acquisitions: Practice & Theory* focused on reorganization of acquisitions departments, and at least three articles described a merger of this function with collection development or of a contiguous role within the technical services division.[25] Of the libraries in the 1989/1990 cohort, only two combined collection development and acquisitions responsibility for the CDO (exclusive of the rest of technical services).

Numerous less drastic changes have taken place in the organization of collection development in many libraries. All such changes increase the complexity of individuals' responsibilities and, hence, affect their time commitments to collection development. The advent of electronic media prompted formation of groups to attend to the broader range of ingredients in a given selection decision, paying attention not only to content, but also to equipment, instruction, and leasing. Collection developers participate to some extent in these bodies. One library has provided small accounts for selectors to use in providing commercial document delivery services when working closely with faculty and graduate students. Any number of collection development librarians are learning multiple software packages to cope with vendor products, learning html and creating WWW home pages, exploring the world of electronic journals, and integrating other offerings on the Internet into the broadening concept of their libraries' collections. In addition, teaching has become an increasing portion of the collection developer's daily workload; whether subject- or product-specific or focused on the Internet, this instructional activity is increasingly recommended by academic departments for both faculty and students. The only compensation offered to collection development librarians for these incredibly time-consuming activities has been some libraries' decisions to depend upon approval plans without local review.

Thus, time endures as the most precious commodity for collection development librarians. In 1986, Bryant examined how collection development officers might apportion workload among a team of collection developers, and Paul Metz followed in 1991 with another methodology for apportioning activities quantitatively among subject bibliographers.[26] Both recognized the increasing tendency of libraries to organize collection development using the team approach or one of Cogswell's Models B through F, all dispersing responsibility for some subjects beyond the confines of a division exclusively devoted to collection development.[27] Schad gave six suggestions for enhancing the services of dual responsibility selectors in the collection development program of a library.[28] A preconference for dual role collection development librarians was conducted by the Association for Library Collections and Technical Services at the 1991 annual conference; its speakers' contributions were described by Winters.[29] In most cases, it is assumed that the dual roles are mostly held by reference librarians. Libraries with multiple branches devoted to specific subject areas and those with separate area studies collections demonstrate the tensions between public services and collection development (and sometimes technical services) for individual librarians, especially when comparing their responsibilities with those of bibliographers in a main library whose sole function is collection development.

A scan of job advertisements in *American Libraries* for six months in 1995 identified 71 positions that included collection development responsibilities. Only half of the ads sought specific subject expertise. Three libraries wanted catalogers who could both build and process collections in specific languages. Most libraries were looking for public services librarians, in five cases suggesting that the person "may" be assigned collection development responsibilities, and in another that the person might be assigned collection development work or online searching. Eighteen of the positions were in science libraries or sought science background for a member of a main library corps of librarians. Titles of positions ranged from the traditional reference librarian to information access librarian, electronic services librarian, or information services librarian; one library described the job as outreach librarian.

FUTURE POSSIBILITIES

It is clear that a longitudinal study of collection development organization does not illuminate what collection development staffing and organization will look like in the library of the future. The clearest evidence is that the role of collection development officer is losing its separate identity in the library organizational structure, though it is too early to determine whether such experiments as team-led collection development will ultimately reveal that CDOs can be done without for the long term. Collection developers' day-to-day inventory of tasks may not have been altered greatly over the past five years, but for much of the past decade these individuals have been grappling with how electronic representations of published knowledge fit in the library of today and tomorrow. They are building a body of literature about the newest manifestations of publishing: Haar asked how new technologies would influence reference collection decision making; with "text mutability and collection administration" Atkinson launched continuing discussions about how electronic publication will affect library collections and collection development practice; Gaunt examined the librarian's role in development of libraries of machine-readable literary texts; Shreeves explored humanities scholarship in an electronic milieu; Britten wrote about Internet "collections," and Demas, McDonald, and Lawrence have explored methods for mainstreaming selection of Internet resources.[30]

Literature germane to speculation about collection development organizations in the 21st century is extensive and, necessarily, less specific. Glimpses of collection development personnel in the library of tomorrow are in most cases simply that—glimpses. Drabenstott reviewed the literature focusing on the library of the future though 1993 with very few references to collection development and collection developers.[31] In a few instances, future roles attributed to reference librarians fit parts of current prescriptions for collection development librarians' positions, for example:

For a while, academic libraries would support the posting of reference librarians to particular schools and departments. . . . Librarians would interact directly with students, faculty, and research staff, learn the culture of the particular unit, understand the various research methodologies that the field employs, discover the specific research interests of faculty and research staff, and identify the strategies that they use to satisfy their information needs.[32]

This role is remarkably like that of the subject specialist that Bastiampillai and Havard-Williams described in 1987; and they concluded that for most libraries "some form of subject specialization seems the best approach . . . [but it] would mean the end of the traditional hierarchical staff structure in libraries."[33] Blewett approaches this concept when describing the extension of the liaison concept to include the bibliographer's keeping office hours in an academic department.[34]

Three recent descriptions of library attempts to accommodate the immediate future instruct us to explore new roles, new organizations, and new perspectives on the world of information as it develops. In 1994, Demas offered a new model of "Collection Development for the Electronic Library" that merits consideration for its usefulness in the library of the future.[35] The Mann Library (Cornell University) concept of genre specialists is intriguing. It has been in operation for five years, and Demas, considering it to be a temporary model for coping with electronic publishing, expects it may be in place for another three to five years or until all genres are mainstreamed. Mainstreaming a genre means "integrating the various new forms of information transfer, as they emerge, into the existing collections, services, policies, and operations of the library."[36] An Electronic Resources Council addresses these issues and includes representatives from each functional unit of the library. Currently, there are five technologies under consideration at Mann Library: microfilm, floppy disk, CD-ROM, magnetic tape, and remote access. Each is in varying stages of approaching the mainstreamed target for one or more genres: applications software, bibliographic files, full text, numeric files, or multimedia. The genre specialist may or may not be a subject bibliographer, may have primary assignment in reference or technical services, and spends about 25 percent of the work week on genre questions. The genre specialist selects titles for purchase and consults the subject bibliographer or a faculty member if there is question about the content involved. The Mann Library has chosen to assign selection responsibility to the genre specialist because the technical issues are more difficult to resolve than subject considerations. It is clear that this model works well in the milieu of a science library, but it has not been attempted in a large library covering a broad scope of subjects. There is great potential here for coping with the challenges of new media, and Demas urges other libraries to try modifications of the Mann model to determine what works best for them. These concepts are described with specific reference to the Internet in a 1995 treatment, "The Internet and Collection Development."[37]

Stanford University Libraries announced in September 1995 that it would recruit six Information Resources Specialists (IRS) to explore for two years the efficacy of placing computing specialists in academic departments to assist faculty in advancing their computer literacy and in using computing technologies for their teaching and research. Each of these positions requires a specific subject background at the baccalaureate level combined with experience in the academic computing field. There is no indication that these IRS agents will work in tandem with bibliographers assigned to the same academic units. Although the IRS agents will work in the main library about 20 percent of their work week, there is no indication how they will work with librarians. This is an interesting experiment and one that librarians will be watching closely, but it would have more potential interest for this discussion if it were linked with the library's collection development personnel.

A December 1995 job description for a collegiate librarian information officer holds more promise for ascertaining the future role of collection development librarians. This position locates a librarian with an engineering background in the College of Engineering for 50 percent of the time and in the main library for the balance. Its specifics are as follows:

offers faculty and students in the College of Engineering on-site, intradepartmental, discipline-related consulting to expand their awareness and use of information and technological resources . . . the CLIO will work with the College to advance the use of computing and information resources in research and teaching . . . assisting faculty with the use of the World Wide Web technology . . . collaborating on the development of information literacy programs within the College . . . promote the use of information services and technologies to support the College's program in writing across the curriculum and to facilitate communication among the members of the College.[38]

When in the main library, this librarian will provide reference, instructional, and collection development services in the sciences.

Whatever collection development and library organizations look like at a given point in the new century, it seems certain that they will be changing as the corporate vision, the technologies, and the demands of library users change. Bucknall's mandate for experimentation will no doubt characterize the last few years of the present century and several decades of the next. It will be exciting and daunting to forge ahead in the effort to provide quality information to an increasingly technology-based, yet ever-human, community.

NOTES

1. David Tyckoson, "Access vs. Ownership: Changing Roles for Librarians," *The Reference Librarian* 34 (1991): 41.

2. Ross Atkinson, "Access, Ownership, and the Future of Collection Development," in *Advanced Collection Management and Development Institute, 1993, Chicago, Ill.* (Chicago: American Library Association, 1993), pp. 93–94.

3. Ibid., pp. 105–6.

4. Michael Buckland, "What Will Collection Developers Do?" *Information Technology and Libraries* 14 (September 1995): 155–59.

5. Bonita Bryant, "The Organizational Structure of Collection Development," *Library Resources & Technical Services* 31 (April 1987): 111–22.

6. Jeanne Sohn, "Collection Development Organizational Patterns in ARL Libraries," *Library Resources & Technical Services* 31 (April 1987): 123–34.

7. James E. Bobick, comp., *Collection Development Organization and Staffing in ARL Libraries.* SPEC Kit 131 (Washington, DC: Association of Research Libraries, Office of University Management Studies, 1987).

8. Carol W. Cubberley, "Organization for Collection Development in Medium-Sized Academic Libraries," *Library Acquisitions: Practice & Theory* 11 (1987): 320.

9. James A. Cogswell, "The Organization of Collection Management Functions in Academic Research Libraries," *Journal of Academic Librarianship* 13 (1987): 268–76.

10. Ibid., pp. 274–76.

11. Carolyn Bucknall, "Organization of Collection Development and Management in Academic Libraries," *Collection Building*, nos. 3/4 (1988): 11–17.

12. Sheila Creth, "The Organization of Collection Development: A Shift in the Organization Paradigm," in Association of Research Libraries, Minutes of the [Joint Meeting at the University of York, September 19–22, 1988] (Washington, DC: Association of Research Libraries, 1989), pp. 105–15.

13. Sheila Creth, "The Organization of Collection Development: A Shift in the Organization Paradigm," *Journal of Library Administration* 14 (1991): 67–85.

14. Nancy M. Cline, "Staffing: The Art of Managing Change," in *Collection Management and Development: Issues in an Electronic Era. Proceedings of the Advanced Collection Management and Development Institute, Chicago, Ill., March 26–28, 1993*, ed. Peggy Johnson and Bonnie MacEwan (Chicago: American Library Association, 1994), pp. 13–28.

15. William C. Robinson, "Academic Library Collection Development and Management Positions: Announcements in *College & Research Libraries News* from 1980 through 1991," *Library Resources & Technical Services* 37 (1993): 134–46.

16. Peggy Johnson, "Collection Development Officer, a Reality Check: A Personal View," *Library Resources & Technical Services* 33 (1989): 153–60.

17. Jasper G. Schad, "Managing Collection Development in University Libraries That Utilize Librarians with Dual-Responsibility Assignments," *Library Acquisitions: Practice & Theory* 14 (1990): 165–71; Cline, "Staffing."

18. Chuck Hamaker, "Is Collection Development Narcissism?" *Against the Grain* 4, no. 2 (April 1992): 20+.

19. Samuel Demas, "Collection Development for the Electronic Library: A Conceptual and Organizational Model," *Library Hi Tech* 12, no. 3 (1994): 71–80.

20. Cogswell, "The Organization."

21. Cubberley, "Organization for Collection," p. 308.

22. Carla J. Stoffle, "Organizational Transformation: New Structures for New Realities," unpublished paper presented as part of "New Ways of Knowing, New Ways of Doing: Rethinking Collection Management in an Electronic Age," at the American Library Association Annual Conference, Chicago, 1995.

23. Kay A. Flowers, Kerry A. Keck, and Janice L. Lindquist, "Collection Development and Acquisitions in a Changing University Environment," *Library Acquisitions: Practice & Theory* 19 (1995): 463–69.

24. Cynthia M. Coulter and Katherine F. Martin, "Defining Boundaries: Acquisitions and Collection Management Responsibilities in a Changing Environment," in *Acquisitions 90: Conference on Acquisitions, Budgets, and Collections: Proceedings*, comp. and ed. David C. Genaway (Canfield, OH: Genaway, c1990), pp. 67–72.

25. Richard P. Jasper and Jane B. Treadwell, "Reorganizing Collections and Technical Services: Staffing is Key," *Library Acquisitions: Practice & Theory* 16 (1992): 361–66; Judith Niles, "Acquisitions and Collection Management Reorganization: An Exercise in Crisis Management," *Library Acquisitions: Practice & Theory* 16 (1992): 379–82; and Kathleen Wachel and Edward Shreeves, "An Alliance Between Acquisitions and Collection Management," *Library Acquisitions: Practice & Theory* 16 (1992): 383–89.

26. Bonita Bryant, "Allocation of Human Resources for Collection Development," *Library Resources & Technical Services* 30 (1986): 149–62; Paul Metz, "Quantifying

the Workload of Subject Bibliographers in Collection Development," *Journal of Academic Librarianship* 17 (1991): 284–87.

27. Cogswell, "The Organization."

28. Schad, "Managing Collection Development," p. 170.

29. Barbara A. Winters, "Dual-Role Collection Development Librarian: Personal and Organizational Management Issues: An ALCTS Preconference," *Library Acquisitions: Practice & Theory* 16 (1992): 295–98.

30. John M. Haar, "The Reference Collection Development Decision: Will New Information Technologies Influence Libraries' Collecting Patterns?" *The Reference Librarian* 22 (1988): 113–24; Ross Atkinson, "Text Mutability and Collection Administration," *Library Acquisitions: Practice & Theory* 14 (1990): 355–58; Marianne I. Gaunt, "Machine-Readable Literary Texts: Collection Development Issues," *Collection Management* 13 (1990): 87–96; Edward Shreeves, "Between the Visionaries and the Luddites: Collection Development and Electronic Resources in the Humanities," *Library Trends* 40 (1992): 579–95; William A. Britten, "Building and Organizing Internet Collections," *Library Acquisitions: Practice & Theory* 19 (1995): 243–49; Samuel Demas, Peter McDonald, and Gregory Lawrence, "The Internet and Collection Development: Mainstreaming Selection of Internet Resources," *Library Resources & Technical Services* 39 (1995): 275–90.

31. Karen M. Drabenstott, *Analytical Review of the Library of the Future* (Washington, DC: Council on Library Resources, 1994), p. 130.

32. Ibid., p. 169.

33. Marie Angela Bastiampillai and Peter Havard-Williams, "Subject Specialization Re-Examined," *Libri* 37 (1987): 209.

34. Daniel K. Blewett, "The Librarian Is in," *College & Research Libraries News* 56 (November 1995): 701–3.

35. Demas, "Collection Development for the Electronic Library."

36. Ibid., p. 71.

37. Demas, "The Internet and Collection Development."

38. *Chronicle of Higher Education*, December 1, 1995, p. B36.

11

Budgeting for Information Resources: Current Trends and Future Directions

William Fisher and Barbara G. Leonard

INTRODUCTION

As libraries and information centers move into the 21st century, they will continue to be faced with an array of challenges in developing and maintaining their collections. Some of those challenges are relatively minor and may have an impact on microlevel day-to-day operations, while other challenges are forcing the profession to reevaluate how we operate at the macrolevel and even question why we exist at all. Here is one collection-related example: in the opening of both the first (1979) and second (1987) editions of his text *Developing Library and Information Center Collections*, Evans quotes, "No Library of One Million Volumes can be all BAD!", and cites it as coming from a cover of the *Antiquarian Bookman*; in the third edition (1995) that quote is not used. Gone are the days when big is the same as good, or when libraries can think solely in terms of volumes or even primarily of ownership. The absence of that quote is no accident—it signifies a new way of thinking about library collections.

But there are no easy answers, and when the role of budgets in the collection picture is considered, it becomes a "chicken-or-egg" situation. Some will argue that it is the fiscal constraints faced by virtually all libraries that affect collection development today and force libraries to find new ways of making information available to their clients. Others will argue instead that new ways of building collections and acquiring material are partly responsible for the fiscal problems. Rather than try to resolve this specific debate, this chapter will look at some of the budgetary issues affecting the delivery of information resources by libraries to their clients.

One of the first issues that needs to be addressed by libraries is the increasing variety of formats that information resources can take and how that information would be ''acquired'' in a very broad sense of the word, and especially whether the information would physically reside within the library. The old dichotomy between print and nonprint takes on an entirely new meaning: Is it the way in which the information is created, stored, accessed, used, or physically transported from one location to another that matters? With these options in how information is packaged, libraries now find a variety of options for gaining access to these packages.

BUYING INFORMATION

The first option is to buy the material so that the library has outright ownership of the information package in question. This is one of the traditional ways libraries have provided access to their clients. The fiscal advantage of this option is that the library spends money once to acquire the material, and while there are costs involved in processing and housing the material, the acquisition cost is incurred only once—short of acquiring additional copies of the same material due to demand, damage, or loss. It is the purchasing library's property to do with as it wishes, within certain limitations such as existing copyright laws and any local regulations. The major drawback to this method of providing access is that money spent on one item cannot be used for other material if the original purchase is not being used or no longer meets clients' needs.

BORROWING INFORMATION

One of the primary alternatives to purchasing material is for the library to borrow the needed material from another library that already owns it. This usually takes the form of interlibrary loan, although variations on this method are prevalent. The most notable of the latter are arrangements that allow clients from one library to directly access material from another library without going through their own library first. Historically, there have been many advantages to this method of information access, since most of these arrangements were set up with the requesting library or its client paying little, if any, of the direct costs. This method has allowed libraries to provide access to low-demand material and meet clients' needs without purchasing the material. Funds that might have been used to acquire little-used items could be reallocated to access specifically requested items, thus permitting libraries to maximize access to information within their budgetary limits.

There are, however, some drawbacks to this method of access. In the case of interlibrary loan, at least within the United States, copyright law limits the number of times a library can borrow a title before it has to purchase the item, so a document could end up costing the library more than if a purchase had been made originally. Some libraries, primarily those with a significant imbalance between their roles as lender and as borrower, charge a fee to accept a loan request without any guarantee that the material will be provided. It is conceivable that a borrowing library could pay this fee many times and still not obtain the information sought without finally purchasing the material. For some libraries, the cost of not being able to provide immediate access to neeeded information for clients may be a big price to pay. Personal reciprocal arrangements have undergone changes as libraries experience greater pressure to demonstrate that they are using their available funds to deliver information services to their primary clientele. Although not universal, in-house use may still be available without direct charges. However, borrowing privileges may necessitate payment of a fee, although that fee may vary for different types of secondary clients. Finally, libraries that depend on interlibrary loan to supply low-demand material are finding that some of the newer information packages are not ''loanable'' in the traditional sense. Putting a book in the mail is a reasonably straightforward process; sending material in a nonprint format requires both the lending and borrowing libraries (or at least the borrowing client) to have similar equipment so the information can be accessed and used upon receipt.

DOCUMENT DELIVERY

The middle ground between outright purchase and interlibrary borrowing comes in the form of vendor-based document delivery systems. The basic model currently in use allows the client to search a database listing thousands of journal article citations. If certain articles are wanted, the client can order the information online directly from the vendor. Then, depending on how the individual library has structured the system, the client pays for the information or the cost is charged to the library's deposit account. The actual cost will also depend on the way in which the information is delivered from a range of options, including: fax transmission, file transfers to e-mail accounts, overnight mail, or standard mail delivery. Copyright fees are assessed directly by the vendor, so the same article can be requested as often as needed. (Of course, if the library is paying for this service, the repeated purchase of a specific item would need to be evaluated.) While this option nicely bridges the gap between purchase and borrowing, some drawbacks exist. As these services are currently structured, they only provide journal articles, and then only those from a core list of journals. Other types of information packages are not available, and there is a good deal of overlap of the journal titles covered by the major vendors. Since there are still relatively few vendors providing document delivery services on a wide basis, there is not a great deal of pricing flexibility or competition. This last point is important, since it leaves room for libraries with rich serials collections, especially in highly focused subject areas not covered by the commercial vendors, to introduce document delivery services of their own. However, what has not been clearly established is the financial impact of these delivery systems, especially in comparison with the costs of acquisition.

TRANSFERRING INFORMATION

Another method of acquiring information is electronically transferring information from a central repository (or multiple sites) into the library or information center that needs the information, or even directly to the client who has requested the information. The much touted ''virtual library'' would operate in this fashion, with a very small (if any) local collection but wide access to global information. The advantages and disadvantages of this electronic collection development are the topic of much discussion within the profession, as indeed is the possibility of developing universal access to any form of digitized information. While the cost of the technology to make this a useful reality is high, it is not as expensive as building new libraries, renovating existing structures, or acquiring remote storage facilities to accommodate larger, paper-based collections.

However, there is still a long way to go to get to a point of global electronic delivery. While the amount of digital information is growing, it will be some time before a significant percentage is obtainable in this manner. And that just emphasizes printed text; when options such as sound, video graphics, non-Roman alphabets, or handwritten materials are included, the time span required stretches even farther. Rigidly applied standards and/or universal interfaces are also needed for various systems to communicate successfully. This scenario also assumes levels of ''information literacy'' and of technological access which simply do not exist, even in highly developed countries like the United States. Less highly developed nations are even further away from having such infrastructures in place.

There are also numerous copyright issues that need to be addressed, both for older works and for newly created works. Existing copyright laws require modifications; and for this kind of access to be truly global, international copyright laws need revision, as well as cooperation in enforcement. Better monitoring of what is being acquired will also be needed to make copyright effective. This, however, brings up questions of privacy and whether these ''access'' records will be analogous to current circulation records, which are protected by law as confidental, at least in the United States. These concerns must be addressed as the shift from ''just-in-case'' collection development to ''just-in-time'' collection development continues.

ACCESS OR OWNERSHIP

Given the emphasis on accessibility to and not the ownership of materials, future allocation of library collection funds will be made for two purposes: to purchase materials for addition to the on-site library collection and to acquire materials for immediate delivery to library users, with or without consideration of later retention by the library.[1]

If these assumptions are correct, how will the information resources budget of the future be allocated? What can fiscal and collection development officers learn from the current situation that will assist them in future budgetary decisions?

The information resources budget was historically known as the acquisitions or materials budget, with materials being primarily print in nature. As information provided by libraries grew to include materials of a nonprint nature such as recordings, microform, and videos, the costs of these materials were also included in the information resources allocation schemes. In the early 1980s, online searching costs generated debates in librarianship as to the appropriateness of including their costs in the "materials budget." In the 1990s, no one blinks at the inclusion of leasing information such as CD-ROM databases in the information resources budget. In fact, there is such a wide disparity of formats and services within the realm of information resources that the budgets bear little resemblance to those of earlier libraries. And it is suspected that in the 21st century the library's information resources budget will undergo further transformations.

What is happening today that influences the allocation of information resources budgets? The problems of rising prices, increasing amounts of materials produced, the changing process of scholarly communication, and declining library budgets have been discussed at length elsewhere. It does not appear that these influences will change much for the better in the foreseeable future; therefore, librarians must come to grips with these problems and seek workable solutions.

In discussing the current state of libraries and the concern for costs, Lynden summarizes ten factors that have direct impact on the library budget: high inflation, declining proportion of funds received from parent institutions, increased range of materials purchases, equipment required for newer materials, electronic equipment, a sophisticated and knowledgeable staff, reduction in staff, inadequate and outmoded library buildings, deteriorating collections and the necessity for preservation and conservation, and education and training of staff.[2] These factors will continue to influence not only library services but also library collection growth as well as the distribution of library funds in a shift from "just-in-case" to "just-in-time" collections. Is it realistic to expect that collections shift from "just-in-case" to "just-in-time" and that the entire library budget will be restructured so that less is spent on personnel and more on information resources? Is that what library administrators and collection development personnel should expect?

JUST-IN-CASE TO JUST-IN-TIME: THE ACADEMIC PICTURE

As Saunders indicated, academic libraries in the year 2000 and beyond will purchase a basic core collection for use on-site and will purchase materials that users request for individual use. Biernan predicts the mix of ownership and access in the following manner: public and school libraries, 70 percent/30 percent; research libraries, 40 percent/60 percent; and special libraries, 20 percent/ 80 percent.[3] Assuming that most university libraries will fall into the research category, the shift to 60 percent of the library's collection being acquired "just-in-time" is an extraordinary change and will require major adjustments in the behavior of librarians, students, and faculty.

If the academic library collection shifts to providing only 40 percent of needed materials as a core collection and up to 60 percent of needed materials on demand, what might these two categories contain? The core collection might consist of the basic books and journals needed by undergraduates to complete their degrees. There will be electronic resources such as OPACs and CD-ROM indexes for accessing the local collections. There will be some librarian assistance, especially for library instruction. The main criteria for determining whether a work will be in the collection is its potential use by the students. Graduate students and faculty will become more dependent on finding their information electronically, and they are likely to do the majority of their work from a workstation away from the library.

How will this scenario affect library budgets? Certain funds will be set aside for the purchase of known items that support the undergraduate curriculum, as is done now. Items such as articles from journals not in the library collection will be acquired from a commercial document delivery service. Generally, these items will not be added to the library collection but will be given to the user requesting them because the costs of processing a specific paper journal article are not cost-effective. Even if the library paid for acquiring the article, it is still less costly than adding a printed article to the collection. On the other hand, libraries may decide to add such an article if it is received electronically and if the library has already established an archive of electronically transmitted journal articles. This would be relatively inexpensive to do.

What is not known at this time is the cost of electronic information in the 21st century. Although we suspect that libraries will be collecting information in electronic formats as well as providing access to information, no data are yet available on what the cost is likely to be to the library for collecting this format. Biernan indicates that the "costs of electronic information in the 21st century are murky at best."[4] Obviously, there are costs associated with the hardware and software necessary to acquire the information. Are there minimal or excessive staff costs associated with acquiring information? Can the user manage this alone and either pay for it or have the library pay for it?

RESTRUCTURING OF LIBRARY BUDGETS

Given the assumption that academic libraries will provide access to information rather than buying and storing information, how will the library's budget be structured in the first ten years of the next century? What influences will other campus services such as computing have on the library budget? Will there be more consolidation of information providers under one budget? Providing information or access to information is no longer the total responsibility of the library. The place of the computing groups on campuses began to be recognized in the 1980s and 1990s in terms of funding. Increasing proportions of university financial resources have been devoted to computing with a decreasing amount being devoted to libraries.[5] Can this continue in the first decades of the next century? New funding sources must be discovered, yet this appears to be highly unlikely; if users do not pay for the information they consume beyond the core collection, then a restructuring of university library budgets may be required.

Battin lists several directions in which institutional budgets could go:

- reallocation of resources within a particular division or department;
- reallocation within the university based on the determination of institutional priorities;
- generation of new revenue . . . by imposing new access fees on the user;
- commitment to new cooperative interinstitutional mechanisms for sharing infrastructure costs—such as networks, print collections, and database development and access.[6]

Assuming that the final three directions above do occur in some manner, the library still must address some sort of reallocation or restructuring of the budget from what has been done in the past. Traditionally, libraries have spent 60 to 70 percent on personnel, 20 to 30 percent on information resources, and 5 to 10 percent on operating expenditures. There have been subtle shifts in these percentages throughout the 1990s, with personnel dropping slightly, information resources remaining relatively stagnant despite the ravages of inflation on serials, and operating costs increasing due to increasing expenditures on automation.

Murray Martin has long advocated that libraries must look at restructuring their budgets; in *Academic Library Budgets* he summarizes four options available to libraries. These were first suggested by Webster in a paper prepared for an Association of Research Libraries Task Force on Staffing in 1984.

1. Maintain of the traditional paper-centered library, modified by the gradual introduction of new technologies. Budget concepts would remain relatively the same.
2. Expand the library role to include information transfer. This would increase the operating portion of the library budget but is not a radical change.
3. Shift the library to provide discipline-oriented information services. The budget would emphasize people and operating costs.
4. Develop a highly automated academic information center, to include a library. The budget would shift emphasis to technology.[7]

In response to the changing library, the structure of the budget must change as well. If the literature is correct and the trends continue toward the "virtual" library, as appears to be the case in the mid-1990s, the library of the future will have a smaller but more technologically-oriented and service-oriented staff that will require continuing retraining and development. Librarians and support staff together will be the "links" between the user and the information, no matter what the format. This being the case, libraries are likely to develop a budget like Martin/Webster's fourth option.

Can predictions be made about the academic library budget in the year 2010? The personnel commitment may decrease to 40 percent or less of the total budget. Technical services divisions might be reduced the most in personnel. Much of the acquisitions and cataloging work would be done by book vendors. Books will arrive in the library ready for shelving, cataloging records will be in the online catalog, and the only labor required by the library will be that of the students who shelve and reshelve the books. The portion of the information resources budget allocated to books will decline. As mentioned, books will be the core collections needed to support the undergraduates' coursework. Circulation will be patron-initiated via the automated circulation system, thus requiring fewer circulation staff members.

The traditional technical services functions of the library of the future will change dramatically. Outsourcing of technical services functions will continue to increase. As the number of books purchased for the core collection decreases, the function of an acquisitions department will become that of acquiring information in any form, and not merely acquiring books and materials. This will mean a smaller staff with differing responsibilities. Rather than buying books in the traditional manner, libraries will allow the vendors to choose the books based on a narrowly defined profile constructed by the library and the vendor. The books will be sent to the library, fully catalogued and shelf ready. Since the intermediate processing functions of searching, ordering, claiming, receiving, cataloging, and processing are eliminated, staff are freed for other functions or, as they retire or leave, their positions are either not replaced or are reassigned. Libraries at the University of Arizona, Stanford University, and California State University at Monterey Bay are already experimenting with this model.

In the library of the future, the acquisitions staff will procure information by means of document delivery. Van Goethem contends that there is a future for acquisitions and document delivery as long as the "library is paying for information" because control over the budget is needed.[8] Electronic access as the method of delivery of information will not reduce the cost of information. Therefore, cost reductions must come elsewhere in the restructuring of staff assignments and a corresponding decrease in staff costs.

Each faculty member will have an office computer workstation and will not need to enter the library to do research. Thus, there will be little need for mediation on the part of librarians for faculty research, although they still will be necessary to assist undergraduates. Fewer librarians will be needed for reference assistance, and such assistance will be by appointment only. Index searching assistance for in-house library users will be done by student assistants—a cheaper source of labor. Faculty members and students will be able to take advantage of delivery of information through commercial services. Such delivery of information will be partially subsidized by the library. Document delivery will replace most journal subscriptions, especially those in science and technology, although the library will continue to subscribe to titles supporting undergraduate education. Like the portion of the information resources budget allocated for books, that for serials subscriptions will also decline.

Delivery of information and access charges will comprise a major portion of the information resources budget. This portion will include the charges of the commercial document delivery service, the hardware and software to support the access to information tools, and the equipment within the library needed by the students and other users for access.

ARE USER FEES THE ANSWER?

In short, all these changes will involve a fundamental change in the way libraries budget for collection development. Under the current ownership model, there is some certainty. The acquisitions librarian knows what the total budget is, and once the decision has been made on how to divide that total, the acquisitions and collection development staff can monitor the funds as they are spent throughout the year. Budgetary controls under the newer access models will be more difficult to maintain. Knowledge of the book trade and how various vendors operate will no longer be enough. Acquisitions personnel will need to become more familiar with leasing arrangements and how to understand and negotiate contracts in order to get the "best deal" for their situations. Leasing information is not new to some libraries; however, it has usually been the exception rather than the rule. Keeping order among all the information formats from a larger variety of vendors will become a greater challenge than ever before.

Another fundamental change will take place in how all this information is paid for. It is clear that with the increasing reliance on electronically delivered information, library costs will not decrease in the 21st century. Young believes that costs to libraries will rise because of the expense of providing the information that library users need. He argues that "costs will take a variety of formats but most will be for equipment, resource purchase, and term access fees, not easily transferred to individual users."[9] Discussion of the additional costs associated with providing information to library users of the 21st century brings up the issue of fees for services. Librarians have long debated the "free versus fee" issue and generally concluded that if a user receives a product such as a printout, fees are permissible because the costs of providing the product (paper, toner, etc.) are being covered.

Malinconico reminds us that fees can be of two types—those that underwrite the costs of delivering a service to the library's basic clientele and those that are charged to other users.[10] In the electronic environment, should fees be charged to recover costs of the library in providing information? Can a distinction be drawn between "basic" and "other" users? Should librarians charge for the actual information?

Current user-fee models exist; however, they may not be transferable from one library to another. Some corporate libraries use sophisticated models that allow them to charge back all their activities and operate as a profit center for the organization. On the other hand, most public and academic libraries do not charge at all, or only charge for "nonbasic" services. The search for some middle ground or compromise position might prove to be worthless. Each library or information center has a unique set of budgetary factors to which it must respond. Using whatever local factors may exist, each library will need to develop or adapt a user-fee model that makes both political and fiscal sense for that library. The model could be source-specific, delivery mechanism–specific, client-specific, or some combination of all these factors. However, without significant changes in funding algorithms for all types of libraries by parent institutions, greater reliance on user fees seems all but inevitable.

CONCLUSION

As libraries and information centers enter the next century, the trends and directions discussed above may have an even more significant impact on the budgeting process than they do already. Some trends have been prominent for only a relatively short time, and new issues appear frequently. The result is that collection developers and acquisitions personnel in concert with fiscal officers must continue to educate themselves, their constituents, their funding sources, and their professional colleagues about how delivery of information resources affects budget development and budget management.

NOTES

1. Laverna M. Saunders, ed., *The Virtual Library: Visions and Realities* (Westport, CT: Meckler, 1993), p. 73.

2. Frederick C. Lynden, "Remote Access Issues: Pros and Cons," *Journal of Library Administration* 20 (1994): 20–23.

3. Saunders, *The Virtual Library*; Kenneth John Biernan, "Costs of Electronic Information," in *Encyclopedia of Library and Information Science* (1994), vol. 54, pp. 132–33.

4. Biernan, "Costs of Electronic Information," p. 134.

5. Patricia Battin, "New Ways of Thinking About Financing Information Services," in *Organizing and Managing Information Resources on Campus* (McKiney, TX: Academic Computing Publishers, 1989), p. 374.

6. Ibid., pp. 381–82.

7. Murray S. Martin, *Academic Library Budgets* (Greenwich, CT: JAI Press, 1993), p. 247.

8. Jeri Van Goethem, "Whether by Byte or by Tome, Buying Information Is 'Acquisitions,' " *Library Acquisitions: Practice & Theory* 17 (1993): 361.

9. Philip H. Young, "Visions of Academic Libraries in a Brave New Future," in *Libraries and the Future: Essays on the Library in the Twenty-First Century* (New York: Haworth Press, 1993), p. 52.

10. S. Michael Malinconico, "Technology and the Academic Workplace," *Library Administration and Management* 5 (Winter 1991): 27.

PART VII

Cooperative Collection Development and Management

12

The Axioms, Barriers, and Components of Cooperative Collection Development

Richard J. Wood

INTRODUCTION

As we enter the 21st century and a period of great technological change in libraries and library networks, it seems appropriate to review, and to speculate about, the two primary aspects of cooperative collection management, cooperative collection development and cooperative collection assessment. More specifically, the facilitators of cooperative collection development, or barriers to it, are the focus of the author. Variables which affect cooperative collection development, such as leadership, turf protectionism, financial support, bibliographic control, electronic publishing, full-text electronic article delivery, integrated library systems, the Internet, and telecommunications, are each examined briefly.

The environments in which the facilitators are more likely to occur are also addressed in the context of library networks, consortia, systems, authorities, or other cooperative arrangements. These cooperative library groups shall be referred to synonymously in this chapter as library networks or consortia, meaning a ''group of individuals or organizations that are interconnected to form a system to accomplish some specific goal. This linkage must include a communications mechanism. . . .''[1] Thus, two or more libraries which have agreed to cooperate with each other for cooperative collection assessment and cooperative collection development would meet Martin's criteria, assuming that the libraries communicate with each other regarding these programs. This broad definition includes public library systems like Philadelphia's, regional networks like AMIGOS or SOLINET, large university library systems with separately administered libraries like the University of Texas, and area library system authorities like those in the state of Indiana.

THE STATE OF COOPERATIVE COLLECTION MANAGEMENT

There are about 600 library networks, consortia, and other cooperative library organizations in the United States, according to the Association of Specialized and Cooperative Library Agencies.[2] The majority (385) of them are single-type library consortia. The *American Library Directory* lists far fewer library consortia, networks, and other cooperative library organizations in the United States and Canada because the publisher, American Library Association, relies on public information or the input of administrators to whom surveys were sent, and not all respond.[3] The *Directory* has long included research, public, academic, school, medical, law, and other types of library consortia or networks located in North America.

Library networks may be classified in a variety of ways. California legislation outlines an "all-in-one" or "multidimensional" model.[4] All-in-one cooperatives are networked together under one regional entity. Multidimensional cooperatives are linked in geographic clusters, or the libraries are linked to like libraries throughout the region. McCrossan classifies library networks as single or multijurisdictional; both types may be loosely or tightly governed, but are nonprofit.[5] Library networks may be categorized by the functions they offer; however, most networks provide both primary and secondary functions. Most library networks in the United States are nonprofit, but another type is a commercial network such as Dialog. A more thorough discussion of network models, types, or paradigms can be read in a basic reader.[6]

The *American Library Directory* specifies the primary functions of the library networks and consortia it indexes. The vast majority of these primary functions involve interlibrary loan, information resources sharing, reciprocal borrowing, union listing, continuing education, and staff development functions. It seems obvious that networks were formed by libraries primarily to share their collections, staff expertise, and an economy of scale made possible by larger orders. In these ways, networks can help member libraries provide better services and collections. The desire to improve services and resources for their users, of course, is the raison d'être for libraries, and should be for networks as well, although they work through, or on behalf of, their member libraries.

It should be obvious that functions of library networks could be classified as primary or secondary. It may be assumed that when functions are not listed in the *American Library Directory*, they are either secondary functions of the library networks or not functions of the networks, because only the primary functions are supposed to be reported. Further, the status of library consortiums' functions may change over time because leadership, technology, and circumstances change continually.

An examination of state legislation and regulations which relate to multitype libraries of thirty-four states within the United States shows that cooperative acquisitions and collection development activities are common elements of the laws.[7] That is, the laws enable library networks to practice cooperative collection management programs, but they do not mandate it. While their long histories offer rich stories of mutually beneficial, multitype library cooperation, it is clear from examining the entries of the *Directory* that cooperative collection development and cooperative collection assessment, or other aspects of cooperative collection management such as preservation and storage, are either secondary functions of library consortia, or not a function at all. Further, a cursory comparison of the functions listed in the *Directory* with those listed in a previous study of academic library networks does not show a significant increase in cooperative collection management practices, except for the implementation of the Conspectus by research libraries, libraries in the Pacific Northwest, and other local and regional cooperatives around the country.[8]

While most libraries of all types and sizes generally have procedures for the selection and acquisition of books, periodicals, and other materials, not all libraries have written collection development manuals—nor wish to write them. Gorman and Howes note that the national libraries like the British Library and Bibliotheque Nationale, as well as many of the historically considered great university libraries existed for many decades without the benefit of such policies because they ''. . . simply relied on their genuine passion for literature and in-bred instinct for what was 'right' when collecting.''[9] Merritt blames the ''natural human procrastination rather than . . . disagreement or opposition, though some disagreement may indeed exist.''[10] No matter what the reason, this author doubts that the situation is different when it comes to wanting to write cooperative collection development policies. In reality, very little information about actual collection development practices and policies of libraries or networks is known, because such policies are not collected anywhere centrally at the state and national levels. We do know more about research level libraries, however, because their policies are often reproduced in the literature, particularly by the Office of Management Studies of the Association of Research Libraries (ARL). The hundreds of libraries that use the RLG, WLN, or other Conspectus approach follow somewhat standard collection coding strategies and practices. The reader may find that this chapter, as a result, reflects this understandable but disappointing state of affairs, which is especially true of public and special libraries. It should be no surprise, then, that we generally know very little about the cooperative collection development and cooperative collection assessment policies and practices of libraries that belong to library consortia.

Nonetheless, cooperative collection management among libraries of all types is a decades-old enterprise which has excited and challenged hundreds of library managers, library network administrators, and collection development librarians.[11] In the preface to his book, Harloe says:

In the last decade, collection management has become a primary concern for all types of libraries. As libraries are confronted by increasing information resources and shrinking fiscal resources, and as online bibliographic access proliferates, coordinated and cooperative collection development as well as shared access to materials become vital to meeting the information needs of all.[12]

There are many reasons for cooperative collection development. Frequent articles and news reports by periodical vendors point out the high cost and continuing price inflation of journals. Roberts discusses science serials specifically.[13] Biggs and Sartori emphasize national and regional collection development of serials.[14] These factors make serials a prime target for cooperative collection management activities. Smith provides us with an example of cooperative collection development for rare books among academic libraries.[15] Cooperative collection development efforts are often directed by the cost of titles; availability of the title in the region; and the need to strengthen subject coverage, to fill gaps in the collection, to replace worn or missing volumes; or to acquire a type of material like microfilm for space or budgetary reasons.

Electronic media, the newest formats "collected" by libraries and library networks, prompt a special discussion because electronic media seem to have overshadowed all other formats during the 1990s. Cooperative collection management discussions need to be broadened to include CD-ROM, tape-loaded, and other electronic media which are acquired or licensed by libraries, or remote databases accessed through the Internet or dial-up connections. We might also, as a result, have to broaden our concept of cooperative collection management to include commercial enterprises, publishers, utilities, government agencies, professional associations, and other entities which are responsible for making electronic resources available to users, including libraries. Whether or not library networks, consortia, authorities, or systems include nonlibrary entities, it is clear that the electronic media have had a profound impact on cooperative collection development, cooperative collection assessment, and other library and library network services. Historically, however, their direct involvement in libraries' cooperative collection management activities has been minimal.

EARLY HISTORY

Prior to World War II, in the United States, there were very few cooperative collection development activities reported by libraries except at the local level. This lengthiest stage of cooperative collection development provides very little documentation in the library literature of those efforts which were centered, for the most part, around union listing of serials, cooperative and centralized acquisitions, reciprocal borrowing, and interlibrary lending. At that time, of course, there were no automated library systems, few audiovisual materials to collect, no national or large regional bibliographic utilities, no integrated library systems, and no computer networks for easy electronic communication to facilitate cooperative library programs. Transportation and communication systems mitigated against cooperation. Despite the appearance of the *National Union Catalog* and the *Union List of Serials* before World War II, libraries largely acted independently of one another in terms of assessing and developing their collections because, except for expensive monographic and serial sets, few librarians or users saw the need for or benefits of cooperative collection development and assessment. Users saw libraries as local warehouses for books, journals, and other printed sources. Any efforts at cooperation were most likely regarded as too costly in terms of time and energy. That is, library directors and collection developers most likely did not see a favorable cost-to-benefit ratio, if they even reflected on this matter.

POST–WORLD WAR PERIODS

It is not necessary to go much beyond World War II, however, to find well-known examples of cooperative collection development, as well as illustrations of facilitators and barriers. The formation of public library systems is probably the most widely known example whereby previously independent public libraries were placed in systems by public officials in order to save taxpayers' money. Many of these systems selected and acquired books and other materials cooperatively. The librarians or library staff who selected and acquired materials in the branch libraries met collectively on a periodic basis to coordinate collection development. This cooperative collection development model has remained enormously effective, despite the apparent lack of methodical collection assessment by the branch and main libraries.

Although the library consortium is now known popularly as the CRL (Center for Research Libraries), it began as the Midwest Inter-Library Center (MILC). It was established in 1949 by ten major midwestern university libraries.[16] After MILC's membership grew beyond the Midwest during the 1960s, its name was changed to the Center for Research Libraries. In response to pressures to cooperate in the acquisition of research materials, the CRL cooperated in collecting rare, expensive, and infrequently used research materials. The CRL now has over 100 members and inputs their records into both RLIN's and OCLC's databases for resource sharing purposes, using either bibliographic utility.[17] Obviously, the development of OCLC and RLIN, as well as the integrated library systems of research libraries, were the chief factors leading to the success of cooperative collection assessment and cooperative collection development efforts by the research libraries. As these systems generally were cost prohibitive for nonresearch level libraries until the 1980s, nearly all cooperative collection development activities that used these technologies were limited to research level libraries which could afford large computers and programming staff.

Dougherty identifies another single-type network which serves a special purpose, the Research Libraries Group (RLG).[18] ARL's publication details the charge of the RLG's Collection Development Committee:

1. the allocation of collection responsibility for subjects, geographical areas and forms of material;
2. the establishment of a mechanism for the sharing of information on the acquisition of materials including expensive items and materials of limited use; and
3. the placement of serial titles wanted in RLG institutions on the basis of collection strengths.[19]

As Dougherty says, the RLG's mission of trying to achieve the broadest possible coverage of relevant materials while reducing duplication might "appear to be overly idealistic, but when one realizes that university research libraries today are able to acquire only about 5 to 7 percent of the world's publishing output, the importance of collaboration becomes more apparent."[20]

The mechanism that RLG developed was the North American Collections Inventory Project (NCIP), which is based on the RLG Conspectus. It provides descriptions of member collections using the Library of Congress Classification Number System (LCCN). Even with this powerful tool, all the research libraries in the United States fail to collect a significant portion of the world's literature. It is little wonder, then, that national libraries in other countries fail in their efforts, too. According to Woodsworth,

The failure of the United States to establish a national library mandate for the Library of Congress is perhaps the single most significant factor in the shape of the present plural and voluntary character of its library cooperative projects.[21]

Later efforts to correct the mistake failed, Woodsworth continued, because of lack of funds, inadequate technology, and insufficient organizational commitment in early efforts during the 19th century.[22] The failure to establish a single national library in the United States gave rise to the multipronged approach to collection development we see today. Our "national" libraries in the United States—the Library of Congress, the National Library of Medicine, and the National Library of Agriculture—are the direct result of the federal role in supporting library efforts to collect the world's literature. All the efforts of these three national libraries are still far from sufficient in this regard.

The collective efforts of other federal and major research-level libraries in the United States, mainly those by ARL, RLG, and CRL institutions, have been responsible for the greatest percentage of cooperative collection development activities in library history. In addition, federal libraries in the United States formed a single-type library network called FEDLINK, which now includes well over 1,000 federal government libraries and information centers. Although the federal funds that have gone into the establishment, support, and maintenance of the collections of these hundreds of libraries are modest in comparison with defense or social agency budgets, the sums are evidence of federal investments made to support U.S. libraries.

Several federal programs have assisted libraries in cooperative collection development efforts: the Farmington Plan in 1942, the Cooperative Acquisitions Project for Wartime Publications in 1946, the Library Services Act (1956), the Latin American Cooperative Acquisitions Project in 1959, the Public Law 83–480 program in 1962, the Higher Education Act of 1963, the Library Services and Construction Act (1964), and the Medical Library Assistance Act of 1965, to name the most commonly reported.[23] The statewide cooperative collection development efforts of Illinois, Alaska, and the Pacific Northwest libraries are perhaps the most frequently cited and best-known examples.[24] Alabama, California, New York, and other states provide other examples.[25] The RLG or WLN Conspectus is the cooperative collection assessment or development framework used in these states, as well as many regional, specialized, or other geographic areas.[26]

Perhaps the best-known example of cooperative collection development exists among the members of Research Libraries Group (RLG) who use the RLG Conspectus.[27] The Conspectus was conceived initially as an inventory and collection assessment tool by an initial four RLG member libraries (Columbia, Harvard, Yale, and New York Public). The tool they developed became a standard framework to indicate the depth of past collecting and current collection depth, using the Library of Congress system.[28] The Conoco study of the Research Libraries Group documents the impact of cooperative collection development with respect to the German language and geology.[29] According to Dougherty, "the major contribution of the Conoco study is that it highlights the fact that selectors behave in a way that makes shared collection programs a practical option."[30] German and geology bibliographers changed their selection decisions 40 percent and 50 percent of the time respectively.[31]

Collecting collaboratively by country is one of the earliest examples of cooperative collection development among North American research libraries. It is odd to think of World War II as a facilitator of cooperative collection management, but one library historian connects the two in this way:

An outgrowth of the war was a recognition that American collection efforts had been primarily Western European in orientation. World War II revealed major gaps in . . . Eastern Europe, especially the Soviet Union. There was also a notable lack of materials about Africa, the Middle East and Asia. The Farmington Plan, certainly one of the most ambitious collection efforts ever undertaken by a group of librarians, was conceived in 1942 and initiated in 1948.[32]

Libraries that participated in the Farmington Plan accepted acquisitions and cataloging responsibilities for specific geographic areas.[33] Weber's review shows how the federal government supported this and other efforts for the acquisition and cataloging of research materials in the national interest.[34] The Farmington Plan and the Latin American Cooperative Acquisitions Project both ceased in 1972 due to inadequate finances, withdrawal of members, and the somewhat overlapping program of the Library of Congress.[35] Readers interested in pursuing federal and state roles in library cooperative efforts can consult a number of readings.[36]

Additional federal dollars have supported some profound technological changes in libraries. Millions of public dollars have supported research and development of OCLC and its regional networks, and the development of integrated library systems. These have significant direct and indirect impact on cooperative collection management. Millions of federal dollars, for example, have supported the preservation efforts of the Library of Congress, research libraries, library networks, and other libraries. Most recently, the federal government has been supporting the efforts of libraries and educational entities to gain free and easy access to the Internet through local or regional utilities. Federal funding attempts to involve libraries and library networks in preservation imaging has resulted in cooperative collection management efforts of libraries and library networks through grant opportunities.

If the library literature accurately reflects new cooperative collection management efforts, the failure over the past decade of more library networks to embrace cooperative collection assessment and cooperative collection development activities is hard to explain in light of any number of variables and technologies which should act as facilitators. These include:

• the pervasive use of large bibliographic utilities such as OCLC and its subsystems or services;

• retrospective conversion projects of existing collections;

• implementation of integrated online library systems;

• the increase in the number of local area networks;

• the growth of the Internet and libraries' access to it;

• the increase in citation and full-text electronic document delivery providers;

• access to and use of the databases available through electronic networks; and

• use by patrons of the same electronic databases and Internet resources as are used by librarians or available in libraries.

An interesting phenomenon is that citizens of democratic countries not only expect free access to library and information resources through public libraries and tax supported academic libraries, but they also expect inexpensive access to such databases from their home workstations through commercial services. Several major commercial providers of the Internet connection and/or a variety of electronic databases are waiving subscription fees for a limited time in order to entice customers into becoming regular, paying monthly users.

ANALYSIS AND PROGNOSIS: THE PARADIGM SHIFT

As access to both citation and full-text databases has increased during the 1990s, the idea of building library collections seems to have become a more distant thought, or is being questioned by more librarians or other administrators in the parent organization. As vendors and library networks have offered libraries more electronic products, and as libraries have offered more electronic databases to their clients, many librarians and library network managers have worried about their future viability. This chapter shows that a paradigm shift is leaving some librarians out of the collection management decision-making process for electronic databases. Not all librarians are sure that more cooperation among libraries helps to maintain libraries and library networks as vital organizations in the collection, assessment, storage, retrieval, and dissemination of information and literature. Librarians who are able to affect such cooperation need to realize not only the potential value of the electronic media, and cooperative collection management, but also the ramifications discussed here.

It is important to understand, however, that the cooperation which is essential if libraries are to remain useful to their clients is not just limited by formal, interlocal government agreements, bylaws of library consortia, and network agreements. Academic libraries and computing centers, for example, have been cooperating on many campuses and in many systems for decades without agreements or bylaws. Such alliances have seemed natural, expected, and taken for granted. Some directors of both the library and computing services have been reporting to the same chief university administrator for many years; the practice may increase as libraries become more dependent on campus area networks and computing resources. Many academic libraries have become almost totally reliant on the campus computer services department for library automation, database management, and related services, unless they maintain their own computer systems. The similarity of their information-related goals has led some computer centers to install CD-ROM databases on their systems independently of the library. This is likely to be the case with public libraries and school libraries, where teachers will ask system staff, not librarians, to install CD-ROM titles on the system. This is but one example of collection development decision making being taken from the librarian.

At the same time, a growing percentage of the budgets of all libraries, as well as library networks, is earmarked for the purchase of electronic databases, licenses, development and maintenance of integrated library systems, microcomputers, computer printers, related supplies, microcomputer maintenance agreements, and software. The types of decisions associated with these matters are more managerial, often based on costs, license agreements, computer support, and the like. Academic reference librarians are spending less time helping students with printed sources and more time teaching them how to access the electronic databases. For more academic librarians, collection development responsibilities should represent a decreasing percentage of the total hours worked.

None of the foregoing discussion is meant to suggest that collection management programs in any type of library or library cooperative organization are or should be any less important today than before. The author believes that the opposite is true. For one thing, there has been no decline in book or journal publishing. For another, the electronic media have been limited thus far to the types of information and data suited for this medium, not retrospective or current literature. Rather, the point is to suggest that the technological advances have shifted priorities in the budgets and staffing of libraries and library networks. More important and relevant to the discussion, the advances have shifted decision making for some electronic databases and access questions from bibliographers and selectors to managers, sometimes nonlibrary managers.

Future library cooperative collection management and resource sharing activities are likely to include electronic media and telecommunications for rapid retrieval and dissemination of information and text because library budgets are not growing fast enough to keep pace with inflation and the demand for print materials. It seems to follow that the attention of librarians will be refocused on working cooperatively through their library consortia to share the costs of electronic databases. These technological advances have led to dramatic changes in how library staff and patrons access bibliographic information, obtain the holdings information of their home library and those of other libraries, and use (or do not use) collections and libraries. These factors, which this chapter now explores, should also be factored into the paradigm shift.

Dougherty emphasizes that the availability of large databases such as OCLC and RLIN stimulates greater participation in resource sharing activities.[37] Libraries with Internet access can easily, conveniently, and inexpensively check the holdings of libraries with known strong collections in any subject area. Cooperative collection assessment and development efforts, then, have been enhanced by the ease with which librarians and users are able electronically to consult local and other libraries' holdings. Librarians may decide not to consider the purchase of an expensive title or series because another library's online catalog shows that a copy is held in that location. Moreover, less importance has been attached to the proximity of the holding location as more and more libraries around the world input their bibliographic records into OCLC's union catalog and use its ILL subsystem.

Likewise, OCLC member libraries, and members of its regional or state GACs, as they are called, have little need to maintain additional regional or area union databases. The success of OCLC's Group Access Capability (GAC) demonstrates the need for more cooperative collection management, not less. GACs make the collections of smaller libraries accessible across the group of participating libraries and establish the advantages of cooperation. Many of these smaller libraries have a surprising number of unique holdings which become more widely used across the GAC membership. Atkinson, for example, notes that in Illinois the lending by small libraries increased once their holdings were input into the OCLC database.[38] If the limited budgets of all libraries are used to strengthen each library's collections in particular subject areas, there is more, not less, reason to be interested in cooperative collection assessment and cooperative collection development programs.

The costs of all materials, as well as database licenses, management, and maintenance, are major considerations of library managers today. The costs of many CD-ROM products are comparable to their printed counterparts and, therefore, compete with them favorably even though the electronic technologies require computer hardware, software, maintenance, and telecommunications. These associated costs are sometimes justified by library and network managers because the purchase of electronic media results in (and from) high customer satisfaction, as well as demand for more electronic databases. The costs and benefits associated with the electronic media, of course, must be compared with the costs associated with acquiring, cataloging, processing, shelving, shelf maintenance, binding, and preservation for monographs. Fortunately, features of the electronic databases such as keyword searching, hypertext links, online help, and the like have become fairly standard in each of the major vendors' systems—again due to competition and universal user satisfaction with these features. Otherwise, such factors would be extremely difficult for decision makers to consider.

Many directors are trying to account for the "hidden" costs associated with electronic databases (for instance, reformatting and refreshing tapes, reconverting data for new automated systems, switching vendors, simultaneously acquiring print versions of the same or similar databases, public relations, training, maintenance). It is becoming clear to many library managers that some print databases are far less expensive or more cost-justified when all factors are considered.

Because most libraries generally have shouldered all of the costs of electronic databases without receiving additional funds for them, we have to question whether their budgets will soon reach the breaking point. This is the point in the decision-making process when materials considered core or absolutely essential have to be cut in order to continue the electronic database subscriptions or purchases—or any other acquisitions considered absolutely essential. If yet another new electronic format or title is being marketed when most libraries have reached this breaking point, it seems unlikely that any new format will be supported, especially if it depends upon the purchase of more powerful computer hardware and software. There should be little doubt that the electronic technologies have exacerbated the situation, because more, not fewer, books, journals, and other materials are printed and needed than ever before. The need to acquire printed materials, that is, has not decreased with the purchase of or subscription to electronic databases. In any case, both the demand for electronic databases and the increased strain on libraries' budgets should have acted as facilitators of cooperative collection development. Healthy libraries and library networks seem never to have enough electronic databases, or access to them at affordable costs. The prospect of obtaining access to databases, files, and conversational areas of bulletin board systems on the Internet holds some promise for smaller and rural libraries, although it will be well into the 21st century before most of them have access to the Internet.

Library consortia and networks with paid training staff have helped members plan for, acquire, and learn how to use telecommunication systems and electronic databases available through the Internet. These network services may be crucial for public and other libraries that do not have a centralized computing center on which to rely. If they cannot rely on the network or a cooperative arrangement for hardware, telecommunications, computer memory, software and hardware maintenance, and staffing costs associated with accessing the electronic media, they will not have access. Library networks offer an economy of scale similar to universities, which are able to "charge" computing and telecommunication costs over many administrative and academic departments. Library networks should be able to charge such costs over a number of member libraries, thereby reducing substantially the costs to any one member. The alternative might be to rely on one or more stand-alone microcomputer workstations, if funds allow.

While access to the Internet might be a minor cost to academic libraries served by campus computing centers, Internet access for the users of school and small public libraries is still largely lacking. For most schools and school districts, the costs of telecommunications, networking, multimedia work stations, printer, paper, and maintenance are too burdensome to consider at the campus level. If school libraries enjoy such services, they are likely to experience limitations in terms of the number of workstations, location, use, and training time. Busy reference librarians and media specialists typically lack the time to learn and maintain Internet skills. Providing quality database service with only one or two library professionals and paraprofessionals seems to be an insurmountable challenge for any understaffed library; yet the electronic media and Internet hold out the promise of leveling the playing field so that size and location of the library is irrelevant for cooperative collection development purposes.

Anyone who predicted the demise of libraries and library networks when telecommunications, automation, and electronic databases became publicly available and relatively inexpensive has been proven wrong well before the end of the 20th century. Not only does it appear that books and journals will be published in greater numbers than ever before, but their use has increased in most libraries, as can be seen from comparing circulation statistics. The "electronic revolution" appears to be but one more revolution survived by libraries and librarians and can be added to the others: the microcard, microform, Xerox, audiovisual materials, teaching machines, and computer-assisted-learning revolutions of the decades following World War II.

Most people continue to prefer print formats for fiction, philosophy, literature, poetry, textbooks, and subject matter where critical thinking and understanding are essential for comprehension. Scholars continue to show higher regard for scholarly monographs because most undergo critical review prior to publication—that is, they have been subject to peer and editorial review. Most academics generally regard the types of material found on the Internet so far as mostly conversational, unreliable, and nonauthoritative. Scholarly publications do not often cite bulletin boards, listserv messages, or other electronic material in their publications. Librarians have already begun to treat electronic databases as they have other formats by developing written collection development policies which include selection criteria for them. These selection criteria have generally excluded conversational areas of the Internet and local electronic bulletin boards.

Library networks also have been affected by a number of technological changes. When most of their large academic and public library members, for example, had converted their bibliographic holdings, the large OCLC networks, which had their own computer systems, began revealing financial losses. The revenue from large retrospective conversion projects was no longer providing sufficient funds during the 1990s to compensate for computer and staffing expenses. By 1995, this environment had forced AMIGOS to sell off its relatively new computer system, cut staff, eliminate its computer services division, and otherwise simplify its organizational structure. AMIGOS increased its research and development efforts, added potentially profitable new services, dropped unprofitable ones, and implemented a new dues and fee structure designed to attract new members. AMIGOS had already put in place a diversified list of services and products beyond those related to OCLC.

As early as the 1980s, AMIGOS began brokering the OCLC Collection Analysis Compact Disk (CACD) product in the United States. It also offered another collection management service whereby an academic library's holdings were compared with *Books for College Libraries*. SOLINET and AMIGOS also obtained grants enabling them to move into preservation services, mostly training and consulting. Both networks offered other vendors' CD-ROM databases for sale to members along with training and installation. Other networks have made similar adjustments and responses.

Strong competition among library automation, periodical, and other vendors has produced such a wealth of affordable electronic products that cooperative purchasing and licensing agreements are being negotiated at many levels. Texas state universities in 1995, for example, successfully completed a bidding process for a statewide contract which resulted in contracting with UMI for its general and business databases, including ASCII full text when available. The costs of such databases are far less than what even the largest individual member libraries would pay.

Librarians are beginning to see more than just a wider range of options for the purchase or licensing of electronic databases, including full-text services. While the options are desirable, one should be aware that there has been a major paradigm shift in library collection management practices and policies. The decision-making process for electronic databases in some cases has moved from the selector level to the library management level. Reference librarians can suggest or advise which databases they prefer, but the ultimate choice has shifted higher up the hierarchy because of the sums of money involved, the need to analyze licensing agreements, or to meet critieria of library network agreements. The important differences between electronic and printed media become obvious when technical specifications for computer hardware and telecommunication or other devices must be planned before the database can be used. Also important in the acquisition of electronic periodical indexes is the impact on stack maintenance and interlibrary loan. As users find more citations to library journals, use of bound or microfilmed journals increases. More of the library's budget, therefore, might have to go toward stack maintenance, interlibrary loan, and full-text article delivery services, thus making electronic formats more costly than print format.

Internet and some electronic databases raise additional problems because of their lack of bibliographic control, file organization, indexing and abstracting, or lack of search capabilities. Librarians must now weigh—and weight—a host of different variables than those used for book selection. While library catalogers worry about what standards are applicable and wonder how they can classify or describe moving electronic targets on the Internet, standard markup languages and other bibliographic control methods are being developed by nonlibrarians.

The fear that electronic technologies, including document delivery services, will lead to the demise of cooperative collection management and resource sharing seems, in the final analysis, to be unfounded. There simply are too many electronic titles for each school, college, university, public, and special library in any multitype library network to acquire. Each library can acquire only a percentage of those electronic databases and services that are appropriate to their clientele. The same is true for electronic document delivery services. There is very little evidence that the document delivery services of the various vendors has adversely affected the benefits of cooperative collection development among consortia members. If libraries could offer their users free electronic document delivery services on the same basis as their interlibrary loan services, it might potentially result in cancellation of periodical subscriptions which are expensive and infrequently used. At this time, however, commercially supplied full-text article delivery is too costly for this to happen. Moreover, a library which offers free interlibrary loan service is not likely to cancel subscriptions if librarians believe that the number of interlibrary loan requests will increase to a point that counteracts the savings, or shifts costs back to interlibrary loan. Librarians are more likely to cancel subscriptions and standing orders to titles which they believe have low demand, or which they know are held by a consortium library in close proximity, and available through interlibrary loan or reciprocal borrowing.

BARRIERS TO COOPERATIVE COLLECTION MANAGEMENT

Despite the paradigm shift evident in the growth of cooperative collection development activities, there are many barriers to effective cooperation. This section discusses some of the more significant barriers. Turf protectionism, or a desire to be self-sufficient, is a major blockage in cooperative collection management efforts. This "custodial attitude" is characterized by a library director whose limited vision fosters the belief that cooperation will decimate the collection, take too much staff time and money for committee meetings, and result in spending local funds on materials or programs that will benefit the users of other libraries more than the local library.[39] Sharing cooperative collection development responsibilities with members of a local consortium, therefore, might mean loss of autonomy as well as loss of resources. Mosher notes that "each institution's natural desire for academic self-sufficiency . . . helps to foster competition among American university research libraries and a myth of the self-sufficient 'comprehensive' collection necessary for any library with pretensions to greatness."[40] Research libraries are not unique in this feeling and spirit. "Cooperative resource sharing arrangements must be perceived as being mutually beneficial," says Dougherty. He adds that this does not mean "absolute borrowing/lending parity is essential."[41]

A lack of support, commitment, or leadership on the part of library directors or their governing board weakens cooperative collection management efforts. The unwillingness of some library directors to share decision making through committees, or their reluctance to obtain input about procedures, methodologies, and public relations leads to lack of backing on the part of staff involved in cooperative collection development. Lack of support and commitment on the part of some or all of those charged with collection development responsibilities can limit progress in selection and ordering procedures.

The failure to develop and operate a cooperative collection management program under the auspices of a formally recognized, if not legally constituted, governing structure such as a library system, network, area authority, consortium, or parent institution might deter progress. A school or medical board, for instance, might block or restrict cooperative collection management programs because library services are not one of their primary goals.

Lack of knowledge and training in collection assessment, collection development, or other aspects of collection management by members of the libraries' governing bodies, administrative superiors, or members of the staff with collection management responsibilities is also a handicap. When librarians are assigned collection development responsibilities without training in how to recognize quality materials, many excellent materials may be overlooked or poor materials ordered. Spending scarce dollars on the preservation of titles that contribute to the depth and breadth of the library's and the consortium's collection is also essential for cooperative collection management efforts. It should not be assumed that new librarians or staff with collection development responsibilities inherently realize the criteria to be used for cooperative collection development purposes, much less understand the goals of the network.

The lack of a budget for acquiring the essential monographic, serial, and electronic titles to meet the primary or core needs of users is a further barrier in cooperative collection development. The first priority of collection developers is to acquire the materials needed to serve local users, not the needs of users in other libraries. Also, this barrier might be expressed in terms of cost-to-benefits. Many do not see the benefits of cooperation accruing to the local library; the money spent on travel to attend network meetings is seen as money better spent on the acquisition of essential monographs or serials. These librarians distrust the claims that cooperation results in savings or cost avoidance at the local level. In any case, these librarians find it very difficult to explain the advantages, purposes, or goals of the network because their library's local services seem to be entirely sufficient to meet the demands of users.

Some librarians and library users might believe that cooperative collection development will result in splintering the collection by acquiring low priority materials which contribute little to the depth and quality of the collection. Although the number of people who acknowledge the need for resource sharing might be increasing, Dougherty says "there is a fear among faculty that, over time, such programs of divided collection responsibility will diminish the luster of their own program's reputation and could ultimately influence academic decisions regarding appointments, promotion, and tenure."[42]

The rationale that interlibrary loan, commercial electronic document delivery services, or other means of resource sharing can fill voids in a library's collection has not gained favor among a large percentage of users. Dougherty notes that many faculty at his institution were

adamant in their view that performance of the existing document delivery systems—i.e., ILL—was "woefully" inadequate for their needs. It is probably true that the attitudes of some users toward interdependence have changed; it is probably also true that others remain staunchly opposed to the proposition that access to collections should be dependent on document delivery. For this latter group, the memory of four- to six-week interlibrary loan delivery performance may never fade away.[43]

Librarians, bibliographers, faculty and other users share a spirit of interdependence. Most libraries embrace cooperative collection management in the hope that their libraries will be able to offer improved access to materials by reshaping collection behavior to reflect greater reliance on resources held in a range of libraries. Dougherty, however, acknowledges that few faculty he talked to had developed this spirit of interdependence; he also discusses the problem of dealing with accreditation standards, adding:

Clearly, so long as accrediting agencies and academicians use size of library collections as the principal criterion for judging quality, and fail to give consideration or recognition to cooperative collection development programs, faculty and librarians will continue to view with suspicion cooperative programs which divide up responsibility for collection development along disciplinary lines.[44]

Human procrastination and avoidance of the difficult or time-consuming activities, especially if failure might be likely, is another chief hurdle in the way of cooperative collection management activities. Bishop adds clash of personalities, jealousy, stubbornness, indifference, unwillingness to experiment, mistrust between librarians, and an assumption that each library has unique rather than common needs and goals as attitudes of librarians which act as barriers.[45]

This section has noted the many variables which make cooperative collection management efforts difficult, time-consuming, and frustrating at times due to natural barriers involving board politics, the egos of library directors, the book budgets of member libraries, the subject or format biases of collection development librarians, the acquisition practices of the various entities, the buying regulations of the various governmental agencies to which members must account, and the growing competition for libraries' materials budgets.

FACILITATORS OF COOPERATIVE COLLECTION DEVELOPMENT

If there are substantial barriers to cooperative collection development, there are also numerous factors that facilitate positive growth in this area. This section discusses some of the more important facilitators. The ever-increasing inflation in the cost of library materials, particularly serials, is a chief facilitator of cooperative collection management. When cooperative collection management can be viewed as a strategy for stretching library budgets and coping with inflation, the spirit of cooperation and interdependence increases. Cooperation manifests itself first for periodical titles because of the more rapid inflation in their prices. Faxon's and Ebsco's customer newsletters and correspondence regularly note factors in serial price increases such as size of issues, rising cost of paper, and changes in the value of U.S. currency. Increases in the output of book publishers, the need to publish in new formats such as CD-ROM, and the growing emphasis on access have resulted in subscription cancellations and reliance on commercial document delivery and interlibrary loan services of other libraries. The price that remaining library subscribers must pay increases further as the total number of subscriptions declines.

Harloe identifies a specific benefit of cooperation as ''promotion of more systematic collection development planning to permit calculated responses when library income becomes flat or decreases.''[46] Dougherty identifies the importance of each institution being able to contribute unique titles to the consortium. Union listings and agreements to hold the last remaining subscription and backruns are often first programs because the libraries should be able to obtain and analyze lists of subscriptions by title or call number without much difficulty.[47] Library consortium or network members can analyze the results in concert with each other far more easily than for monographs.

Since the 1980s there has been greater pressure from educators, librarians, and residents of rural areas all across the United States for parity of access to library materials. Distance and rural education programs, including rural librarianship programs, have increased since then. In the 1990s, this effort is being fed by expansion of the Internet and rural education networks which will take fiber optic cable to rural areas. The impact on collection management which the Internet will have in small and rural libraries, both public and school, will be dramatic once such systems are firmly in place. As rural residents gain access to the world's literature through electronic means or interlibrary loan, it is likely that rural libraries will have to spend a higher proportion of their budgets on electronic access, thereby putting more strain on their materials budgets.

The need for new types or methods of storing, retrieving, cataloging, and preserving the new formats and electronic databases will challenge and invigorate cooperative collection management efforts, if funding can be found and if costs continue to decline. Digital imaging systems, for example, are just beginning to become economical as a means of full-text delivery and preservation of brittle materials, photographs, and archives.

How the cooperative collection management program is implemented and who is involved—or not involved in implementation—is as important as its structure and methodologies. Dougherty adds, "there is another requirement for the efficient and effective operation of the model—that is, the ability of selectors to communicate with one another in an easy and timely fashion."[48] Strong leadership, broad support, and unfailing commitment on the part of library directors or others who make decisions regarding the funding for cooperative collection management activities, including training, training materials, committee meetings, staff support, and time, are absolute requirements.

The involvement or representation in decision making of those who will be participating in the cooperative collection development activities is essential to gaining their commitment. Unless they are involved, or represented through committees or other processes in the decision-making processes, they will not facilitate the successful implementation of cooperative collection development programs.

A widely understood, readily accepted, and easily taught cooperative collection development and cooperative collection assessment framework and methodology are other prerequisites for success. The RLG and WLN Conspectus provide the best-known collection coding methodologies. The Conspectus has become a standard cooperative collection assessment and cooperative collection development method used around the world. Furthermore, the availability of easily identifiable bibliographies, catalogs, or other authoritative works, standards, or guidelines for collection assessment and development programs enhances cooperative collection management activities. AMIGOS, for example, will compare a library's holdings on OCLC tapes against *Books for College Libraries* tapes for local or cooperative collection assessment purposes. OCLC's CACD service provides an instant database for bibliographers to compare the holdings of their library with those of peer institutions, thereby revealing collection gaps and strengths.

It should be apparent that the implementation of cooperative collection assessment and development projects is long, arduous, complex, and time-consuming, and that it requires considerable commitment in terms of planning, organization, time, and funds. Some ARL librarians express a sense of relief that responsibility is being shared in the area of expensive materials, or ''. . . those items which a selector might have been required to consider or even purchase if RLG-coordinated collection development facilities had not been available.''[49] Any steps that can facilitate such a program by overcoming the many potential barriers, or capitalize on the facilitators which propel all members of a library network into the cooperative collection management project, should be considered. It is helpful to keep in mind that "One of the key behavioral factors in library cooperation is leadership. It is through leadership that other components for successful networking can be identified and addressed.''[50]

A FACILITATION PROCESS

This discussion assumes that there is an existing consortium, because it is unlikely that such a group will be formed initially for the primary purpose of cooperative collection management. The idea of cooperating for purposes of cooperative collection development will arise somewhat informally in most cases—at meetings of either library directors or librarians. It does not take long for informal discussions to turn to the rising costs of serials and then to discussions about the need for and benefits of cooperation. From this point, though, it is a giant step to put in place any program for cooperative collection assessment and development, because it is easy for any of the barriers to thwart such initiatives.

A facilitative process and positive environment are essential for *interest* in cooperative collection assessment and cooperative collection development to develop into an agreement and a program. Strong leadership by library directors or collection development librarians is essential if a cooperative collection development program is to be implemented. A network governance structure may be essential; as one writer claims:

When two or more libraries agree to engage in an exchange of information for some interdependent purpose, they have to define the mechanisms through which their interdependent activities will be guided or directed. The participants must have procedures and processes for regulating activities, for restraining unwanted activities, and for making decisions. It must be clear who has legal and fiduciary responsibility for products, services, and roles of staff (if any) who are working for the joint enterprise.[51]

Woodsworth provides her readers with examples of different types of governance structures, as well as legal issues, issues of staff involvement, and other governance issues.

Whoever initiates the cooperative collection management idea, library directors are needed to facilitate initial steps such as developing a sample cooperative collection management agreement or letter of understanding, asking key librarians to participate, and gathering the library literature, including as many sample cooperative collection management agreements as possible. The involvement of collection development, acquisitions, and serials librarians in the process is likely to be crucial. Directors might, for instance, be reluctant to spearhead such efforts without the demonstrable support of librarians responsible for cooperative collection management. Collection development librarians can be especially effective facilitators after a cooperative collection management agreement is reached, because library network committees will undoubtedly be necessary. Once the cooperative collection management program as a concept gains acceptance at the library management level, plans and proposals should be studied in more detail by those responsible for overseeing collection management at the member level. To begin obtaining involvement and commitment, it is advisable for the directors to refer the proposal to an existing committee of collection development or acquisitions librarians for study, or otherwise to form such a study committee. This committee can be charged by the directors to study the concept and develop a recommendation for consideration. The directors of the individual libraries can work closely with the librarians who serve on the committee. In small or understaffed libraries, such delegation may not be possible. In large academic and public libraries, however, the director can delegate tasks, form multiple committees, and assign specific responsibilities for drafting policy statements and gathering and analyzing information. The larger libraries may have so many involved in collection development that only one or two can be appointed to the network-level study committee. This brief description, of course, does not represent a blueprint for action, but rather a suggestion for how one might proceed in an existing library network to get the idea "on the decision-making table."

There are a number of concurrent preliminary steps that should occur prior to writing a draft cooperative collection development policy. Each of the member libraries will find it useful to review their own existing collection development policies, goals, and objectives. If necessary, they should be revised to reflect current practices and policies. They then should be shared with other network members for information purposes, as opposed to critical review— inviting critical review would erect barriers to further cooperation. This information sharing and examination stage should reveal common concerns and areas for discussion.

User surveys are often a part of each member's assessments and should also be examined. Each member's community analysis should be provided to every other member of the consortium. An examination of all the members' community analyses will be the basis of the consortium's comprehensive environmental scan. Many factors revealed by such a scan might have a bearing on the cooperative collection development program. Knowing the demographic characteristics of the populations is important for decision making by those with collection development and selection responsibilities.

The final drafts of proposals, of course, must ultimately be put on the agenda of library directors for discussion. Once the decision to develop a library consortium for cooperative collection development has been made, the hard work of developing and implementing the collection development policy begins. After completing the first cooperative collection development policy, it is necessary to consider a revision to reflect changes which occur. Having a broadly stated cooperative collection management policy is also recommended if administrative procedures and policies can be used to flesh out the more detailed statements that members might want written; these should not require formal approval of governing boards or managers. Otherwise, if the first policy required approval of a board or the individual administrators of each institution, it is a good idea to follow the same process for revisions.

After training in basic collection development and assessment methodologies, librarians should be ready to begin work with their own collections. Training must focus on where and how librarians and library staff should begin the project. In assessing the strength of the collection in a particular Library of Congress classification range, for instance, training should emphasize how librarians can compare their libraries' collections with recognized collections having the same subject strength. For the first collection analysis, members should find it helpful to choose a common subject area which is of general interest to all members. No matter how thorough training is, an implementation committee made up of peers will prove useful. Members can compare assessment procedures, work forms, and results. If a collection coding scheme is used, there are bound to be discussions about what the codes mean, why one collection is better or worse than another, how work forms can help to assure that the recommended steps are taken, and so on.

Assuming that a cooperative collection development program or an agreement is accepted, the leadership of a library network might identify and adopt key objectives or collection development priorities to meet cooperative collection management objectives. These should be general in nature, because the network cannot impose specific collecting objectives successfully on members unless the members are willing. Some examples of general goals are:

- to educate and train collection developers, selectors, and library staff who are involved in collection development and assessment activities by means of workshops, seminars, training sessions, and other continuing education programs;
- to establish primary collectors for subjects by LC or Dewey ranges;
- to share bibliographies and other collection assessment tools, as well as expertise in their use, the interpretation of results;
- to share public relations programs that show the merits of the cooperative program.

By concentrating the attention of library staff, librarians, and others on positive aspects of the cooperative collection management program, library leaders improve the program's chances of success. Such efforts are necessary because all members need to move carefully and deliberately toward the same goals.

AXIOMS OF COOPERATIVE COLLECTION MANAGEMENT

After reviewing much of cooperative collection assessment and development literature, at least fifteen principles or axioms may be proferred as the foundation on which successful cooperative collection management rests.

Axiom 1. Cooperative collection assessment and development programs of library networks provide the best solutions at the local, state, regional, or national levels to the continuing explosion of publications and information resources and their rising costs.

Axiom 2. There are many budgetary, psychological, environmental, philosophical, educational, political, and societal variables which can act at any time as barriers to, or facilitators of, developing and maintaining cooperative collection development programs. A variable which might be a barrier in one instance might be a facilitator in another instance.

Axiom 3. Cooperative collection development programs are less likely to be developed when barriers such as turf protectionism, fear of dependence, or lack of knowledge by some governing board members, library directors, or collection development librarians stand in the way.

Axiom 4. Collection assessment is the cornerstone of successful cooperative collection development programs.

Axiom 5. The support and commitment of the network's library directors alone is not enough for the success of network level cooperative collection development programs.

Axiom 6. Successful cooperative collection development programs are characterized by the following:

- broad support of the library's governing board or officers, as well as library directors, librarians, library staff, and the library's primary clientele;
- strong leadership by key library and network directors;
- a spirit of interdependence by collection development librarians, an effective network organization and administration;
- a common database of the members' holdings;
- use of and access to online library catalogs by all members; and
- adoption of an agreed-upon cooperative collection assessment and cooperative collection development structure.

Axiom 7. Support and commitment can be dictated by the library's governing board, or parent organization, as a cost saving measure, or it can be pursued by collection developers or library directors. In any case, cooperative collection management programs should operate under the auspices of recognized, if not formally and legally established, library governance structures including inter-local government agreements, incorporation, bylaws, constitutions, or similar governance structures. Unless some document serves as a guide to selectors and acquisition librarians, the intended goals of the original library managers or board members will go unmet.

Axiom 8. The success of and support for cooperative collection management programs by professional and paraprofessional library staff are more likely when they feel it is necessary to meet the basic needs of users.

Axiom 9. Successful cooperative collection development programs assign primary collecting responsibilities to the member libraries having the strongest collections and collecting interest in particular subjects or topics.[52] Unless cooperative collection assessment and cooperative collection development structures and methodologies take advantage of the members' collection strengths, cooperative collection objectives are likely to remain unmet.

Axiom 10. Library directors and librarians of consortium libraries are likely to see cooperative collection assessment and cooperative collection development programs as successful when those programs are perceived to support institutional missions, goals, and collection development objectives, and if each library has control over its own collection development and assessment policies, procedures, selection, and acquisitions. Successful cooperative collection development programs must be perceived as having benefits to the clients of the member libraries and their users.

Axiom 11. Conversely, if the resource sharing provisions of cooperative collection development agreements or understandings ask member libraries to consider the collection needs of the library network as greater than their own local needs, the program will not generate the necessary spirit of cooperation and support, particularly when the libraries' material budgets are generally insufficient to meet local needs. Cooperative collection development must be seen as a way of enhancing or complementing a member library's collection rather than taking from it resources needed by other members.

Axiom 12. As material budgets decrease in buying power, libraries will focus acquisitions and subscriptions on developing or maintaining a core collection. As the percentage of each library's materials budget spent on core material increases, however, the percentage that is free to be spent on supporting cooperative collection development will decrease; this is likely to be reflected in declining collection depth and collecting intensity across the network.

Axiom 13. It is essential that the network structure and administration or process for cooperative collection development is flexible enough to

- adapt to changes in electronic/computing technologies;

- be adaptable by libraries of all sizes;

- be adaptable by library consortia, systems, and networks of all types and sizes;

- identify the member library with the strongest collection in any specific subject;
- be able to be used by libraries using either LC or the DDC;
- identify collection assessment tools readily available and easily used by staff.

Axiom 14. Beyond the core collection needed for minimal effective service, libraries need access to the materials outside the core. The focus of public relations material should emphasize each library's services in meeting users' needs rather than acquisitions or collecting materials. Such complementary library services include reciprocal borrowing privileges, interlibrary loan, electronic document delivery, and telefacsimile of reference materials.

Axiom 15. A cooperative collection development program which is based on meeting the collection goals and mission of each member library provides the clientele of all the member institutions with access to more materials than each library would otherwise provide without sacrificing the quality of its own collection development program.

CONCLUSION

Although cooperative collection assessment and development programs are not a primary function of the several hundred library networks, consortia, or systems in the United States, they are essential in making as much of the world's literature as possible available to users through their member libraries. Print resources should continue to be published and collected by libraries for many decades into the 21st century because books, journals, and documents are preferred by scholars and recreational readers. Electronic media, on the other hand, might someday overtake printed resources for reference sources, as well as scientific, technical, medical, and similar fields where information and data change rapidly. Growing user preferences for electronic periodical and other databases have already severely affected the budgets of libraries because they represent yet another format that must be acquired. Many barriers in the way of cooperative collection development have been suggested: turf protectionism, the difficulty in obtaining commitment, lack of leadership by library or network directors, restrictions by the parent consortium. Lack of support, lack of commitment, lack of training, lack of funds to acquire materials beyond a core collection—such barriers can put an abrupt halt to cooperative collection assessment and development programs. At the same time, any number of facilitators working in concert can result in a successful cooperative collection assessment and development program: Strong leadership by a library director; pressure from a parent consortium, board, or taxpayers to save money; the lack of an adequate materials budget; and the inability of any library to acquire the materials needed by its primary clientele because the number of titles steadily increases. The retrospective conversion and automation projects of libraries that have contributed their holdings to the OCLC and RLIN databases have greatly facilitated collection assessment and development activities in libraries and library consortia by making resources of one library known to others who have access to the appropriate bibliographic utility. Collection management services of OCLC, WLN, AMIGOS, Ebsco, Faxon, and many other vendors or bibliographic networks also have increased cooperative collection management activities. These and other developments such as statewide and regional OCLC/GACs should increase the prospects for more, not less, cooperative collection management programs in the 21st century.

A successful cooperative collection assessment and cooperative collection development program can be a highly positive public relations tool which helps to convince taxpayers that the libraries are maximizing their resources. Cooperation in the collecting of materials with other libraries does not need to lessen the quality of the member's own collection, but it can lead to strengthing the quality of all the members—assuming that each member has ready access to the others' collections through other resource sharing practices such as interlibrary loan and reciprocal borrowing. At the very minimum, each member should have and maintain a strong collection for its primary clientele. Members can at the same time, however, cooperate with many other libraries to build a stronger collection across the network. By providing all of the member libraries' clients with easy access to the consortium's collection, every user and each library benefits significantly from being able to provide more materials than it could have alone.

NOTES

1. Susan K. Martin, *Library Networks, 1986–87: Libraries in Partnership* (White Plains, NY: Knowledge Industry Publications, 1986), p. 2. The reader wanting more complete definitions of terms or concepts such as library network, bibliographic utilities, library cooperative, regional network, and library consortium should see Anne Woodsworth, *Library Cooperation Networks: A Basic Reader* (New York: Neal-Schuman, 1991), chapters 1 and 3.

2. J. E. Wilkins, ed., *The Report on Library Cooperation, 1989*, 7th ed. (Chicago: Association of Specialized and Cooperative Library Agencies, 1990).

3. The *American Library Directory* makes note of this data collection method in the preface of each volume.

4. Keith M. Fiels, Joan Neumann, and Eva R. Brown, *Multitype Library Cooperation State Laws, Regulations and Pending Legislation* (Chicago: Association of Specialized and Cooperative Library Agencies, 1991), p. 12.

5. J. A. McCrossan, "The Role of Library Systems and Networks," *Local Public Library Administration* (Chicago: American Library Association, 1980), pp. 199–212.

6. Woodsworth, *Library Cooperation*, pp. 24–29.

7. Fiels, et al., *Multitype Library Cooperation*.

8. Ruth J. Patrick, *Guidelines for Library Cooperation* (Santa Monica, CA: System Development Corporation, 1972), p. 71.

9. G. E. Gorman and B. R. Howes, *Collection Development for Libraries* (London: Bowker-Saur, 1989), p. 4.

10. LeRoy Charles Merritt, "Writing a Selection Policy," in *Background Readings in Building Library Collections*, 2nd ed., ed. Phyllis Van Orden and Edith B. Phillips (Metuchen, NJ: Scarecrow Press, 1979), p. 67.

11. Paul H. Mosher, "Cooperative Collection Development Equals Collaborative Interdependence," *Collection Building* 9 (1988): 29–32.

12. Bart Harloe, ed., *Guide to Cooperative Collection Development*. Collection Management and Development Guides, no. 6. (Chicago: American Library Association, 1994), p. vii.

13. Elizabeth P. Roberts, "Cooperative Collection Development of Science Serials," *Serials Librarian* 14 (1988): 19–27.

14. Mary Biggs, "The Proposed National Periodicals Center, 1973–1980: Study, Dissension, and Retreat," *Resource Sharing and Information Networks* 1 (1984): 1–22; Eva Martin Sartori, "Regional Collection Development of Serials," *Collection Management* 11 (1989): 69–76.

15. Martha M. Smith, "Cooperative Collection Development for Rare Books among Neighboring Academic Libraries," *College & Research Libraries* 46 (1985): 160–67.

16. Woodsworth, *Library Cooperation*, p. 8.

17. Ibid.

18. Richard M. Dougherty, "A Conceptual Framework for Organizing Resource Sharing and Shared Collection Development Programs," *Journal of Academic Librarianship* 4 (1988): 288.

19. *Resource Sharing*. SPEC Kit 42 (Washington DC: Association of Research Libraries, Office of Management Studies, 1978), p. 72.

20. Dougherty, "A Conceptual Framework," p. 289.

21. Woodsworth, *Library Cooperation*, p. 128.

22. Ibid.

23. Edward G. Holley, "North American Efforts at Worldwide Acquisitions since 1945," *Collection Management* 9 (1988): 89–99; Robert W. Frase, *Library Funding and Public Support* (Chicago: American Library Association, 1973); Jean B. Wellisch et al., *The Public Library and Federal Policy* (Westport, CT: Greenwood Press, 1974).

24. Peggy Forcier and Nancy Powell, "Collection Assessment in the Pacific Northwest; Building a Foundation for Cooperation," *Advances in Library Automation and Networking* 3 (1989): 87–121; A. Haley and D. K. Ferguson, "The Pacific Northwest Collection Assessment Project," in *Coordinating Cooperative Collection Development: A National Perspective*, ed. Wilson Luquire (New York: Haworth Press, 1986), pp. 185–97; Karen Krueger, "A System Level Coordinated Cooperative Collection Development Model for Illinois," in *Coordinating Cooperative Collection Development: A National Perspective*, ed. Wilson Luquire (New York: Haworth Press, 1986), pp. 49–63; Georgine N. Olson, "Community-Based Reference Services in Central Illinois—a Multitype Cooperative Collection Development Project," *Illinois Libraries* 71 (1989): 4–11; Dennis Stephens, "A Stitch in Time: The Alaska Cooperative Collection Development Project," in *Coordinating Cooperative Collection Development: A National Perspective*, ed. Wilson Luquire (New York: Haworth Press, 1986), pp. 173–84; Robert Wallhaus, "Library Resource Sharing: The Illinois Experience," in *Coordinating Cooperative Collection Development: A National Perspective*, ed. Wilson Luquire (New York: Haworth Press, 1986), pp. 11–19.

25. Linda M. Cohen, ''Resource Sharing and Coordinated Collection Development in the Network of Alabama Libraries,'' *Collection Management* 10 (1988): 149–62; Fred Heath, ''An Assessment of Educational Holdings in Alabama Academic Libraries: A Collection Analysis Project,'' in *Cooperative Collection Development: Proceedings of the June ASCLA Multi-LINCS Preconference* (Chicago: Association of Specialized and Cooperative Library Agencies, 1992); Deborah K. Jensen, ''Resource Sharing—New York State,'' *Advances in Library Resource Sharing* 1 (1990): 120–26; William A. Pettas and Henry Bates, ''Cooperative Collection Development: An Inexpensive Project in Northern California,'' *Collection Management* 11 (1989): 59–67.

26. Suzanne Fedunok, ''Metro Collection Inventory Project: A Conspectus Case Study,'' *Advances in Library Resource Sharing* 1 (1990): 95–119; Christopher A. Millson-Martula, ''The Greater Midwest Regional Medical Library Network and Coordinated Cooperative Collection Development: The RLG Conspectus and Beyond,'' *Illinois Libraries* 71 (1989): 31–39; Mary Y. Moore, ''Washington State's Cooperative Collection Development Project,'' in *Cooperative Collection Development: Proceedings of the June ASCLA Multi-LINCS Preconference*, comp. Diane Macht Solomon (Chicago: Association of Specialized and Cooperative Library Agencies, 1992), pp. 15–18.

27. Paul H. Mosher, ''A National Scheme for Collaboration in Collection Development: The RLG-NCIP Effort,'' in *Coordinating Cooperative Collection Development: A National Perspective*, ed. Wilson Luquire (New York: Haworth Press, 1986): pp. 21–35; Joe A. Hewitt and John S. Shipman, ''Cooperative Collection Development among Research Libraries in the Age of Networking: Report of a Survey of ARL Libraries,'' *Advances in Library Automation and Networking* (Greenwich, CT: JAI Press, 1987), pp. 189–232.

28. Anthony W. Ferguson, Joan Grant, and Joel S. Rutstein, ''The RLG Conspectus: Its Uses and Benefits,'' *College & Research Libraries* 49 (1988): 198.

29. *Report on the Conoco Project in German Literature and Geology* (Palo Alto, CA: Research Libraries Group, 1987).

30. Dougherty, ''A Conceptual Framework,'' p. 191.

31. Report on the Conoco Project.

32. Holley, ''North American Efforts,'' p. 92.

33. Ibid.

34. David G. Weber, ''A Century of Cooperative Programs among Academic Libraries,'' *College & Research Libraries* 37 (1976): 205–21.

35. Woodsworth, *Library Cooperation*, p. 113.

36. Fiels, *Multitype Library Cooperation*; Frase, *Library Funding*; Wellisch, et al., *The Public Library*; George Jefferson, *Library Co-operation* (London: Andre Deutsch, 1977); Redmond Kathleen Molz, *Federal Policy and Library Support* (Cambridge, MA: MIT Press, 1976).

37. Dougherty, ''A Conceptual Framework.''

38. Hugh C. Atkinson, ''Atkinson on Networks,'' *American Libraries* 18 (June 1988): 432–39.

39. Martin, *Library Networks*, p. 90.

40. Mosher, ''A National Scheme,'' p. 29.

41. Dougherty, ''A Conceptual Framework,'' p. 288.

42. Ibid.

43. Ibid.

44. Dougherty, ''A Conceptual Framework,'' p. 289.

45. D. F. Bishop, *Not Alone . . . But Together: A Conference on Multitype Library Cooperation*, ed. A. F. Trezza (Tallahassee, FL: Florida State University, 1987), p. 19.

46. Harloe, *Guide*, p. 3.

47. Dougherty, ''A Conceptual Framework,'' p. 288.

48. Ibid., pp. 290–91.

49. *Resource Sharing*, p. 32.

50. Woodsworth, *Library Cooperation*, p. 47.

51. Ibid, p. 49.

52. Richard J. Wood and Katina Strauch, *Collection Assessment: A Look at the RLG Conspectus* (New York: Haworth Press, 1992); Stephens, ''A Stitch in Time''; Mosher, ''A National Scheme''; Hewitt and Shipman, ''Cooperative Collection.''

13

Cooperation Is the Future of Collection Management and Development: OhioLINK and CIC

Gay N. Dannelly

INTRODUCTION

Following the tradition of their institutions, academic libraries have usually found it difficult to develop organized and effective cooperative resource sharing and collection development programs. Academic libraries have a long history of independent activity and intense and continuing competition. They and their institutions vie for state and private funding, faculty, students, grants, resources of all kinds, as well as status and prestige within the academic community. Libraries in particular are evaluated primarily on the size of their collections, the amount of institutional funding provided, and the number of staff. The very nature of academic and library evaluation mitigates against cooperative ventures. Despite these circumstances, library cooperation also has a long history. With increasingly severe cost pressures on the university and college communities, the changing nature of publishing, escalating rates of publication and publication formats, and the rapidly evolving role of electronic access to information, cooperation extending beyond resource sharing has become a much more strategic approach to the provision of library services.

While recent concern has been directed primarily at the efficacy of interlibrary loan and commercial document delivery systems, other efforts are being made to determine the future of library collections and services within the library community itself. As Perrault has noted, "It is apparent . . . that problems in resource sharing have become the focus of national concern."[1] The recent publication of the American Library Association's *Guide to Cooperative Collection Development* has also served to highlight the changing nature and importance of cooperation within the library community.

There are many reasons why institutions come together to share current and future resources. Academic libraries, in particular, have long recognized that

even the most affluent . . . libraries cannot possibly acquire sufficient portions of the world's available literature to satisfy all their user groups. They must, in fact, begin to delimit the fields of knowledge in which they will build extensive library collections. As this occurs, they will be forced to rely more and more on access, through reciprocal arrangements, to the specialized collections of companion libraries.[2]

Such cooperation is aimed at supplementing the resources and services of the local library, not becoming a substitute for them. "Its primary purpose is to increase the range and depth of library resources and services available to users . . . and to provide all . . . citizens and institutions with adequate access to the human record. . . ."[3] The developing pattern of access to electronic resources is allowing consortia to expand on this approach as they provide such databases in a shared environment that makes the most efficient use of both human and financial capital. As such capacity expands, it will make these programs even more attractive both to users and to university and state financial officers.

Present conditions in higher education have made university administrators very aware of what is at stake and how libraries might join together to improve the conditions for each institution. Kenneth Gros Louis, Provost of Indiana University, has eloquently supported the concept of library cooperation:

As I cannot imagine universities doing business as usual in the next several decades so too I cannot imagine libraries doing business as usual. I understand how enormously complex it will be for regional libraries to cooperate in collection development, resource sharing, perhaps even personnel sharing. I do not know how to do it, I am not sure it can be done, but I do believe that responses of academic officers, faculty budgetary advisory committees, and university presidents will be much more favorable if the level of cooperation among libraries is greater than it has been in the past. The real challenge is how to enhance collections with an existing or even shrinking budget by sharing collection development policies as well as databases and other means of accessing material. Ownership, like ownership of some exotic degree program, must be abandoned in favor of access.[4]

While Gros Louis' views are those of many academic officers, the concept of sharing the "ownership of some exotic degree program" has not yet penetrated to the heart of academia, and this illustrates one of the great barriers in establishing cooperative library programs.

NATURE OF COOPERATION AMONG LIBRARIES

The nature of cooperative enterprises in the academic library community is as varied as the participants. True cooperative collection programs and services are dependent on the desire of the participants, at all levels, to join the effort and to support it in daily activities and in the establishment of local priorities. The goals of a program must be developed and agreed upon, procedures established to support these goals and, perhaps most important of all, the users of the libraries must be educated to see the advantages of cooperation. Such programs ". . . require clear consensus on what the role of the local library should be, and what the obligations are of the regional and/or state-wide network—what materials, for example, should be duplicated in local collections, what supplied from other sources, how costs of library service should be shared. . . ."[5] Cooperation is no longer considered an option by many libraries but, due to external forces, has become a necessity. However, the effectiveness of cooperative programs is still based on the willing participation of members. While it may no longer actually be voluntary, it is the perceived ". . . quality of being voluntary which distinguishes cooperation from other forms of interaction and which creates some of its peculiar difficulties."[6]

ADMINISTRATIVE ISSUES

Cooperative agreements, depending on their nature and origin, often have programmatic obligations that require participants to make contractual commitments. In such cases, the program must have support from ". . . the highest organizational levels. That is, those responsible for funding in the organizations or political entities intending to cooperate must be prepared to address any legal, financial, political, or administrative issues that may be involved in the cooperative effort."[7] In fact, the effectiveness of any cooperative program requires the ". . . full support of library administrators at both the conceptual and operational level. . . . If the program is simply imposed from above, there will likely be resistance from below."[8] Even the most narrowly defined agreements should have administrative support in principle and in fact, or there is little likelihood that either the selectors or the faculty will take them seriously.

In part, resource sharing and cooperative collection development require that the "custodial" role of libraries be expanded to provide more varied and dynamic concepts of libraries as a source of information and services, rather than solely as keepers of books. "New concepts of availablity are also needed by the user and users' needs require further study in terms of delay tolerance, format required and specificity of material for different categories of reader."[9]

BENEFITS OF COOPERATION

Cooperative programs can provide welcome breadth of support in a variety of ways to beleaguered libraries. In order to respond to the increasingly complex information needs of library users, whether faculty, students, or staff, libraries must find effective ways of expanding the resources available to them and of providing efficient and quick delivery mechanisms. There are many potential benefits of such programs. For example, users will have access to a much broader range of materials, services, and in-depth collections. More effective collection development and resource allocation can take place, including the elimination or limitation of unnecessary duplication of little-used materials, subject specialization, and shared information and reference capabilities. Effective, efficient, and economical delivery mechanisms that reduce costs to both library funds and time of the user can be instituted. Cooperative preservation, microfilming, and retention policies and practices can be established. Participation in the academic library community's efforts to provide consistent, equitable, and effective delivery of information and information services can become more effective. And expanded training and participatory opportunities for library staff at all levels will not only be available, but will be necessary.[10]

CHALLENGES TO COOPERATION

The primary purpose of cooperation is to expand the resources available to local users and to establish a set of relationships that each library can depend on and that lend themselves to the further development and expansion of library and information resources through a variety of mechanisms. Unfortunately, many university administrators, particularly at smaller institutions, view cooperation as a way of saving money, not as a way of improving the information available to local faculty and students.

While there are strong administrative, budget, and collection incentives to move further into cooperative relationships, there are equally strong local issues that may result in cooperation being viewed as a direct threat to traditional collections, services, and local independence and autonomy. Libraries have long regarded themselves, and particularly their collections, as institutionally based and more than adequate to provide for local needs. While selectors consistently request additional funds for collection development, they simultaneously want to develop local resources that do, indeed, answer all needs, and they do not want to have to consider any external policies or practices that limit their flexibility in the selection of specific materials. The faculty are usually even more committed to such views. They may be quite eager to borrow the resources of other libraries, but they are dismayed at the reality of having any of "their" resources used by others. Intellectually, of course, faculty and librarians understand the values of cooperation, but the practice is fraught with complexities and the need for change and development.

One concern voiced by many researchers, in particular, is the frustration caused by the unwillingness of libraries to lend specific types of materials such as rare books, microfilm, and other special collection items. It is these very items, so hard to find and to use, that cause many of the negative perceptions of resource sharing among faculty and graduate students. Libraries need to change the meaning of resource sharing to include a greater commitment, not only to cooperative collection development, but also to the provision of such materials across the consortia. As libraries develop further cooperative programs and have even greater dependency on other institutions, it is imperative that they consider the impact not only on students, but even more importantly on the scholarly process and the intellectual tradition of the university, and seek ways to go beyond the custodial role and to develop more effective ways of delivering the information required.

The most critical issue in cooperative collection development is the need for continued development and support of collections of the scholarly record for current and future use. "Librarians know that research libraries are unaffected by the parable of loaves and fishes, and cannot feed their multitudes by sharing impoverished collections."[11] Without local collections of continuing depth and breadth there will be nothing to share among libraries. As Shaughnessy has noted, "access depends on ownership; a network does not create new resources, it facilitates the sharing of existing resources."[12] A distinction has been made between the "virtual library," which is able to access information, and the "virtuous library," which also collects resources both for local use and for contribution to the broader library and information communities. This is an important point and one that research libraries, as well as all participants in consortial agreements, must continue to support in order to be sure that there is a continuity of the historical record and that it is not restricted by the commercial market. Libraries simply cannot be dependent upon commercial publishers or document suppliers to provide information on a permanent and long-term basis. It may not be in a company's best interest to do so; companies go out of business; it is unlikely that all information resources required by library users are going to be transferred to or maintained online; and history should not make libraries confident that any of this will improve significantly.

Perhaps the largest stumbling block to effective resource sharing has been the available delivery mechanisms. It is all very well to share bibliographic information in catalogs or databases, but the actual provision of the information has been slow and inefficient, despite the best efforts of libraries. The academic calendar allows for little or no lag time in the provision of needed articles and books, particularly for undergraduates. The interlibrary loan system, with the advent of online bibliographic databases in particular, has been overrun by demand. Delivery, even through the use of commercial services, cannot fulfill all, or even most, of the information needs of library users. The single most important change necessary to the successful development of effective resource sharing and subsequent cooperative collection development programs is the development of quick and efficient ways of delivering the information required to the user.

There is also an administrative perception that cooperation is a free good and has little or no cost associated with it. This is far from true. Cooperation costs money, time, and personnel. While there may be ways for each local library to change internal procedures to minimize these costs, it is still an expensive process. And there has been little work done on the actual costs of cooperation, no matter what benefits are realized. This perception seems to be due to the nature of the cooperative process itself. People simply change what they spend time on or add it to already full-time positions, thus making it an indirect and comparatively hidden cost. However, when cooperative activities take so much time that local responsibilities cannot be fulfilled, then the costs become obvious, and institutional and library commitments may be questioned.

While technology has certainly made cooperation and document delivery more realistic, it is important to be aware of the role of the Internet in the effectiveness of these efforts. Rapid and easy communication has lowered the geographic barriers that have often damaged or made impossible past attempts to develop cooperative collection management and resource sharing programs. However, recent reviews of the operation and nature of the Internet by a variety of government agencies and the widening role of information utilities has generated great concern among the users of the current systems. As Lynch has noted, ''Particularly threatening is the possibility that the restrictions on information transfer in the evolving network environment will undermine the long and valuable tradition of interlibrary cooperation through such activities as coordinated acquisitions and interlibrary loan.''[13]

CHARACTERISTICS OF RESOURCE SHARING AND COOPERATIVE COLLECTION DEVELOPMENT CONSORTIA

Resource sharing and cooperative collection development programs tend to develop in a limited number of ways. They are usually organized around one or more of six primary characteristics: geography, type of library, type of administration, political jurisdiction, funding source, and commercial versus nonprofit.[14] There are specific kinds of shared information that characterize such groups, no matter what the organizational origin: bibliographic information (shared automated catalog and/or integrated systems and shared management information); shared electronic bibliographic or other databases; shared physical access to member collections; agreed-upon delivery mechanisms, whether jointly or individually funded; shared information about current acquisition activities to avoid expensive duplication or duplicate cancellation of serials. This last element is usually of an informal nature through personal communications, since automated systems do not yet easily provide ready access to such information.

The most effective organizations are those that have some kind of central organization and are able to provide support for specific projects, expertise in the exploitation of systems, and leadership or consultation as necessary. Those organizations that are entirely dependent on volunteer work alone are usually not effective over a long period of time. The commitment to central staffing is perceived as both an institutional commitment and a way of furthering agreed-upon goals by supporting the efforts of the consortium.

CHANGING COLLECTION DEVELOPMENT IN THE COOPERATIVE ENVIRONMENT

As resource sharing expands to encompass cooperative collection management and development, the perceptions of these activities change, not only at the local level but also through the administrative hierarchies at member institutions. The first phase of such programs usually focuses on sharing current resources. This may involve the sharing of materials formerly considered to be for local use only, such as microforms or other media. The expansion of such arrangements to include such additional elements as special formats, expanded loan times, or agreed-upon arrangements for reimbursement for lost items usually indicates a desire on the part of at least some members to begin moving beyond such limited agreements and to expand cooperative efforts to future acquisitions.

As interest shifts to the future, a variety of cooperative efforts can be initiated. Shared purchases, made with either centrally funded monies obtained through special allocations from external sources or through voluntary assessments, are common. Planned, distributed responsibilities for specific subjects can be established either through collection analysis and agreement or, more simply, through recognition of traditional strengths and current program interests. Specific programs for the acquisition of materials, often modeled on the Center for Research Libraries Area Microform Projects, are also common.

Although publishers regularly protest, a regular subject of discussion in cooperative programs is serial cancellations, particularly esoteric or very expensive titles. These discussions may concentrate on specific topics, countries of publication, formats, or other criteria. Mechanisms for sharing subscription information and retention priority are underway in several cooperative groups, spurred on by ever-increasing prices, multiple formats, choices in delivery methods, and decreasing purchasing power of library budgets.

The expansion of cooperative collection development into other areas of library services indicates a mature program in which the participants are committed to the consortium, depend upon its programs and resources, and consider participation outside collection development as a primary part of their obligations to the group. These programs include cataloging commitments for subject areas or specific areas of responsibility; cooperative cataloging of shared resources; cooperative reference, automation, and other expertise; cooperative decisions for storage and retention of both print and nonprint resources; and shared preservation programs.

CASE STUDY ONE: OHIOLINK

In Ohio in the mid-1980s a series of capital improvement projects was submitted by several state-supported higher education institutions to renovate or build new library facilities. Subsequently, a detailed study of information, facility, and technology needs led to the decision to establish a series of remote storage facilities and a cooperative network among the state-supported higher education institutions, beginning with the four-year institutions and their branch campuses. Phase two was to encompass the two-year and technical institutions supported by the state. The project was to include a shared central catalog with local systems that could, to a certain extent, be controlled by the local institution. The local systems would allow for patron-initiated borrowing, as would the central catalog, thus turning a technological base into a new kind of resource sharing program and providing the ability for library users to request materials from distant locations to be delivered to their local campuses. This was expected not only to ease the overburdened ILL load but also to increase the variety of resources available to students, faculty, and staff, decrease unnecessary duplication, and further stretch the state dollars spent on library materials. At last count (August 14, 1995) there were 5,305,285 bibliographic records, of which 3,088,682 (or 58%) are unique in the state. This latter figure, of course, represents various editions, decisions to catalog collections as sets rather than monographs, and similar conditions.[15] Clearly, however, the hope of increasing the scope of materials available to library users has been realized.

Following the development of a very detailed request for a proposal including sections on acquisitions and serials, cataloging, circulation, public services and, most unusually, collection management and development, and an excruciating demonstration and review process, Innovative Interfaces, Inc. was selected as the vendor for the system. The first group of institutions to install the system included all the four-year institutions, the State Library of Ohio and two private institutions that were considered to have valuable collections for state use.

Initial funding was approved by the Ohio Board of Regents, which provides a central point for the funding and review of all state-supported institutions of higher education. This funding continues and has also allowed for the installation of a wide variety of shared electronic databases within the OhioLINK system or provided via gateways, including some with document delivery capabilities. At present there are more than thirty databases in place, with another twenty-five expected to be made available in the next several months.

A central OhioLINK management was in place from the beginning of the project and now includes an executive director, a systems director, and a variety of other positions as the system expands. This skilled central support has made a variety of programs available that volunteer effort could not have hoped to encompass. The nature of OhioLINK, however, is such that governance, while mandated by the state, resides in the universities. A general advisory board composed of university administrators provides the highest level of policy review. In addition, a technical board and task force groups provide expertise in specific areas. The working group of library directors, however, provides the day-to-day governance of the project. This board is supported by four committees: database management, which includes acquisitions, cataloging and related services; collection management; intercampus services, including circulation policies; and user services. Each of the support committees has a specific charge, representative membership from the consortium, and the responsibility for overseeing specific aspects of the project's programs. Specific staff at OhioLINK work with each committee to provide consultation, expertise, and support for projects. In some cases, such as the installation of databases, the programs are carried out by OhioLINK staff. In others, the program is run primarily by the members of the committee. This is particularly true in the case of collection management and cooperative collection activities at the selector level.

At present, the collection management group is concerned with selection of databases and their recommendation to the other members of OhioLINK, the establishment of cooperative subject collection efforts through projects using the Conspectus, and the establishment of statistical report mechanisms and capabilities to support cooperative collection management. This is strategic in an era when new programs are expanding and graduate programs are losing state support through a statewide review process. For example, the recent review of doctoral programs in history reduced the number of these state-supported programs to two. The collections of those institutions will be of great importance over time to the remaining members of the consortium. The companion concern to such programmatic cancellations is where library funds formerly used to support such programs will be applied, or whether such funds will simply become part of the general budget used to support the rapidly increasing costs of serials in all disciplines.

Although the project is still very young, the influence of OhioLINK in the local selection process is becoming clear. Large, expensive purchases are regularly reviewed at the local institution with the holdings of the state in mind. Decisions to purchase such materials are beginning to be made in concert with institutions who hold complementary or supplementary collections. While this process is tentative at present, it is becoming more a part of the purchase decision process at many of the member institutions, and it is certainly part of the approval process at the administrative level. The ability to see readily what other institutions hold certainly changes the selection process, as does the ability to count on the actual provision of the materials to the patron at a location remote from the owning library. At present, patron-initiated request is functional only for monographs, but planned enhancements will also provide for article requests and the ability to readily request large microform materials. At present the latter are available through a preferred partner ILL system.

CASE STUDY TWO: COMMITTEE ON INSTITUTIONAL COOPERATION

Since 1958 the Committee on Institutional Cooperation (CIC) has acted as a voluntary, regional institutional cooperative active in many areas of academic programs. Composed initially of the Big Ten institutions (Universities of Illinois, Indiana, Iowa, Michigan, Minnesota, Wisconsin, and Michigan State University, Ohio State University, Northwestern University, and Purdue University) and the University of Chicago, CIC has expanded to include the University of Illinois, Chicago and Pennsylvania State University, the latter upon its acceptance in the Big Ten athletic conference. Directed jointly by the presidents of all member institutions, programs include cooperative efforts at the academic subject level, international cooperative programs, joint course offerings, and long-term library cooperation at the directorial level. This last area of cooperation led to initial agreements for broad resource sharing and on-site loan of materials to visiting graduate students and faculty. The library directors continue to provide the leadership in program development assisted by a number of other groups with specific responsibilities.

In 1983, the collection development officers began meeting to try to establish cooperative collection development programs. Part of the impetus was provided by increasing costs and the loss of purchasing power in library acquisitions budgets; part was based on a recognition that it would be most advantageous for all the members of CIC if more effective ways could be found to use limited financial and collection resources. From this group grew a preservation officers' group and subsequently public services, ILL, and technical services groups, as well as task forces to address specific topics.

Until 1994, the Director of the CIC and his small staff provided the only administrative support for the various grant and project activities of the libraries. However, in 1994 the library directors agreed to establish a position named Director, Office of Library Initiatives. The convergence of several other initiatives and the establishment of this position have led to significant progress since August 1994, including shared database acquisition, a conference on the potentials for shared electronic full-text resources, an additional grant proposal, and the furtherance of several subject projects. Funding for all these activities, outside those funded by grants, must be provided by the libraries themselves. This has, of course, limited the amount of time and commitment that individual libraries have been able to provide to specific activities.

In addition to the CIC administration, the consortium is assisted by CICNet, the upper Midwest provider of network interconnectivity. Founded by the CIC institutions and with expansion into the provision of connectivity to other academic and commercial organizations, the special expertise of CICNet has provided technical support and enthusiasm that individual members could not have afforded.

Initially, the collection development officers concentrated efforts on bringing together groups of selectors in the hope that each subject group would find mutual benefit not only in meeting face-to-face, but in beginning to develop cooperative programs. Two such meetings were held for science selectors and for social science selectors. While communication did improve within the various groups, there was no move toward specific programs with definable goals and objectives. The university presidents and provosts, faced with spiraling library budgets and increasingly limited resources, instructed the library directors to begin to establish broader cooperative initiatives. In 1993, the library directors requested that the collection development officers establish a plan that would bring about a series of specific subject cooperative efforts. In addition to earlier cooperative preservation grants and programs, the CIC libraries also applied for a grant to establish a virtual electronic library to provide many of the same patron capabilities available through OhioLINK. This project was seen as a way to provide ready searching of the catalogs of each member through a Z39.50 search engine. A subsequent phase would include the consideration of patron-initiated borrowing with delivery via a shared system, thus moving much of the current ILL traffic into a circulation function and limiting the manual labor involved in providing resources across the consortium.

At the same time, the collection development officers were working on a plan for ''systematic coordinated collection development within the CIC'' that would provide means for subject groups to establish cooperative programs.[16] The report also suggested a series of test projects to make the initial investment of time and funds from each institution reasonable, and also to provide information regarding the nature of such cooperative programs and to test the effectiveness of such groups. While the effort expended in each of the projects was considerable, they all made clear the need for a shared database that could be easily consulted, particularly in the area of serial subscriptions. The actual implementation of the Virtual Electronic Library will be a major step in providing this information.

In 1993, the library directors also appointed a Task Force on the CIC Electronic Collection to ''explore the management and use of shared electronic resources and to consider relevant issues for the CIC libraries.''[17] Although reporting to the directors, this group has also been instrumental in assisting the cooperative collection development efforts of several subject groups as well as initiating, with the approval of the collection development officers, specific subject selectors, and technical support of CICNet, a variety of projects. Among the best known is the CIC Libraries Electronic Journal Collection. Initiated by CICNet at the request of the collection development officers, this archive was subsequently reviewed by the Task Force and a number of organizational issues clarified and policies established. At present awaiting the results of a grant application prior to a planned expansion, the more organized collection (as opposed to the archive) has become a major test of consortial cooperative efforts in technology, selection, and processing and cataloging. The provision of a variety of databases through mounting at member institutions and cooperative costing, cooperative price negotiations, and similar methods has also assisted the members in their efforts to expand resources available to their users.

CONCLUSIONS

It is clear from the literature that a variety of cooperative programs have become not only highly visible, but a functional part of many library programs throughout the nation. Based on the two case studies briefly described above, several common characteristics emerge, most of which should be expected.

The most productive programs are those supported by institutional administrative levels of both governing bodies and sources of financial support. This does not mean that those groups essentially run out of a hip pocket cannot succeed, but that there are more barriers and more is required of the individual participants than an institution can support easily. In addition, administrative support indicates the importance of cooperative programs to the institution and minimizes the need for program justification.

The provision of central management personnel enables projects to succeed. It does not guarantee success, but it provides a pivotal communication point both within the consortium and beyond it that eases many processes and provides both greater speed of response and much more effective negotiation power when representing the consortium. The assignment of staff specific to a project or group also enhances that group's ability to function and provides important expertise and concentration on shared goals. In addition, the presence of an ex officio member from the central management improves the likelihood that a program will indeed move forward and provides a focal point for the consortial agenda rather than a series of institutional agendas.

Central funding makes life much simpler in terms of supporting cooperative activities and acquiring materials in any format. Such funding clearly provides an incentive for cooperation. However, that is likely to be only a part of the process. It can make movement and accomplishments much easier, but cooperation still requires the investment of library time, attention, and resources. The political process of cooperation can itself be very costly, requiring the investment of personnel that are also central to local programs.

Technology is providing new means of delivering information that is much more amenable to remote access and delivery across time and space. Even the ability to deliver books, with vans and trucks, has become more realistic in the consortium setting as libraries take advantage of commercial delivery services under cooperative contracts. The sharing of electronic resources, including bibliographic, full-text, and image materials, is not necessarily dependent on local collections, but allows for the expansion and augmentation of local collections through technology.

The most important enabling factor, however, is to convince the selectors and the faculty that academic institutions must recognize mutual dependence as a normal part of the academic process and a survival mechanism in the shrinking higher education economy. In addition, the library reward system should recognize and provide incentives to selectors who participate in cooperative projects at the behest of their libraries. After all, rewards are a recognition of the importance of a particular activity to a library's programs.

Establishing successful cooperative academic library programs has much in common with herding cats. First, many of the potential participants do not want to be part of a group, each wants to go in its own direction, and their owners may not want them to play nicely together. However, when institutions commit to a cooperative program, systematic cooperative collection development, in concert with efficient delivery programs and provision of additional electronic and other resources, can enhance the usefulness of each member's collection. By providing an alternative means to fill curricular and research needs, the responsible academic library must exploit all the resources at hand and, in turn, expect to be a participant in the supply of information to others. The systematic development of cooperative collection management can be a dependable part of this process and greatly enhance both the role of the university library and the resources that it can offer to its users. Technology, need, and recognition of reality are all converging to make cooperative programs a vital part of an effective academic library program.

NOTES

1. Anna H. Perrault, "Improving Resource Sharing: The Service Imperative in an Access Environment," *Advances in Library Resource Sharing* 2 (1991): 1.

2. Ruth J. Patrick, *Guidelines for Library Cooperation: Development of Academic Library Consortia* (n.p.: System Development Corporation, 1972), pp. 3–4.

3. Genevieve M. Casey, *Interlibrary Cooperation in Ohio: A Background Paper Prepared for the Ohio Multitype Interlibrary Cooperation Committee* (Dayton, OH: Wright State University, 1978), p. 1–1.

4. Kenneth R. R. Gros Louis, "The Real Costs and Financial Challenges of Library Networking: Part 1," in *Networks, Open Access, and Virtual Libraries: Implications for the Research Library. Papers Presented at the 1991 Clinic on Library Applications of Data Processing, April 7–9, 1991* (Urbana-Champaign: University of Illinois, Graduate School of Library and Information Science, 1992), p. 121.

5. Casey, *Interlibrary Cooperation*, p. 1–2.

6. Robert H. Blackburn, "Interlibrary Cooperation," in *Research Librarianship: Essays in Honor of Robert B. Downs*, ed. Jerrold Orne (New York: Bowker, 1971), pp. 51–52.

7. *Guide to Cooperative Collection Development*, ed. Bart Harloe. Collection Management and Development Guides, no. 6 (Chicago: American Library Association, 1994), p. 2.

8. Ibid.

9. Philip H. Sewell, *Resource Sharing: Co-operation and Co-ordination in Library and Information Services* (London: Andre Deutsch, 1981), pp. 131–32.

10. Ibid.; *Guide to Cooperative Collection Development*, pp. 3–4.

11. Robert H. Blackburn, "Interlibrary Cooperation," in *Research Librarianship: Essays in Honor of Robert B. Downs*, ed. Jerrold Orne (New York: Bowker, 1971), p. 52.

12. Thomas W. Shaughnessy, "The Real Costs and Financial Challenges of Library Networking: Part 2," in *Networks, Open Access, and Virtual Libraries: Implications for the Research Library. Papers Presented at the 1991 Clinic on Library Applications of Data Processing, April 7–9, 1991* (Urbana-Champaign: University of Illinois, Graduate School of Library and Information Science, 1992), p. 123.

13. Clifford A. Lynch, "Networked Information: A Revolution in Progress," in *Networks, Open Access, and Virtual Libraries: Implications for the Research Library. Papers Presented at the 1991 Clinic on Library Applications of Data Processing, April 7–9, 1991* (Urbana-Champaign: University of Illinois, Graduate School of Library and Information Science, 1992), p. 23.

14. Anne Woodsworth, *Library Cooperation and Networks: A Basic Reader* (New York: Neal-Schuman, 1991), pp. 25–28.

15. "OhioLINK Database Statistics, August 14, 1995" (Columbus, OH: OhioLINK, 1995), p. 1.

16. *CIC CDO Cooperative Collection Project Report to the CIC Library Directors, May 1, 1994* (http://www.cic.net/cic/cdo.html), p. 1.

17. Task Force on the CIC Electronic Collection, *Report to the CIC Library Directors, October 1, 1993* (http://www.cic.net/cic/elecfin.html), p. 1.

14

Cooperative Collection Development: Compelling Theory, Inconsequential Results?

Dan C. Hazen

INTRODUCTION

Librarians commonly complain about inadequate collections budgets. One frequent rejoinder promises an inevitable cooperative fix, and each new collaboration then generates its own insistent triumphalism. But a sense of failure nonetheless persists: the initial fanfare, hype, and hope too often trail off into disappointed cynicism. Are we questing for a bibliothecal grail, or merely chasing a will-o'-the-wisp? If cooperation is such an obvious solution, why do its fruits seem so elusive?

This chapter, by focusing on concrete examples concerning Latin American Studies, explores what cooperation in building collections has achieved and what it might accomplish. Following a quick recapitulation of the rationale for cooperative collection development, it describes and then assesses a suite of cooperative North American efforts to acquire Latin Americanist materials. This analysis, together with more speculative reflections on today's changing technologies, highlights the achievements, potential, and challenges of cooperative collection development.[1]

THE CASE(S) FOR COOPERATION

Cooperative collection development is typically expected to meet one or several of the following, not necessarily compatible, needs:

Broadening access. Scholars require ready access to the full printed record, yet comprehensive acquisitions are beyond any library's reach. Distributed collecting responsibilities will enable groups of libraries to acquire a wider variety of materials than any one could manage on its own.

Containing cost. Research libraries spend a great deal to duplicate materials held at other institutions. Coordinated acquisitions will save money by minimizing redundancy. Cooperative collection development is the best way to contain library costs.

Improving coverage. Publications from some world areas remain uncontrolled and unsystematic. Even the richest and most conscientious library will miss some materials. Cooperation improves the chances for complete coverage.

Ensuring the exotic. Universities face intense fiscal pressure. Most academic libraries are charged with supporting present and future scholarship, implying acquisitions that may receive neither early nor frequent use. Cost-cutters may see such purchases as a frill. "Esoteric" acquisitions can be justified in the context of a national cooperative plan.

Arguments asserting the virtues of cooperative collection development are buttressed by two technological trumps. In the first place, successful cooperation presumes both a common knowledge of what has been acquired and efficient mechanisms for document delivery. Online bibliographic databases and electronically based interlibrary loan support these requirements as never before. The second and still embryonic development centers on electronic formats. Digital communications and electronic storage nullify the logic of ownership and the logistics of location. The promise—and challenges—of electronic cooperation are fundamentally new.

Librarians and scholars concerned with Latin American Studies have, for more than fifty years, practiced cooperative collection development. Their efforts have taken many forms, from limited projects to comprehensive plans. Impacts have similarly ranged widely. While Latin Americanists' cooperative efforts have not spared the field from the cutbacks and pressures common to other library collections, the results (at least relative to each project's objectives) have often been both positive and substantial. Examining some of these projects demonstrates how cooperation has arisen and also suggests the bases for continued activity.

LATIN AMERICANIST COOPERATION: SEVEN CASE STUDIES

Every discipline has unique characteristics which, among other things, shape its need for information and the way it uses scholarly resources. These attitudes and patterns, possibilities and constraints, establish the broad context for cooperative collection development. This section thus begins with a broad overview of Latin American Studies. It then describes and analyzes several Latin American cooperative efforts. These specific descriptions will provide the grounding for a general discussion of collections cooperation.

The Academic Setting: Latin American Studies and Its Library Collections

Several features of Latin Americanist scholarship have affected library programs as well as academic priorities. The field only emerged in the early 20th century. The study of societies whose documentary resources were limited and for which research questions were broad soon became self-consciously interdisciplinary. Methodological eclecticism, while reinforcing inclusive needs for information, also promoted enduring alliances between librarians and scholars as partners in the research process.

The consolidation of Latin American Studies dates at least to the 1918 inauguration of the *Hispanic American Historical Review*. However, the *Handbook of Latin American Studies*, initiated in 1936, is for our purposes more interesting. This annual publication serves as both an interdisciplinary research guide and an annotated bibliography.[2] From the first it has been the collaborative product of librarians (who identify materials for potential inclusion), scholars (who edit each of its sections), and an academic publisher (who actually produces the book). The *Handbook* has built upon but also extended the field's interdisciplinary perspective and its reliance on librarian-academic partnerships.

Area studies programs, with strong support from the federal government and foundations, were propelled to the forefront of academic expansion during the 1950s and 1960s. Interest in Latin American issues intensified noticeably following the Cuban Revolution. The 1966 formation of the Latin American Studies Association marked the field's maturity.

Latin American Studies is today fully international. Scholars from the region are highly visible in foreign universities and on the conference circuit; non-Latin Americans are likewise active in the region's universities, think tanks, and action organizations. The field is also thoroughly dispersed. Latin Americanists may be found at National Resource Centers and prominent specialized programs, but also in hundreds of more isolated settings.

Early Latin American library collections were, for the most part, constructed by acquiring specialized private libraries. Acquisitions skyrocketed as new academic programs were created through the 1950s and 1960s. Budgets have since stagnated, and collections may have become more uniform as the same high profile materials have been acquired by many institutions. Perhaps two dozen libraries now comprise the top tier of major collections.[3]

Latin Americanist library cooperation boasts a substantial history of its own. This chapter focuses on seven noteworthy examples that illustrate both problems and possibilities. Our selective overview will set the stage for a broader-gauged discussion of cooperative collection development as a whole.

While the following seven examples of cooperative collection development for Latin American materials by no means exhaust the roster, they do represent its range. The cases vary in complexity, so their descriptions vary in length. Each discussion addresses the project's origin and organization, as well as its relationship to the four possible goals for cooperation cited above.

Bilateral Cooperation: The Duke University–University of North Carolina Model

One of the field's earliest collaborative efforts was constructed around strong Latin American programs and preexisting library cooperation in neighboring institutions. Beginning in 1940, foundation support for Latin American programs and library collections at Duke University and the University of North Carolina (UNC) enabled each library to develop particular country strengths.[4] Administration was easy, while access to materials was quick and simple due to shared catalogs and physical proximity. Faculty on both campuses were strongly supportive. The two collections were expected to function as one, with minimal overlap for high-use materials. The specializations continue to this date. The University of California at Berkeley and Stanford University have embraced a similar model of cooperation through complementarity. Several more extended regional groupings are now seeking to combine the advantages of geographic proximity with the benefits of scale.

Bilateral arrangements particularly address the cooperative goals of broader access (among a limited number of participants) and cost containment. Specialization in support of intensive collecting, and measures to secure exotic materials, have in the Duke-UNC case been secondary. The bilateral model could certainly support such priorities.

Programmed National Cooperation: The Farmington Plan

The Farmington Plan, a national initiative inaugurated in 1948 (though with roots extending back to the late 1930s), initially focused on subject-specific collecting assignments for Western European materials: the goal was to ensure that all materials of scholarly value were acquired in some North American library.[5] The Plan eventually expanded to include about 60 participating libraries which covered 16 (mostly European) countries through subject assignments, and another 120 countries via country assignments. Participants followed a host of special procedures, particularly for European acquisitions. Materials from Latin America, like those from other world areas, were encompassed within the Plan.

The Farmington Plan generated increasingly mixed reactions, for reasons both good and bad. Its efforts were associated first and foremost with Western European imprints. Coverage for this region was based on subject assignments implemented through obligatory collecting arrangements with specific booksellers. The bureaucratic and organizational complexities provoked a steady undercurrent of participant frustration. Misgivings over administrative costs, the adequacy of Plan coverage, and the very need for the Plan during an era of university and library expansion likewise undermined support. The Association of Research Libraries (ARL) dismantled the Plan's central office at the end of 1972, following vocal dissatisfaction and the withdrawal of several major libraries. While only Western European arrangements were officially affected, and while ARL urged continued efforts for coordinated acquisitions, the Plan was effectively dead.

Latin American coverage through the Farmington Plan was, at least nominally, fairly complete. Most assignments reflected participants' long-standing academic and collecting emphases. For Latin America, as for other non-European collecting areas, libraries were entrusted to make their own acquisitions arrangements rather than being constrained to specific dealers. On the other hand, and as for most world areas, the Plan never devised means to track receipts or to evaluate results. When the general Plan superstructure was abolished, its Latin American manifestation quickly faded away.

The "Mini-Farmington Plan," launched by Latin American librarians in the late 1970s, was a fairly straightforward, region-specific revival of the original scheme. Bibliographers again assumed institutional responsibility for acquisitions from particular countries. Their library directors, who again signed the resulting agreements, pledged ongoing support for both collection development and prompt cataloging. However, this revival again lacked any formal structure to report problems and triumphs, to encourage participants, or even to publicize the arrangement's existence. Momentum dwindled fairly quickly.

Collecting commitments from the two Latin American incarnations of the Farmington Plan have tended to endure. Since assignments were from the first associated with each institution's programmatic and collection strengths, these ongoing effects may reflect local continuities more than cooperative commitment. The Farmington Plan was designed to guarantee North American access to the world's output of research materials. Cost containment was not at all prominent, while the goal of esoteric acquisitions was by and large subordinated to pursuing materials of probable scholarly interest. The central goal, maximized coverage, related closely to that of ensuring broad representation of the region's research output.

Cooperation to Support Local Collections: The Latin American Cooperative Acquisitions Project (LACAP)

A different focus for cooperation arose in response to the complexities of Latin American acquisitions. The region's book trade remained notoriously difficult, at least into the 1960s. Specialist librarians, meeting through the Seminar on the Acquisition of Latin American Library Materials (SALALM), began in the late 1950s to explore on-site purchasing. This impulse, which overlapped with the Farmington Plan's concern for strengthened coverage of foreign publications, eventually matured into the Latin American Cooperative Acquisitions Project (LACAP).[6]

LACAP began in 1960 as the Stechert-Hafner firm commissioned North American librarians, chief among them Nettie Lee Benson, to scour Latin America for publications. The endeavor gradually expanded to include a permanent staff, ongoing relationships with Latin American booksellers, numerous library participants, and increasingly sophisticated procedures to manage new acquisitions. Twenty-three of forty-six ARL libraries surveyed in the early 1970s relied on LACAP for at least some Latin American materials. Most libraries with Farmington Plan responsibilities for Latin America, however, did not employ this source.

Crowell, Collier, Macmillan acquired Stechert-Hafner in 1972. LACAP ended, on financial grounds, shortly thereafter. The program was in any event controversial. Many libraries preferred their own acquisition channels, and the participants themselves often complained of high prices, poor selection, and mediocre service. On a more positive note, LACAP helped foster a group of Latin American booksellers willing and able to operate in the international sphere. The Project's demise had surprisingly little impact on collections and collecting. The times had changed through a process in which LACAP itself played a major role. LACAP, as an effort to strengthen the infrastructure for Latin American collection development, did not directly address any of the four general objectives of cooperation. Like automated bibliographic control or quicker interlibrary loan, LACAP affected the broad context of library operations and thereby made other things possible.

LACAP, along with virtually all other cooperative initiatives following the Duke-UNC consortium and the Farmington Plan, owed a great deal to SALALM. Just as LACAP focused on the infrastructure for Latin American acquisitions, so SALALM created a supportive context for Latin Americanist librarianship as a whole. SALALM evolved out of an original meeting in 1956. The first seminars were convened in order to resolve concrete problems associated with Latin American acquisitions. Despite significant growth, the organization's central concern remains the same. Members have expanded beyond librarians to include the major Latin American booksellers as well as publishers and scholars. They thus represent a broad cross-section of those involved with the dissemination of Latin Americanist scholarly information.

SALALM in and of itself embodies area-specific cooperation. Its committee structure and its programs are concerned with the flow of Latin American scholarly publications to North American libraries. Some of its projects, such as multilingual correspondence manuals and lists of potential exchange partners, have been eminently practical. One standing committee brings together librarians and booksellers to address both specific irritations and broader concerns. SALALM's annual programs, as they highlight emerging trends in scholarship and scholarly information, have laid the foundations for continued cooperative efforts. Perhaps most important, SALALM enables area specialists to meet and to work together—trust, respect, and shared values are among the results.

Simple Tasks and Straightforward Structures: The Intensive Cuban Collecting Group

The Intensive Cuban Collecting Group (ICCG) is the recent, informal, and task-specific creation of interested bibliographers from libraries with strong Cuban holdings.[7] ICCG took shape in 1988 as a means to guarantee that the most important Cuban serials would remain available. Its participants together identified significant (mostly retrospective) titles and then decided whose library would acquire or microfilm each one. Scholars were widely consulted, but arrangements rarely involved library bureaucracies. ICCG, which was coordinated at Princeton University, functioned as a voluntary consortium without outside funds. It declared its work complete after ensuring the availability of several hundred Cuban serials. Groups like ICCG have addressed specific sets of materials, whether esoteric or mainstream. Cost containment—indeed, almost any consideration of costs—has been largely irrelevant. Enhanced access, beyond ensuring that titles are held somewhere within the country, has been secondary as well.

An Independent Agency for Cooperation: The Latin American Microform Project

The Latin American Microform Project (LAMP) follows a different pattern. LAMP was created in the mid-1970s when a group of bibliographers sought to preserve endangered research materials by pooling their resources.[8] LAMP, now with thirty-five institutional members, funds its efforts through a combination of annual dues and occasional outside grants. Many of its microfilming projects have been carried out in conjunction with Latin American libraries and archives.

The LAMP model varies from those already described in several respects. Perhaps most obvious, LAMP enjoys both an independent budget and organizational autonomy. Its policies are decided by the membership and an elected executive committee. Administrative support is provided by the Center for Research Libraries, which manages LAMP's money and also stores and services its film. LAMP's independent status, plus its ability to draw on the expertise of members' librarians and scholars, have enabled it to tackle needed preservation efforts that are beyond the reach of any single institution. Autonomy has also encouraged flexibility and innovation. A current foundation grant thus supports an experiment to digitize previously filmed Brazilian serial documents and then mount the files on the Internet.

LAMP is noteworthy for its impact within Latin America. Preservation microfilm must meet rigid standards. LAMP has sought out the best filmers in many Latin American countries and then worked with them to improve their products. Just as LACAP encouraged a network of Latin American booksellers, so LAMP has strengthened the region's capabilities for preservation microfilming.

LAMP's prospectus identifies the primary goals of enhanced access (through preservation) of regional research materials and the preservation of esoteric or hard-to-find resources. As a budget-conscious organization largely funded by member dues, LAMP is deeply concerned with cost efficiency. Cost containment, however, is not particularly central.

Large-Scale Cooperation: The Conspectus

The Research Libraries Group (RLG), an organization built around the twin bases of its bibliographic utility (RLIN) and programs specifically targeted to research libraries, emerged as a national force in the 1980s. Coordinated collection development was then, as now, a central concern. RLG sought to redefine the scope and nature of cooperative collection development by devising a more powerful instrument to describe both collection topics and collecting practices.[9] The Conspectus, initially RLG's and later shared with the Association of Research Libraries (ARL), consists of an exhaustive division of knowledge through which libraries report the strength of their collections and their current collecting levels. The combined values from many different libraries comprise a topical map of overall coverage. The North American Collections Inventory Project (NCIP) denoted a concerted effort to complete this grid, which in turn was expected to facilitate cooperative collecting assignments.

Latin Americanist librarians pitched in to create and then complete their own Conspectus. As with the document as a whole, the Latin American Conspectus established a new conceptual framework from which cooperative arrangements were expected to emerge. The actual impact, however, has been limited. Many libraries have completed the Conspectus, but projects to identify and address areas of national weakness have not borne fruit. There are several explanations.

As with other fields, calibrated evaluations of Latin American collections across different institutions require carefully constructed verification studies which are almost prohibitively expensive. With about 600 separate Latin Americanist lines, the chances for confusion—and exhaustion—are high. The structure of the Latin American Conspectus has also proved problematic. The Conspectus's categories, which are framed in terms of the Library of Congress Classification, only occasionally correspond to scholarly concerns. These pigeonholes also carry little prospective value for library acquisitions, since it is often impossible to anticipate a book's eventual call number. The instrument's descriptive powers have not been fully exploited, and its predictive force remains in doubt.

For all its practical limitations, the Conspectus has had a major impact. It has provoked unprecedentedly acute evaluations of many local collections. The weight of RLG and ARL sponsorship has made it the focus of extended speculation concerning cooperative collection development. And the difficulties in implementing its apparently straightforward potential have fostered ever more realistic expectations.[10] Early Conspectus rhetoric encouraged predictions that it would establish the framework to address all four of the general objectives for cooperative collection development. This broad appeal may itself have induced some of the enthusiasm that the Conspectus continues to engender.

Our Last, Best Hope? The AAU/ARL Latin Americanist Research Resources Pilot Project

The Association of American Universities (AAU) and the Association of Research Libraries have taken the lead in confronting what they identify as an incipient crisis in foreign acquisitions. This endeavor, to a degree not found in our other cases, also coincides with what is widely perceived as a more generalized, and problematic, transformation in the entire structure of scholarly communication.[11]

The Latin Americanist Research Resources Pilot Project was established in order to create "a prototype for fully connected collections for Latin American Studies that could also serve as a model for other scholarly fields." The Project thus expects to increase the range of Latin Americanist resources available to students and scholars, while minimizing the costs of sustaining these (ideally enlarged) collections. At some level it responds to all four general objectives of cooperative collection development—though different constituencies have different favorites. Scholars and bibliographers thus focus on enhanced coverage, while university and library administrators more often emphasize cost containment.

Three specific efforts are now underway. The Project's 32 participating libraries have distributed collecting assignments for 300 serials from Argentina and Mexico. An online table of contents database and expedited (Ariel-based) interlibrary loan ensure broad awareness of these materials and rapid transmission of needed articles. Collecting responsibilities have also been distributed for the publications of various nongovernmental organizations, again from Argentina and Mexico, again in conjunction with enhanced cataloging and rapid interlibrary loan. Presidential messages from Argentina and Mexico are being digitized and made available over the Internet. In a second phase, five test libraries will explore the internal adjustments in organization and staffing required to implement large-scale cooperation through a distributed model.

The Pilot Project capitalizes on several strengths of previous Latin Americanist efforts. The bibliographers at participating institutions are committed to the project and in regular contact. An advisory committee of scholars and librarians is continuing the partnership that has long characterized the field as a whole. Project libraries have pledged significant cash contributions. Library directors have uniformly signed off on the project, which affects a host of operations within each institution.

The Pilot Project also moves beyond its predecessors. Tightly defined collecting assignments make it easy to monitor compliance and evaluate results. The Project places a heavy emphasis on the availability of bibliographic information. Other improvements reflect such new technological capabilities as fax-based interlibrary loan and a generalized use of electronic communications. The creation of digital files is, of course, new as well.

Perhaps most important of all is the Project's explicit formulation of goals that suggest cutbacks in participant acquisitions and heavier reliance on shared resources. The other cases we have examined have at best only implicitly and eventually proposed local reductions. This conceptual shift has major implications, both for the participating libraries and for other actors in the process of scholarly communication.

Even in its current formative state, the Pilot Project raises a number of issues. Some are particular to this effort, while others will apply to almost any cooperative endeavor. Since the Project seeks to exploit existing capabilities for sharing in-print hard-copy originals as fully as possible, the sticking points deserve careful attention.

Growing a Project. Special routines have been imposed on Project participants in order to provide prompt indexing and cataloging, speed up interlibrary loan, and gather special statistics. These unusual procedures, applied to very small sets of materials, have reduced efficiency within many of the affected units. Cooperative efforts generally assume savings as a result of their large scale of operation. However, most libraries now lack both the means to pursue extensive cooperation and the proof of cooperative economies that would spur them to substantially change their structures. Large-scale organizational shifts, moreover, will work best if groups of libraries change together: a single library structured for an environment of distributed, networked collections can accomplish but little. The second phase of the Pilot Project will address some of these issues.

The Pilot Project might expand in any number of directions. While its set-up costs have been high, the necessary level of continuing administrative overhead is not yet clear.[12] Expansion is also likely to involve additional actors in the chain of scholarly communication. Some book dealers have already voiced fears of reduced sales as subscriptions are consolidated. Publishers may feel the same. And scholars, our users, need to decide whether the Project offers an acceptable trade-off between breadth of coverage and delivery speed.

The Dismal Science and Shared Collections. In the long run, successful cooperation must make economic sense: a structure that replicates existing capabilities at a higher price should not survive. Economics remains central. Nonetheless, the rhetoric that links planned cooperative collection development to enhanced service and reduced costs has not yet been tested. To begin with, the economic prospects for cooperative collection development can, at a rather simple level, be assessed within and among libraries.

As we well know, library acquisitions range in cost from the cheap to the expensive. The costs of ownership include the initial purchase or subscription price, but also the expenses of ordering, receipt, and claims; cataloging and processing; binding; shelf space; circulation; and preservation. Materials similarly vary in terms of their local use, from no demand to heavy consultation.

Each title held in a library will show a particular combination of cost and use. Every library also incurs real expenses for interlibrary loan.[13] It makes economic sense for libraries to rely on interlibrary loan when the cost of borrowing a particular item is less than that of purchase and processing. Conversely, purchase is appropriate when interlibrary loan would be more expensive.

Similar calculations apply at an aggregate level. Cooperation is questionable for inexpensive, high-use materials; it provides a likely response for little-used items that cost a lot. Even though we are too often unable to measure either cost or use, the frameworks for analysis are straightforward.

The cost balance between ownership and remote access may shift as a result of several developments beyond the Pilot Project's immediate scope. More complete indexing and bibliographic control are likely to increase demand and thereby encourage broader local collections. Cheaper interlibrary loan would have far greater effect. In a longer term, shifts in document formats—for instance the substitution of electronic files for paper copies—will change the premises of both cooperation and collection development itself.

This section has described seven projects for cooperative collection development that either originated within the Latin Americanist library community or encompassed Latin American materials. The projects, some still active, have had varying impacts. Most have focused on only one or two of the general goals commonly cited to justify collection cooperation, even when (as in most cases) additional objectives could have been adduced. Another way to assess these projects is to consider the extent to which they satisfy a series of conditions that have been suggested as necessary for cooperative success.

CONDITIONS FOR COOPERATIVE SUCCESS

Cooperative endeavors can be evaluated in different ways. Many of the Latin Americanist efforts just described have accomplished their stated goals. These successes, however, have not spared the field from the fall-off in collections coverage that seems to affect libraries as a whole. The triumphs have not turned the tide. Our Latin American examples can also be assessed in order to determine the conditions under which cooperative efforts will succeed or fail. Evaluation can likewise focus on each cooperative project's impact on the overall system of scholarly communication. Finally, the meaning of cooperation can be gauged in terms of the changing nature of information and information technology.

This section begins by comparing our Latin American cases to one recent article's proposed conditions for cooperative success. Additional elements are suggested as well. We then consider how other players in the structure of scholarly communication have been affected by the sample projects. The chapter's concluding section briefly addresses the issues associated with technological change.

Conditions for Success

One recent and very detailed survey of cooperative collection development focuses on North Carolina's Research Triangle University Libraries (and therefore includes the Duke-UNC collaboration). The authors suggest seven necessary conditions for success: "propitious circumstances, visionary and committed individuals, supportive organizational structures, appropriate staff participation, bibliographic and physical accessibility to collections, outside funding, and a history of successful cooperation."[14] This list provides a useful starting point for analysis.

Propitious Circumstances

Latin Americanist cooperative initiatives have benefitted from "propitious circumstances" in several respects. The field as a whole prizes interdisciplinarity and collaboration. Since the mid-1950s, SALALM has served as a library seedbed for cooperation, collegiality, and exchange. A sense of impending crisis— a paradoxical yet extraordinarily powerful "propitious circumstance"—has likewise underlain all these efforts. Mobilization has thus proved relatively easy.

Individual programs reflect more immediate conjunctures. Foundations supported the Duke–UNC arrangement, and also the AAU/ARL Latin Americanist Research Resources Pilot Project. The Latin American Cooperative Acquisitions Project, the Latin American Microform Project, the Mini-Farmington Plan, and the Intensive Cuban Collecting Group are direct responses to fairly immediate concerns of bibliographers and scholars. The AAU/ARL Pilot Project, the Conspectus, and the original Farmington Plan reflect Latin Americanist applications of general initiatives within the library community. It is probably safe to conclude that cooperative efforts will not arise, much less survive, without propitious circumstances. While important, this condition lacks predictive power.

Visionary and Committed Individuals

The Latin Americanist library community has from the start been blessed with strong, far-sighted personalities. The roster of pioneers is long, though Nettie Lee Benson of the University of Texas and Marietta Daniels Shepard of the Organization of American States particularly stand out.[15] The field continues to attract individuals of vision and generosity. Each of the projects we have described has been particularly beholden to a few leaders. The role of these individuals has been articulated within an academic field and area studies specialization that encourage cooperation. Latin Americanist leaders have worked closely and well with their colleagues. Without champions, cooperative programs simply will not get off the ground. The factor is again necessary but not predictive.

Supportive Organizational Structures

This condition implies institutions committed to cooperation and capable of providing necessary operational support. Latin Americanist efforts, including the

Latin American Cooperative Acquisitions Project and the Latin American Microform Project, have devised special interinstitutional frameworks. Other efforts, for instance, the Intensive Cuban Collecting Group, have deliberately avoided bureaucracy. The muted success of the Mini-Farmington Plan in part reflected its lack of structure. Both the original Farmington Plan and the Conspectus, on the other hand, were fairly massive operations centered outside the Latin Americanist community. One of the challenges facing the current AAU/ARL Pilot Project is to sustain a high degree of specifically Latin Americanist involvement, while responding to the general collections concerns of library managers and university administrators.

Cooperative structures need to foster active participation among their librarian and scholarly constituencies. Communications must be broad and open, projects must respect existing areas of aspiration and strength, perceived needs must be addressed with care. Several cooperative programs—LACAP, as it moved outside the sphere of participant control, seems an especially good example—have faltered for want of this base.

Appropriate Staff Participation

Successful projects must involve line staff as well as administrators: goals are met by addressing myriad practical details, as well as by articulating broad visions of change. Staff involvement requires appropriate reward structures as well as inclusive mandates for participation. Our case studies have taken root at various points within the library hierarchy, and have then made use of different sorts of staff expertise. All seven projects eventually involved area specialists. The Intensive Cuban Collecting Group, the Latin American Cooperative Acquisitions Project, and the Latin American Microform Project originated within this specialist community and were by and large successful in matters over which participants had direct control. At the other extreme, the Conspectus was administered by the Research Libraries Group and the Association of Research Libraries. While high-level sponsorship ensured the instrument's complete elaboration and widespread application, the practical experiences of line librarians established the limits of its utility.

Tensions are normal when projects impinge upon different units within the library. Since bibliographers cannot usually speak for catalogers or interlibrary loan staff, administrative involvement is essential in activities that cut across functions. Even efforts like the AAU/ARL Pilot Project, which built in directorial support from the first, are finding that cross-divisional compliance is far from certain. Mobilizing a full range of appropriate staff members remains both necessary and problematic.

Bibliographic and Physical Accessibility to Collections

Accessibility, whether bibliographic or physical, is a concept heavily conditioned by the changing possibilities of the times. The Duke–University of North Carolina collaboration is based in next-door institutions whose shared catalogs date back to the 1930s. Adequate access was initially possible with entirely manual systems, even though automated records are now the rule. More dispersed consortia have, through online bibliographic utilities, provided reasonable (though not yet complete) bibliographic access to member holdings. On the other hand, as monograph and serial titles have become more accessible in bibliographic terms, expectations have changed. The frontier for intellectual access now centers on such hitherto overlooked resources as the journal articles and ephemeral publications addressed in the AAU/ARL Pilot Project.

Physical access is still based on the slow, costly, and cumbersome process of interlibrary loan. Efficient document delivery is indispensable for effective cooperation. Assessments of interlibrary loan, however, must also recognize scholars' often increasing difficulty in working with local holdings. Collection growth has filled many libraries to overflowing. Remote storage, while a common response, generally comes at the cost of easy accessibility. Local library holdings are less and less browsable, and specific stored volumes require ILL-like transactions for retrieval. The practical distinction between local ownership and shared access may be smaller than we think.

The impact and scope of almost all cooperative programs have been limited by the practicalities of access. The Latin Americanist exceptions—for instance, the Latin American Microform Project, in which interlibrary loan was assured from the start; the Intensive Cuban Collecting Group, in which access was not part of the project's objectives; or the Duke–University of North Carolina Consortium, in which close geographic proximity made other measures superfluous—prove the rule. These variations also suggest, somewhat paradoxically, that successful projects for cooperative collection development need not include easy access among their primary goals.

Outside Funding

Outside funding, while a major boost to many projects, is not essential. The Duke–UNC collaboration, the AAU/ARL Pilot Project, the Farmington Plan, and the Conspectus effort were launched with external support. Other efforts, like LAMP, have used external resources only to enhance their programs.

Outside funds have been more crucial in sustaining the overall structure of area studies scholarship. Cold War fears and the Sputnik shock stimulated broad federal support for area studies programs beginning in the 1950s. Competitive grants for what are now known as National Resource Centers have been fundamental to Latin American Studies and to other area enterprises as well. Most area studies specialists feel that the programs have benefitted students, scholarship, and the country as a whole. Any cooperative program must ultimately sustain itself. External support, as either catalyst or stimulant, will be short-lived and episodic. The dilemma of long-term support affected both the Farmington Plan and the Conspectus. Solvency is now one of the central challenges facing the AAU/ARL Pilot Project.

A History of Successful Cooperation

Latin American Studies and librarianship have developed a lasting culture of cooperation. This long history has in and of itself fostered a willingness to experiment with new possibilities. The limited scale of Latin American librarianship also means that area specialists know one another: Informal contacts bolster formal arrangements. This condition, which again reflects a Latin Americanist constant, has by consequence only limited predictive value.

The seven proposed conditions for cooperative success apply in different degree to our seven test cases. A closer look at the reasons for some programs' decline underscores some of the most essential elements. Four of our examples (the Duke–University of North Carolina consortium, the Latin American Microform Project, the Intensive Cuban Collecting Group, and the AAU/ARL Pilot Project) are still in operation, successfully concluded, or too new to evaluate. The immediate cause of the Latin American Cooperative Acquisition Project's demise was its lack of profitability. This in turn reflected the Latin Americanist community's lukewarm adherence to the program, LACAP's reportedly indifferent service, and the emergence of improved channels for direct acquisitions. The Farmington Plan, for its part, was perhaps prematurely abandoned. Mixed reactions while it was in effect, several major defections, and a near-total lack of means for evaluation largely eliminated a constituency to sustain it. The Conspectus, finally, established an elegant conceptual infrastructure that proved impractical as a basis for concrete activities. The elements whose absence underlay these failures appear straightforward: economic viability, mechanisms for constructive feedback, means for evaluation, and on-the-ground practicability.

Other Dimensions

Our examples suggest several other dimensions of cooperative activity that have little effect on projects' viability. While many programs have limited themselves to libraries in North America, some have been more adventuresome in terms of either their geographic scope or their involvement with nonlibrary actors within the chain of scholarly communication. SALALM, LACAP, and LAMP have been inclusive by design. Projects whose geographic scale and range of actors transcend the United States or the library community are complex. Their potential benefits are correspondingly large.

Administrative arrangements can likewise vary without a clear impact on project success. Our examples encompass structures ranging from the simple (Intensive Cuban Collecting Group) to the complex (the Conspectus, the AAU/ARL Pilot Project). Decision makers range from bibliographers alone (ICCG), to bibliographers and library directors (the Mini-Farmington Plan), to a host of players including local staff and broadly based institutions (the Conspectus). Mechanisms to monitor progress again vary widely. While complex efforts imply larger superstructures, cost imposes its own limits. Complexity also requires special efforts to ensure participants' continuing engagement.

Different projects have followed separate paths in planning their efforts. The Farmington Plan and the Conspectus evolved into or began as comprehensive endeavors affecting all collecting areas. The Latin American Microform Project, while it has established a mechanism to identify and approve preservation candidates, has consciously refrained from comprehensive priorities. The AAU/ ARL Pilot Project, though starting small, carries the implicit, albeit long-term promise of comprehensive coverage. Collection cooperation admits of more and less ambitious proposals. Thus far, tighter focuses have correlated with success.

Latin Americanist cooperation is striking for its diversity of approach. Given engaged leaders, necessary start-up funds, and a reasonable plan, almost any project can find both peer support and some degree of success. The field's varied history of cooperative achievement suggests that Latin Americanists will continue to benefit from a range of initiatives. On the other hand, little in this survey suggests that cooperation will forestall the incipient crisis we now confront.

Other Players and Their Interests

The chain of scholarly communication, in oversimplified synthesis, begins with scholars-as-authors and proceeds through publishers, booksellers, and libraries, to end with scholars-as-consumers. Each player is responsible for one or several functions. Scholars produce manuscripts. These enter the editorial process as publishers select specific texts, review and revise them for accuracy and style, and mass produce and market the finished versions. Publishers also authenticate each final copy, ensuring that it is faithful both to the original and to every other copy. Intermediaries including bibliographic agencies and trade groups, but first and foremost booksellers, organize and manage the publications market. Libraries (and individuals) then decide what they will acquire. Libraries ensure access to scholarly resources through bibliographic control, arrangements for physical consultation, and preservation. As the products of scholarship become available to scholars, the cycle begins anew.

University Libraries and Scholarly Communication is perhaps the most ambitious of several recent studies that attempt to untangle this structure's ever more precarious economics.[16] By focusing on the economic forces constraining academic publishers and research libraries, this work describes a system in which two principal players are increasingly at odds. The ARL Foreign Acquisitions Project, in its draft final report, confirms a sustained decline in scholarly access to foreign publications. While only peripherally concerned with scholarly communications' nonlibrary players, the document again demonstrates a system in flux.

Most studies addressing current challenges to the structure of scholarly communication overlook the role of booksellers as the principal intermediaries between publishers and consumers. Bookseller competition, which varies widely by field and country, is (among other things) reflected in different levels of service, coverage, and markup. Diminishing sales to libraries may result from shrinking acquisitions budgets or effective cooperative programs. Either way, the probable consequences include higher prices, less competition, and—eventually—a reduced availability of scholarly materials.

Cooperative collection development, libraries' most common response to the pressures they face, seeks to limit local costs while increasing aggregate holdings and improving access. Better means for interlibrary loan and vastly improved bibliographic databases have made effective library cooperation ever more plausible. At the same time, the prospect of reduced sales increasingly threatens many publishers and booksellers. Cooperative projects that might once have been considered within the library's exclusive domain now produce widespread misgivings.[17]

Issues of intellectual property, as codified by copyright law, impose an additional layer of complexity. Mounting pressure on publishers, vendors, and libraries, along with the emergence of free-flowing electronic resources, have generated sweeping but also contradictory calls for reform. Continuing confusion, legislation, and litigation are likely. We are far from achieving workable arrangements.

Latin Americanist projects for cooperative collection development have focused on different combinations of current and retrospective materials. The distinction is immediately significant for the potential impacts on nonlibrary players in the structure of scholarly communication. Efforts like the Latin American Microform Project or the Intensive Cuban Collecting Group have for the most part addressed materials in the public domain. They have had very little impact on authors, publishers, or booksellers. The Farmington Plan, the Conspectus, and the AAU/ARL Pilot Project have shared much broader ambitions. The Pilot Project, which has emerged in a period of general uncertainty, particularly espouses a rhetoric of contained costs and limited acquisitions. All the ramifications are not yet clear.

AN ELECTRONIC ANTICIPATION

Discussions of shared resources increasingly focus on the digital technologies which at once foster and reflect new perspectives on scholarly information. Futurist scenarios range wildly in predicting the evolution of formats and the implications for scholarship. The consequences for cooperation vary every bit as much. We thus need to assess the relationship between electronic information and both the structure of scholarly communication and the research process.

Most mainstream scholarship, at least in the humanities and social sciences, has until recently been based on the printed record as supplemented by investigations in laboratories, archives, and the field. The library has been central. The situation is changing, and some students find the motor in technology. They argue that electronic products, including nonprint materials as well as texts, will become more and more prominent simply because the medium affords fluidity, flexibility, and easy access. Digital formats and media, location free and content neutral, will necessarily move to the center of scholarship.

Another explanation focuses on different types of information instead of technology. Some forms of data are best captured and utilized by machine, while other information is better suited to traditional platforms. Digital files of text or data lend themselves to counts and string retrievals: number-crunching applications or simple word matches are well served by electronic data. Marked-up files, with embedded equations or formatting codes, can facilitate analyses of structures and trends. Page images or bit maps visually recapitulate original sources—although a poem, for instance, may still be most effectively conveyed on paper. Scholarly information comes in different forms, some almost requiring digital representation and others most compellingly provided through print or other analog media. While the eventual equilibrium is far from clear, the long-term scenario is likely to combine electronics and print.

Still other analysts focus on research agendas and methodologies, rather than either technology per se or "natural" associations between data types and information formats. New technologies and media allow, but do not mandate, changes in each discipline's most urgent questions and approaches to research. Linguists' agendas, for instance, might be supported by the full-text databases that simplify word counts and correlations. But many literary scholars still ask questions that may be better answered with books. The utility of digital information—its costs and benefits vis-à-vis specific research purposes—will determine each field's decision on how its information should be provided. Fields that are not now dependent on electronic technologies are not necessarily "behind": their agendas may simply be different.

However we understand the changing relationship between scholarship and scholarly information, research resources encompass an expanding variety of formats. Publishers and booksellers have traditionally been responsible for selecting, editing, producing, authenticating, marketing, and distributing scholarly products. Digital formats are in almost all senses malleable, and the corresponding organizational and functional responsibilities are not yet settled. The library's print-based role of acquiring, organizing, providing intellectual and physical access, and preserving scholarly information is by no means assured for the digital age.

The possible rupture of long-standing relationships between actors and functions may fundamentally alter our assumptions about scholarly access to research materials. But the fluidity of the moment also provides opportunities for experimentation and creativity: One need not assume a future in which information as a commodity is only available on the profit-based terms of a digital cartel, just as one need not expect a golden age of free and unfettered exchange. As libraries and other actors delineate the functions essential to scholarly communication in an electronic environment, new roles and responsibilities will gradually take shape. Scholars' needs must help drive the process.

The creation, transmission, preservation, and use of digital information will comprise core concerns of the emerging electronic age. Another dimension of this still incipient transformation centers on materials now available only in print, or precisely those resources most closely associated with libraries.

Print publications are objects that, even when still protected by copyright, can be owned and (within certain limits) shared. They lend themselves to cooperative programs. A tiered, demand-driven, digitally conscious strategy for cooperation and shared access might thus distinguish between several categories of hard-copy materials. High-use resources, particularly if scattered or scarce, could be digitized. The choice between page images, plain text files, and marked-up files would reflect both cost-benefit analyses and the scholarly utility of each potential product.[18] Other materials might be targeted for coordinated projects of hard-copy preservation and access, for local preservation, or in some cases for benign neglect. Different disciplines might find their information needs addressed by efforts centering on different points along this continuum. In fields like Latin American Studies, in which print resources continue to dominate, choices among these sorts of cooperative strategies will for some time remain central.

The emerging challenges of cooperation take us beyond the Latin Americanist context to more general questions of organization, technology, innovation, and information. The Latin Americanist example, nonetheless, suggests the utility of limited efforts in fields marked by a sense of shared commitment and need. This example also suggests the imagination and energy that may enable cooperative efforts to transcend their uneven past and provide a stronger basis for our collective scholarly future.

NOTES

1. This chapter centers almost exclusively on North American institutions and initiatives. Other approaches have been tried in other areas; the analysis is admittedly partial.

2. Dan C. Hazen, "The *Handbook of Latin American Studies* at (Volume) Fifty: Area Studies Bibliography in a Context of Change," *Revista Interamericana de Bibliografía/Inter-American Review of Bibliography* 41 (1991): 195–202.

3. See David B. Bray and Richard E. Greenleaf with the assistance of Bruce D. Tobias, *A Directory of Latin American Studies in the United States* (New Orleans: Published by the Roger Thayer Stone Center for Latin American Studies, Tulane University, for the Consortium of Latin American Studies Programs, 1986). Annual statistics from about twenty major collections are being compiled by SALALM and reported in its October *Newsletter*. See, for instance, "Latin American Collections: An Annual Statistical Report," *SALALM Newsletter* 22 (October 1994): 50–53.

4. Patricia Buck Dominguez and Luke Swindler, "Cooperative Collection Development at the Research Triangle University Libraries: A Model for the Nation," *College & Research Libraries* 54 (1993): 470–96. For a less rosy view, see Deborah Jakubs, "Resource Sharing in the Research Triangle: A Challenge Unmet," *Caribbean Collections: Recession Management Strategies for Libraries. Papers of the Thirty-Second Annual Meeting of the Seminar on the Acquisition of Latin American Library Materials, Held Jointly with the Eighteenth Conference of the Association of Caribbean University,*

Research, and Institutional Libraries, May 10–15, 1987 (Madison, WI: SALALM Secretariat, 1988), pp. 86–89.

5. For the Farmington Plan, see Edwin E. Williams, "Farmington Plan," in *Encyclopedia of Library and Information Science* (1972), vol. 8, pp. 361–68; also Edwin E. Williams, *Farmington Plan Handbook: Revised to 1961 and Abridged* (n.p.: Association of Research Libraries, 1961). The Farmington Plan and the Latin American Cooperative Acquisitions Project are both treated in Robert K. Johnson, ed., "The Acquisition of Latin American Library Materials in ARL Libraries: A Report to the ARL Foreign Acquisition Committee from the Latin American Farmington Plan Subcommittee," *Foreign Acquisition Newsletter*, no. 36 (Fall 1972): 1–15; "The Acquisition of Latin Americana in Non-ARL SALALM Libraries and in Selected Non-SALALM Libraries, 1967/68–1970/71: Part II of a Report from the Latin American Farmington Plan Subcommittee of the Association of Research Libraries and the Seminar on the Acquisition of Latin American Library Materials prepared for the ARL Foreign Acquisition Committee and SALALM," *Foreign Acquisition Newsletter*, no. 37 (Spring 1973): 8–17; also Hendrik Edelman, "The Death of the Farmington Plan," *Library Journal* 98 (April 15, 1973): 1251–53.

6. M. J. Savary, *The Latin American Cooperative Acquisitions Program . . . : An Imaginative Venture* (New York: Hafner Publishing, 1965).

7. Peter T. Johnson and Francisco J. Fonseca, "Cuban Serials and Primary Source Collections: A Bibliography of Microfilm Negatives," *Cuban Studies* 22 (1992): 231–47. A more inclusive listing is scheduled for publication by SALALM under the title, "Cuba from Colony to Revolution: A Bibliography of Microforms."

8. Carl W. Deal, "The Latin American Microform Project: The First Decade," *Microform Review* 15 (Winter 1986): 22–27; Latin American Microform Project *Prospectus* (1993 version).

9. See, for instance, the three papers concerning the Conspectus in the section entitled "The Conspectus Ten Years On: Achievements and Future Prospects," in *Latin American Studies into the Twenty-First Century: New Focus, New Formats, New Challenges. Papers of the Thirty-Sixth Annual Meeting of the Seminar on the Acquisition of Latin American Library Materials, June 1–6, 1991* (Albuquerque: SALALM Secretariat, 1993), pp. 235–64.

10. The Conoco Project, named in recognition of its corporate sponsor, was conducted by RLG in the mid-1980s in loose conjunction with the Conspectus effort. This effort assessed librarians' willingness to forego local acquisitions in exchange for timely remote access to materials in the earth sciences and German literature. Despite encouraging results, follow-through has been limited.

11. Mark Grover et al., "Our Last, Best Chance? The ARL Latin Americanist Research Resources Pilot Project," in *Latin America in the World Economy: Research Trends in Globalization and Regionalism. Papers of the Fortieth Seminar on the Acquisition of Latin American Library Materials, April 29–May 3, 1995*, forthcoming.

12. An analysis of costs and benefits must consider alternatives as well as optimization within a given structural scenario. For instance, what are the trade-offs between such carefully constructed efforts as the AAU/ARL Pilot Project and, at the other extreme, relatively spontaneous plans in which participants would dedicate some percentage of acquisitions funds to deliberately "unlikely" materials within predefined collecting areas?

13. The Association of Research Libraries/Research Libraries Group's 1993 study of

Interlibrary Loan indicated average costs of about $18.60 to borrow an item, with the total cost of an ILL transaction almost $30.00. Marilyn M. Roche, *ARL/RLG Interlibrary Loan Cost Study: A Joint Effort by the Association of Research Libraries and the Research Libraries Group* (Washington, DC: Association of Research Libraries, 1993).

14. Dominguez and Swindler, "Cooperative Collection," pp. 487–89. The Introduction to Patricia Brennan and Jutta Reed-Scott, *Cooperative Strategies in Foreign Acquisitions.* SPEC Kit 195 (Washington, DC: Association of Research Libraries, Office of Management Services, 1993) recapitulates other factors and "organizing principles" that affect cooperation.

15. See John Wheat, "Nettie Lee Benson: Beyond the Orthodox," in *SALALM and the Area Studies Community. Papers of the Thirty-Seventh Annual Meeting of the Seminar on the Acquisition of Latin American Library Materials, May 30–June 4, 1992* (Albuquerque: SALALM Secretariat, 1994), pp. 106–12. For Marietta Daniels Shepard, see "In Memoriam," *SALALM Newsletter* 12 (September, 1984): 1–2.

16. Anthony M. Cummings et al., *University Libraries and Scholarly Communication: A Study Prepared for The Andrew W. Mellon Foundation* (Washington, DC: Association of Research Libraries for The Andrew W. Mellon Foundation, 1992); Jutta Reed-Scott, "Scholarship, Research Libraries, and Foreign Publishing in the 1990s: Final Report" (Draft, October 19, 1995) [definitive version forthcoming]. Region-specific analyses include Lynne Reiner, "Is the Sky Falling? Scholarly Publishing in the 1990s," and the section entitled "Latin American Studies, Information Resources, and Library Collections: Whither and How," both in *Latin American Studies into the Twenty-First Century*, respectively pp. 159–64 and 267–302.

17. Current instabilities have provoked numerous proposals to shift responsibilities within the structure of scholarly communication. Many libraries, though perhaps most ambitiously Stanford University, seek heavier reliance on booksellers for bibliographic control. Electronic scenarios vary even more as actors propose systems which (in many cases) would perpetuate their own role, often at the expense of other current players. For but one of many examples, see Ross Atkinson, "The Acquisitions Librarian as Change Agent in the Transition to the Electronic Library," *Library Resources & Technical Services* 36 (January 1992): 7–20. Calls for universities to exert presumed intellectual property rights over faculty output represent yet another approach to a system that no longer seems to work.

18. Cost analyses remain tentative and scarce. One interesting, though incomplete, model has been developed at Yale University. See the synopsis in "Preserving Digital Information: Draft Report of the Task Force on Archiving Digital Information, Commissioned by The Commission on Preservation and Access and The Research Libraries Group," Version 1.0 (August 23, 1995), pp. 30–35.

PART VIII

The Recent Literature

15

Selected Review of the Literature on Collection Development and Collection Management, 1990–1995

Ruth H. Miller

INTRODUCTION

In the fourteen chapters constituting the substantive part of *Collection Management for the 21st Century*, all of the authors maintain that collection development or collection management is undergoing, and will continue to undergo, significant changes in focus and function in the coming decades. In their discussions a broad range of supporting literature has been cited. Indeed, what emerges from these chapters is the recognition that published output in the constituent topics of collection development has been little short of phenomenal. It is partly to give some structure to this literature that the following literature review, focusing on the period 1990–1995, is offered as a conclusion to the volume.

Most contributors to this volume recognize that the nature of library collections has been altered substantially by the increasing prominence of electronic access to information from a variety of sources, from CD-ROM and magnetic tape to the Internet. These changes in what is owned, even temporarily, and what can be accessed by borrowing, copying, or online viewing require accompanying responses from those who select and manage collections. The discussion of the larger issues has sometimes been lost in catchy slogans, but the balancing act of obtaining the optimum resources for library users with limited funding pivots on resource sharing, from interlibrary loan to coordinated collection development, and the critical nature of serials within the changing aspects of scholarly communication and electronic publishing.

A key image in the shift from the library as warehouse to the library as gateway is the "electronic library," often described as "the scholar at his workstation—a computer linked to national and international networks and providing access to bibliographic information," full-text documents, numeric data, and much more.[1] Saunders, in suggesting a reengineering of acquisitions and collection development, notes that the virtual library is a "metaphor for the networked library, consisting of electronic and digital resources, both local and remote."[2] These terms, "electronic," "digital," or "virtual libraries," are used variously, but all indicate the search for a new vision of libraries.[3]

Whether called a paradigm shift or not, the changes are pervasive. Some would say that if there is any shift, it is only "in the range of materials we can provide," whereas others would agree that libraries are going through "a fundamental and revolutionary rethinking of institutional missions and an examination of the presuppositions involved with information relationships."[4] Despite talk of the paperless society, the end of the book, and the end of libraries, the evidence for any of this is hard to find, at least for the foreseeable future. What seems more likely is an increasingly complex mix of formats and means of locating and retrieving information during a transitional period from print collections to a mix of print and electronic resources.

As has been noted, "new technologies rarely completely supplant the old, and . . . new points of balance eventually are achieved."[5] Indeed, "New technology . . . supplements or layers . . . [old technology] in unforeseen ways, and may add to existing costs rather than displace them."[6] Crawford and Gorman make this same point with comments on the real economic limits inherent in this process; they note further that "libraries are *not wholly or even primarily about information*. They are about the preservation, dissemination, and use of recorded knowledge in whatever form it may come. . . ."[7] This agrees with Buckland's four roles of collections: preservation, dispensing, bibliographic, and symbolic (having to do with status and prestige). He makes a distinction between localized media (paper) and nonlocalized media (electronic).[8] Perhaps the single biggest current challenge to collection management is making appropriate use of these "nonlocalized media," most notably at present, the Internet. The 1990s show a shift from "building" collections in the sense of emphasis on locally held collections, and a related interest in resource sharing of a widening variety as well as defining collections differently (to include electronic resources, links, and pointers to Internet resources).[9]

Collection Management: A New Treatise, edited by Osburn and Atkinson, is one of the more important contributions to the literature during this period, with articles covering the whole range of collection management and defining its changing nature.[10] Those changes continue, and this literature review attempts to follow some of them. Of the many topics treated in the literature, the following will be looked at here: access and ownership, acquisitions and budgeting, the Internet, cooperation, resource sharing, scholarly communication, serials, electronic publishing, organization, policy statements, selection and evaluation, and preservation.

ACCESS AND OWNERSHIP

Discussions of access and ownership have been prominent in the writing of recent years. This topic is necessarily bound up with discussions of scholarly communication, changing technology, the Internet, serials pricing, and resource sharing. Whatever initial value there may have been in positioning the discussion as "access versus ownership," the phrase is now appropriately criticized for "its lack of utility and its contribution to obfuscation."[11] It is time to "get beyond fretting about the oversimplified dichotomy of access versus ownership, and on with the complexities of beginning to actually build collections/connections which include networked resources."[12] Both these articles emphasize the importance of focusing on the content, not the form, of the information and offer suggestions on how to do so. The notable published discussion of access and ownership from 1989 is well summarized as part of a report on a University of Arizona Task Force on access and ownership.[13]

Shaughnessy discusses the difficulty of maintaining collection strengths during a shift in focus; he notes that bigger is not necessarily better, contrasts the "supply-oriented" to the "demand driven" library, and calls for evaluating the costs of access with costs of ownership as well as development of measures for access.[14] Woodsworth notes, more basically, that "Librarians have had neither the time nor the capital to implement a sensible shift in philosophy and operations that might make access an acceptable substitute for ownership to most faculty and students."[15] Truesdell supports Woodsworth in looking at cost, turnaround time, and fill rate for evaluating "access" performance (defining this as interlibrary loan and document delivery) and says the question is "whether access can perform well enough to substitute for ownership.... Standards of performance upon which borrowers and lenders can depend must be developed if access is to be a viable alternative to ownership."[16]

"The shift away from ownership as the primary form of access" marks the changing map of discourse. Atkinson makes the point that "while the shift from paper-based to electronic scholarly information exchange doubtless will be gradual and incremental," it is a transformation that will eventually come about.[17] Similarly, Rutstein et al. say, "What matters is that . . . a metamorphosis is occurring in the way we produce, store, and disseminate information, due largely to the impact of computerized technologies."[18] Owens notes that libraries must decide not only what is a "core collection" but also what is "core access": "that body of information that is not locally held but is nevertheless considered essential to meeting the needs of the local clientele."[19]

One of the more useful studies done in this connection is Perrault's "The Shrinking National Collection." Having looked at the shifting of funds from monographs to serials and the subsequent decline in holdings in research libraries, she finds that an access model "based on a combination of commercial document delivery and library resource sharing will not work if no library owns the material sought. Commercial document delivery may supply current journal contents, but printed monograph materials will continue to be borrowed for the foreseeable future." Foreign language materials will probably require global cooperation.[20] Similarly, Schwartz tries to assess "the declining ability of the nation's research libraries to maintain comprehensive book collections in the face of extraordinary growth and price inflation of scholarly literature since the 1970s." Looking at total book publication output and Association of Research Libraries (ARL) acquisition patterns, he presents a model "for coming to grips with the concepts of 'access, not ownership' and literature loss."[21] Some of the materials that Perrault and Schwartz consider are the least likely to be made available online in the near future, if ever. The implications of such studies are that cooperative efforts are critical if the electronic library is to work effectively; if everyone borrows, someone must own what is borrowed. The relatively limited overall success of cooperative efforts does not offer great encouragement for a quick resolution to the problem.

In addressing "just-in-time rather than just-in-case acquisitions," Lynch says that the approach "abdicates one of the primary roles of the research library: to preserve the scholarly record and the materials for future research." He offers a "two-tiered system of a handful of very large, collection-oriented 'traditional' research libraries that function as service centers to smaller, more agile, acquisition-on-demand-oriented libraries."[22] Limited budgets and the omnipresence of electronic information have forced collection management librarians to respond to an increased need for materials. It is ultimately a matter of needing both access and ownership, both local priorities and broader cooperation, both paper-based and electronic materials; but the way to incorporate and provide all of these is neither clear nor simple, nor is it uniform from library to library.

ACQUISITIONS AND BUDGETING

Acquisitions remains an essential element in collection management, and the reporting functions available on most automated systems are valuable in supporting collection management by permitting assessment of expenditures, vendor performance, holdings, and use. There has been discussion about a shift in focus from "just-in-case" to "just-in-time" purchasing, though the latter probably represents the majority of a library's purchases only rarely. Acquisitions may be more on-demand than previously, though, especially if interlibrary loan and document delivery are considered as part of that process. The shifting of funds from the materials budget for document delivery, partly as a response to serials cancellations, is indicative of this change.

Among a number of useful books published is Schmidt's *Understanding the Business of Library Acquisitions*, which brings together chapters on the publishing industry, vendors, out-of-print and secondhand markets, nonprint publications, and accounting methods. Practical tips are offered by *Managing the Purchasing Process: A How-to-Do-It Manual,* and *Collection Development and Finance: A Guide to Strategic Library-Materials Budgeting,* which provides practical help for planning and monitoring the budgeting process. Two issues of the *Journal of Library Administration* concentrating on acquisitions are "Collection Assessment and Acquisitions Budgets," which includes papers on evaluation, automation, serials cancellation projects, and vendors, and "Declining Acquisitions Budgets: Allocation, Collection Development and Impact Communication," a collection of conference papers with discussions of serials vendors, access and ownership, indexing costs, and allocating budgets.[23]

Allocation Formulas

Allocation formulas remain of interest, though they now have to cover not only disciplines but formats and services. In reviewing the literature on allocation formulas for about 60 years, Budd finds that differences among formulas are "frequently subtle and constitute variations on a theme." They attempt to provide objectivity by dealing with such measures as faculty size, enrollment, cost, and number of publications, but quality of the collection and user needs are less successfully dealt with.[24] Houbeck describes a materials budget divided into subject and language funds with subdivisions for continuing and noncontinuing materials, with ceilings for serials prices (to keep continuations at or below 55% of the total allocation).[25] Lowry offers a matrix formula for allocating funds for monographs and serials based on disciplinary needs and publishing patterns.[26] Carrigan proposes allocating the book budget in accordance with proportional use, including interlibrary loan requests with circulation figures for maximum benefit.[27] Cubberley presents a "formula-based plan for redistributing materials funds that uses data on program level and the price of materials available in each discipline."[28] Jones and Keller discuss acquisitions in small college libraries, where selection is a collaborative effort between faculty and librarians. Factors in allocation are the number of faculty, average cost of materials, and number of students.[29] Webster provides an overview of the major allocation methods over the last fifty years, which she labels historical, zero-based, formulas, ranking, and percentages. She notes differentiation by types of payments (one-time, standing orders) and recommends use studies and annual reviews as well as moving from allocation by academic department toward larger subject groupings (humanities, social sciences, sciences). Finally she notes, "Access services, including document delivery should also be included as standard budget categories."[30]

Approval Plans

An important acquisitions method is the approval plan. Carpenter relates approval plans to collection development policies, the latter informing the former, and says that since approval plans need updating, they can be useful collection development tools.[31] Calhoun recommends approval plans for academic mainstream collection development in medium-sized to large research libraries as a means of freeing selectors to identify more difficult materials.[32] Based on two surveys of ARL libraries' use of approval plans, Loup and Snoke question "to what extent is resource sharing among these research libraries at risk from use of approval plans." After looking at alternative acquisitions methods (standing orders, gifts and exchange, retrospective, supplementary), they say that participating in approval plans does not put resource sharing at risk: "It is the failure to keep pace with more complex and time-consuming selection activities, leading to strong unique research collections that might do so."[33] This activity needs to be maintained, despite staffing problems. Franklin tests approval plans for engineering and physical science books and finds them well represented in a timely manner but recommends better coordination for interdisciplinary subject areas.[34] Nardini says that approval plans are "inherently political in nature, . . . [because they] challenge library boundaries" within the library, between librarians and faculty, and between libraries and vendors. They are hard to measure, but evaluation is necessary.[35]

Automation

The automation of acquisitions may now be taken for granted, but there are still refinements and improvements to be made. Sasse and Smith see automation of acquisitions as changing the roles and processes of collection development, the relationships between libraries and vendors, and library organization. They discuss the bibliographer's workstation as an aid to collection development, especially cooperation: "[a]s library automation matures, collection developers will have use of better information on which to base decisions for collection building and management."[36] Sasse and Smith see collection development as moving toward expert systems and increased use of paraprofessional staff. Hawks focuses on "automation support from the acquisition department *other* than from automated acquisitions systems," such as The Bibliographer's Workstation and Selection Advisor, and vendor services such as *BIP Plus*, B&T Link, EBSCONET, and OCLC Collection Analysis CD-ROM.[37] Meador and Cline describe The Bibliographer's Workstation, a hypertext tool which they developed, as a mechanism for identifying, evaluating, selecting, and acquiring materials.[38] In a later article, Hawks looks again at expert systems and notes that "the work in acquisitions and serials control has focused on monographic vendor selection and approval plan receipts." She considers Selection Advisor, Monograph Selection Advisor, Journal Expert Selector, and The Bibliographer's Workstation, none of which are in widespread use.[39] Ray considers the limitations for acquisitions in being tied to an integrated library system; he stresses the need for a better interface between the ILS and vendor-automated systems and the need to reassess what acquisitions is about.[40]

Acquisition of Electronic Resources

Nissley notes that the first CD-ROM ''appeared in the library marketplace in 1985.'' Based on a survey of how CD-ROMs are being acquired in twenty-five libraries, she notes departures from regular acquisitions practices because of funding, equipment considerations, and the need for demonstration of the software.[41] Davis reports on acquisitions challenges in acquiring CD-ROMs for a LAN—problems of subscription and pricing options, licensing, variations from printed format, backfiles, and so on, and notes that acquisitions, collection development, and automation skills are needed.[42] Marshall reports on electronic ordering via the Internet to Blackwell North America, noting reduced OCLC search costs, reduced paperwork and postage, and use of data entry clerks to enter data into the online system; and Kara discusses new responsibilities for processing electronic items, such as acquiring datasets and electronic journals.[43] Questions remain of evaluating resources, pricing, measuring delivery, comparing vendors, considering duplication of material in different formats, and licensing and copyright restrictions; but as Van Goethem says, ''we will continue to carry out an acquisitions function by buying information in bits and bytes, on paper or electronically.''[44]

THE INTERNET

The Internet Index (No. 12, January 2, 1996) reports that there are 37 million people over the age of sixteen in the United States and Canada with access to the Internet.[45] This statistic lends support to the statement that ''By the end of the decade, the Internet . . . will be as pervasive in our lives as radio has been for seven decades and television for four.''[46] The rapid growth of gopher sites since 1991 has now been overshadowed by the increase in World Wide Web pages.

In one of the most significant articles on the Internet and collection development, Demas et al. report on an impressive one-year project ''to adapt the principles and practices of collection development to the world of Internet resources.'' They note that use of the Internet is still limited for scholarly publications because of continuing issues of copyright, the economics of electronic publishing, and ''the rudimentary nature of network organization and retrieval tools.'' Indicative of the effort required, they examined 1,000 Internet sites from which 41 were selected. Included are a good summary of what has been done on selection of Internet resources (''Systematic selection of Internet-accessible resources has not been treated in the literature.'') along with policy statements, project goals, and methods. ''[W]hat many Internet users are demanding is the kind of selection and organization that libraries have traditionally brought to the world of published information resources.'' They address the broad collection issues related to the electronic library, such as ''text mutability, potential for cooperative collection development with virtual collections, access versus ownership, and the library's role in the evolving system of scholarly communication."[47]

Starr evaluates physics literature on the Internet and recommends tracking sources and evaluating them as is done for any reference source, and Santa Vicca offers specific criteria for evaluation.[48] Swann and Rosenquist-Buhler see collection development in an electronic environment as requiring selection similar to traditional collection development, with the addition of such criteria as whether an Internet site is authoritative, current, and provides unique information on a topic.[49] Johnson indicates some of the problems of selecting online. "One problem is that no convention like the title page exists with on-line resources." Electronic journals usually follow the conventions of printed journals and therefore are easy to cite; books in full text may also be reasonably consistent, but the Internet has many documents of value without clear identifiers (name, title, date). "Even the most dedicated bibliographer has trouble monitoring on-line resources and selecting among the possibilities. Consistently applied conventions for preparing on-line documents will do much to create order in the chaos of the Internet."[50]

Monty and Warren-Wenk report on use of the Internet by faculty in the social sciences and humanities. The Internet is used for informal SDI, communication at all stages, discussion groups, electronic journals, and even for some aspects of research design and data gathering. Concerns remain about incorporating peer review, loss of authorial control, and accuracy and integrity of the record.[51] Gurn says new measurements are "needed for services provided on the Internet. Four characteristics . . . [are] accessibility, authority, interactivity, and conviviality."[52] Britten says "The idea of a virtual network library is attractive, but the library profession needs to formalize the process of assigning responsibility for building these virtual subject collections."[53] Zhou notes that electronic resources on the Internet "require selectors to extend their traditional expertise to include knowledge of various electronic resources and acquisitions skills using computer-facilitated tools and procedures. He proposes three phases of evolving change: traditional formats acquired traditionally; traditional formats with computer-facilitated acquisitions; and electronic formats acquired with computer-facilitated acquisitions.[54] Tedd, in an introduction to resource sharing via the Internet in European academic libraries, mentions accessing other libraries' catalogs, document delivery, shared information products, and development of campus-wide information systems. She also mentions electronic document delivery, electronic journals, on-demand publishing, and other resources likely to become available within the next few years.[55]

COOPERATION

While cooperation becomes more important than ever if "access" is to work, Branin is one of many sounding the note that cooperative collection development does not have an especially good track record, but he predicts that more "centralization and more consolidation of print collections in the next ten years" can be expected.[56] Hacken comments on the aftermath of the RLG 1985 Conoco study, "Although small efforts have been made in light of the Conoco Study findings, acquisitions in the vast majority of institutions . . . proceed in the traditional manner. . . . Experience since the Conoco Study has shown that the consortium serves its members best when each member acquires materials primarily according to local needs."[57]

One response to factors driving libraries to more cooperation (economic tightening, the need for quality improvement, an expanding information universe, and the growth of information technology) is OhioLINK, a network of state-supported academic institutions, providing "both a local and central online catalog." It further provides online databases and "digital library services and cooperative lending services." Reports indicate that it is successful and "an overwhelmingly positive experience."[58] Dominquez and Swindler report on six decades of experience in cooperative collection development in North Carolina. They identify seven "major factors that promote successful cooperative collection development: propitious circumstances, visionary and committed individuals, supportive organizational structures, appropriate staff participation, bibliographic and physical accessibility to collections, outside funding, and a history of successful cooperation."[59] Medina reviews a cooperative collection development program established in Alabama in 1984 to support graduate education.[60] Hightower and Soete describe a project to share translation journals in the physical sciences among California academic libraries. They offer twelve steps to success in collaborative collections projects, and present a model "in which consortia continually try new strategies, view each trial as a learning experience, and adjust as they learn."[61]

Wood and Strauch's book on the Conspectus provides a history and overview, discussion of issues involved in its use, its utility, and criticisms; the book also includes an annotated bibliography.[62] Among the many articles about the Conspectus, Ferguson suggests using it for training, and Biblarz discusses methods of using Conspectus data for developing a policy that is a blueprint for planning, priorities, and budgeting.[63] On the negative side, Blake and Tjoumas express reservations regarding its utility ("a sophisticated but paradoxical instrument"), noting what others have noted about difficulties of translating it to smaller collections, the need for clearer definitions for describing acquisitions activities, and the need to determine whether it can perform the functions claimed for it.[64]

Among the mechanisms supporting cooperation, Paskoff and Perrault recommend automated shelflist sampling for comparative collection analysis. "The resulting collection profile provides a multidimensional quantified description of the collection using a different analytical approach than either a shelflist measurement or the RLG Conspectus." This method would "permit collection profiles . . . to be created on a large scale, with more analysis than existing methodologies have permitted."[65]

Harrell describes how, in 1989, OCLC and the AMIGOS Bibliographic Council's new product called "Collection Analysis CD-ROM" was developed to assist libraries in measuring their collections against those of peer institutions. She recommends the product for "seeking to analyze a library's holdings in specific subject fields, as well as identifying retrospective titles for possible addition. . . ."[66] Radke notes that the OCLC/AMIGOS Collection Analysis Compact Disc (CACD) can generate statistical and bibliographic reports to find holdings gaps, overlap, and uniqueness in a collection for various collection development uses.[67] According to Vellucci, the system allows for both "quantitative assessment that produces a variety of statistical reports, such as Counts, Proportions, Overlap, Holdings Distribution, Gap, and Uniqueness," and "qualitative assessment that produces reports in the form of bibliographic record citations rather than numeric data."[68] She suggests such uses for CACD as course analysis, desiderata lists, or management information systems.

The point has been made that resource sharing and cooperative collection development have usually been on separate administrative tracks, and ways to improve connections between these forms of cooperation are needed.[69]

RESOURCE SHARING, INTERLIBRARY LOAN, AND DOCUMENT DELIVERY

Resource sharing has become an essential component in collection management, though not necessarily close organizationally. The organization of interlibrary loan (ILL) and document delivery is quite varied. LaGuardia and Dowell's survey of 100 ARL libraries finds ILL units variously organized with circulation, reference, or elsewhere; document delivery is offered by fewer than half the responding institutions.[70] McKee, in calling for an access rather than acquisitions budget, says document delivery should be treated as an extension of reference rather than part of interlibrary loan.[71] Ray makes a useful distinction about the function of acquisitions in this context. "Acquisitions departments have not been formed to procure information but rather to procure materials, usually very specific materials. . . ." If there is any link between acquisitions and document delivery, "it is the management and delivery of materials. . . . [A]cquisitions exists to serve the library" in keeping down costs and confusion, whereas document delivery "is driven by specific patron needs in which library interests, outside the specific service, are irrelevant."[72]

Overviews of this area are provided by Higginbotham and Bowdoin's *Access vs. Assets*, which offers a practical and thorough discussion of interlibrary loan issues and document delivery methods, giving evaluation criteria and recommending a balance of access and assets, and by Gilmer's *Interlibrary Loan: Theory and Management*, which provides a historical overview, and discusses copyright, organization, and policies. A 1994 *Journal of Library Administration* issue on "The Future of Resource Sharing" offers articles on various aspects of the subject; and "DocuShock," a symposium on document delivery, includes coverage on Faxon Finder, UnCover, LOANSOME DOC, as well as use of the

Internet for electronic document delivery, automated ILL, and legal concerns. And the ARL/RLG Interlibrary Loan Cost Study provides critical information in reporting that it cost almost $30 (in 1993) for two academic libraries to borrow ($18.62) and loan ($10.93) a completed ILL transaction.[73]

Resource Sharing

Shaughnessy identifies copyright, reciprocity, and costs as involved in resource sharing and suggests strategies for improvement. He notes that "just-in-time" service is not yet being provided, and recommends creating virtual electronic libraries by using the Z39.50 protocol to link OPACs to "assure the availability of important information at one or more locations in the U.S."[74] Reed-Scott mentions some current initiatives in resource sharing, such as the ARL/AAU Research Libraries Project, one aspect of which focuses on collecting foreign imprint publications; and the Committee on Institutional Cooperation (CIC) Libraries of the Midwest is planning for a "CIC Virtual Electronic Library."[75] Jackson defines resource sharing broadly, to include ILL, document delivery, on-site access, and local ownership. She reports on ARL efforts to develop a new service model for ILL in which "library users will only use ILL departments when they are unable to locate materials themselves." Services such as RLG's Ariel should improve delivery and "with access to databases and online ordering capabilities, electronic delivery technologies offer the promise of desktop delivery to support unmediated service."[76]

Interlibrary Loan

The number of monographs added to research collections has decreased, many serial subscriptions and standing orders have been cancelled, and approval plans cut back; therefore, there is greater reliance on interlibrary loan to supply these items. Added to this is the greater ability of patrons to find citations via electronic indexes. It is easy to see why interlibrary loan units are overwhelmed. Jackson documents "the 99 percent increase in ILL borrowing recorded from 1986 to 1994" and suggests that, to keep ILL from collapsing under the weight, increased reliance on commercial document delivery suppliers, increased user-initiated ILL requests, and limiting ILL services are options for coping with this growth.[77]

Roberts reports on a survey of how physics, chemistry, and biochemistry faculty members use ILL, and their level of satisfaction; timeliness remains a problem. "It is time to reshape library priorities to give interlibrary loan/document delivery a high priority. While there will be costs for a service such as this, enormous savings are possible with the cancellation of little-used journals."[78] Kurosman and Durniak sent requests to OCLC's ILL subsystem as well as to four commercial firms and concluded that traditional ILL is the quickest and most cost-effective method.[79] Rottmann notes an earlier study stating that unless a journal is "used more than 6 times per year, it was less expensive to photocopy an article than to buy a subscription." He notes that it seldom is feasible to conduct detailed analysis of ILL data for collection development purposes, but reporting repeated requests, particularly for back issues of serials, could easily be shared.[80] Lahmon and Mellendorf suggest ways in which interlibrary loan can communicate better with collection development on what library users request.[81] Though ILL is also costly, there are indications that in some cases it is less expensive than purchase.

Bonk contrasts the United Kingdom's centralized and the United States' decentralized systems of interlibrary loan and document delivery and says that not enough information is known about the costs of ILL. U.K. librarians have been more vocal than those in the United States about a worldwide view of these matters.[82] Bradbury and Cornish point out problems of cost, inadequate information on what is available, political barriers, legal constraints, technical barriers, professional attitudes, and user ignorance; Cornish also points out a trend for charging for national but not for international requests.[83] Carrigan gives a brief history of the British Library Document Supply Centre.[84]

ARL's North American Interlibrary Loan and Document Delivery (NAILDD) Project aims at giving the user "transparent access to the most relevant information through appropriate local and remote library catalogs, citation databases, and electronic resources" and the ability to "transfer bibliographic citations or details about non-bibliographic items into electronic requests or orders." These would be checked through the library online system for local availability, the request directed to a supplier electronically, and the materials, in whatever format, received at the desk or workstation. Lynch says "NAILDD is about supplying *print* more efficiently," and "improvements in the ability of users to initiate such intersystem document delivery requests should be a high priority" driven by service and economic needs but also taking advantage of the new technologies of Z39.50 and the Internet.[85]

Document Delivery

Bluh recommends "creating customized, in-house document delivery services that anticipate users' needs according to detailed profiles of specific titles, subject interests, and current research pursuits." The goal is "carefully managed acquisitions, enhanced by improved access to the existing collection, combined with adroit anticipation of users' needs, and augmented by a number of carefully selected document delivery products."[86] Everett considers the use of full-text online databases as a supplement to ILL for document delivery. Benefits include cost, speed, and copyright compliance; disadvantages include varying definitions of full-text and a limited number of journals available in this form.[87] Finnigan reviews technologies for requesting (e-mail and fax) and receiving (fax, online, microform, and CD-ROM) document delivery.[88] Friend notes that "the problems [with document delivery] are not principally technological problems but organizational or political in the widest sense."[89]

Gasaway reviews the various forms of document delivery in light of U.S. copyright laws.[90] Getz makes a useful distinction about internal and external services: "If document-delivery service is faster and cheaper from an external source than it is from the campus collection, and if delivery service is available from external sources but not from the campus library, then the nature of the university library could change radically." He says that just as journals have "replaced books as the primary vehicle for communication in many disciplines" so may electronic documents replace print journals.[91] New models of document delivery are discussed by Harricombe and Lusher, such as the use of funds from acquisitions and collection development (if fees are not charged) and the patron's making requests directly to the vendor rather than the library serving as intermediary.[92] Martin and Kendrick similarly present a scenario of a scholar finding and retrieving documents quickly without library staff intervention.[93] Hewison et al. say policies and service levels should be set for document delivery and suppliers evaluated. The ideal document delivery service "would feature a transparent, seamless electronic service incorporating searching and browsing, identification and marking of desired items, and transmission and fulfillment of requests." The relationship between collection development and document delivery is more important than is often recognized; as one example of the relationship, the overall use of a journal title should be tracked and correlated with subscription prices.[94]

In a significant article, Juergens and Prather note the expansion of commercial suppliers into document delivery, such as CARL's UnCover, offering direct user purchase and "thus bypassing librarians' long-articulated ponderings about unmediated ILL by selling directly to the end user." With improved systems and additional players in resource sharing, they see the library as either a clearinghouse or a marketplace, with the latter of limited value to users and hard to manage, since profits would go to vendors and not to libraries. In the clearinghouse model libraries would add value and become "resource sharing brokers"; "the distinction between 'reference' and 'interlibrary loan,' and between 'interlibrary loan' and 'acquisitions' will be erased."[95] Several overviews of services (such as ADONIS, British Library, CISTI, Dialog) are useful, though with the rapidity of change, frequent updates are needed.[96] Potter notes that when considering copyright and resource sharing, the focus is on scholarly journals. The problems are not technical but economic, legal, and social. "The biggest problem facing academic libraries today is the high and escalating cost of scholarly journals, especially in the sciences."[97]

Bluh sees the range of document delivery services as including full-text online and full-text CD-ROM databases as well as table of contents services. "The decade of the 1990s may be dubbed the 'Decade of Document Delivery' to acknowledge the widespread use of the term and the diversity of definitions it has attracted." But issues of copyright and intellectual property remain.[98] Trau-

ner compares collection-centered and client-based delivery services and describes the benefits of the latter. If users contact the home library, librarians can
direct them to sources. "Information is provided without concern for whether
materials are located in-house, in another campus library, in another research
collection, or in an online database."[99]

Cooperative Efforts

Hawks describes OhioLINK arrangements for rapid interlibrary loan and document delivery and suggests additional needs. Some of her comments are updated in other reports on OhioLINK: "the network will cooperatively develop
collections, offer a growing number of electronic resources to all member libraries, and improve the interlibrary loan of printed material across all institutions to the point that access is virtually equivalent to ownership."[100] Stockton
and Whittaker discuss cooperative ventures such as TULIP and Red Sage and
a pilot project with Wiley and UnCover. The future belongs to document delivery that is "better, faster, cheaper. Yet it needs to have a human touch as
well."[101] Medina reports on a consortium's resource sharing, eliminating fees,
use of fax or a commercial courier, and cutting delivery time.[102]

SCHOLARLY COMMUNICATION

Rogers and Hurt's suggestions for a new system "five years from now"
(1994) have not come to pass, though it seems truer than ever that at least in
some disciplines "Scholarly journals are obsolete as the primary vehicle for
scholarly communication."[103] In a 1989 symposium, Shaughnessy set out the
problems and actions for dealing with the strains on the scholarly communication system. Some of those suggestions have moved forward, though they are
far from resolved: linking of bibliographic systems, better means of interlibrary
loan and document delivery, and making use of new technologies.[104]

The 1992 Mellon study, "University Libraries and Scholarly Communication," concludes that it is unlikely that an alternative model will overtake the
current one in the near future; instead, incremental changes will be made to the
current model. However, "it is equally inconceivable that there will *not* eventually be a more-or-less complete transformation of scholarly communication.
The new technologies are too powerful and their advantages too clear for current
practices to continue indefinitely."[105] Okerson discusses the effects of copyright
on scholarly publishing and says that copyright law "can act as a barrier to the
wide sharing of ideas." She sees the increasing number of electronic journals
as a hopeful sign.[106]

Brown notes that changes to the scholarly communication system come about
"both as the result of societal changes and new areas of inquiry and technological advances." The necessity for providing full access to so much data with
limited finances requires "collaborative efforts between publishers, electronic

information intermediaries, libraries and scholars. . . ."[107] Desirable as that is, it is unlikely to happen, as Schwartz explains: "scholarly communication is not an interdependent system in any meaningful sense, even theoretically. Rather, it is a loosely coupled system, comprised of largely autonomous components with little communication, coordination, or even direct cause and effect relationships." He sees the development of the Internet as reinforcing this separation. The benefits are flexibility, innovation, and local autonomy; but restructuring scholarly communication is unlikely in this context.[108] Franklin emphasizes the role research libraries play in collecting and providing access to the primary records humanists need. Neither photocopies nor digital records satisfy bibliographers, textual editors, literary scholars.[109]

Lynch offers a distinction between "modernization" and "transformation" in discussing the "impact of technology on scholarly communication." The former uses new technology to continue doing the same things but in a more efficient way; the latter "addresses the use of new technology to change processes in a fundamental way."[110] Atkinson says, "The growing capacity of the network, combined with the eventual ability to link any textual units with any others, may well have profound effects on scholarly communication and higher education." Examples of responsibilities that academic information services may assume are "(a) assistance with institutionally based publication, (b) work with authors on the indexing of their publications, and (c) the design of new, network-based document structures."[111]

SERIALS

"While the journal is essentially obsolete for rapid communication at the research frontiers, it has successfully retained its archival function along with the closely related functions of priority claiming and quality control." Bennion sees the 20,000-plus primary research journals as an "expensive and endangered species."[112] And it is the need to cancel serial subscriptions that is the crux of academic libraries' financial, and political, stress. The latter is shown when Hayes reports on Louisiana State University library's cancellation of 1,569 scholarly journals costing $446,000, and its guarantee to provide article copies within two days. Over the next year it provided 2,092 articles for $25,000; later, faculty were able to request their own copies directly from UnCover via fax within 24 hours. Hamaker provides the background to this story in his discussion of having tried a zero-based budget approach after years of serials cancellations. He found that "faculty could usefully differentiate between titles for which they needed physical, onsite in-house subscriptions and titles where access via expedient document delivery and table of contents services would be appropriate."[113] Widdicombe reports on eliminating all journal subscriptions at Stevens Institute of Technology, though what seems to be working in a special library within close proximity of many research libraries probably might not work so well in other places.[114] Metz describes a serials cancellation project, relying on a use study, indexing coverage, citation study, price, and faculty evaluation. He elsewhere lists thirteen steps in serials cancellation, including: measure use, have one person in charge, automate the process as much as possible, supply a list of titles for cancellation to faculty, be flexible, publicize what is done.[115]

Hughes ranks journals in molecular and cellular biology to create a core list for protection from cancellation; it is not a use study but uses faculty citations and faculty publication with ISI's *Journal Citation Report*.[116] Chrzastowski and Schmidt survey five midwest ARL libraries on serial cancellations from 1987 to 1990 and find that 40 percent of cancellations were in the Q, R, S, T classes and 82 percent cost less than $200, most published in English in the United States. They note the loss of diversity as unique titles are dropped. Chrzastowski also studies serials use in a chemistry library as part of a pilot project for providing document delivery through Chemical Abstracts Document Delivery service. It proves to be cost-effective and satisfactory to users. "The conclusions do not support completely replacing serial ownership with serial access. Instead, they do support a method for making a good collection even better through collection analysis and for employing a strong service model to extend subject-specific collection."[117]

Coons and McDonald offer criteria for substituting electronic journals for paper ones in a discussion of commercial document delivery. This method is used to aid selection, substitute for new or some current subscriptions, and supplement ILL. Use, costs, historical value, language, geography, publisher type, and accessibility are considered.[118] Calhoun uses citation analysis in working with a relational database file of 13,000 serial titles from ISI's *Current Contents* and *Journal Citation Reports*, Bowker's *Magazines for Libraries*, and the Wilson databases; he suggests ways to use these data to manage academic journal collections.[119] Haas and Kisling use Dialog's online rank command in Scisearch and Agricola databases to determine which serials are used by the science and agriculture researchers at the University of Florida.[120] Stein uses the Internet to identify core periodical titles in a specialized subject collection. She compares periodicals holdings in eight university libraries, produces a core list, identifies ILL sources, and pinpoints collection strengths and weaknesses.[121]

Gossen and Irving say, "if a periodical is used fewer than five times per year in a given library, it is generally more cost-effective to rely on access, even if the subscription cost is modest." If it is used ten times, the decision depends on the discipline. This is based on a one-year use study of bound and unbound periodicals. Their conclusion is that "considerable savings can be generated by offering access to low-use journal titles rather than owning them."[122] Ferguson and Kehoe observe that "it is better to access than to own if the cost of borrowing . . . is less than the cost of subscribing," but cost "is not the only factor to be considered when building library collections."[123]

The Advisory Panel for Scientific Publications report, "The Cost Effectiveness of Science Journals," offers criticism to be taken seriously: "Most library managers are isolated from the publishers and scientists that their institutions deal with daily." They find offensive the evaluation of science journals on a cost-per-citation basis, saying that "Value can be assigned only by a user, no matter what the citation count, word count or cost might be." And they find anachronistic the "absence of reliable indicators to show use of research information in science libraries. . . ."[124]

ELECTRONIC PUBLISHING

In a *Library Trends* issue on networked scholarly publishing, Lancaster discusses the evolution of electronic publishing from the early 1960s.[125] Butler thinks electronic publishing will not mature in the 1990s, sees copyright as *the* issue, and believes that the "strongest influences on the scholarly communication process are . . . factors that are beyond the control of the internal processes," such as academic pressure to publish, accreditation demands for large collections, university budget cuts, and so on.[126] For basic coverage, the two volumes *Electronic Journals in ARL Libraries: Policies and Procedures* and *Electronic Journals in ARL Libraries: Issues and Trends* provide useful information, and the ARL *Directory of Electronic Journals, Newsletters, and Academic Discussion Lists* has become as basic a tool as the *Gale Directory of Databases.*[127]

Clark looks at cost differences and finds that because there are fewer steps in electronic book publishing, "publishing books electronically is cheaper." [128] Valauskas offers a useful corrective on how people actually use electronic text. "We have to accept that readers will not bother to read a great deal of text on a monitor." And we "should not fall into the seductive trap of thinking that all books will become electronic and that paper is dead." [129] Grochmal offers tips for selecting full-text/full-image products and says librarians should influence the way electronic products are being developed (in accuracy of content, data storage, omissions, and so on).[130] LaGuardia and Bentley note a different problem: "too much information is being put into electronic format that just doesn't belong there. . . . [L]ess than 50 percent of the titles coming out have been developed because that's the best way to deliver the information." They list such collection development considerations as format and cost, time, learning curve, multiple formats, content, and user preferences.[131]

Hickey says, "the more highly used a source is and the more that currency is important, the more quickly electronic versions become available." Hence, indexing and abstracting services developed first, then reference works, then journals and books. He lists advantages of online journals (customization, integration with other work, full-text searching, speed of access, speed and cost of publication, availability, hypertext links, portability, less paper) and disadvantages (frustrating interfaces, reliance on equipment, less permanent, higher and more obvious costs, lower quality, requirement to log-on, incompatible software, less material available, network speeds remain too low). He predicts that the switch from primarily paper to primarily electronic access to journals will occur within the next decade and finds the main barriers now to be mostly economic, though there are also "social barriers in acceptance, the time it takes publishers to become familiar with the technologies and start to use them, and the time it takes to develop usable software and make it widely available."[132]

As Schaffner says, "Peer-reviewed science journals, presented to readers in an electronic form are still rare." Changes within science continue to drive this development of a new form of communication.[133] Hunter notes that electronic journals are still (in 1994) "less than one-fifth of 1 percent of the serious scholarly literature in English." She discusses such projects as CORE, Red Sage, and The University Licensing Program (TULIP). A special section more fully describes TULIP, with case studies from eight universities working with Elsevier Science Publishing to provide access to materials science journals.[134] Metz says that if electronic journals are to succeed, all involved must see these as distinctly separate from unedited listservers; indexing services should cover them; and libraries must welcome them. Then might come the recognition that they can represent quality as well as printed material can.[135]

Barden offers an overview of electronic publishing and discusses the Digital Libraries Initiative, which is more fully discussed in the April 1995 issue of the *Communications of the ACM*. There Samuelson says, "the expectation is that there will be many digital libraries, most of which will have specialized collections and will be internetworked together in a way loosely resembling today's Internet."[136] The goals of digital libraries, according to Huser et al., are to provide users with opportunities to access and use information in flexible, user-oriented ways. To meet these goals "one has to adopt a new perspective . . . [by] no longer viewing documents as static entities published . . . in a definite form, but as dynamic and networked collections of information composed on demand and presented with possibilities for interaction."[137] In the same issue, Wilensky takes a more extreme view, and says that if digital libraries are to succeed, the traditional idea of the library must be abandoned: "Libraries in the traditional sense are nowhere to be found in this model (i.e., the notion of a limited intermediary containing some small fraction of preselected material available only to local patrons is replaced by a system providing to users everywhere direct access to the full contents of all available material)."[138]

ORGANIZATION FOR COLLECTION DEVELOPMENT

Pitschmann gives the historical background of organizational models for collection development as well as current practice and projections for the future: "Perhaps the four strongest catalysts" for the transition "from selection-driven collection development activities to a more inclusive management approach to collection issues" have been development of the RLG Conspectus, fiscal constraints, deterioration of existing print formats, development of electronic formats. He suggests that "perhaps we should henceforth talk not of collection management but rather of resource management lest our own terminology influence the scope of our development and management activities.'' He finds no agreement on an ideal organizational method.[139]

Schad examines the difficulties of doing collection development under dual-responsibility assignments and recommends ways to improve part-time selectors' effectiveness: "1. Create a more effective organization. 2. Select and develop librarians suited to such assignments. 3. Improve the management of collection development."[140] Johnson discusses using matrix management as an organizational structure. Despite potential for conflict, matrix structures "encourage flexibility, professional independence, and the sharing of information and expertise."[141]

This topic has taken on new importance as the work and the focus change; a flatter, less hierarchical library organizational structure is currently being touted. A 1992 issue of *Library Acquisitions: Practice & Theory* features articles on reorganization of acquisitions departments; another issue in 1995 focuses on library reorganization for the 21st century.[142] Creth sees a functional design as inadequate for the future and prefers a team approach using subject orientation, with teams for art and humanities, social sciences, and sciences. Collection development should be a "bridge or link to establish an integrative structure in the research library" with "strong orientation for both information resources and the end user."[143] Gossen and Irving note that "the relationship between the periodicals collection, interlibrary loan, and collection development should be more fluid and dynamic than it has been in the past."[144]

POLICY STATEMENTS

In one of the more thought-provoking articles on this topic, Hazen says that collection development policies

have outlived their purpose. Research libraries will better serve both themselves and their users by devising flexible guides to all the information associated with particular fields of study. Local collections will comprise a part of these "information maps," but only within the context of a richer and less bounded universe of scholarly resources.[145]

Hazen may be indicating the new direction, but until everyone else catches up, such items as the third edition of *Collection Development Policies and Procedures* continue to be useful, as is "The Relevance of Collection Development Policies," which reviews "selected classic writings on collection development policy. . . ."[146]

Ferguson lists four problems to be considered: "Which electronic access medium will best meet the needs of our library user community? . . . Which criteria should be employed when selecting a specific title within an access medium? . . . Who pays for new electronic titles? . . . Can the Conspectus be used to describe electronic text and data collections?" He sees the writing of collection development policy statements as still useful because the process forces the selector to think through the issues.[147] LaGuardia says there is a need to add new criteria (and offers 11 questions) to cover selection of electronic materials (vendor support; administration of costs, maintenance, security; searching and system capabilities).[148] Mardikian and Kesselman recommend having "access development statements for the resources accessible over the network."[149]

SELECTION AND EVALUATION

In some ways selection and evaluation may be more important than ever because of the need to provide essential materials for local needs, even while working out ways to access additional materials. Nisonger's *Collection Evaluation in Academic Libraries* is a significant bibliographical contribution to collection evaluation, describing over 600 publications since 1980 in a topical arrangement.[150]

In a thought-provoking article, Buckland says selection is made for demand versus value; considerations of demand and value diverge because they require different courses of action. He talks about "privileging networked resources." "Access and ownership always separate in principle but hitherto rarely separate in library practice, are expected to diverge in the electronic network environment. . . . This new need for the evaluative skills of collection developers arises from the emergence of the new environment of networked resources, not from changes in the roles of local collections."[151]

Atkinson says "collection development perceives the universe of publication as bifurcated into the local collection and what we might call the *anti-collection*, i.e., the set of all publications not held in the local collection. Selection is, therefore, to a great extent, a continuous series of decisions about which items in the anti-collection should be moved into the collection."[152] Those may have to be looked at differently in the future, as Demas's focus on "mainstreaming" electronic materials indicates. Collection development principles don't change from print to electronic materials, but the "methods of decision making and specific selection guidelines must be adjusted." He calls for a collection development model "that gets us beyond the segregation of resources by publishing format" and offers Cornell's "information genres" and "tiers of access" as part of a new model. "Regardless of the format, the primary selection criteria are the same. These include subject relevance, intellectual content, level of presentation, and reputation of author and publisher. But with each new format, unique considerations are introduced."[153]

Cassel points out that "collection development issues relating to Internet resources have yet to be addressed in the literature, although some discussion has occurred on COLLDEV. . . ." She recommends a distinct policy adhering to the general criteria for print materials, plus additional considerations.[154] Ciliberti attempts to correlate library practice to higher education assessment and reports on a study using the OCLC AMIGOS Collection analysis CD.[155] Using citation analysis to examine information use by scientists in a chemistry department,

Hurd looks at how interdisciplinary their research is and finds that over 49 percent of journals cited in a sample were classed in other disciplines.[156] Herubel and Buchanan discuss the distinctive elements of citation studies in the social sciences or humanities, and Heidenwolf evaluates an interdisciplinary public health library by means of citation checking; she includes a literature review on citation checking.[157] White's *Brief Tests of Collection Strength* offers useful ways to "assign libraries a score for existing collection strength in a subject area" and "produce readings on the RLG scale" of collecting levels.[158]

PRESERVATION

Preservation, as it relates to collection management, seems mainly now to be about how to integrate it into existing programs with competing resources for electronic resources and traditional acquisitions.[159] Atkinson says collection development and preservation "can be effectively coordinated only when the underlying political forces that drive these two operations are defined and compared." Risks must be taken to protect these materials' survival; this requires altering political values. "It is in the best interest of those long-term goals that academic libraries accept the risks and exploit the benefits of a vastly expanded, nationally coordinated preservation program as a basic component of the national collection effort." [160]

Cunningham-Kruppa makes a case for having preservation officers report to, or at least work closely with, collection development, since "All collection management decisions . . . are embodied in that item's physical deterioration and its ultimate need for preservation intervention." [161] Gracy reports on the Second Preservation Intensive Institute, which focused on preservation of moving images.[162] Mareck gives a framework for preservation selection process at collection level and item by item, looking at technical decisions and preservation options.[163]

Isenberg surveys books in one library published between 1980 and 1993 in the United States, England, and India, and charts percentages for acidity, binding, and so on, with handling procedures recommended.[164] Gertz reports on ten years of preservation in New York State with the eleven largest research libraries committing over $15 million to this program, based on "planning, education, cooperation, and flexibility."[165]

CONCLUSION

The old questions remain: how to select for collections, how to make optimal use of limited budgets, how many serials and which ones are sufficient, how to evaluate collections and determine use. Newer concerns have been added about how best to select not only print but also electronic resources and what to own and what to acquire "just-in-time"; how to provide for preservation along with other costs; how to combine and balance resource sharing, cooperation, and document delivery; and how to deal with the changes in scholarly communication.

Many of these changes will continue with or without librarians, being driven as they are by technology and other forces beyond libraries and educational institutions. The increasing importance of electronic resources has forever changed the way libraries work. If ways can be found to develop the electronic library out of the traditional library with systematic procedures and policies, at a time when new products and technology change the situation more rapidly than most organizational structures can respond to, then libraries can continue to offer valuable services to users; if not, users almost certainly will find other means of obtaining what they need.

Two contributors to the *Communications of the ACM* offer reminders of what should be known:

the highest priority of a library, digital or otherwise, is to serve the research needs of its constituents. . . . Among librarians, there is sometimes a tendency to focus on collection acquisition and maintenance and to lose sight of the library's role in supporting the community's research.[166]

A positive effect of the current situation is that librarians and administrators have learned to question their roles and goals and find new ways to fulfill both. As for solutions, no single model will work for all libraries, but many choices are being developed.

NOTES

1. Kate Herzog, "Collection Development for the Electronic Library," *Computers in Libraries* 10 (1990): 9.

2. Laverna M. Saunders, "Transforming Acquisitions to Support Virtual Libraries," *Information Technology and Libraries* 14 (1995): 41.

3. "The 'virtual' library may be dead, but the digital library—which is very much alive—has some problems of its own." Cheryl LaGuardia, "Virtual Dreams Give Way to Digital Reality," *Library Journal* 120, no. 6 (1995): 42.

4. Charles A. Hamaker, "Re-Designing Serials Collections," *Journal of Library Administration* 20 (1994): 47; Peter R. Young, "Changing Information Access Economics: New Roles for Libraries and Librarians," *Information Technology and Libraries* 13 (1994): 111.

5. Edward A. Fox, Robert M. Akscyn, Richard K. Furuta, and John J. Leggett, "Digital Libraries," *Communications of the ACM* 38 (1995): 24.

6. Paul H. Moser, "*Real* Access as the Paradigm of the Nineties," *Journal of Library Administration* 21 (1995): 44.

7. Walt Crawford and Michael Gorman, *Future Libraries: Dreams, Madness & Reality* (Chicago: American Library Association, 1995), p. 5.

8. Michael Buckland, *Redesigning Library Services: A Manifesto* (Chicago: American Library Association, 1992), pp. 55–57.

9. Books like the following serve as useful correctives to the hype about the In-

formation Superhighway and the Internet's all-encompassing benefits. Benefits there certainly are, but not without challenges as well. William F. Birdsall, *The Myth of the Electronic Library: Librarianship and Social Change in America* (Westport, CT: Greenwood Press, 1994); Crawford and Gorman, *Future Libraries*; Theodore Roszak, *The Cult of Information: A Neo-Luddite Treatise on High Tech, Artificial Intelligence, and the True Art of Thinking*, 2nd ed. (Berkeley: University of California, 1994); Clifford Stoll, *Silicon Snake Oil* (New York: Doubleday, 1995); Steve Talbott, *The Future Does Not Compute: Transcending the Machines in Our Midst* (Sebastopol, CA: O'Reilly, 1995).

10. Charles B. Osburn and Ross Atkinson, eds., *Collection Management: A New Treatise*, 2 vols. (Greenwich, CT: JAI Press, 1991). There have been good contributions in such basic works as SPEC Kits, CLIP notes, and ALA Collection Management and Development guides. Noteworthy also is the listserv COLLDV-L, which provides information and communication, among the more useful examples being the Issues & Trends Document (by the Association for Library Collections & Technical Services, Resources Section, Collection Management and Development Committee, of the American Library Association) distributed October 7, 12–14, 1992.

11. Bart Harloe and John M. Budd, "Collection Development and Scholarly Communication in the Era of Electronic Access," *Journal of Academic Librarianship* 20 (1994): 87.

12. Samuel Demas, Peter McDonald, and Gregory Lawrence, "The Internet and Collection Development: Mainstreaming Selection of Internet Resources," *Library Resources & Technical Services* 39 (1995): 277.

13. Beth Brin and Elissa Cochran, "Access and Ownership in the Academic Environment: One Library's Progress Report," *Journal of Academic Librarianship* 20 (1994): 207.

14. Thomas W. Shaughnessy, "From Ownership to Access: A Dilemma for Library Managers," *Journal of Library Administration* 14 (1991): 1–7.

15. Anne Woodsworth, "In the Midst of a Paradigm Shift: The Ownership Dilemma," *Library Issues* 12 (1992): 3.

16. Cheryl B. Truesdell, "Is Access a Viable Alternative to Ownership? A Review of Access Performance," *Journal of Academic Librarianship* 20 (1994): 201, 204.

17. Ross Atkinson, "Access, Ownership, and the Future of Collection Development," in *Collection Management and Development: Issues in an Electronic Era: Proceedings of the Advanced Collection Management and Development Institute, Chicago, Illinois, March 26–28, 1993*, ed. Peggy Johnson and Bonnie MacEwan (Chicago: American Library Association, 1994), p. 93.

18. Joel S. Rutstein, Anna L. DeMiller, and Elizabeth A. Fuseler, "Ownership versus Access: Shifting Perspectives for Libraries," in *Advances in Librarianship*, vol. 17, ed. Irene P. Godden (San Diego: Academic Press, 1993), p. 56.

19. Genevieve Owens, "Managing Transition," COLLDV-L no. 651, November 4, 1994.

20. Anna H. Perrault, "The Shrinking National Collection," *Library Acquisitions: Practice & Theory* 18 (1994): 16.

21. Charles A. Schwartz, "Empirical Analysis of Literature Loss," *Library Resources & Technical Services* 38 (1994): 133–38.

22. Clifford A. Lynch, "The Transformation of Scholarly Communication and the Role of the Library in the Age of Networked Information," *The Serials Librarian* 23 (1993): 13–14.

23. Karen A. Schmidt, ed., *Understanding the Business of Library Acquisitions* (Chicago: American Library Association, 1990); Barbara A. Winters and Arnold Hirshon, *Managing the Purchasing Process: A How-to-Do-It Manual for Librarians* (New York: Neal-Schuman, 1993); Murray S. Martin, *Collection Development and Finance: A Guide to Strategic Library-Materials Budgeting* (Chicago: American Library Association, 1995); "Collection Assessment and Acquisitions Budgets," *Journal of Library Administration* 17, no. 2 (1992): 1–148; "Declining Acquisitions Budgets: Allocation, Collection Development and Impact Communication," *Journal of Library Administration* 19, no. 2 (1993): 1–138.

24. John M. Budd, "Allocation Formulas in the Literature: A Review," *Library Acquisitions: Practice & Theory* 15 (1991): 95, 105.

25. Robert L. Houbeck, Jr., "Who Gets What: Allocating the Library's Materials Budget," *Journal of Library Administration* 14 (1991): 99–119.

26. Charles B. Lowry, "Reconciling Pragmatism, Equity, and Need in the Formula Allocation of Book and Serial Funds," *College & Research Libraries* 53 (1992): 121–38.

27. Dennis Carrigan, "Improving Return on Investment: A Proposal for Allocating the Book Budget," *Journal of Academic Librarianship* 18 (1992): 292–97.

28. Carol Cubberley, "Allocating the Materials Funds Using Total Cost of Materials," *Journal of Academic Librarianship* 19 (1993): 16.

29. Plummer Alston Jones, Jr., and Connie L. Keller, "From Budget Allocation to Collection Development: A System for the Small College Library," *Library Acquisitions: Practice & Theory* 17 (1993): 183–89.

30. Judith Webster, "Allocating Library Acquisitions Budgets in an Era of Declining or Static Funding," *Journal of Library Administration* 19 (1993): 60, 74.

31. Eric J. Carpenter, "Collection Development Policies Based on Approval Plans," *Library Acquisitions: Practice & Theory* 13 (1989): 39–43.

32. John C. Calhoun, James K. Bracken, and Kenneth L. Firestein, "Modeling an Academic Approval Program," *Library Resources & Technical Services* 34 (1990): 367–79.

33. Jean L. Loup and Helen Lloyd Snoke, "Analysis of Selection Activities to Supplement Approval Plans," *Library Resources & Technical Services* 35 (1991): 202, 215.

34. Hugh L. Franklin, "Sci/Tech Book Approval Plans Can Be Effective," *Collection Management* 19 (1994): 135–45.

35. Robert F. Nardini, "Approval Plans: Politics and Performance," *College & Research Libraries* 54 (1993): 418.

36. Margo Sasse and Patricia A. Smith, "Automated Acquisitions: The Future of Collection Development," *Library Acquisitions: Practice & Theory* 16 (1992): 142.

37. Carol Pitts Hawks, "In Support of Collection Assessment: The Role of Automation in the Acquisitions and Serials Departments," *Journal of Library Administration* 17 (1992): 14.

38. John M. Meador, Jr., and Lynn Cline, "Displaying and Utilizing Selection Tools in a User-Friendly Electronic Environment," *Library Acquisitions: Practice & Theory* 16 (1992): 289–94.

39. Carol Pitts Hawks, "Expert Systems in Technical Services and Collection Management," *Information Technology and Libraries* 13 (1994): 208.

40. Ron L. Ray, "The Dis-Integrating Library System: Effects of New Technologies in Acquisitions," *Library Acquisitions: Practice & Theory* 17 (1993): 127–36.

41. Meta Nissley, "Handle with Care! Delicate Package! CD-ROMs and the Acquisitions Process," *Library Acquisitions: Practice & Theory* 14 (1990): 251.

42. Trisha L. Davis, "Acquisition of CD-ROM Databases for Local Area Networks," *Journal of Academic Librarianship* 19 (1993): 68–71.

43. David L. Marshall, "The Internet Connection for Electronic Ordering," *Computers in Libraries* 13 (1993): 26–28; William J. Kara, "Acquisitions in Transition: On the Road to the Electronic Library," in *Continuity & Transformation: The Promise of Confluence, Proceedings of the Seventh National Conference of the Association of College and Research Libraries, Pittsburgh, Pennsylvania, March 29–April 1, 1994* (Chicago: Association of College and Research Libraries, 1995), pp. 203–7.

44. Jeri Van Goethem, "Whether by Byte or by Tome, Buying Information Is 'Acquisitions,' " *Library Acquisitions: Practice & Theory* 17 (1993): 362.

45. The Internet Index, no. 12, January 2, 1996 (http://www.openmarket.com/info/internet-index/).

46. Dan Lester, "I May Be a Cyclops, but I'm Not an Internaut!" *Technicalities* 14 (1994): 9. See Peggy Johnson, "Collection Development and the Internet," *Collection Management and Development: Issues in an Electronic Era: Proceedings of the Advanced Collection Management and Development Institute, Chicago, Illinois, March 26–28, 1993,* ed. Peggy Johnson and Bonnie MacEwan (Chicago: American Library Association, 1994), pp. 63–79 for a brief history and description of the Internet.

47. Demas, "The Internet and Collection Development," pp. 275–77.

48. Susan S. Starr, "Evaluating Physical Science Reference Sources on the Internet," *The Reference Librarian*, nos. 41/42 (1994): 261–73; Edmund F. Santa Vicca, "The Internet as a Reference and Research Tool: A Model for Educators," *The Reference Librarian*, nos. 41/42 (1994): 225–36.

49. Julie Swann and Carla Rosenquist-Buhler, "Developing an Internet Research Gopher: Innovation and Staff Involvement," *Journal of Academic Librarianship* 21 (1995): 371–75.

50. Peggy Johnson, "Desperately Seeking Sources: Selecting On-Line Resources," *Technicalities* 15, no. 8 (1995): 4–5.

51. Vivienne Monty and P. Warren-Wenk, "The Impact of the Internet on the Scholarly Research Process in the Social Sciences and Humanities," in *Continuity & Transformation*, p. 51.

52. Robert M. Gurn, "Measuring Information Providers on the Internet," *Internet Librarian* 15 (1995): 42.

53. William A. Britten, "Building and Organizing Internet Collections," *Library Acquisitions: Practice & Theory* 19 (1995): 249.

54. Yuan Zhou, "From Smart Guesser to Smart Navigator: Changes in Collection Development for Research Libraries in a Network Environment," *Library Trends* 42 (1994): 648.

55. Lucy A. Tedd, "An Introduction to Sharing Resources via the Internet in Academic Libraries and Information Centres in Europe," *Program* 29 (1995): 43–61.

56. Joseph J. Branin, "Delivering on Promises: The Intersection of Print and Electronic Information Systems in Libraries," *Information Technology and Libraries* 10 (1991): 328, 330.

57. Richard Hacken, "The RLG Conoco Study and Its Aftermath: Is Resource Sharing in Limbo?" *Journal of Academic Librarianship* 18 (1992): 22.

58. Arnold Hirshon, "Library Strategic Alliances and the Digital Library in the

1990s: The OhioLINK Experience," *Journal of Academic Librarianship* 21 (1995): 384.

59. Patricia Buck Dominguez and Luke Swindler, "Cooperative Collection Development at the Research Triangle University Libraries: A Model for the Nation," *College & Research Libraries* 54 (1993): 487.

60. Sue O. Medina, "The Evolution of Cooperative Collection Development in Alabama Academic Libraries," *College & Research Libraries* 53 (1992): 7–19.

61. Christy Hightower and George Soete, "The Consortium as Learning Organization: Twelve Steps to Success in Collaborative Collections Projects," *Journal of Academic Librarianship* 21 (1995): 91.

62. Richard J. Wood and Katina Strauch, eds., *Collection Assessment: A Look at the RLG Conspectus* (New York: Haworth Press, 1992); Georgine N. Olson and Barbara McFadden Allen, eds., *Cooperative Collection Management: The Conspectus Approach* (New York: Neal-Schuman, 1994); Association for Library Collections & Technical Services. Collection Management and Development Section. Subcommittee on Guide to Cooperative Collection Development, *Guide to Cooperative Collection Development*, ed. Bart Harloe. Collection Management and Development Guides, no. 6. (Chicago: American Library Association, 1994).

63. Anthony W. Ferguson, "The Conspectus as an On-Site Training Tool," in *Recruiting, Education, and Training Librarians for Collection Development*, ed. Peggy Johnson and Sheila S. Intner (Westport, CT: Greenwood Press, 1994), pp. 171–81; Dora Biblarz, "The Conspectus as a Blueprint for Creating Collection Development Policy Statements," *Acquisitions Librarian* 4 (1992): 169–76.

64. Virgil L. P. Blake and Renee Tjoumas, "The Conspectus Approach to Collection Evaluation: Panacea or False Prophet?" *Collection Management* 18 (1994): 27.

65. Beth M. Paskoff and Anna H. Perrault, "A Tool for Comparative Collection Analysis: Conducting a Shelflist Sample to Construct a Collection Profile," *Library Resources & Technical Services* 34 (1990): 199.

66. Jeanne Harrell, "Use of the OCLC/AMIGOS Collection Analysis CD to Determine Comparative Collection Strength in English and American Literature: A Case Study," *Technical Services Quarterly* 9 (1992): 14.

67. Barbara A. Radke, "OCLC/AMIGOS Collection Analysis CD," *OCLC Micro* (October 1991): 28–30.

68. Sherry L. Vellucci, "OCLC/AMIGOS Collection Analysis CD: Broadening the Scope of Use," *OCLC Systems and Services* 9 (1993): 49.

69. Genevieve Owens, "Education for Collection Management," COLLDV-L No. 643, October 29, 1994.

70. Cheryl LaGuardia and Connie V. Dowell, "The Structure of Resource Sharing in Academic Research Libraries," *RQ* 30 (1991): 370–76.

71. Anne McKee, "Article Delivery: Shifting Paradigms," *Serials Librarian* 23 (1993): 207–15.

72. Ron L. Ray, "A Skeptic's View of the Future for Combined Acquisitions and Document Delivery," *Library Acquisitions: Practice & Theory* 17 (1993): 348–49.

73. Barbara Buckner Higginbotham and Sally Bowdoin, *Access vs. Assets: A Comprehensive Guide to Resource Sharing for Academic Librarians* (Chicago: American Library Association, 1993); Lois C. Gilmer, *Interlibrary Loan: Theory and Management* (Englewood, CO: Libraries Unlimited, 1994); "The Future of Resource Sharing," *Journal of Library Administration* 21 (1995):1–202; "DocuShock: Options for the Document

Delivery in the Nineties," *Bulletin of the Medical Library Association* 82 (1994): 161–87; Marilyn M. Roche, *ARL/RLG Interlibrary Loan Cost Study* (Washington, DC: Association of Research Libraries, 1993), p. 34.

74. Thomas W. Shaughnessy, "Resource Sharing and the End of Innocence," *Journal of Library Administration* 20 (1994): 11–13.

75. Jutta Reed-Scott, "Future of Resource Sharing in Research Libraries," *Journal of Library Administration* 21 (1995): 67–75.

76. Mary E. Jackson, "The Future of Resource Sharing: The Role of the Association of Research Libraries," *Journal of Library Administration* 21 (1995): 198–201.

77. Mary E. Jackson, "Library to Library: Redesigning Interlibrary Loan and Document Delivery Services," *Wilson Library Bulletin* 69 (May 1995): 68.

78. Elizabeth P. Roberts, "Ill/Document Delivery as an Alternative to Local Ownership of Seldom-Used Scientific Journals," *Journal of Academic Librarianship* 18 (1992): 33.

79. Kathleen Kurosman and Barbara A. Durniak, "Document Delivery: A Comparison of Commercial Document Suppliers and Interlibrary Loan Services," *College & Research Libraries* 55 (1994): 129–39.

80. F. K. Rottmann, "To Buy or to Borrow: Studies of the Impact of Interlibrary Loan on Collection Development in the Academic Library," *Journal of Interlibrary Loan & Information Supply* 1 (1991): 18.

81. Jo Ann Lahmon, "Using Interlibrary Loan Data in Collection Development," *OCLC Micro* (October 1991): 19–22; Scott A. Mellendorf, "A Practical Method for Using Interlibrary Loan Data to Assist Librarians with Collection Development," *OCLC Systems and Services* 9 (1993): 45–48.

82. Sharon Bonk, "Interlibrary Loan and Document Delivery in the United Kingdom," *RQ* 30 (1990): 230–40.

83. David Bradbury and Graham P. Cornish, "Worldwide View of Information: Availability of Publications and International Interlibrary Loan," *RQ* 32 (1992): 185–92; Graham P. Cornish, "Charging for Interlibrary Loan Nationally and Internationally, *Interlending and Document Supply* 20 (1992): 102–7.

84. Dennis Carrigan, "From Interlibrary Lending to Document Delivery: The British Library Document Supply Centre," *Journal of Academic Librarianship* 19 (1993): 220–24.

85. "The Future Direction of Library Access and Delivery Services," *ARL: A Bimonthly Newsletter of Research Library Issues and Actions* 176 (1994): 3; Clifford A. Lynch, "System Architecture and Networking Issues in Implementing the North American Interlibrary Loan and Document Delivery (NAILDD) Initiative," *Journal of Library Administration* 21 (1995): 148, 164; see also Mary E. Jackson, "The NAILDD Project," *Wilson Library Bulletin* 68 (1993): 66–68.

86. Pamela Bluh, "Document Delivery 2000: Will It Change the Nature of Librarianship?" *Wilson Library Bulletin* 67 (1993): 50, 112.

87. David Everett, "Full-Text Online Databases as a Document Delivery System: The Unfulfilled Promise," *Journal of Interlibrary Loan & Information Supply* 3 (1993): 17–25.

88. Georgia Finnigan, "Document Delivery Gets Personal," *Online* 16 (1992): 106–8.

89. Frederick J. Friend, "Document Delivery: A World Solution to a World Problem?" *IFLA Journal* 19 (1993): 374–84.

90. Laura N. Gasaway, "Document Delivery," *Computers in Libraries* 14 (1994): 25–32.

91. Malcolm Getz, "Economics: Document Delivery," *The Bottom Line* 5 (1991/ 92): 41; Malcolm Getz, "The Electronic Library: Analysis and Decentralization in Collection Decisions," *Journal of Library Administration* 14 (1991): 74.

92. Lorraine J. Haricombe and T. J. Lusher, "You Want It When? Document Delivery in the 1990s," in *Continuity & Transformation*, pp. 357–64.

93. Harry S. Martin, III and Curtis L. Kendrick, "A User-Centered View of Document Delivery and Interlibrary Loan," *Library Administration & Management* 8 (1994): 223–27.

94. Nancy S. Hewison, Vick J. Killion, and Suzanne M. Ward, "Commercial Document Delivery: The Academic Library's Perspective," *Journal of Library Administration* 21 (1995): 140.

95. Bonnie Juergens and Tim Prather, "The Resource Sharing Component of Access," *Journal of Library Administration* 20 (1994): 88.

96. Mounir Khalil, "Document Delivery: A Better Option?" *Library Journal* 118 (February 1, 1993): 43–47; Ronald G. Leach and Judith E. Tribble, "Electronic Document Delivery: New Options for Libraries," *Journal of Academic Librarianship* 18 (1993): 359–64. Also of use is Mounir A. Khalil and Suzanne R. Katz, "Document Delivery: An Annotated Selective Bibliography," *Computers in Libraries* 12 (1992): 25–30.

97. William Gray Potter, "Scholarly Publishing, Copyright, and the Future of Resource Sharing," *Journal of Library Administration* 21 (1995): 65.

98. Pamela Bluh, "Striking a Balance: Document Delivery in the Nineties," *Law Library Journal* 85 (1993): 600.

99. Meg Trauner, "Client-Based Document Delivery Services," *Law Library Journal* 85 (1993): 412.

100. Carol Pitts Hawks, "The Integrated Library System of the 1990s: The OhioLINK Experience," *Library Resources & Technical Services* 36 (1992): 61–77; Judith A. Sessions, Richard N. Pettitt, Jr., and Scott Van Dam, "OhioLINK Inter-Institutional Lending Online: The Miami University Experience," *Library Hi Tech* 13 (1995): 11–24, 38; Phyllis O'Connor, Susan Wehmeyer, and Susan Weldon, "The Future Using an Integrated Approach: The OhioLINK Experience," *Journal of Library Administration* 21 (1995): 110.

101. Melissa Stockton and Martha Whittaker, "The Future of Document Delivery: A Vendor's Perspective," *Journal of Library Administration* 21 (1995): 180.

102. Sue O. Medina, "Improving Document Delivery in a Statewide Network," *Journal of Interlibrary Loan & Information Supply* 2 (1992): 7–14.

103. Sharon J. Rogers and Charleen S. Hurt, "How Scholarly Communication Should Work in the 21st Century," *College & Research Libraries* 51 (1990): 5.

104. Thomas W. Shaughnessy, "Scholarly Communication: The Need for an Agenda for Action—A Symposium," *Journal of Academic Librarianship* 15 (1989): 68–78.

105. Anthony M. Cummings et al., *University Libraries and Scholarly Communication: A Study Prepared for the Andrew W. Mellon Foundation* (Washington, DC: Association of Research Libraries, 1992), p. 165; see also *Scholarly Communication in an Electronic Environment: Issues for Research Libraries*, ed. Robert S. Martin (Chicago: American Library Association, 1993).

106. Ann Okerson, "With Feathers: Effects of Copyright and Ownership on Scholarly Publishing," *College & Research Libraries* 52 (1991): 425.

107. Rowland C. W. Brown, "Changing Patterns of Scholarly Communication and the Need to Expand the Library's Role and Services," *Library Acquisitions: Practice & Theory* 14 (1990): 377.

108. Charles A. Schwartz, "Scholarly Communication as a Loosely Coupled System: Reassessing Prospects for Structural Reform," *College & Research Libraries* 55 (1994): 102.

109. Phyllis Franklin, "Scholars, Librarians, and the Future of Primary Records," *College & Research Libraries* 54 (1993): 397–406. She refers to Eldred Smith, *The Librarian, the Scholar, and the Future of the Research Library* (Westport, CT: Greenwood Press, 1990).

110. Lynch, "Transformation of Scholarly Communication," p. 8.

111. Ross Atkinson, "Networks, Hypertext, and Academic Information Services: Some Longer-Range Implications," *College & Research Libraries* 54 (1993): 199–215.

112. Bruce C. Bennion, "Why the Science Journal Crisis?" *Bulletin of the American Society for Information Science* 20 (1994): 25. The *Newsletter on Serials Pricing Issues* (http://sunsite.unc.edu/reference/prices/prices.html) and *Against the Grain* help to keep librarians informed on issues of costs and cancellations.

113. John R. Hayes, "The Internet's First Victim?" *Forbes* 156 (December 18, 1995): 200–201; Hamaker, "Re-Designing Serials Collections," p. 39.

114. Richard P. Widdicombe, "Eliminating All Journal Subscriptions Has Freed Our Customers to Seek the Information They Really Want and Need: The Result—More Access, Not Less," *Science & Technology Libraries* 14 (1993): 3–13.

115. Paul Metz, "Making the Most of a Bad Situation: A Successful Journal Cancellation Project," *Library Issues* 12 (March 1992): 1–2; Paul Metz, "Thirteen Steps to Avoiding Bad Luck in a Serials Cancellation Project," *Journal of Academic Librarianship* 18 (1992): 76–82.

116. Janet Hughes, "Use of Faculty Publication Lists and ISI Citation Data to Identify a Core List of Journals with Local Importance," *Library Acquisitions: Practice & Theory* 19 (1995): 403–13.

117. Tina E. Chrzastowski and Karen A. Schmidt, "Surveying the Damage: Academic Library Serial Cancellations 1987–88 through 1989–90," *College & Research Libraries* 54 (1993): 93–102; Tina E. Chrzastowski, "Seeking the 99% Chemistry Library: Extending the Serial Collection Through the Use of Decentralized Document Delivery," *Library Acquisitions: Practice & Theory* 19 (1995): 152.

118. Bill Coons and Peter McDonald, "Implications of Commercial Document Delivery," *College & Research Libraries News* 56 (1995): 626–31.

119. John C. Calhoun, "Serials Citations and Holdings Correlation," *Library Resources and Technical Services* 39 (1995): 53–77.

120. Stephanie C. Haas and Vernon N. Kisling, Jr., "The Use of Electronic Ranking to Analyze Scientific Literature Used in Research at the University of Florida," *Collection Management* 18 (1994): 49–62.

121. Linda L. Stein, "What to Keep and What to Cut? Using the Internet as an Objective Tool to Identify 'Core' Periodical Titles in a Specialized Subject Collection," *Technical Services Quarterly* 10 (1992): 3–14.

122. Eleanor A. Gossen and Suzanne Irving, "Ownership versus Access and Low-Use Periodical Titles," *Library Resources & Technical Services* 39 (1995): 43, 51.

123. Anthony W. Ferguson and Kathleen Kehoe, "Access vs. Ownership: What Is Most Cost Effective in the Sciences," *Journal of Library Administration* 19 (1993): 97.

124. The Advisory Panel for Scientific Publications, "The Cost Effectiveness of Science Journals," *Publishing Research Quarterly* 8 (1992): 77–80. They find the following studies methodologically unsound: Dorothy Milne and Bill Tiffany, "A Survey of the Cost-Effectiveness of Serials: A Cost-Per-Use Method and Its Results," *Serials Librarian* 19 (1991): 137–49; Marifran Bustion, John Eltinge, and Joh Harer, "On the Merits of Direct Observation of Periodical Usage: An Empirical Study," *College & Research Libraries* 53 (1992): 537–50.

125. F. W. Lancaster, "The Evolution of Electronic Publishing," *Library Trends* 43 (1995): 518–27.

126. Brett Butler, "Electronic Editions of Serials: The Virtual Library Model," *Serials Review* 18 (1992): 103.

127. *Electronic Journals in ARL Libraries: Policies and Procedures*, comp. Elizabeth Parang and Laverna Saunders. SPEC Kit 201 (Washington, DC: Association of Research Libraries, Office of Management Services, 1994); *Electronic Journals in ARL Libraries: Issues and Trends*, comp. Elizabeth Parang and Laverna Saunders. SPEC Kit 202 (Washington, DC: Association of Research Libraries, Office of Management Services, 1994) provide useful information; and the *Directory of Electronic Journals, Newsletters, and Academic Discussion Lists* (Washington, DC: Association of Research Libraries, Office of Scientific and Academic Publishing, 1991–) has become as basic a tool as the *Gale Directory of Databases* (Detroit: Gale Research, 1993–).

128. Tom Clark, "On the Cost Differences Between Publishing a Book in Paper and in the Electronic Medium," *Library Resources & Technical Services* 39 (1995): 28.

129. Edward J. Valauskas, "Reading and Computers: Paper-Based or Digital Text: What's Best?" *Computers in Libraries* 14 (1994): 46.

130. Helen M. Grochmal, "Selecting Electronic Journals," *College & Research Libraries News* 56 (1995): 632–33, 654.

131. Cheryl LaGuardia and Stella Bentley, "Electronic Databases: Will Old Collection Development Policies Still Work?" *Online* 16 (1992): 43.

132. Thomas B. Hickey, "Present and Future Capabilities of the Online Journal," *Library Trends* 43 (1995): 529, 540, 542.

133. Ann C. Schaffner, "The Future of Scientific Journals: Lessons from the Past," *Information Technology and Libraries* 13 (1994): 239.

134. Karen Hunter, "Issues and Experiments in Electronic Publishing and Dissemination," *Information Technology and Libraries* 13 (1994): 127–32; Clifford Lynch, ed., "The TULIP Project," *Library Hi Tech*, no. 52 (1995): 7–74.

135. Paul Metz, "Electronic Journals from a Collection Manager's Point of View," *Serials Review* 17 (1991): 82–83.

136. Philip Barden, "Multimedia Document Delivery—The Birth of a New Industry," *Online & CD-ROM Review* 19 (1995): 321–23; Pamela Samuelson, "Legally Speaking: Copyright and Digital Libraries," *Communications of the ACM*, pp. 15–21.

137. Christoph Huser, Klaus Reichenberger, Lothar Rostek, and Norbert Streitz, "Knowledge-Based Editing and Visualization for Hypermedia Encyclopedias," *Communications of the ACM*, p. 49.

138. Robert Wilensky, "UC Berkeley's Digital Library Project," *Communications of the ACM*, p. 60.

139. Louis A. Pitschmann, "Organization and Staffing," in *Collection Management: A New Treatise*, pp. 125–143.

140. Jasper G. Schad, "Managing Collection Development in University Libraries That Utilize Librarians with Dual-Responsibility Assignments," *Library Acquisitions: Practice & Theory* 14 (1990): 166.

141. Peggy Johnson, "Matrix Management: An Organizational Alternative for Libraries," *Journal of Academic Librarianship* 16 (1990): 229.

142. "Special Section: Reorganization of Acquisitions Departments," *Library Acquisitions: Practice & Theory* 16, no. 4 (1992): 345–89; "Special Section: Library Reorganization for the 21st Century," *Library Acquisitions: Practice & Theory* 19, no. 4 (1995): 415–85.

143. Sheila D. Creth, "The Organization of Collection Development: A Shift in the Organization Paradigm," *Journal of Library Administration* 14 (1991): 78.

144. Gossen and Irving, "Ownership versus Access," p. 51.

145. Dan C. Hazen, "Collection Development Policies in the Information Age," *College & Research Libraries* 56 (1995): 29.

146. Elizabeth Futas, ed., *Collection Development Policies and Procedures*, 3rd ed. (Phoenix, AZ: Oryx Press, 1994); Collection Development Policies Committee of the Collection Development and Evaluation Section, Reference and Adult Services Division, "The Relevance of Collection Development Policies: Definition, Necessity, and Applications," *RQ* 33 (Fall 1993): 65.

147. Anthony W. Ferguson, "Interesting Problems Encountered on My Way to Writing an Electronic Information Collection Development Statement," *Against the Grain* 7 (1995): 16–19.

148. LaGuardia, "Electronic Policies," p. 61.

149. Jackie Mardikian and Martin Kesselman, "Beyond the Desk: Enhanced Reference Staffing for the Electronic Library," *Reference Services Review* 23 (1995): 27.

150. Thomas E. Nisonger, *Collection Evaluation in Academic Libraries: A Literature Guide and Annotated Bibliography* (Englewood, CO: Libraries Unlimited, 1992); Michael R. Gabriel, *Collection Development and Collection Evaluation: A Sourcebook* (Metuchen, NJ: Scarecrow Press, 1995).

151. Michael Buckland, "What Will Collection Developers Do?" *Information Technology and Libraries* 14 (1995): 157–59.

152. Atkinson, "Access, Ownership," p. 97.

153. Samuel Demas, "Collection Development for the Electronic Library: A Conceptual and Organizational Model," *Library Hi Tech* 12 (1994): 71.

154. Rachel Cassel, "Selection Criteria for Internet Resources," *College & Research Libraries News* 56 (1995): 92–93.

155. Anne C. Ciliberti, "Collection Evaluation and Academic Review. A Pilot Study Using the OCLC/AMIGOS Collection Analysis CD," *Library Acquisitions: Practice and Theory* 18 (1994): 431–45.

156. Julie M. Hurd, "Interdisciplinary Research in the Sciences: Implications for Library Organization," *College & Research Libraries* 53 (1992): 283–97.

157. Jean-Pierre V. M. Herubel and Anne L. Buchanan, "Citation Studies in the Humanities and Social Sciences: A Selective and Annotated Bibliography," *Collection Management* 18 (1994): 89–137; Terese Heidenwolf, "Evaluating an Interdisciplinary Research Collection," *Collection Management* 18 (1994): 33–48.

158. Howard D. White, *Brief Tests of Collection Strength: A Methodology for all Types of Libraries* (Westport, CT: Greenwood Press, 1995), pp. 3–4.

159. Ross Harvey's *Preservation in Libraries: A Reader* (London: Bowker-Saur, 1993) and *Preservation in Libraries: Principles, Strategies and Practices for Librarians* (London: Bowker-Saur, 1993) provide broad, current coverage for the subject. See also *The Changing Role of Book Repair in ARL Libraries*, comp. Randy Silverman and Maria Grandinette. SPEC Kit 190 (Washington, DC: Association of Research Libraries, Office of Management Studies, 1993); *Preservation Organization and Staffing*, prep. Jutta Reed-Scott. SPEC Kit 160 (Washington, DC: Association of Research Libraries, Office of Management Studies, 1990).

160. Ross Atkinson, "Preservation and Collection Development: Toward a Political Synthesis," *Journal of Academic Librarianship* 16 (1990): 98, 102.

161. Ellen Cunningham-Kruppa, "The Preservation Officer's Role in Collection Development," *Wilson Library Bulletin* 67 (November 1992): 29.

162. Karen F. Gracy, "Film and Television Preservation Concerns Come of Age: An In-Depth Report on the Second Preservation Intensive Institute," *Library Hi Tech* 117 (November 1994): 1–6.

163. Robert Mareck, "Practicum on Preservation Selection," *Collection Management for the 1990s*, ed. J. J. Branin (Chicago: American Library Association, 1992), pp. 114–26.

164. Laurie Isenberg, "Planning for Preservation: A Public Health Library Conditions Survey," *Collection Management* 19 (1994): 111–19.

165. Janet Gertz, "Ten Years of Preservation in New York State: The Comprehensive Research Libraries," *Library Resources & Technical Services* 39 (1995): 198–208.

166. David M. Levy and Catherine C. Marshall, "Going Digital: A Look at Assumptions Underlying Digital Libraries," *Communications of the ACM*, p. 80.

Index

About the Editors and Contributors

BONITA BRYANT (B.A., M.A.L.S.) has been Assistant Director for Collection Development at the State University of New York at Albany's University Libraries since 1981. Previously, she was Chief Bibliographer at the University of Northern Iowa for fourteen years. She was a member of the founding Executive Committee of the Collection Management and Development Section (CMDS) of the Association for Library Collections and Technical Services (ALCTS) of the American Library Association, and has served on various CMDS committees. She has published two articles on the topic of collection management and development staffing and organizations.

JOHN M. BUDD (B.A., M.A., M.L.S., Ph.D.) is Associate Professor in the School of Library and Informational Science at the University of Missouri–Columbia. He is active in the Reference and Adult Services Division's Collection Development and Evaluation Section and the ALCTS Collection Management and Development Section of the American Library Association. His recent publications have appeared in *Library Quarterly*, *RQ*, *Library Resources & Technical Services*, and the *Journal of Academic Librarianship*

PHILIP J. CALVERT (B.A., M.Sc., M.L.S.) is Senior Lecturer in the Department of Library and Information Studies at the Victoria University of Wellington. His first jobs were in public libraries in England, and he also spent some years as a librarian in Fiji and Papua New Guinea before returning to England for a short while in the library supply industry. He has been with Victoria University since 1990, where he teaches mainly information technology subjects. Together with Rowena Cullen he is the author of several articles on library effectiveness, which are the product of four years of research in public and university libraries in New Zealand.

MARY F. CASSERLY (M.L.S., Ph.D.) is currently the Division Head for Collection Development at the University of Maine. Her previous publications have included work on self-study and accreditation, collection development in college libraries, and training and evaluation of collection development personnel.

ANNE C. CILIBERTI (M.L.S., Ph.D.) has been the Collection Development Librarian at William Patterson College since 1992. Dr. Ciliberti's previous library experience includes academic reference work and administration of a multitype library cooperative. Her research interests focus on academic library performance measurement, collection analysis and evaluation, and decision making in collection development.

GRAHAM P. CORNISH (B.A., L.Th., F.L.A., F.I.Inf.Sc.) studied theology at the University of Durham and information science in Liverpool. He joined what is now the British Library in 1969 and has worked in many areas, mostly concerned with document supply. Since 1983 he has been responsible for copyright matters in the British Library and from 1985 has managed the IFLA Office for International Lending and subsequently the Universal Availability of Publications (UAP) Programme. He is involved in several European Commission projects on electronic document supply and copyright, and regularly writes on such issues as copyright, document supply, audiovisual archives, and international librarianship.

GAY N. DANNELLY (B.A., M.A.L.S.) is Collection Development Officer and Associate Professor at Ohio State University. She is active in the American Library Association, Center for Research Libraries, Committee on Institutional Cooperation, and OhioLINK committees. She has presented papers at a variety of professional conferences and published on topics in collection management and development, budgeting, and resource sharing.

WILLIAM FISHER is Professor and Associate Director of the School of Library and Information Science at San José State University. He teaches in the areas of collection management, management of information organizations, business information resources, and special libraries. He has published numerous works, including a number of articles on education for acquisitions and collection development.

G. E. GORMAN (B.A., M.Div., S.T.B., Grad.Dip.Lib., M.A., Th.D., F.L.A.,

F.R.S.A.) is Associate Director of the Centre for Information Studies and Senior Lecturer in the School of Information Studies at Charles Sturt University–Riverina, where his special interest is in the areas of collection development, collection management, and research methods. He is the author of several books in these areas, and of more than 70 articles in such journals as *Library Acquisitions: Practice & Theory, Libri, Serials Librarian, Asian Libraries, Australian Library Review*, and *Australian Academic and Research Libraries*. He is a series editor for publishers in Britain, North America, and Australia, and also an editor of *Library Acquisitions: Practice & Theory, African Book Publishing Record*, and *Australian Library Review*.

BART M. HARLOE (B.A., M.A., M.L.S.) is University Librarian and Director of Libraries at St. Lawrence University. Prior to holding this position, he was Assistant Director for Collection Management at the Libraries of the Claremont Colleges and Head of Collection Management at New Mexico State University. A member of ALA, Harloe has been active in ACRL and ALCTS/CMDS. Most recently, he edited *The Guide to Cooperative Collection Development* (ALA, 1994) and co-authored an article with John Budd on collection development and scholarly communication, which appeared in the *Journal of Academic Librarianship*.

ROSS HARVEY (B.Mus. (Hons.), Ph.D., Dip.N.Z.L.S., A.A.L.I.A., A.N.Z.L.A.) is Senior Lecturer in the Division of Information Studies at Nanyang Technological University. His publications include *Preservation in Libraries: Principles, Strategies and Practices for Librarians* and *Preservation in Libraries: A Reader* (1993), and the second edition of *Preservation in Australian and New Zealand Libraries* (1993). Other professional interests include the organization of information and newspaper history, and he has recently established the Elibank Press to promote interest in book trade history.

DAN C. HAZEN (M.L.S., Ph.D.) is Librarian for Latin America, Spain, and Portugal in the Widener Library at Harvard University. He previously served as Librarian for Hispanic Collections at the University of California, Berkeley; as Visiting Curator in the Stanford University Libraries; and as Latin American Librarian at Cornell University. He is an active member of the Seminar on the Acquisition of Latin American Library Materials (SALALM), of which he was president in 1985; and he currently chairs the Executive Committee of the Latin American Microform Project (LAMP). He has been involved in, and published on, numerous projects concerning research resources for Latin American Studies.

SHEILA S. INTNER (B.A., M.A., Ph.D.) is Professor in the Graduate School of Library and Information Science at Simmons College, where she teaches in a number of areas, including collection development, preservation management, and research methods. Her most recent research grant from the Council on Library was for "Ownership or Access? A Study of Decision Making in Collection Development," which was published in *Advances in Library Administration and Organization* (1995). She has written numerous books and journal articles and columns, and edits *Technicalities* and the ALA series, Frontiers of Access to Library Materials.

PEGGY JOHNSON (B.A., M.A., M.B.A.) is Head of Planning and Special Projects, University of Minnesota Libraries. She has consulted on collection management issues in the United States and on library development projects in Rwanda, Uganda, and Morocco. Her publications include *Automation and Organizational Change in Libraries* (1991); *Guide to Technical Services Resources* (1994); *Collection Management and Development: Issues in an Electronic Era* (1994); *Recruiting, Educating, and Training Librarians for Collection Development* (1994); and *The Searchable Internet Bibliography* (1996). She writes a bimonthly column on collection management for *Technicalities*.

BARBARA G. LEONARD (M.L.S.) is Coordinator of Collections and Fiscal Planning in the Library at San José State University. She also teaches collection management and library fiscal management for the School of Library and Information Science at San José State University. She is active in the Library Administration and Management Association of the American Library Association, serving on the Budget and Finance, Publications, and Acquisitions Systems Committees. She has published journal articles on library science practicums, systems librarians, library finance, and collection management.

RUTH H. MILLER (B.A., M.A., M.L.S.) is Associate University Librarian, Collections and Information Services, at Hong Kong University of Science and Technology. From late 1996 she will be Director of Library and Media Services, David L. Rice Library, University of Southern Indiana, Evansville, Indiana. She was previously Head, Department of Collection Development and Preservation, Cunningham Memorial Library, Indiana State University. Her papers have appeared in *Library Acquisitions: Practice & Theory, College and Research Libraries, Library Resources & Technical Services*, and other professional journals.

WILLIAM S. MONROE (B.A., M.S., M.A., M.Phil.) is Head of the Collection Development Department at Brown University. He has published articles on both librarianship and historical subjects, and is undertaking Ph.D. research in medieval history at Columbia University.

THOMAS E. NISONGER (M.L.S., Ph.D.) is Associate Professor at Indiana University's School of Library and Information Science, where he teaches collection management and evaluation of library resources and services. He has

published over 75 articles, book reviews, and reports in such journals as *Library Resources & Technical Services, Library Acquisitions: Practice & Theory, Journal of the American Society for Information Science, Serials Review*, and *College and Research Libraries*. He is also the author of *Collection Evaluation in Academic Libraries: A Literature Guide and Annotated Bibliography* (1992).

RICHARD J. WOOD (M.L.S., Ph.D.) has served as the Director of Library Services at Sam Houston State University since August 1990. From 1986 to 1990, he was Director of Library Services at The Citadel, the Military College of South Carolina, in Charleston. Prior to that he was Head of Circulation (1971–1986) and Coordinator of User Services (1979–1986) at Slippery Rock University of Pennsylvania. He has written numerous articles and, with Katina Strauch, edited *Collection Assessment: A Look at the RLG Conspectus* (1992). His latest edited work is *Library Collection Policies: A Reference and Writers' Handbook* (1996). He is currently a contributing editor to Meckler's *Library Software Review*.